Peter Oborne is an award-winning writer, reporter and broadcaster who has worked for various newspapers, including the *Spectator*, the *Daily Mail* and the *Daily Telegraph*, where he was the chief political commentator until his resignation from the paper in 2015. He now writes for *Middle East Eye* and *Byline Times*. He is the author of numerous books, including *The Rise of Political Lying* (2005), *The Triumph of the Political Class* (2007), *Wounded Tiger* (2014) and *The Assault on Truth* (2021). He lives in Wiltshire.

Praise for *The Fate of Abraham*

'I cannot tell you how very, very good *The Fate of Abraham* is . . . It is an extraordinary book: fresh, hard-hitting and documented. Been a long time since I could say "I couldn't put it down"' **John Esposito**

'Over the years, Oborne has left no stone unturned to speak the truth and dismantle many of the myths surrounding British Muslims, without fear or favour' **Muhammad Abdul Bari**

'Meticulous . . . *The Fate of Abraham* is an *aide mémoire* that reminds one of the chains of causation that get buried under the froth of soundbites and institutionalised amnesia that combine to gaslight us. It is a good read, and a valuable resource for the connected history of why the West is wrong about Islam' **Professor Salman Sayyid, University of Leeds**

'An admirable piece of sustained investigative journalism . . . genuinely breaks new ground and deserves to be widely read and debated' *Church Times*

'Masterly . . . Oborne is probably one of the last remaining inheritors of the distinguished tradition of investigative, humanitarian journalism. One of the rare breed of journalists who dare to take up the cause of the dispossessed and voiceless, such as Muslims' *Muslim World Book Review*

THE FATE
OF ABRAHAM

Why the West is Wrong About Islam

PETER OBORNE

SIMON &
SCHUSTER

London · New York · Sydney · Toronto · New Delhi

First published in Great Britain by Simon & Schuster UK Ltd, 2022
This edition published in Great Britain by Simon & Schuster UK Ltd, 2023

3 5 7 9 10 8 6 4 2

Simon & Schuster UK Ltd
1st Floor
222 Gray's Inn Road
London WC1X 8HB

www.simonandschuster.co.uk
www.simonandschuster.com.au
www.simonandschuster.co.in

Simon & Schuster Australia, Sydney
Simon & Schuster India, New Delhi

A CIP catalogue record for this book
is available from the British Library

Paperback ISBN: 978-1-3985-0105-8
eBook ISBN: 978-1-3985-0104-1

Typeset in Perpetua by M Rules
Printed and bound by CPI Group (UK) Ltd, Croydon, CR0 4YY

CONTENTS

PART TWO:
Britain and Islam

PART THREE:
France and Islam

PART FIVE:
Fate of Abraham

PROLOGUE

It has taken nearly twenty years to research and write this book. The Iraq War and its terrible aftermath was the trigger. Until then, I regarded the British state as virtuous.

I loved and was thankful for the monarchy, Parliament, the army, the rule of law, the NHS, the Foreign Office, the BBC and everything that the United Kingdom stood for. I considered liberal capitalism the best system of economics the world has had. I was a conventional Conservative. I wrote for Conservative newspapers.

I was brought up in the British establishment. My father was a career army officer. Lt-Col Tom Oborne, my grandfather, was awarded a DSO for building bridges after D-Day. Recently I went to the National Archives at Kew and obtained a copy of his citation. I read how he would make perilous journeys into the centre of rivers 'under accurate German small-arms fire'. I examined the citation carefully because he had never talked about his DSO when alive. If pressed, he said it was given not to him at all but the men under his command. It hangs above my desk as I write. My mother's father served in the British navy during both world wars.

Her grandfather in turn fought at Omdurman, in the Boer War and then for three years on the Western Front where he commanded the Cameron Highlanders and acquired a bar to his DSO. Winston Churchill, according to family tradition, was his fag at Harrow. My great uncle, aged just nineteen years old, was killed in the First World War. My mother, who was brought up in the same house in Devon where he spent his childhood, says she used to see this young man with his gentle, innocent, kindly face on the landing when she was growing up in the 1930s.

You had to look quite hard to find a male member of my family who had not served at some point in the armed forces. I was taught that all these brave men fought for tolerance and decency, and stood up for the underdog against fascism and bullying.

This was the atmosphere I breathed while I grew up, and I eventually took some of it with me into a career in British journalism. In 2001, when the planes flew into the Twin Towers, I was political correspondent on *The Spectator*, the political magazine of the former ruling class.

Boris Johnson was the editor, and we would spend much of our time describing doomed attempts by the Tory party to cope with the calamities and humiliations inflicted by Tony Blair's New Labour. Johnson would say: '*The Spectator* is not a political magazine: we are a journal of manners.' New Labour ran Britain, but not *The Spectator*.

This idyll could not last. The turning point was Iraq, and my realisation that the British state was party to a lie about the existence of weapons of mass destruction in order to justify an illegal war. This led me to re-examine everything that I believed.

Then came the Hutton Report into the death of the government scientist David Kelly. I read this document and realised that this too was a deception. I had not grasped that judges could be bent. I reeled, bent down and placed my head in my hands. I had liked the look of Lord Hutton, with his clipped speech and grey, sober suits. He made a fool of British justice. I had followed the Hutton Inquiry closely, and knew the evidence as well as he did.

I went mentally into opposition to the British state. I wrote a book, *The Rise of Political Lying*, which explored the collapse of integrity which had permitted the Iraq War. I read deeply and started to understand that truth as I had been brought up to understand it – based on empirical evidence which could be independently tested – no longer existed. It had turned into an instrument of power, a weapon to be used and manipulated for political advantage. This was years before the term 'fake news' had become current with the emergence of the alt-right and Donald Trump, so that was more of an original insight then than it is now.

Then I turned to a more ambitious enterprise. It had become plain that Tony Blair and the war party couldn't have got away with telling their lies if the state – the judiciary, the civil service, the Foreign Office, the intelligence services – had not been party to the deceit. So I wrote a larger book, *The Triumph of the Political Class*, which explored how traditional British institutions had abandoned their integrity in order to become part of a broader political project.

It also hit me hard in the course of writing these books that I had been wrong to share the conventional assumption that the British media told the truth and by doing so held government to account. I concluded that many British journalists were actually instruments of power and part of a client media class that worked alongside and formed part of the governing elite.

My experience was the mirror image of the journey made by many of my former adversaries on the left. Iraq didn't shock them because they had always believed that the British state was rotten. Lying didn't shock them because they always assumed that the British state lied. A venal press couldn't shock them because they'd always assumed the media was biased. War crimes couldn't shock them because they always believed that the British state was illegal. They had never considered, as I had, that the British state could be fair-minded and decent. They opposed almost all the things I as a young man had as a whole supported: the Cold War, the nuclear deterrent, British foreign policy, spending on arms, the alliance with the United States, the first Gulf War in 1991.

Then there occurred the historic split on the left between those who saw Iraq as a just war and those who saw it as an act of aggression. A significant group abandoned their former comrades and became advocates for the American alliance, Tony Blair, the CIA and George W. Bush's 'war on terror'. They joined the establishment just as I was leaving it. Some time in 2003, they and I passed one another, like ships in the night.

How I came to write this book

I started to investigate attacks on Muslims, just as a traditional reporter sets out to expose a miscarriage of justice or unsolved murder. I opened a file on the anti-Muslim stories which worked their way almost every day into the pages of British newspapers, including the ones I worked for, many from political and security sources. The first case I examined concerned an alleged plot by suicide bombers to attack Old Trafford football stadium, home of Manchester United. The story was a national sensation, dominating ITN and Sky News for two days. The front page of the *Sun* splashed 'MAN U SUICIDE BOMB PLOT' with a two-page spread inside.[1] This inflammatory press reporting was given ample assistance by the Manchester police, while politicians cheerfully joined in.

I went to Manchester and tracked down one of the suspects, a Kurd. He was a refugee from Saddam Hussein's Iraq who had always supported Manchester United: perhaps it was his most meaningful emotional connection with Britain. The *Sun* reported that the suspects had planned to sit at different parts of the ground in order to inflict maximum damage with their bombs. In fact, they'd bought the tickets off touts, which is why their tickets were for seats in different parts of the stadium. This information had not been made public, and could only have come from the Manchester police. The Kurdish refugee was never charged. But he had suffered so badly from having his name linked to a terrorist plot that he asked to remain anonymous.[2]

The Manchester police, having promoted this false story,

refused to launch an investigation into the press leaks. This kind of deceitful private collaboration between police (or security services) and media in the manufacture of fabricated stories about Muslims has become endemic in British public culture. In Part Four of this book, entitled 'The Enemy Within', I will set out more examples of this false reporting, promoted with immense vigour by award-winning columnists and reporters from Britain's most respectable newspapers. I will name names, while providing proof of an abuse of media power so systemic and ruthless that it cannot be regarded as traditional news and is more accurately described as a sustained, calculated assault on a minority.

This ugly discourse differs from other bigotries. It's not just a phenomenon of the tabloid press. It is also sanctioned and permissible in highbrow circles. In 2006 Martin Amis, one of the UK's most acclaimed novelists, gave an interview in *The Times*. 'There is a definite urge – don't you have it?' remarked Amis, 'to say, "the Muslim community will have to suffer until it gets its house in order".' He went on to describe this suffering: 'Not letting them travel. Deportation – further down the road. Curtailing of freedoms. Strip-searching people who look like they're from the Middle East or from Pakistan . . . Discriminatory stuff, until it hurts the whole community and they start getting tough with their children.'[3]

Amis was using the language of fascism. His books continued to sell, and his work is celebrated.[*]

In the weeks after Amis's outburst, his fellow author Ian

---

[*] Significantly, and to his credit, Amis has since retracted his remarks. In his words: 'It was a rash remark made at a terrible time. Ten years on from September 2001, we have still not got a usable word for what we mean. People think you are talking about Islam but you are not. "Islamism" is hopeless because it has got too many letters in common with Islam. I suggest we call it al-Qaeda. What I said was that there was an urge. No one can tell me that there was not. By the next day, I had changed my mind because that is collective punishment, but people were saying that. More than 95 per cent of Muslims are horrified by this ridiculous, nihilistic wing and should not be connected verbally or otherwise with these extremists.' 'Martin Amis: "I wish my sister had converted to Islam"', *Guardian*, 16 March 2010.

McEwan came to his defence. 'A dear friend had been called a racist,' he said. 'As soon as a writer expresses an opinion against Islamism, immediately someone on the left leaps to his feet and claims that because the majority of Muslims are dark-skinned, he who criticises it is racist.' This was, according to McEwan, logically absurd and morally unacceptable. 'Martin is not a racist. And I myself despise Islamism, because it wants to create a society that I detest, based on religious belief, on a text, on lack of freedom for women, intolerance towards homosexuality and so on – we know it well.'

Likewise, the celebrated journalist Christopher Hitchens spoke out in support of Amis. Writing in the *Guardian*, Hitchens said: 'It is much worse than pointless, in the face of genuine worry about the spread of real bigotry and awful violence, to try to pin the accusation of prejudice on those who are honestly attempting to ventilate the question, and to clarify it.'[4]

It is important to understand that in the view of many mainstream British politicians, newspaper editors and writers, hostility to Islam is justified. 'Islamophobia?' says the *Sunday Times* columnist Rod Liddle. 'Count me in.'[5] Liddle (like many writers on *The Spectator*, the *Daily Telegraph* and the Murdoch press) denies the existence of Islamophobia, saying that it 'seems to me an entirely rational response to an illiberal, vindictive and frankly fascistic creed'. This is a position which validates, not refutes, the existence of Islamophobia.[6]

The history of the post-war United Kingdom is in part the story of enlightenment: the steady eradication of irrational fears and resentments. Some of the prejudice against foreigners, gays, Jews, Irish and Black people had softened, though much remains. One resentment is stronger than ever. Prejudice against Islam – often given the cumbrous portmanteau name Islamophobia – is arguably the UK's last remaining socially respectable form of bigotry. This means there is very little social, political or cultural protection for Muslims: as far as the British political, media and literary establishment is concerned, the normal rules of engagement don't apply. I started to understand that a special form of discourse has emerged to define, ostracise and isolate Muslims, and set myself the task of exploring how it works.

Every year, as part of my duties as a political correspondent, I would attend the Conservative Party Conference. I noted that Muslim organisations were treated especially badly. They found it nearly impossible to find speakers for their events, which were often cancelled at the last moment, and the authorities treated them with barely concealed hostility.

Out of support for the underdog, I started to accept Muslim invitations to speak or chair their panels. At one, a Muslim businessman made a particularly strong presentation. He argued that Muslims were naturally conservative: hard-working and family-minded people who want to stand on their own feet. He made much of the paradox that very few Muslims vote Conservative, explaining this was a legacy of Conservative hostility towards immigration in the post-war era. He argued that this hostility was now history, meaning that Muslims were now a promising Tory target group.

The Conservative Party chairman Grant Shapps had promised that a Tory MP would speak at the event. As so often, none turned up. The organisers felt insulted. I agreed with them.

Later that evening the *Daily Telegraph* held its annual conference party. This was always an enormous event, and the prime minister, Chancellor of the Exchequer, and the bulk of the Cabinet invariably attended. I was there in my then role as the paper's chief political commentator. I spotted Grant Shapps and strolled across the room to ask him why he had broken his promise.

The Conservative chairman blamed administrative oversight and confusion. I replied that other organisations the Conservatives valued never suffered in this way. I cited the Conservative Friends of Israel event the same evening, which had been attended by plenty of Cabinet ministers and scores of MPs. After all, the Muslim organisation had only asked for one solitary MP.

Mr Shapps changed tack. He claimed that there was a security issue. I replied that his insinuation that the Muslims at the meeting posed a threat to life and limb was ridiculous. In any case, since the Muslim event took place inside the secure zone, everybody present had been obliged to undergo security checks in advance, in addition to being screened and frisked. The Conservative chairman had no answer.

I made further enquiries, only to learn that all mainstream political organisations, including Labour, behaved in the same way. One example was the Global Peace and Unity Conference, billed as the largest Muslim get-together in Europe, which was to be held the following weekend. The organisers had invited a number of MPs, party spokesmen and ministers. They had all refused. I rang up the GPU and told them I was available to speak if needed.

The conference was held in East London. When I got off the train at Stratford, agitators were harassing visitors. They turned out to be followers of Anjem Choudary, a Muslim preacher since convicted of encouraging support for the terror group Islamic State. His supporters were distributing pamphlets. I picked one up. It warned that the conference was haram – an Arabic word which means forbidden. The protesters were annoyed by a number of issues, including the fact that men and women were mingling together inside. The pamphlet stated that women were being 'paraded in front of others as objects of desire and where they show off their beauty as opposed to being people who are honoured and whose integrity is protected'.[7]

The pamphlet also objected to the presence of politicians: 'The first pillar of belief is to reject anything worshipped, obeyed or followed other than Allah. This includes members of the British Parliament or indeed anyone taking the role of legislator in contradiction to sovereignty and supremacy belonging solely to Allah.'

The pamphlet's authors were wrong about this. When I got inside, not a single MP was present. They had all been told by their party machines not to attend. However, the pamphleteer reserved his greatest contempt for fellow Muslims, who were declared to be apostates from Islam, since the conference was a den of un-Islamic iniquity. Yet women and men were dressed decently. Children were running around. Families were on a day out. I met the Imam of Copenhagen, a British army officer who later tried to get on the Conservative Party candidates list, several Haredi Jews,* pro-Palestinian activists and a former Anglican Bishop of Jerusalem.

I had a long conversation with the leader of the Parliament of the World's Religions, who spoke urgently of the plight of the Rohingya Muslims, urging me to travel to Myanmar to report on their plight. This was several years before the majority of the Rohingya were driven over the border to neighbouring Bangladesh, with many thousands being shot, burned alive or raped.

I found the event's organiser, a businessman called Mohammed Ali Harrath, almost prostrate with despair because of the boycott. Later, I made a point of getting to know Harrath (he turned out to be one of the bravest men I have met) and I will tell the harrowing story of how he escaped from prison in Tunisia and made his way to Britain when I deal with Western foreign policy and Islam.

His Global Peace and Unity Conference existed in a political and social vacuum. Its denizens were despised by the British political establishment. But they were also hated by the terror groups al-Qaeda and Islamic State. They were simultaneously within the law and outside the bounds of respectable discourse. None of the people there were criminals, let alone terrorists.

They were the enemy within, to be monitored and harassed. When my turn came to speak, I told the audience that I found that the way they were being treated was contrary to the British tradition of fairness and decency. And here they were, a collection

---

* I believe from the Neturei Karta group of anti-Zionist Jews.

of (mainly) British citizens who were not welcome in British society, even though they had done nothing illegal. Why weren't they welcome? Who had they offended? What laws had they broken? Who indeed made the unacknowledged, unspoken rules that turned them into pariahs?

This book is in part the story of my attempt to answer this question. I travelled round Britain listening to community leaders, imams, scholars, students and politicians. I spoke at Islamic meetings. I have talked at length to the (often basically brave, kindly and decent) people who dislike British Muslims to try and understand why they feel that way. I have gained some understanding of what it is like to be Muslim in Britain, making me wonder whether Britain really is the decent, open and tolerant country that most of us think we live in.

Of course I can understand why it feels that way for many people. That's how it still feels to me too, as a white, middle-class Briton. My freedoms are not under threat. Muslims, however, are subject to arbitrary arrest. Their bank accounts get frozen, for no apparent reason. They get libelled and insulted at will in the national press and broadcasting media, and slandered, spat at or physically attacked in the streets. Cancel culture is a relatively new phrase in public discourse, but prominent British Muslims, as I show in this book, have lived with it for years.

All this is greeted with national indifference. Very few people care about the predicament of British Muslims. Many resent them or feel afraid. I found it hard to get articles highlighting the problem published. Embarking on this work caused me to question many ideas and concepts that are today taken for granted. Words and phrases (Islamism, extremist, moderate, non-violent extremism, British values, radical, radicalisation, terrorism) form part of a pseudo-scientific discourse that relies heavily on abstract concepts and technical terms which are often used to stigmatise Muslims.

An innocent-sounding term – 'fundamental British values' – has been constructed as an officially sanctioned attack phrase against those Muslims who deviate from approved conduct and language.

Later in the book, I will set out in detail how think tanks and politicians have deliberately constructed or moulded these words in order to categorise and control British Islam. Since I will use these terms throughout the book, I provide definitions below, along with short notes on their use and abuse.

Islamism

Many Western writers argue that Islamists (supporters of Islamism) are hell-bent on the destruction of the West and indeed any institution or nation state which refuses to impose Islamic law.[8] The Conservative political thinker Roger Scruton wrote that Islamism was a term 'recently introduced in order to distinguish Islam, as a religious creed and devout practice, from Islamism, which is the belligerent attempt to impose Islamic government and Islamic law on people regardless of whether they consent to it'.[9]

In Western discourse, the term has come to be attached to violent groups such as al-Qaeda and Islamic State. In 2013, the Council of American-Islamic Relations took issue with this definition of Islamism. It complained that the Associated Press news agency's definition of an 'Islamist' – a 'supporter of government in accord with the laws of Islam [and] who view the Quran as a political model' – had become shorthand for 'Muslims we don't like'.

AP altered its style guide, telling reporters:

Do not use as a synonym for Islamic fighters, militants, extremists or radicals, who may or may not be Islamists. Where possible, be specific and use the name of militant affiliations: al-Qaida-linked, Hezbollah, Taliban, etc. Those who view the Quran as a political model encompass a wide range of Muslims, from mainstream politicians to militants known as jihadi.[10]

The International Crisis Group usefully divides Islamist groups into three categories. The first is political Islamist groups, the most famous of which is the Muslim Brotherhood, founded in Egypt in 1928 with the dramatic announcement that 'The Quran is our constitution'. It is certainly the case that the Muslim Brotherhood promises to use Sharia (Islamic law) and challenge Western cultural influences.[11] Yet it works within national political systems, renounces violence and claims to discern no contradiction between democracy and Islamism.

Secondly, there are revivalist groups, interested not in political power but spiritual and moral regeneration. A notable example is the Tablighi Jamaat movement, which began in India but now works across continents.

The final category embraces groups that employ armed struggle to fight regimes in the Muslim world which they deem un-Islamic, as well as non-Muslim occupiers and the West. Outside the territories they control, they are no more than fringe movements.[12] Though they claim inspiration from the Quran, their doctrine about the killing of innocent civilians is not supported in Islamic scripture according to the overwhelming majority of Muslim scholars.[13] A great deal of mainstream discourse in Britain and the West elides violent Islamist groups like Islamic State with mainstream Islamist groups, treating all as a common threat.

Radical

Over lunch ten years ago, I asked the then rising Conservative star Jeremy Hunt, later Foreign Secretary, to describe his political philosophy. Hunt replied: 'I am a radical.' Mainstream politicians, whether from the right or left, tend to define themselves as 'radical'. When applied to Muslims, the word means subversive, dangerous, opposed both to society and to the state. A radical Muslim attracts the unwelcome attention of the authorities and may be locked up.

The term 'radicalisation' describes the journey from the approved state of being a 'moderate' to becoming a radical extremist, or an Islamist Muslim. A Muslim can only be rescued from this predicament if she or he agrees to undergo a process of 'deradicalisation'.

Note the important difference between Western radicalism and Muslim radicalism. Politicians view Western radicalism as a sign of modernity and a willingness to take on the supposedly backward institutions of the twenty-first-century state. Not so Muslim radicalism. Official doctrine holds that radicalised Muslims have repudiated modernity itself. The authorities consider that signs of radicalisation include conservative social attitudes, exemplary devotion and refusal to adopt the sartorial conventions of Western civilisation. This is sometimes called the 'conveyor belt' theory: the more Islamic an individual becomes, the more likely he or she is to commit an act of violence. According to this thesis, Islamist extremism (often used as if synonymous with Islamism) inexorably propels individuals towards terrorist violence.[14]

Extremism

In 1912, Viscount Helmsley, destined to die on the Western Front a few years later, became the first MP to use the term in Parliament when he warned against female 'extremists' who wanted to vote. Once women won the vote, politicians employed the term to describe supporters of independence for India. Today, *opponents* of universal suffrage or Indian independence would be regarded as extremist. These and other examples illustrate the problem of the term extremist.

In the 1970s, the British left was routinely accused of extremism, leading the Labour leader Michael Foot to reply that 'most of the great reforms in history have been carried through by people who originally were extremists'.[15] Senator Barry Goldwater, the Republican candidate for the presidency in 1964 and seen by many as godfather of modern American conservatism, agreed with Foot and told his party's nominating convention in 1964 that 'extremism in the defence of liberty is no vice'[16]

This proposition was defended by Malcolm X at an Oxford Union debate. He said: 'As long as a white man does it, it's all right, a black man is supposed to have no feeling. But when a black man strikes back, he's an extremist, he's supposed to sit passively and have no feelings, be non-violent and love his enemy no matter what kind of attack, verbal or otherwise, he's supposed to take it.'[17]

From 2001 onwards, the term extremism has come to be associated in particular with Islamism, leading to a series of recent attempts to define 'extremism' by statute. It proved impossible to do this. This is not surprising. Extremist is a modern term for heretic, and should be used with caution.

Non-violent extremism

Before the term came into use under David Cameron's premiership, the phrase 'non-violent' was only used to describe forms of peaceful political action or civil disobedience.[18] Non-violence was not seen as dangerous or sinister, indeed rather the reverse: as another method of laudable democratic political engagement.

Non-violent extremism was based on the same core assumption as the theory of radicalisation explored in the section above: namely, that there is within Islam a pool of ideas which, while not in themselves violent, are nevertheless dangerous because they are conducive to terrorism.

The first use of the term on the floor of the House of Commons came from Theresa May as Home Secretary, when she announced her new Prevent strategy in June 2011. May said that Prevent would be aimed at stopping al-Qaeda, but crucially added that the strategy 'must also recognise and tackle the insidious impact of non-violent extremism, which can create an atmosphere conducive to terrorism and can popularise views that terrorists exploit'.[19]

This was the first explicit parliamentary articulation of non-violent extremism. Though not recognised as such at the time, it was a significant moment in political history because it implied massive new powers for the state to police not just criminal activity but also opinion.

Traditionally, British citizens have been allowed to think and conduct themselves as they wanted, so long as they stayed within the law. Thanks to the concept of non-violent extremism, this is no longer the case. Citizens may be harassed, put on secret lists or barred from public life without having committed an offence. I will consider the practical aspects of this new situation in Part Four.

British values

One definition of non-violent extremism is opposition to 'British values'. The presence of one can therefore be taken as the absence of the other, and vice versa. The British government describes British values as 'democracy, the rule of law, individual liberty and mutual respect and tolerance of those with different faiths and beliefs'.[20] At first sight, there appears little to object to here.

But what makes these values British? These are liberal values shared across much of the world. Britain is a well-established country which has evolved a set of institutions and ideas over centuries. Many of these do not adhere to official British values. Public schools of the sort attended by two of the last three British prime ministers are single sex. The monarchy is hereditary. Legislators in the House of Lords are appointed.

There is also a chronological problem. Britain only became a full democracy in 1928 when women over the age of twenty-one were given the vote. Likewise, religious tolerance and respect is a very recent phenomenon in Britain. Does this mean that before this we had no values, or that the values we did have were not British?

No one is more self-deprecating about national identity than the British. Some liberal democracies, such as France and the United States, celebrate their nationhood through specific values. But Britain has no equivalent to *liberté, égalité, fraternité*. As the Conservative writer Janet Daley has noted, the British have 'arguably the most un-solemn, unselfconscious, unobtrusive sense of national identity of any people in the known world. Indeed, it is precisely this ironic diffidence which could be regarded as the essence of the British national character.'[21] I will show in this book how ministers have promoted this most un-British of notions as an attack phrase to isolate and attack Muslims.

These terms can be used in various combinations as in 'Islamist extremist,' 'extreme Islamist', 'Islamist terrorist', etc. Sometimes they are treated as if they were synonymous (i.e. Islamist and extremist). On other occasions, the terms are used as opposites. Thus moderation is opposed to extremism, radical to moderate. I will show how they have been designed to separate 'good' Muslims from 'bad' Muslims. The effect is to encourage prejudice against all Muslims, along with the belief that Islam itself is an enemy of British and Western society.

Whenever the terms are encountered, they should be treated with suspicion. They will all recur from time to time in this book, and I ask readers to bear in mind these misleadingly simple words and phrases as they read, and to remember they do not always mean what you think.

INTRODUCTION

The term 'Judaeo-Christian tradition' has played an important role in the construction of the most successful political narrative of our time: that Western civilisation (and, above all, the Judaeo-Christian religion it represents) is under mortal danger from forces which threaten to destroy everything we stand for, and must therefore be defended at all costs.

The very concept of the 'Judaeo-Christian' tradition may at first appear to be a statement of the obvious: Europe has been Christian for roughly fifteen centuries, and Christianity emerged out of Judaism. The Christian and Jewish traditions therefore share a magnificent literary, moral and religious inheritance. The stories which we learn in our childhood – about Adam and Eve, Cain and Abel, Abraham and Isaac, Moses and Joshua – are Jewish stories. The same applies to the moral teachings embodied in the Ten Commandments and the words of the Old Testament prophets.

It is no coincidence that this term emerged from theological circles in the 1930s. It was employed by writers horrified by the rise of fascism and with it anti-Semitism. One of the first to adopt it was George Orwell in a review of a biography of the French novelist Stendhal, written in the final weeks before the outbreak of the Second World War.*

He and other users of the neologism would have been aware that the Christian church had, for many centuries, played a poisonous role in fostering anti-Semitism. In the 1930s, certain prominent churchmen across Europe were anti-Semitic, and flirted with emerging fascist movements. Meanwhile in the United States, American fascists inspired by Adolf Hitler and Benito Mussolini set themselves up in organisations like the Christian Front, Christian American Crusade, and the Christian Aryan Syndicate.[1]

In reaction to this, American politicians and intellectuals rejected the foundation legend of the United States as a Christian project and instead started to talk about a Judaeo-Christian nation. So did churchmen. In 1941, the influential *Protestant Digest* described itself not as a Christian publication, but for the first time as a periodical 'serving the democratic ideal which is implicit in the Judaeo-Christian tradition'. Priests and rabbis toured the country (and US military units), emphasising that Jews and Christians had more in common than previously acknowledged.

After the war, American public figures naturally used the term 'Judaeo-Christian' instead of simply 'Christian'. As the threat of fascism faded into a memory, atheistic communism was deployed instead to fill the role of political enemy number one. Mark Silk, professor of religion in public life at Trinity College Hartford,[2] notes in his study of the term that 'having proved itself against the Nazis, the Judaeo-Christian tradition

---

* Orwell wrote: 'Admittedly it is a queer kind of magnanimity that the characters show, but that is just where Stendhal's genius comes in. For what one is obliged to feel is not merely that the Duchess of Sanseverina is superior to the ordinary 'good' woman, but that she herself *is* a good woman, in spite of a few trifles like murder, incest, etc. She and Fabrice and even Mosca are incapable of acting *meanly*, a thing that carries no weight in the Judaeo-Christian scheme of morals. Like several other novelists of the first rank, Stendhal has discovered a new kind of sensitiveness. He is deeply sentimental and completely adult, and it is perhaps this unlikely combination that is the basis of his peculiar flavour.' George Orwell, review of F. C. Green, *Stendhal, New English Weekly*, 27 July 1939.

now did duty among the watchfires of the Cold War'. In 1953, Eisenhower became the first US president to use the term. 'Our form of government,' he said, 'has no sense unless it is founded in a deeply felt religious faith . . . With us of course it is the Judaeo-Christian concept.'

After the end of the Cold War, the term was once again redeployed. With Soviet Communism no longer the mortal enemy of the West, the Anglo-American historian Bernard Lewis wrote a paragraph which defined much of the following three decades:

> We are facing a mood and a movement far transcending the level of issues and policies and the governments that pursue them. This is no less than a clash of civilisations – the perhaps irrational but surely historic reaction of an ancient rival against our Judaeo-Christian heritage, our secular present, and the worldwide expansion of both.[3]

He was talking, of course, about Islam.

Three years later, the revered political scientist Samuel P. Huntington took up the theme. 'Nation states,' said Huntington, 'will remain the most powerful actors in world affairs, but the principal conflicts of global politics will occur between nations and groups of different civilisations. The clash of civilisations will dominate global politics. The fault lines between civilisations will be the battle lines of the future.'[4]

The most urgent and influential element of Huntington's theory concerned Islam. Huntington argued that with the end of the Cold War between the USSR and the West, it would be replaced by a new struggle between two irreconcilable enemies: Islam and the West. Huntington asserted that identity, rather than ideology, lay at the heart of contemporary politics. 'What are you?' he asked. 'And as we know, from Bosnia to the Caucasus to the Sudan, the wrong answer to that question can mean a bullet in the head.'

He added that 'Islam has bloody borders'. Writing in the wake of the Iranian Revolution and the displays of anti-American rage on the streets of Tehran (by no means surprising given longstanding US support to the Shah of Iran's bloody repression), he left readers with the impression that 1.5 billion Muslims all thought the same way – and had little to think about except animosity towards the West.

Within a few years, the obscene horror of 9/11 seemed to prove him right. This view – that Islam and the West (defined in terms of the Judaeo-Christian tradition) are embroiled in a mortal battle for survival which only one side can win – took hold. It shapes public thinking to this day. It has shaped policy across Europe and the US, and defined the popular understanding of Islam. President Macron's attacks on French Muslim citizens carry echoes of the Huntington thesis. It has become one of the primary assumptions driving official discourse in the UK today.

Unfortunately, the term 'Judaeo-Christian tradition' has increasingly been appropriated by the far right. In recent years, Donald Trump's former chief strategist Steve Bannon has set up an 'Academy for the Judaeo-Christian West' in a former Carthusian abbey in Italy.[5] Nigel Farage urged Europeans to be more courageous in standing up for what he called 'our Judaeo-Christian culture', alleging that a 'fifth column' was operating, one 'that is utterly opposed to our values'.[6] In Hungary, the right-wing President Orbán claims to embody what he calls the 'Judaeo-Christian heritage', something of an irony as he is frequently accused of toying with anti-Semitism.[7] But this dark irony should alarm us: eighty years ago, liberal intellectuals and politicians worried that the term 'Christian civilisation' was coming to be used in an ominously exclusive way because it excluded Judaism. And yet today the term Judaeo-Christian is being used to exclude Islam, the second most followed religion in Europe beside Christianity.

And this at a moment when the forces of supremacist

nationalism which manifested themselves in anti-Jewish Nazi Germany are emerging in France, Hungary, Greece, India, China, the US – and also in the UK. Anti-Semitism has not gone away. Jews are still a target.[8] But Islamophobia is the most virulent phenomenon of recent decades, fuelled by migration which has brought millions of Muslims to Europe. It is becoming more powerful every year, and moved with ease from the far-right fringes to the political mainstream.

Across the globe murderous hostility to Islam has been driven by a powerful, elemental narrative that Muslims are dirty, foreign, terroristic, anti-social and an existential threat. This has resulted in two genocides of Muslims in the last twenty-five years, the first in Bosnia in 1995 and the second in Myanmar in 2017. The Communist regime in mainland China has carried out extreme repression of the Muslim Uyghur people in Xinjiang province, with more than a million people being 're-educated' in concentration camps. In February 2020, an anti-Muslim pogrom swept through parts of New Delhi, the capital of India.

In the United Kingdom, it is becoming an open question whether Islam, our second most followed religion, will evolve into a welcome addition to our national identity, or be seen as a malign force only serving to corrupt our national ideals. The dominant view expressed by ministers, think tanks and in the press is that Islam is indeed a bad thing. Critics of Islam, who exist at senior levels in both major political parties, in general concur that the British state has become too accommodating to Muslims. Some even allege that certain Muslims are conspiring to take over parts of the state. This discourse may well win votes, but is dangerous and wrong. One of the purposes of this book is to dismantle these lies and falsehoods told about Muslims and Islam, and to open the way to a clearer and more truthful mutual understanding within the British tradition of religious toleration.

I will show that the United Kingdom is currently replaying an unpleasant debate about religious and national identity that has emerged time and again in history. Many of the moral panics today being mobilised against Islam duplicate or echo the torrent of murderous hatred that was directed against Muslims during the Middle Ages – and even more so Jews, who had the misfortune to live in England in much larger numbers until they were expelled by Edward I in 1290.

This in turn means going far back in time to show the ancient origins of the divide between Islam and the West. The book is divided into four parts, the first of which focuses on the history of Islam and the United States. This must be the starting point because, for the last twenty-five years, the US has been the primary source of global Islamophobia, and to understand why we must track this back to its source. I begin in colonial times, tracing the immense influence of the Holy Bible on so many early settlers, particularly the notion that they represent a second chosen people of Israel, in covenant with God, fulfilling his mission.

Their treatment of Native Americans as savages, outside God's covenant, anticipates much present-day American thinking about Muslims. I examine the first major foreign war fought by the US – against the Muslim 'Barbary pirate' states of North Africa. Again, this war uncannily anticipated the 'war on terror' and created stereotypes of American heroes securing the triumph of Christianity and civilisation over Muslim savagery that would endure for centuries.

I shall trace the way that this ancient notion of Muslim barbarism was developed and embellished by recent intellectuals, particularly the 'clash of civilisations' theorists Lewis and Huntington, and how their ideas were advanced by the media, and by bloggers and conspiracy theorists, as well as well-paid opportunists posing as academics or professional 'good Muslims'. The anti-Muslim diatribes of American politicians and intellectuals may therefore be understood as part of a continuum dating back to the earliest days of colonial settlement. I will show that hostility to Islam has also become an American business, promoted by special interests competing for both government and private money. Finally, I show how tens of millions of Evangelical supporters, obsessed by theories about the apocalypse and the end times, have driven US policies towards the Muslim world.

PART ONE

The United States and Islam

'As long as a white man does it, it's all right, a Black man is supposed to have no feeling. But when a Black man strikes back, he's an extremist, he's supposed to sit passively and have no feelings, be non-violent and love his enemy no matter what kind of attack, verbal or otherwise, he's supposed to take it.'

MALCOLM X, speaking at an Oxford Union debate on 3 December 1964, eleven weeks before his assassination

THE AMERICAN
RELATIONSHIP WITH ISLAM

The American relationship with Islam has always been determined by imagination rather than reality.

There have been Muslims on the North American continent
since Columbus – perhaps even before. Many arrived as African
slaves, and their character, beliefs and culture were almost totally
unknown to the white majority who shaped early American
society.[1] Removed from their homelands and living a marginal
existence, many adapted to a Christian-dominated environment
before and after emancipation by outright conversion to orthodox
Protestant Christianity or by inventing new forms of religious
practice in which Islam played a minor and private part.

During the first century of the United States, very few white
Americans would ever have encountered a Muslim at all, let
alone on equal terms. This meant that Americans were free to
view Islam through travellers' tales which had a great vogue in
early American life. These generally presented Islamic societies
in distant lands as cruel, despotic and backward, tempered by the
romantic mystery of the Orient and barely suppressed eroticism.

Although some of the Founding Fathers, notably Thomas
Jefferson, treated Islam seriously and respectfully, negative
stereotypes were established early in American history and were
powerfully reinforced by the two so-called Barbary Wars of
1801–05 and 1815. These wars are often ignored in histories of
the United States (for example, Paul Johnson does not mention

them at all in over 800 pages of his 1997 book *A History of the American People*), but they were hugely important, both politically and culturally.

They were the first wars fought by the US on overseas soil, in this case North Africa, nominally against the fading Ottoman Empire but actually against the independent rulers of Tripoli, Tunis and Algiers, whose fleets preyed freely against American merchant ships, kidnapped sailors and traders, and extorted heavy ransoms and tributes (what would now be called protection money). The Barbary pirates, as they were called, made early Americans as frightened of militant Islam as those of today became after 9/11. As with all foreign wars fought by the US, the Barbary Wars were preceded by a barrage of propaganda and fake news, mostly featuring enslaved Americans enduring appalling cruelty. (These accounts were exploited by abolitionists, who pointed out the irony of the US going to war against Muslim slavery while preserving Christian slavery on a far larger scale.)

The Barbary Wars established a lasting image of valorous Christian Americans prevailing over backward, cruel Muslims and spreading the blessings of civilisation to benighted lands. They are celebrated to this day in the opening words of the official hymn of the US Marine Corps: 'From the halls of Montezuma / To the shores of Tripoli / We fight our country's battles / In the air, on land, and sea.'[2]

After the Barbary Wars, the United States had almost no contact with any Muslim society for another seventy years, with the exception of minimal and usually inaccurate accounts from traders, missionaries and travellers.

The Holy Bible and its impact

Unlike the British and French, who ruled millions of Muslims through their colonial empires, the Americans encountered few Muslims in the conquest of the continental United States, nor in the Caribbean and central and southern American regions where they became the dominant power.

Up to the twentieth century, the most widely read book in the US was the Holy Bible. Until the nineteenth-century many Americans read nothing else,* and had little regular entertainment other than listening to sermons. In the early part of the century, the US underwent a series of religious revivals which engendered sects such as the Mormons, the Shakers, the Millerites and the Seventh-day Adventists. Although these sects argued fiercely with each other, they shared two powerful ideas in common.

The first was that Americans were a people chosen by God, like the Jews. Indeed, the Mormons professed that Americans were descendants of lost tribes of Israel (some believe that they managed to cross the Mediterranean and the Atlantic in midget submarines).³ The second was that Americans and Jews had a special role in the end of the existing world and the Second Coming of Christ, events which were imminent and precisely foretold in biblical prophecy. As we shall see below, the latter belief is still held by millions of American voters incited by popular (and profitable) Evangelical media in alliance with the Israeli government. This belief was the single most powerful influence on the overseas policy of the Trump administration.

The Bible, of course, makes no mention of Islam, as the religion followed its last book by several hundred years. The Bible therefore gives readers no understanding of Muslims. Anyone from Donald Trump upwards who relies *only* on the Bible as a source of authority can view Muslims at best as an aberration, ignorant and deluded people unaware of the will of God, and at worst, as enemies of the will of God and of his chosen people. For Americans increasingly obsessed by the imminent apocalypse, it

---

* However, *Arabian Nights* was also popular and contributed a countervailing image of Islamic societies as places of magic and mystery and erotic delights. See M. B. Oren, *Power, Faith and Fantasy: America in the Middle East, 1776 to the Present* (Norton, 2007), pp. 44–45.

has become easier and easier to identify Muslims as the shadowy figures mentioned in biblical prophecy who will dominate the world in the end times before being destroyed at God's hands. I shall return to this troubling subject in much more detail, but I want first to tell the forgotten story of the Muslim population of early America.

Muslim slaves

Muslims went to the Americas with Columbus and all the other early European explorers. Indeed, there are persistent legends that they got there first, exploited notably in 2014 by Turkey's President Erdogan.[4]

Columbus is said to have followed navigation charts created by Portuguese Muslims as far back as the twelfth century. However, because these Muslims were unpaid sailors and labourers, they are almost all anonymous and unknown. One exception is a certain Istafan, described as a 'black Arab originally from Azamor' in Morocco, renamed by his Spanish masters Estevanico de Dorantes. Istafan's story is as dramatic as that of any European explorer, but he barely figures in any history of exploration. He survived desert and shipwreck, and was the first non-American to meet many American Indian peoples, who adopted him as a medicine man.[5] Other exceptions barely count, as they involve invention such as the semi-fictional Kunta Kinte, the young Muslim from Gambia kidnapped and transported into slavery, who is the progenitor of the dynasty in Alex Haley's novel *Roots* (1975). He probably was a real person, son of a Muslim merchant and sold into slavery in 1767. But the facts remain obscure and Haley's imaginative treatment of his central character paradoxically drives home the anonymity of the Muslims who travelled to America. Very few early African American Muslims became known in the eighteenth and early nineteenth centuries because they were taken up by powerful white men to further their political, commercial or religious agendas – especially if they had become identified as Christian converts.[6]

Muslims were part of the slave population of the Americas from the earliest times but there is no consensus about the actual numbers. The lowest estimate is about 40,000 from a total slave population of 4.5 million in the 1860s. Given the incentives and pressures for slaves to convert to Christianity a figure of 40,000 professing Muslims in the 1860s is striking.[7]

There is some evidence (from the records of their masters) that Muslim slaves considered themselves superior to others and that they were used as supervisors and in skilled occupations.[8] 'Moorish' slaves were regularly identified as the leaders of slave rebellions in the Caribbean and South America from 1526 to the early nineteenth century.[9]

Within the slave population, there are accounts of men who maintained a knowledge of Arabic and kept up Muslim rituals as both a mark of separation from the rest and in an attempt to find a better place in white-dominated society. Such efforts had little or no success, and indeed when emigrants from Syria and Palestine reached the United States on a large scale in the late nineteenth century, they had a better chance of being classified as white if they were Christians rather than Muslims.

The general pattern was for Muslim slaves in the US to lose their identity as Muslims. One reason was the absence of Muslim women slaves, who had a high death rate and were outnumbered by men. The 'surplus' male Muslim slaves formed unions with non-Muslim women and had children by them who were not raised as Muslims. Islam survived in isolated island communities off Georgia and South Carolina. Elsewhere, Muslim men gravitated to Black Baptist churches which gave them a degree of protection from the worst conditions as slaves and, after emancipation, from the lynchings of the Jim Crow era.[10] As a result, Islam virtually disappeared from the US until the Muslim revival among African American communities in the early twentieth

century. Living a marginal life, as a fraction of the slave population of the US, it is not surprising that a substantial native Muslim
population had no influence on early American society. By contrast, Muslim powers overseas had a profound impact.

The United States fights its first foreign wars

American independence ended the protection of the British navy
(and British tribute money) for the new nation's merchant ships in
the Mediterranean and the Atlantic approaches to it. They therefore became easy prey for pirates based in North Africa.

The United States in 1783 had no navy, no money and no constitution. Its government was largely in the hands of individual
states, with limited powers for the Continental Congress. The
convoy which took the American delegates home from the peace
negotiations with Britain encountered Algerian pirates in the
Atlantic. The pirates' swift, three-masted xebecs were lightly
armed, but they did not need to be well armed against the virtually defenceless Americans.

A year later, three American merchant ships were seized by the
Algerians, and their crews taken hostage. In Algiers, they were
imprisoned, tortured and enslaved. The pirates created widespread panic: even the bold sailor John Paul Jones thought they
could 'extend themselves as far as the western islands', by which
he probably meant the Canaries or Azores. Fear of the enemy
within meant that four innocent Virginian Jews were banished
as suspected agents of the Algerians.[11]

Much as it would two centuries later in the Iraq War, the United
States tried to organise a coalition of willing European powers to
suppress the pirates, which the French refused to join, even though
they were still formally allied to the Americans. (As over Iraq,
the French became very unpopular and were widely suspected
of secretly conspiring with the pirates to destroy American commerce in the Mediterranean.) The French response was a bitter

disappointment to the American envoy to Paris, Thomas Jefferson, who oscillated between a policy of force against the Barbary pirates and the use of diplomacy (with the payment of tribute).[12]

Jefferson had more understanding of Islam than any American leader then or since. He kept a much-studied copy of the Holy Quran in his library. He had campaigned for religious freedom in his native Virginia and demanded recognition of the religious rights of the 'Mahamdan [sic], the Jew and the pagan'. Later, in the long debates on the future American Constitution, he would campaign for Article VI, which ensures to this day that no public office in the United States, including the presidency, may be withheld on religious grounds.[13]

However, he and his colleague John Adams (then minister to London, later the second president) were shocked by the response of Abd al-Rahman, the negotiator for the Barbary State of Tripoli, with whom they sought to negotiate America's first international treaty. 'It was written in the Koran that all nations who should not have acknowledged [the Muslims'] authority were sinners, that it was their right and duty to make war upon whoever they could find and to make Slaves of all they could take as prisoners, and that every Mussulman who should be slain in battle was sure to go to Paradise.'[14] Whether or not the Americans reported this response accurately in translation, it established for the first time a template of militant Islamic fanaticism which has now become familiar.

For lack of a navy, Jefferson and Adams stuck to diplomacy and tribute. They negotiated a treaty not with Tripoli but with the Islamic state of Morocco. It expressly denied any hostility towards Islam, as well as bearing an Islamic inscription and date.[15] However, the treaty brought little or no relief from piracy and hostage-taking. The demand for a navy to defend American lives and commerce was a key component of the nationwide debate on the Constitution and a powerful weapon for the Federalists against the proponents of states' rights. It was even suggested that without a Federal union to finance the navy, the Barbary pirates could cross the Atlantic and invade the American coast.[16] Eventually, in 1794, Congress met President George Washington's pleas by voting to create 'a navy adequate for the protection of the commerce of the United States against Algerian corsairs'.[17]

Meanwhile, early Americans were fed many lurid stories of their compatriots in captivity. As at present, some were fabrications.[18] One of these dubious accounts had the compendious title *The Captivity and Sufferings of Mrs Mary Velnet, Who Was Seven Years A Slave in Tripoli, Three of Which She Was Confined in A Dungeon, Loaded with Irons, and Four Times Put to the Most Cruel Tortures Ever Invented by Man*.[19]

Real or fictional, the enslavement of Americans influenced another key debate. Abolitionists condemned the hypocrisy of national indignation against the Barbary rulers when Americans were practising slavery on a much greater scale. The last writing of Benjamin Franklin made this point ironically in a purported defence of slavery by an Algerian prince. In 1796, the bestselling two-volume novel *The Algerine Captive* by Royall Tyler made the point directly and dramatically. The young hero and narrator Updike Underhill has a series of picaresque adventures, culminating in service as a doctor on an American slave ship. He is captured by Barbary pirates, enslaved in Algiers and becomes an earnest abolitionist on release. However, the most powerful abolitionist text was the first-hand testimony of an American sea captain, William Riley, who submitted to slavery for survival after being shipwrecked off North Africa. His book *Sufferings In Africa* sold nearly a million copies over forty years. One of his admirers was Abraham Lincoln.[20]

Implicitly, such arguments associated slavery with Islam, as the product of a defective religion and society, and not fit for a Christian nation. Abolitionists associated slavery with pre-modern societies ('savage', 'ancient' and 'nomadic') in contrast with modern (Christian) societies which introduced freedom. Understandably, there was a mighty counter-effort by Christians in the Southern states to argue that slavery was sanctioned by God and consonant with the both the Old and the New Testament, even in its most obnoxious form of chattel slavery, which made slaves the personal property of their owner.[21]

In spite of popular indignation against the Barbary states, John Adams, now the second president, maintained the policy of diplomacy and paying tribute.[22] The Barbary rulers increased their demands (besides gold, one asked for a menagerie of zoo animals and a portrait of George Washington) and, by 1800, tribute was absorbing a major part of the national budget. Adams's successor, Jefferson, decided to use the new navy against the Barbary rulers. As with future presidents, he managed to circumvent the constitutional requirements that only Congress could declare war. He ordered the navy to carry out a policing operation to respond to aggression by the pirates. In the event, the Pasha of Tripoli obliged him by declaring war on the United States in May 1801.[23]

The war began with the first American naval victory, a daring attack on the enemy ship *Tripoli*, but this was soon followed by reverses and Jefferson had to ask Congress for more ships. Not for the first time, the United States demonised its principal opponent, the ruler of Tripoli, Yusuf Qaramanli. James Cathcart, the American consul, called him 'a venal wretch, destitute of every honorable sentiment'.[24] The rulers of Tunis, Algiers and Morocco joined Qaramanli. By bad luck, the Americans were forced to surrender the warship *Philadelphia*, which was renamed *The Gift of Allah* by its new masters in Tripoli. With great daring, Stephen Decatur – the first American hero of a foreign war[25] – led a party to set fire to the new *Gift of Allah*, but its former crew remained in cruel captivity. Another daring attempt to destroy the entire fleet of Tripoli ended in failure. As Jefferson entered his second term, the United States was embroiled in an expensive war with a Muslim state with no apparent end in sight.

At this point, the former American consul to Tunis, the bellicose William Eaton, took matters into his own hands.[26] He had detested his assignment and described Tunis as 'a land of sodomy and rapine, whose people know no restraints of honor nor honesty'.[27] He added – in language echoed frequently in our time and comparable to the French 'razzia' visited on Algeria after its conquest in the 1830s – that 'there is but one language which can be held to these people and this is *terror*'.[28] He formed a plan for what would later become known as 'regime change', aiming to replace Qaramanli in Tripoli with his more pliable brother Hamid who was in exile in Egypt (more or less restored to the Ottoman Empire after the ejection of Napoleon's army). He met Hamid and raised a private army to attack Tripoli from the east and depose Qaramanli. Although this private army is remembered in the United States for its marine contingent, there were only 10 Americans (including Eaton himself in a private white uniform) and 90 Tripolitanians, along with 63 European mercenaries (mainly Greek) and 250 Bedouin tribesmen.[29]

Eaton proposed to lead them across 500 miles of the Western desert – a feat not attempted since the Roman wars against Carthage. He soon came to detest the Bedouin, who were essential as guides and labour. 'They have no sense of patriotism, truth nor honor,' he complained, 'and no attachment where they have no prospect of gain.'[30] He also fell out with Hamid. Nonetheless, his force managed to reach Tripoli's second city of Derna and to seize it in hand-to-hand fighting.

At this point, Jefferson abandoned the plan for regime change and made a peace, on favourable terms, with Qaramanli and the other Barbary rulers, which included deliverance for the American prisoners. Eaton was furious. Like another later disappointed general, Douglas MacArthur, he lobbied Congress against Jefferson's betrayal. Jefferson was nonetheless able to present his peace terms as victory, although he asked Congress to finance a massive expansion of the navy, which suggested that he had little confidence that the peace would be lasting.

If so, Jefferson was right. The Barbary rulers were quick

to resume piracy and hostage-taking when the United States was drawn into a naval confrontation with Britain during the Napoleonic Wars, which culminated in the Anglo–American War of 1812. This forced Jefferson to withdraw ships from the Mediterranean, as well as quietly resume the payment of ransoms and tribute. American public opinion demanded fierce action against the pirates when the war against Britain was finally ended by the Treaty of Ghent in December 1814. Reluctantly, President James Madison secured a declaration of war from Congress.

The second Barbary War was fought much more decisively than the first. A strong naval expedition led by Decatur sank the Algiers flagship, off the coast of Spain, in May 1815, before attacking the port of Algiers itself in June. Decatur and his diplomatic colleague William Shaler were able to dictate a Pax Americana to the Dey of Algiers. Shaler was graceless in victory. He belittled the Algerians and remarked that 'Islamism, which requires little instruction . . . seems peculiarly adapted to the conceptions of barbarous people'. He expressed amazement that 'so worthless a power should have been so long permitted to vex the commercial world and extort ransom'.[31]

The peace treaty provided for a permanent American naval presence in the Mediterranean. The wars had finally achieved their main objective and the Mediterranean was safe for American commerce. It also established lasting images of American heroism in the cause of liberty and Christian civilisation against the backward and barbaric power of Islam. An additional term of the treaty meant that seven North African prisoners were taken to the United States and put on exhibition as 'real bona fide imported Turks' in a number of New York theatres, beginning a tradition of presenting the Muslim as both threat and spectacle that would play an ongoing role in the popular American mindset.[32] Apart from the marine hymn already cited, the Barbary Wars supplied the first lyrics by Francis Scott

Key to what became the American national anthem – referring to 'turbaned heads bowed to the brow of the brave' and to 'the star-spangled flag of our nation'.[33]

American neo-conservatives *to this day* characterise the Barbary Wars as part of an inevitable conflict between the United States and militant Islam. One example is Joshua London, writing in the Heritage Foundation's journal in May 2006. Ignoring the powerful economic motives for piracy, London stated that 'America became entangled in the Islamic world and was dragged into a war with the Barbary States *simply because of the religious obligation within Islam to bring belief to those who do not share it* [my emphasis]'.

London continued:

The Barbary pirates were not a 'radical' or 'fundamentalist' sect that had twisted religious doctrine for power and politics, or that came to recast aspects of their faith out of some form of insanity. They were simply a North African warrior caste involved in an armed *jihad* – a mainstream Muslim doctrine. This is how the Muslims understood Barbary piracy and armed *jihad* at the time – and, indeed, how the physical *jihad* has been understood since Mohammed revealed it as the prophecy of Allah.

Obviously, and thankfully, not every Muslim is obligated, or even really inclined, to take up this *jihad*. Indeed, many Muslims are loath to personally embrace this physical struggle. *But that does not mean they are all opposed to such a struggle any more than the choice of many Westerners not to join the police force or the armed services means they do not support those institutions* [my emphasis].[34]

Joshua London's book *Victory in Tripoli* and his interpretation of the Barbary Wars was well received, with reviews focusing on parallels with contemporary Islamic terrorism.[35]

'Manifest Destiny' extends to the Middle East

During the early nineteenth century, the concept of 'Manifest Destiny' caught the imagination of millions of Americans. Invented by the New York journalist John O'Sullivan, it provided the intellectual foundation (as well as divine sanction) for an expanding white population to occupy the whole of the American continent. Its advocates were both anti-foreign and anti-centralist, and who felt that more states in the Union would weaken the power of the Federal government. But they were, above all, moralistic. The contemporary *United States Journal* proclaimed that 'we the American people are the most independent, intelligent, moral and happy people on the face of the earth'.[36]

Acting in the name of progress and civilisation, they would displace the Native American populations who inhabited huge tracts of the United States and conquer the American southwest from Mexico, the weak and troublesome successor to the Spanish Empire.[37]

Buoyed by military, economic and technological success, Americans began to extend the concept of Manifest Destiny to the wider world. American success in the Barbary Wars, combined with the decaying power of the Ottoman Empire, opened up the Middle East to American missionaries, traders and (as they would be called today) tourists. One of their chief exports was Manifest Destiny.

O'Sullivan himself suggested that the United States was ordained 'to establish on earth the moral dignity and salvation of man'. This doctrine was particularly attractive to the Evangelical Protestant missionaries in the Middle East, struggling against great odds to convert Muslims and older local Christian communities to their brand of Christianity. One prominent missionary, William Goodell, told an angry crowd in what is now Lebanon: 'We have come to raise your . . . population from that state of ignorance, degradation and death into which you are fallen, to do all the good in our power.'[38]

In this project, the Jews were seen as the prime allies of the United States, and the local Arabs as, at best, a local obstruction. One proponent of those views was William Lynch, who had led a successful American expedition to Palestine. In his best-selling memoirs, Lynch declared that any Arab's ruling passion was 'greediness of gold, which he will clutch from the unarmed stranger, or filch from an unsuspecting friend', whereas the Jewish people 'were destined to be the first agent in the civilization of the Arab'.[39]

Such ideas had a ready market in the early United States. The Pilgrim Fathers in the seventeenth century, fleeing religious persecution in England, had identified themselves with the Jews, set up a theocratic society modelled on the Old Testament and looked constantly for signs that their American settlements were foreshadowed in the Bible. They were gratified by the apparent discovery of displaced Jews among the American Indian population; as early as 1650, a Presbyterian minister published a book entitled *Jews in America* with far-fetched evidence that 'Indians are Judaicial'.[40]

Above all, they made Bible study the foundation of education. Harvard University was founded in 1636 partly to teach Hebrew to the sons of ministers. It was followed by nine other colleges before the American Revolution – all of them teaching Hebrew.[41]

American travellers, traders and missionaries were all but universal in their contempt for Islam. One traveller, the liberal Walter Colton, suggested that the extinction of Islam was a precondition for the arrival of (American) civilisation in the Middle East. He wrote: 'The same effort which lifts the Mussulman above the broken fetters of his despotism will place him on the ruins of his religion. The sceptre and the crescent, altar and throne, will sink together.' His contemporary Sarah Haight, who wrote a bestselling account of her travels in the Holy Land, called for an international political crusade to humiliate Islam and depose the Sultan and Caliph.[42]

After the Civil War, American travellers in the Middle East

greatly multiplied, encouraged by cheaper and faster steamship travel. They included Lincoln's Secretary of State, William Seward, and three of his generals, George McClellan, William Sherman and Ulysses S. Grant – who was received in state after serving two terms as president himself. None of these visitors returned with a good opinion of Muslim society. Sherman made a revealing comparison when he described Egyptians as 'a race that . . . look . . . and talk and act just like our Indians'. Grant's daughter Julia was depressed that 'Egypt, the birthplace, the cradle of civilization – Egypt, the builder of temples, tombs and the great pyramids – has nothing'.[43] However, the most devastating verdict on Muslims was delivered by Mark Twain in a series of highly paid newspaper articles, later collected into the bestselling 1869 book *The Innocents Abroad*. Twain described them as a 'filthy, brutish, ignorant, unprogressive, superstitious people' hopelessly deluded by the 'wild fables' of *Arabian Nights,* which was actually one of Twain's favourite books (and not, at the time, widely read in the Arab world).[44]

But Twain's comments on Muslims and his caustic account of places in the Holy Land could not wipe out the exotic allure of Islam to some Americans. A fraternal offshoot of the Masons was founded in 1870 called the Shriners, which adopted the trappings of Islam. Their symbols were the scimitar and the crescent, and their (male) members wore fezzes. The Shriners claimed to have been founded by the Prophet Muhammad's son-in-law Caliph Ali in the year of the Hegira 25.[45] The Shriners are still active today as a philanthropic organisation in the United States, supporting hospitals for children and burns victims.

We shall see other examples later of Americans' deeply ambivalent attitude to Islam, alternating horror at its supposed beliefs and imagined threats to American civilisation, while enjoying and appropriating many of its practices and rituals.

THE UNITED STATES ACQUIRES
MUSLIM SUBJECTS

The Spanish–American War of 1898 was one of the least credit-able in history. A weak American president, William McKinley, was pushed into war by newspapers, particularly the Hearst press, peddling fake news. The Americans won a series of rapid and popular victories against the decrepit Spanish Empire. Teddy Roosevelt became a national hero and dramatically accelerated his political career. He was chosen as McKinley's vice-president and shortly afterwards succeeded him as the youngest president in American history.[1]

The United States acquired all of Spain's former possessions in the Caribbean (Cuba and Puerto Rico) and, over considerable domestic opposition, those in the Pacific as well: the island of Guam and the Philippines. McKinley took the Pacific territories partly to keep them out of the hands of a major European power and partly for religious reasons. He was a devout man, much influ-enced by his wife Ida, a strong supporter of American missionary societies. These saw the Philippines as an outlet for civilisation by Protestant evangelism, and were disconcerted to discover that the Spanish had already converted most of the inhabitants to Roman Catholicism.[2]

The Philippines gave the United States colonial responsibility for a Muslim population of around 300,000. They represented less than 5 per cent of the whole population, but controlled Manilla, a territory in the northern island of Luzon and the major southern one of Mindanao, through their native rulers, the sultans and datus. Originally converted by Arab traders who had reached the Philippines a century before the Spanish, the Muslim population was known as the Moros – named pejoratively by the Spanish after the Muslim population expelled from Spain in the fifteenth century. The Moros resisted conversion to Catholicism and had never been subdued by the Spanish, staying loyal to their local Islamic rulers.

From military necessity, the Americans began the occupation of the Philippines by attempting to exploit Islam – a faith which, as we have seen, most Americans despised. The occupation had prompted the US-Philippine War, led by Christian Filipino nationalists, disappointed at their failure to gain independence after the overthrow of the Spaniards. It took the Americans three years to suppress it, at the cost of 5,000 American lives and at least 50,000 Filipinos.[3]

The Americans were worried that the leading Moro ruler, the Sultan of Sulu, might join the uprising. The American ambassador to the Ottoman Empire therefore asked Sultan Abdul Hamid – as Caliph – to appeal to the Sulu Muslims to submit to the Americans, who had promised not to interfere with their Islamic faith. This was ironic, since only recently the Sultan had been pilloried in American newspapers over the massacres of his Christian Armenian subjects. The Sultan obliged with an appropriate letter, and President McKinley expressed his gratitude. It is impossible to assess the letter's influence, but the Sulu Muslims, and the Moros generally, stayed out of the Filipino uprising.[4] In return, the Americans kept their promise and General John Bates negotiated a treaty named after him (by Americans) with the Sultan of Sulu. It promised Sulu autonomy and respect for 'all the religious customs'.[5]

American civilisation reasserts itself

The Bates Treaty was never popular with missionaries and other proponents of American civilisation. It required them to accept what they saw as local despotism and practices of polygamy and slavery. As at present, American administrators claimed to be particularly repelled by punishments including lashings, stonings and amputations.[6] Most importantly, it required them to tolerate Islam, which they blamed for the general backwardness and savagery of their new subjects.

The Americans based their view of the Moros on two main sources: missionaries who had encountered Islam in other parts of the world, particularly the Ottoman Empire; and rival colonial powers who ruled Muslim populations. Ironically, the Americans, who professed to abhor European colonialism and would not let anyone describe the Philippines as a colony, sought detailed advice on Muslims from every single European colonial power – even the Danes, who had almost none in their empire of Greenland, the Faroes and what are now the US Virgin Islands.[7]

Both sources pointed to the same conclusion: the Moros were outside the reach of modern civilisation on the grounds of their Islamic faith. Henry Otis Dwight was a prominent American missionary with extensive experience of the Ottoman Empire but none at all in the Pacific. In 1899, he published a much-read article entitled 'Our Mohammedan Wards' in support of the American annexation of the Philippines, framing it as the protection of their Christian population from the Moros. With arguments frequently copied since, he claimed that *all* Muslims were dedicated to the subjugation or killing of non-Muslims: 'Babies, almost before they are weaned, lisp the word "blasphemer" on sight of a foreigner.' The only language the Moros, as Muslims, would understand was overwhelming force, although eventually Dwight believed that sufficient contact with American Christian soldiers with 'high manly qualities' would induce them to abandon their faith.[8]

Among European colonialists, the most influential was Britain's proconsul in Egypt, Evelyn Baring, 1st Earl of Cromer. He gave long hours of instruction to a visiting American mission, headed by President Roosevelt's favourite general Leonard Wood, whom he had nominated as governor of Moro Province. This province was specially created in the main southern island of Mindanao to isolate Moros from the rest of the Philippines, almost like a Bantustan. Cromer told Wood that the Muslim faith was responsible for all the backwardness he could observe in Egypt. 'Swathed in the bands of the Koran,' said Cromer, quoting a popular British text, 'the Moslem faith, unlike the Christian, is powerless to adapt itself to varying time and place, keep pace with the march of humanity, direct and purify the social life, or elevate mankind.'[9]

Against this background, it is not surprising that American administrators quickly protested against the Bates Treaty's policies of non-intervention against Islam. One of them, O. J. Sweet, was especially incensed at a provision that public education in the Philippines should not attack any religion. 'The Al Koran, a monotheism, is the most colossal forgery of the Christian religion ever perpetuated since the foundation of Christianity. It teaches that it is the duty of those of that faith to convert all peoples to become followers and believers of Mohammedanism.' He wanted the Americans to use public education to counter the 'false doctrine' of Islam.[10]

Meanwhile, the Americans conducted a tribal census of the Philippines. It classified all Christian tribes as 'civilised' and all non-Christian ones, including Moros, as 'wild tribes'.[11] This attitude was reflected in the St Louis World's Fair of 1904. Muslim people were transported from their homelands and exhibited. The Philippines Exhibit cast the Moros as bloodthirsty and dangerous, and visitors were warned against photographing them for fear of rousing them to violence. Perhaps as a result, the captive Moros became one of the fair's biggest attractions. Visitors who lacked the nerve to defy the warnings and take their own photographs purchased and sent thousands of postcards of Moros to impress the folks back home.[12]

The Moros as American Indians

The St Louis World's Fair reinforced the identification of the Moros with American Indians (to use the then current term) – both were inevitable casualties of the march of American civilisation driven by Protestant Christianity. Unsurprisingly, this attitude was particularly prevalent among the American soldiers who had to fight the Moros when a series of local clashes became a major conflict which lasted from 1902 until 1911.

Between the end of the American Civil War in 1865 and the Spanish–American War in 1898, American soldiers had no combat experience outside the 'Indian wars'. As in those wars, American tactics against the Moros were based on the use of overwhelming force and firepower. The suppression of both Indians and Moros was justified as a defence of civilisation itself. In response to his Democratic opponent, who had condemned Republican imperialism, President Roosevelt used this argument when running for re-election in 1904: 'To abandon the Moro country, as our opponents propose, would be precisely as if twenty-five years ago we had withdrawn the army and the civil agents from within and around the Indian reservations in the West, at a time when the Sioux and the Apache were still the terror of our settlers. It would be a criminal absurdity.'[13]

However, the Moros were demonised by Republican politicians and media even more than the Indians – because they were Muslims. This became apparent after the First Battles of Bayang (1902) and Bud Dajo (1906), where more than 1,000 Moros, including women and children, were killed.[14] The latter attracted significant popular criticism at home, even among supporters of the colonial project – most notably a stinging pamphlet by Mark Twain entitled 'The Incident in the Philippines'. In response, the army's defenders briefed visiting Congressmen and journalists that its tactics were an inevitable response to the Islamic fanaticism of the Moros. This was strongly expressed in a letter in the

Christian Observer by a serving soldier. He described the Moros as 'barbarians and Mohammedans of the most intense sort' who were fighting Americans exclusively 'for their religion and we happen to be in their way'. He concluded that 'they are never conquered until dead' and added ominously that 'the women look upon Christians the same as the men'.[15]

The war absorbed 25,000 American troops, supported by Christian Filipino auxiliaries and constabulary, who took heavy casualties. Although the Moros had no unity of command, virtually no modern weapons except those captured from their enemies and no territorial sanctuaries, it took ten years to subdue the last resistance from them. The Americans owed much to their final commander, General John J. Pershing, later to command their forces on the Western Front in the First World War. Although continuing to rely on strength and firepower, Pershing made a genuine effort to understand the mindset of the Moros, including their faith, and inaugurated significant land and economic reforms which improved their condition and gave many a motive to stop fighting.[16]

The war was virtually forgotten at home. Veterans returned from it with no parades or public welcomes from their communities.[17] Few Americans felt any connection with their new colony in the Philippines. As critics predicted at its annexation, it was unprofitable and distant and required an expensive defence, especially from the growing threat of Japan.

The Democratic administration of Woodrow Wilson instituted civilian rule in the Philippines and encouraged Christian Filipinos to penetrate Moro lands. In the longer term, this transferred the United States' 'Moro problem' to the Filipino majority, and set up a new conflict after Philippine independence in 1946. The Moros were forgotten by the American public until their image was briefly revived in 1937 by a Hollywood movie, *The Real Glory*, starring Gary Cooper. This again presented the Americans as heroes defending civilised people from savage fanatics. One entirely fictional scene (starring the hero, played by Gary Cooper), created an enduring myth – later exploited by Donald Trump – that the Americans used pigs' blood and pigskins to prevent Muslim terrorists from entering paradise.[18] The movie had to be withdrawn in 1942 after the Moros fiercely resisted the Japanese occupation of the Philippines, leading to a reversal of roles in which the Moros became briefly visible to movie audiences as 'good guys'.

The British and the French ruled over millions of Muslims through their colonial empires for nearly two centuries, which ensured a lasting Muslim impact on their societies at home, confronting both nations with the problem of replacing relations based on hierarchy with equality. By contrast, the Americans accidentally acquired a small, isolated community of Muslim subjects in their colonial empire for a few decades. They never allowed them into their home country and made almost no effort to understand them or accommodate them.

After repressing them as savages unfit for American civilisation, they forgot about them. I will, however, return to the plight of the Moros later, describing how more recently they have been targeted by Christian settlers from the northern Philippines and inexorably dragged into the global 'war on terror' in a macabre repeat of the Moro wars of the first years of the twentieth century.

3

AFRICAN AMERICANS
REDISCOVER ISLAM

In the first chapter, I showed how Muslims among the slave population of the United States left almost no trace on American society. Emancipation brought no revival of Islam. Former slaves found that some sort of Christian identity made it easier to realise the short-lived gains of Reconstruction or to gain some protection from the 'Jim Crow' regimes of the white supremacists who were restored to power in the Southern states after the Civil War.

However, in the late nineteenth century, the rapid industrialisation and economic dynamism of the United States sucked in labour from all parts of the world. For the first time, the United States acquired a significant free Muslim population by immigration. This was derived principally from the Ottoman province of Syria, and the resulting hyphenated community became known as Syrian-Americans, although many originated in what is now Lebanon or Palestine. Punjabi Muslims from British-controlled India also settled in the United States, usually entering via Canada which was open to them as part of the British Empire.

For a number of reasons, it is especially hard to estimate the total Muslim immigrant population. First, the American immigration authorities did not record the religious affiliation of immigrants, being constitutionally barred from doing so. Second, immigrants often changed their given names, and those of their infant children, to the nearest American equivalent *before* they entered the United States.* Furthermore, the Ottoman Empire made it much harder for Muslims to emigrate than non-Muslims, prompting unknown numbers of Muslims to pretend to be Christians in order to get around the rules.

Once in the United States, an immigrant – just like a former slave – found it easier as a Christian to claim the benefits of American society than as a Muslim. In particular, Christian immigrants (and, for that matter, high-caste Hindus) were more likely to be classified as white and thus avoid specific restrictions on immigration and naturalisation.† American citizenship law in this period allowed naturalisation only to white people or those of African nativity or descent, which made white status for Asian immigrants a vital issue.

Asian Muslims had good reason to fear that Islam would be taken as a marker of non-white status. In a landmark citizenship case as late as 1942, at a time when thousands of Muslims were fighting for the Allied cause in the Second World War, District Judge Tuttle found against a Yemeni Muslim called Ahmed Hassan. He said: 'Apart from the dark skin of the Arabs, it is well known that they are a part of the Mohammedan world and that a wide gulf separates their culture from that of the predominantly Christian peoples of Europe. It cannot be expected that as a class they would readily intermarry with our population and be assimilated into our civilization.' He concluded with a startling piece of circular logic: 'the small amount of immigration of those peoples to the United States is in itself evidence of that fact'.[1]

Allowing for all of these factors, it is estimated that some

---

* The grandfather of my frequent collaborator Richard Heller was one such example. Born Rashid in Beirut, he had become Richard when he was brought by his family as an infant to Ellis Island. Richard's ancestors were in fact Maronite Christians who were assimilated into the Roman Catholic Church in the United States, but the case still illustrates the difficulty of guessing at religious identities from the names on immigration records.

† The Immigration Act of 1891 barred Muslims not on specifically religious grounds, which would have been unconstitutional, but because they were 'persons who admit their belief in the practice of polygamy'.

60,000 Muslim migrants settled in the United States between 1890 and 1924.[2] They were a presence in most great American cities, principally as labourers and shop keepers, while others became homesteaders on marginal land in rural states. Others were recruited as labour for specific industries; for example, in the copper mines near Butte, Montana, which is still home to a significant number of Syrian-American families.

But these Muslims are barely more visible in American history and society in this period than the Muslim slaves before them. They exercised no political influence. When the United States entered the Great War in 1917, it became a potential arbiter of the fate of Arab Muslims. But insofar as there was an Arab lobby seeking to influence President Wilson and the State Department, it was composed exclusively of Arab Christians.[3]

Muslim faith and identity remained a private matter, behind closed doors. The United States' first permanent mosque didn't appear until 1921. It was created in Dearborn, Michigan, to serve the Muslim workers at Henry Ford's automobile factory. The historian Sally Howell describes its distinctly American character:

> The Islam to be practiced in the Moslem Mosque of Highland Park would not be exotic, foreign, or a thing of spectacle. It would be an American faith tradition not unlike those found in nearby churches and synagogues. It would attract worshipers who were American citizens.[4]

The rediscovery of Islam by African Americans

Emancipation did little to change the living conditions for more than four million former slaves in the South, particularly after the corrupt bargain of 1876 in which the Republicans, the party of the late Abraham Lincoln, allowed the restoration of white supremacy in the Southern states in exchange for the election of their candidate in the disputed presidential election.[5]

Over the next four decades, the African American population doubled, but around 90 per cent continued to live in the rural South, prisoners of a backward economy dependent on cotton, deprived of basic civil rights and equal public education, and still subject to beatings and lynchings. Then, around 1910, agricultural depression and demand for labour in Northern cities induced the 'Great Migration' to other parts of the United States which accelerated during the Great War and the boom years of the 1920s. This migration slowed during the Depression of the 1930s, and even partly reversed as the South's economy revived more quickly than the North's. It resumed during the Second World War and into the prosperous 1950s. By 1970, more than six million African Americans had moved to cities in the North, Midwest and West.

The internal migrants saw major gains in their living standards – as long as they remained in work. Around 1916, at the start of the Great Migration, factory wages in the urban North were around three times more than what could be earned working the land in the rural South. These migrants also gained far more freedom around where they could spend their money, and African Americans set up many small businesses to attract them as customers. But rich Northern whites were scarcely less hostile to them than the poor Southern whites they had escaped, an outcome predicted by de Tocqueville in his – usually abridged – chapter on the 'three races' from *Democracy in America*.[6] Although formal segregation was unlawful outside the South, it was applied effectively in housing and education, as well as in access to many public service jobs by informal means, including violence and lynchings.

The summer of 1919, when the United States experienced a post-war slump, saw the worst spate of interracial violence in American history, mostly white on Black. The most violent episode, the Chicago Race Riot of 1919, was instigated by white attacks on Black people, in particular that experienced by a young Black swimmer who had drifted into a 'white' section of a beach.

Returning white war veterans were prominent in attacks on Black people who had moved into the city while they were overseas. The riot lasted for 13 days and left 38 people dead, 537 injured and more than a 1,000 African American families homeless.

Against this background, a number of Islamic movements – for the most part eclectic, syncretic and uniquely American – made headway among African Americans in cities. Their appeal was based on the identification of Islam as an 'African' faith which had never submitted to the white man, and as a pathway to self-respect and personal success, without acceptance of the white man's terms. The appeal of Islamic movements to African Americans was assisted by fissures within the Baptists and the decline of the social gospel movement.

Not surprisingly, these versions of Islam – especially the Nation of Islam, popularised by the brilliant and charismatic Malcolm X – inspired fear and resentment among the white majority and its guardians, notably J. Edgar Hoover's FBI. During the 1950s and 1960s, they also provoked deep splits within the African American community and the civil rights movement.

Freemasonry and Islam

To a striking extent, these movements were influenced by Freemasonry and other fraternal orders, which for years had appropriated many terms and symbols from Islam.[7] Both Sir Richard Burton and Robert Graves traced the origins of Freemasonry to Sufi Islam, while Freemasonry's chief symbol – the compass and square – appears to have been copied from the battle flag of the Ottoman Sultan Selim I.[8]

Masonry was a strong influence on Timothy Drew, renamed the Noble Drew Ali, who claimed Moorish origins and founded the Moorish Science Temple of America in 1913. It has a claim to be regarded as the first specifically Muslim organisation in the United States: although highly syncretic in its teaching, its predominant influence was Islam. Drew Ali blended Masonic and other rituals into the rites of the Temple, and eventually produced his own text, the *Circle 7 Koran*. Although much of this was copied from esoteric, non-Islamic texts, its final appeal was Islamic. He wrote:

> The fallen sons and daughters of the Asiatic Nation of North America need to learn to love instead of hate; and to know of their higher self and lower self. This is the uniting of the Holy Koran of Mecca for teaching and instructing all Moorish Americans, etc. The key of civilization was and is in the hands of the Asiatic nations. The Moorish, who were the ancient Moabites, and the founders of the Holy City of Mecca.

Drew Ali understood the need to combine his Islamic appeal with American showmanship. When he launched his most successful version of the Temple, in Chicago during the 1920s, he promoted it with a vaudeville show that featured a female singer, as well as himself performing not only as a healer but also as a Harry Houdini-style escape artist.[9] In spite of connections with powerful local politicians, including the Illinois state governor, Louis L. Emmerson, Drew Ali alarmed the Chicago police who watched his organisation vigilantly. During a factional dispute, one of his deputies was stabbed to death. Drew Ali was arrested. No charges were brought against him but he died shortly after being released from police custody. He was only forty-three and had no previous record of ill health, which led his most loyal followers to blame the police.[10]

Beneath his more esoteric teachings, Noble Drew Ali had two core ideas about Islam, which were crucially important to leaders who came after him. First, he believed that Islam would restore African Americans to their true heritage as a free Moorish people. Second, he believed that Islam would give them the self-discipline and application to succeed on their own terms, without pleading for favours from white society. John Wesley believed that Methodism would do the same for the English working class by enabling hard-working men and women to succeed on their own terms. Noble Drew Ali himself ran several quite successful businesses within his organisation and published a newspaper, the *Moorish Guide*. (His stabbed deputy was in fact his business manager.)[11]

Both of these beliefs were integral to the career of the much more famous Marcus Garvey, founder of the Universal Negro Improvement Association. Garvey never formally espoused Islam, but made many favourable references to the religion and seems to have accepted its claim to be a means through which African Americans could discover a faith for themselves as a free people. On 17 September 1922, Garvey declared that 'everyone knows that Mohammed was a Negro'. He earlier remarked: 'As Mohammed did in the religious world, so in the political arena we have had men who have paid the price for leading the people toward the great light of liberty.'[12]

Garvey was especially focused on business. He envisaged that African Americans would be empowered by a new sense of personal identity (partly through Islam) to own and develop businesses which would not only challenge white economic hegemony in the United States but enable them to return to Africa and lead its inhabitants to freedom from the white colonial empires. At that time, there were only two independent African states: the empire of Abyssinia and the republic of Liberia, which was virtually a subsidiary of the American Firestone rubber company.

Garvey attracted funds from his supporters to establish the Negro Factories Corporation, which he intended to make and market every major commodity in the United States, and to set up a major shipping company, the Black Star Line. At his peak in the early 1920s, he drew tens of thousands to his open-air meetings in New York and his Universal Negro Improvement Association had developed into a mass movement, with its own newspaper and a membership of at least one million.[13]

The Black Star Line came to grief through a combination of mismanagement, obstruction by employees (especially the white officers it had to use) and record-keeping failures, especially over the alleged purchase of one of its ships.[14] As Garvey had used the US Post Office to solicit funds, the authorities were able to bring charges of mail fraud against him. He conducted a bombastic and over-long defence, the (white) jury turned against him and he alone of the Black Star defendants was convicted and jailed.[15] After two years, President Coolidge had him released and deported to his native Jamaica, where he became influential and revered after his death, even if he were no longer a force in the United States. All this is essential background to understanding the astonishing phenomenon of Malcolm X and the Nation of Islam.

Elijah Muhammad, Malcolm X and the Nation of Islam

The Nation of Islam has been the most successful and durable African American organisation to espouse any form of Islam. Like Garvey and Noble Drew Ali, it too relied heavily on presenting Islam as a faith for free people and a pathway to personal reform and independent success. Its founder was a shadowy figure known variously as David Ford, Wallace D. Fard and, finally by his followers, Master Fard Muhammad. It was given out that he was the son of a Black man and a white woman, born in Mecca, into the tribe of the Prophet Muhammad; in fact, he was probably from what is today Pakistan. The FBI expended much energy trying to establish that he was all-white, born in New Zealand and a racketeer, and later that he was a Nazi agent.[16]

Fard began to preach door to door in Detroit in 1930. Much of his message had nothing to do with Islam, although his idiosyncratic teaching did draw loosely and selectively from certain elements of Islam. He told African Americans that they were a godly race who had originated in Mecca, from which they had been systematically stolen through 'tricknology' and enslavement by white men four centuries earlier. Fard taught that white people had been invented by an evil scientist called Dr Yakub and his followers, through experiments which murdered millions of Black infants.[17] Surviving Black people had been subjugated and enslaved by white people, who had destroyed their cultural identity by introducing them to gambling, alcohol and consumption of 'poisonous animals', especially pork and shellfish. Fard urged his followers to abjure these as Islam prescribed and they would prosper. He prophesied that, through Islam, Black people would be restored to their culture and their divine nature in a final apocalyptic reckoning.*

Fard clashed with the local authorities when he set up separate schools for his followers, and a separate security force, but by 1934 he had about 8,000 followers, nearly all of whom were employed and better-off than their contemporaries in Detroit.[18] Fard disappeared mysteriously and permanently from the record after some of his followers were accused of murdering four white men, but his organisation continued to regard him as an incarnation of God and the leadership of the Nation of Islam passed to his prophet, Elijah Muhammad. The organisation stagnated during the war when Elijah Muhammad went to jail for resisting the draft, but recovered rapidly when it recruited the supremely gifted speaker and writer Malcolm X. He quickly became its main speaker and, in 1961, was the founder-editor of its successful newspaper *Muhammad Speaks*, which achieved sales of 600,000 a fortnight. To its African American readers, it brought sympathetic coverage of Islam in Africa and the Middle East.[19]

Malcolm X offered, through Islam, a totally different vision of power for African Americans from the Christian leadership of Martin Luther King. He rejected King's idea of non-violent

---

* In Fard's words: 'ALLAH would separate us from the Devils and then destroy them; and change us into a New and Perfect People, and fill the Earth with Freedom, Justice and Equality as it was filled with wickedness; and making we, the Poor Lost-Founds, the Perfect Rulers.' Fardi Muhammad, *The Supreme Wisdom, The Final Call* (1993).

democratic change,* arguing that African Americans should prove their capabilities as a separate race and achieve economic and political power on their own terms. 'If you can't do for yourself what the white man is doing for himself,' he told them, 'don't say you're equal with the white man. If you can't set up a factory like he can set up a factory, don't talk that equality talk. *This* is American democracy, and those of you who are familiar with it know that in America, democracy is hypocrisy.'[20] He and the Nation called for a separate state for African Americans; before the Civil War, de Tocqueville had taken an equally bleak view on the prospects of racial equality.[21] It would be a Black-majority state partly financed by reparations to them for the unpaid labour of their ancestors. Malcolm X specifically rejected non-violence and called for them to be ready to defend themselves.[22]

The Nation of Islam reinforced Fard's original teachings about abstinence and personal reform, although its strictures were considered blasphemous by Orthodox Sunni Muslims and Shias alike. For example, it prescribed a month of fasting not during the shifting period of Ramadan but during December, when it believed that all Americans were most subject to temptation. (It also ensured the shortest hours of daylight for the fast.)[23]

The Nation of Islam went from strength to strength. During the 1960s, it invested successfully in a chain of small businesses, trucking concerns, farms, real estate and even a bank of its own.[24]

---

* Malcolm X believed that '. . . it is criminal to teach a man not to defend himself when he is the constant victim of brutal attacks. It is legal and lawful to own a shotgun or a rifle. We believe in obeying the law.

'In areas where our people are the constant victims of brutality, and the government seems unable or unwilling to protect them, we should form rifle clubs that can be used to defend our lives and our property in times of emergency, such as happened last year in Birmingham; Plaquemine, Louisiana; Cambridge, Maryland; and Danville, Virginia. When our people are being bitten by dogs, they are within their rights to kill those dogs.'

'We should be peaceful, law-abiding – but the time has come for the American Negro to fight back in self-defense whenever and wherever he is being unjustly and unlawfully attacked. If the government thinks I am wrong for saying this, then let the government start doing its job.' Malcolm X, 'A Declaration of Independence', 12 March 1964.

Both the organisation and Malcolm X had benefited greatly in 1959 when they were denounced in a celebrated television documentary *The Hate That Hate Produced*. Although tendentious, the programme introduced the Nation of Islam to millions of Americans, including African Americans, who had never heard of it.[25] Malcolm X became a national celebrity and a regular performer on television panels.[26] Membership of the Nation doubled to 60,000 within a few weeks.[27]

The Nation also gained hugely from its most famous recruit: Cassius Clay, the world heavyweight boxing champion mentored by Malcolm X and renamed Muhammad Ali by Elijah Muhammad. From millions of people who might otherwise have been repelled by its doctrines of racial separation, Muhammad Ali won admiration as a supremely gifted man being unjustly punished for his beliefs.

From 1963 onwards, Malcolm X was at odds with Elijah Muhammad over the latter's promiscuous private life. Their rift was aggravated when Elijah Muhammad rebuked Malcolm X for his provocative remarks on President Kennedy's assassination: he had referred to 'chickens coming home to roost', the chickens being a series of murders of Black victims, at home and abroad. In April 1964, Malcolm X went on the hajj. He met many Muslim leaders and, even more importantly, Muslim pilgrims from all races praying together, breaking bread together, sharing a common purpose. This intermingling shattered all his preconceptions. He rejected the Nation's (and his own) doctrines of racial separation as un-Islamic and founded two new organisations: one, the Muslim Mosque, Inc., dedicated to propagating mainstream Sunni Islam; another, the Organization of Afro-American Unity, to make common cause between African Americans and independence and human rights movements overseas. He maintained his commitment against white racism in the United States. Renaming himself el-Hajj Malik el-Shabbaz, he was, however, given little time to develop these new initiatives before his assassination by members of the Nation in 1965.*

After Elijah Muhammad's death in 1975, his son Warith took over the Nation. He tried to reconstitute it as a mainstream Sunni Islamic organisation, and renamed it the American Muslim Mission. He was resisted by his father's lieutenant – and long time rival to Malcolm X – Louis Farrakhan, who revived the Nation with a considerably reduced role for Islam.[28] Since the 1980s, Farrakhan has survived severe illness and multiple accusations of racism, anti-Semitism, homophobia, sexism and, not least, complicity in the murder of Malcolm X. He maintains the Nation's doctrines of Black separatism, abstinence and 'family values'.[29]

The impact of American Islam: an assessment

Since around 1910, a number of charismatic leaders have used Islam as part of an appeal to African Americans to shake off the enduring shackles of slavery and as a means of personal empowerment. They have offered a fierce alternative to the civil rights movement's programme of non-violent persuasion of the white majority and its hopes of reform through the institutions of American democracy and justice.

For all their efforts, they did not succeed in converting African Americans to Islam to any significant degree. In 2009, the respected Pew Research Center presented a report entitled 'A Religious Portrait of African Americans'. It found that just 1 per cent identified as Muslims – the same proportion who identified as Jehovah's Witnesses.[30] It would be presumptuous for a white Christian foreign writer to speculate why Islam had such a limited appeal to African Americans despite its charismatic leaders and prominent converts. Malcolm X was certainly revered by

---

* In 2021 one of the two alleged murderers was in fact exonerated. 'US man exonerated in Malcolm X murder sues New York state', Al Jazeera, 14 December 2021.

vast swathes of African Americans. We shall observe later the splits within Islamic American organisations and the growing identification of Islam itself as an existential enemy of the United States. However, it may simply be that most African Americans were unwilling to accept the degree of separation from American life which Islamic movements prescribed for them, and did not see Islam, as these esoteric movements interpreted it, as a means of social, political and economic advance, especially in the era of success for the civil rights movements inspired by the Baptist, Martin Luther King.

African American Muslims simply have not mustered the numbers to form a significant lobby, interest group or voting block in mainstream American politics, nationally or locally. One can trace no success for them in achieving any political demand, either for themselves or for African Americans as a whole. Ironically, their main political achievement may have been to create a fear of Islam among the white majority.

4

ISLAM AND THE UNITED STATES
AS A GLOBAL SUPERPOWER

In this chapter I shall be retracing the United States' international history to follow how its assumption of global superpower status in the aftermath of the Second World War affected its perception of Islam. I will argue that Muslims both at home and abroad have been judged against US ambitions in its relations with Muslim-dominated countries.

Since the Second World War, the US has divided the Muslim community in two – and continues to do so. There are 'good' Muslims who supported American global ambitions, and 'bad' Muslims who resisted them. Even among American policy-makers, let alone the general public, this division reflects little or no understanding of Islam, nor its different strands.

Muslims with absolutely no commitment to American concepts of democracy and justice – along with a positive hostility to free market capitalism, American consumer lifestyles, equality for women and sexual minorities – became 'good Muslims' and 'freedom fighters' when they fought the US enemy, the Soviet Union in Afghanistan. The mujahideen in Afghanistan are the textbook example of this. President Reagan and his administration equated them with the heroes of the American Revolution. Meanwhile, nationalist leaders of Muslim countries and democratic opponents of Arab despotisms – both more closely aligned with American values – were barely tolerated because they either challenged the narrative of American supremacy or threatened the stability of US client regimes.

Since the 1970s, the American people have discovered that, for the first time since the Barbary Wars, Muslim states and non-state Muslim agents have the power to harm them. They experienced this first through the impact of the oil embargo and the quintupling of oil prices, then through hostage-taking and murders, casualties in unsuccessful conflicts and attacks on American soil, culminating in 9/11.

At this point, the distinction between 'good' and 'bad' Muslims was seriously eroded: Islam itself was regarded – even by scholars and politicians who should have known better – as an existential enemy of the United States and its way of life.

In spite of active efforts by American Muslims to establish their rightful status in the mosaic of American society, and a growing willingness to engage in the political system, they have never acquired enough influence to be judged *in their own right* by the majority. They remain prisoners of the country's relations with a Muslim outside world which it still barely tries to understand.

The Saudi alliance

The United States played no serious role in the Middle East settlement after the First World War. Woodrow Wilson had never declared war on the Ottoman Empire, and he had no troops in the Middle East. Already fixated on establishing the League of Nations, he had limited appetite for challenging the British and French carve-up of the defeated empire. Although there was much domestic sympathy in the United States for the Armenians, and to a lesser degree for the Zionist cause, there was no political pressure on Wilson to intervene in the Middle East. On the contrary, the great mass of the American people wanted to bring their soldiers home and avoid future foreign entanglements, particularly in a region that very few of them knew.

Succeeding administrations kept the United States out of the Middle East until, somewhat fortuitously, it entered a relationship in the 1930s with Ibn Saud, ruler of the Kingdom of Hejaz-Nejd, home to the two holiest sites in Islam and which Ibn Saud renamed Saudi Arabia.* Initially of interest only to missionaries who were spellbound by its desert landscape, the country became of great strategic importance when American oil interests, fending off competition from the British, discovered oil there in immense quantities in 1938.[1]

Since that time, maintaining a good relationship with the Saudi dynasty has been the one constant in US policy in the Middle East. To give a rather poignant example, Ibn Saud was the very last foreign leader to be met by the dying President Franklin D. Roosevelt at the close of the Second World War. FDR received the king on the American cruiser *Quincy* and allowed him and his entourage to treat the warship as their personal plaything, even firing its guns. More importantly, under pressure from his guest, FDR retreated in his support for Zionism.[2]

The relationship has entailed wholesale acceptance of the Wahabi sect of Islam which helped Ibn Saud to power, and which remains the kingdom's pervasive religious ideology. Of all forms of Islam, Wahabism is the one most hostile to non-Muslims and most opposed to Western values. In eighty years of turbulent American relations with Islamic states, Saudi Arabia has always been placed in the category of 'good Muslims'. Since the 1930s, there has been a constant pretence that Saudi Arabia is a pillar of American values. Karl Twitchell, the American engineer who led the team which discovered the country's oil, solemnly assured fellow Americans: 'Though outwardly autocratic in several respects, the [Saudi] government . . . shows certain aspects of democracy.' He described Ibn Saud himself as 'a man of wisdom and righteousness . . . of justice, generosity and hospitality . . . who ranks among the foremost figures of this age'.[3]

---

* Saudi Arabia remains the only state in the world to be named after its current ruling dynasty – a symbol of its treatment as its personal property.

Since then, American and Western media have made constant attempts to present each succeeding Saudi autocrat as a moderniser and a reformer,[4] the latest beneficiary of this corrupt but profitable system being Crown Prince Mohammed, currently overseeing a murderous war in Yemen. One can only speculate on the impact of this relationship on American perceptions of Islam.

In spite of all the pro-Saudi propaganda, the American people have never admired the Saudi regime. In March 2018, when the Crown prince was feted by Donald Trump, opinion research suggested that Americans viewed it even less favourably than long-term enemies Cuba and Communist China.[5] Americans know of the grotesque opulence founded on massive corruption in Saudi society, of the long subjugation of women, of fierce censorship, repression and the torture of dissidents, of punishments by stoning, mutilation and beheading, of virtual slavery for servants and labourers. They know that the Saudis have funded violent groups — including the 9/11 bombers — and madrassas and other institutions which preach constant hatred of the United States and Western values. They have seen the Bush administration give the Saudis a free pass over their involvement in 9/11. More recently, the murder of my colleague at *Middle East Eye*, Jamal Khashoggi,[6] sliced to pieces in Turkey by a murder squad, reportedly on the orders of Crown Prince Mohammed bin Salman, did little to disrupt the US–Saudi alliance. The American people are still told that the Saudis are good Muslims. What does that say to them about the 'bad Muslims' and about Islam itself? This question goes to the heart of this book. The US and its allies (including the UK and France) have formed self-serving alliances with some of the most barbaric regimes in the Muslim world, honouring and feting their leaders in Western capitals. This is likely to be one important reason why so many Western voters regard Islam as a barbaric religion.

The Second World War

The United States became more deeply involved in the Middle East during the Second World War. In November 1942, the Americans launched a massive invasion – Operation Torch – of Morocco and Algeria, then ruled by the French collaborationist Vichy regime of Marshal Pétain. The two countries were of little strategic interest to the United States, but were selected in June as the easiest way for the Americans to create a 'second front' against the Axis, to support the hard-pressed Russians in Stalingrad and the British in Egypt. The military necessity for the operation had largely disappeared after the Russian and British victories at Stalingrad and El Alamein respectively, but the Americans were committed nonetheless.

They prepared for the invasion with a massive propaganda campaign towards both the local Muslim populations and their own troops. American aeroplanes dropped thousands of leaflets in Arabic, borrowing Islamic language to claim that 'the American Holy warriors had arrived . . . to fight the great Jihad of freedom'. This high-flown language, which misappropriated the term 'jihad', was a deliberate attempt to echo that of the Quran while stopping short of actually declaring themselves warriors of Islam.[7] Meanwhile, GIs were issued with a fifty-page pamphlet containing advice on how to behave towards Muslims. For example, they were warned that men walking hand in hand were 'not queer', and told not to speak to a Muslim woman in public. 'Never try to remove her veil. This is most important.'

GIs were also reminded of those very first wars against the Barbary pirates. They were told that the US had returned to the Middle East not for gain or conquest but to ensure that 'men will be free and humanity will have a chance for a decent existence'.[8]

The United States faced limited military resistance in Morocco and Algeria from weak Vichy French forces, although they were badly mauled by the German Afrika Korps when they pushed on to the Kasserine Pass in Tunisia. The Americans faced few problems in their relationship with the local Muslim population, but out of expediency, they shamefully reversed their initial decision to liberate the local Jews from the iniquitous laws imposed by the Vichy administration, accepting Vichy propaganda that any action for the Jews would inflame the Muslim majority.[9]

Eventually, the Americans ejected Vichy — without restoring the position of the Jews — and began to assert themselves against the Free French and the British. They won credit among local nationalists for vetoing the restoration of French colonial rule in Syria and Lebanon, and for encouraging independence for Morocco and Tunisia,[10] and also among local people generally for improving healthcare, access to water, transport and infrastructure — all blessings of American civilisation.[11]

Before the war, as already noted, only a very limited number of Americans had any direct experience of any Muslim society. The war increased this number by tens of thousands, in both military and civilian roles. For most of them, who knew the Middle East only through romantic films such as *Casablanca*, contact with real Arab societies and Muslim culture was disillusioning. Their letters home railed at the ignorance and the dirtiness of the local population, their propensity for thievery and their brutal treatment of women. Few of them, however, made any study of Islam or local culture.[12]

With the exception of Elijah Muhammad's Nation of Islam, America's Muslims enlisted enthusiastically for America's war effort. The military participation ratio for their small community at least equalled that of the United States as a whole.[13] In considering this, it is worth recalling that the Muslim Moros in the American Philippines put up a fierce resistance to the Japanese occupiers in 1942. The Moros terrorised the Japanese who, in spite of their technical superiority and long record of success in jungle warfare, avoided conflict with them and abandoned large parts of the country.[14] But the Moros' resistance to the Japanese did nothing to improve their status in the United States. No Moro received an American decoration, there was no change in their immigration status and, above all, the Americans did nothing to reverse their policies of Filipinisation or to secure them autonomy in the post-war independent Philippines.

The post-war apogee of American relations with Islam

Despite Arab resentment at the United States' role in the foundation of Israel (to be discussed later), the post-war era was a happy period for American relations with the Muslim world in general – and for American Muslims at home. The United States received some credit from newly independent Muslim states for its wartime opposition to colonialism and its contributions to technical development. For example, during his early years of power, the Americans considered Egypt's military leader Gamal Abdel Nasser an ally, while he welcomed their support against enduring British influence in his country.[15] This receded with America's instrumental involvement in the overthrow of the democratically elected Iranian leader, Mohammad Mosaddegh, in 1953. He was replaced by the young Shah Mohammad Reza Pahlavi, who installed an autocratic regime under American tutelage. Credit receded still further when a hard-line US Secretary of State, John Foster Dulles, tried to corral Muslim states into anti-Soviet alliances, and treated the nationalist regimes who resisted as crypto-communists.[16]

This did not deter a massive rise in the number of students from Muslim-majority countries in the United States from 1948 to 1965, an increase of more than 400 per cent. The largest contingent came from Iran, followed by Egypt, Pakistan and Turkey. The great majority were ambitious and hard-working, eager to acquire the technical skills needed to modernise their countries. While adhering to their Islamic faith and building new mosques, they integrated readily into their campuses and into American life generally. Some were Islamists, out of favour with the secular nationalist governments running their countries, and they introduced for the first time to American soil the Islamic renaissance ideals of the Muslim Brotherhood.[17] Among them was the Egyptian poet, teacher and revolutionary Sayyid Qutb, a prominent member of the Muslim Brotherhood. He announced his aversion to the United States, declaring that Americans had closed 'the windows to faith in religion, faith in art, and faith in spiritual values altogether'.[18] Qutb railed against the Westernisation of Muslim society and called for the re-establishment of Islamic values. Although on his return to Egypt he was at first courted by Nasser, the relationship turned sour and, after years of imprisonment and torture, Qutb was hanged in 1966. His teachings would be a significant influence on Osama bin Laden.

However, these students were far less representative of the United States' Muslims than the native-born second-generation Americans who formed the Federation of Islamic Associations in the United States and Canada in 1952. The FIA generally had a patriotic integrationist outlook that linked Islamic ideals to American values. The first founder, Abdallah Igram, successfully lobbied President Eisenhower shortly after he took office to add an identifying 'I' to the dog tags of American Muslim soldiers, so that they could receive a proper burial if killed in combat.[19] As far as I can discover, this is the only successful piece of lobbying by Muslims for Muslims in US political history.

The apogee of US–Islamic relations came in June 1957 with the opening in Washington DC of the giant Islamic Center, paid for with contributions from Muslims in the US and overseas. It was attended by President Eisenhower, who spoke warmly of Islam. This was somewhat ironic since early in his first administration he became the first president to define the US as a Judaeo-Christian civilisation. But now Eisenhower went out of his way to include Islam as a contributor to global (that is, American-led) civilisation. 'With their traditions of learning and rich culture, the countries of Islam have added much to the advancement of mankind,' he announced. 'This Center, this place of worship, is as welcome as . . . any similar edifice of any religion. Americans would fight with all their strength for your right to have your own church and worship according to your conscience. Without this, we would be something else than what we are.'[20]

The US turns against Muslims

In 1965, the United States made major changes in its immigration laws, which removed the barely covert discrimination against Muslim countries in Asia and Africa. This formed part of a general advance in civil rights which removed the pressure on American Muslims to identify with the white majority.* As a result, the number of American citizens born in Muslim-majority countries rose from 134,615 in 1960 to 871,582 in 1990. Nearly a quarter of the new immigrants came from Iran, approximately an eighth from Pakistan and a similar proportion from Lebanon.[21] The majority were professional and technical workers (rather than the labourers who were the main source of earlier Muslim immigration), along with members of their families. Some were refugees from military conflict or political persecution. They were, in general, educated, ambitious and reasonably affluent, normally ingredients for acceptance and success in American society.

Unfortunately for them, they were hit by international politics. In the words of the scholar Zain Abdullah, the Six Day War of 1967 between Israel and an Arab coalition brought negative portrayals of Arabs in the American media. After that, 'the 1970s oil embargo against the US further exacerbated harsh views of Muslims and the Middle East. Long gas lines angered Americans, and Muslims in the United States felt the brunt of their rage.

---

* The horrible term 'passing' (as white) had applied to Asian-Americans as well as African Americans, and skin bleaches were marketed for their use.

Major news outlets sketched caricatures of Arabs as rich oil sheikhs holding the world to ransom.[22]

American perceptions of Arabs in general worsened during the 1970s in response to Palestinian hijackings and terrorist attacks, notably the massacre of Israeli athletes at the 1972 Munich Olympics. Arab-American Muslims pushed back by forming a number of lobbying organisations, although the most successful counter to stereotyping was the election to the Senate in 1972 of an Arab-American Christian, Senator James Abourezk of South Dakota. He served one term: to this day, no Arab-American has reached a rank higher than senator in US politics.[23]

In 1979, American prejudice against Arabs was converted into hostility against Islam in general as the result of the Iranian Revolution and the subsequent hostage crisis. The latter revived memories of the Barbary pirates. Like Adams and Jefferson before him, President Carter oscillated between force and paying tribute. The crisis opened in January 1979. Although preceded by years of smouldering revolt against the corruption, economic mismanagement and repression of his regime, the shah's fall shocked Western policy-makers. Few Americans, even at the highest level of policymaking, had been aware that Iran's prosperity had bypassed the great majority of its people and that the shah's regime, far from progressing towards Western-style democracy, had been sinking ever deeper into corruption, repression and torture.

This last problem was not confined to Iran. Oil-rich regimes supported by the West found they could support themselves from oil revenues (sovereign wealth funds for sovereigns) and had no need of domestic taxation which would require the strengthening of the middle classes and civil society. Paradoxically, organisations like the Muslim Brotherhood depended on a more robust civil society and were keenly resented by Middle Eastern dictators.

The shah went into exile, with an Islamic dictatorship succeeding him, dominated by the ultra-conservative Ayatollah Khomeini. Relations with the United States, dubbed the 'great

Satan' by Khomeini, steadily worsened, but erupted into violence when, in October, Carter allowed the shah, mortally ill, to travel to the United States for medical treatment. On 4 November, militant students invaded the US embassy and took the occupants prisoner. They released a few but kept fifty-three people hostage.

Ignoring the advice of his Secretary of State, Cyrus Vance, to secure their release by diplomacy, Carter dramatised the crisis, expelling Iranian students from the United States, freezing Iranian assets and halting American purchases of Iranian oil. Carter may have hoped that a tough posture would help him secure re-election in 1980, and it did indeed score him re-nomination for the Democratic Party against the challenge of Ted Kennedy. However, his tactics only encouraged the Iranians to demand a higher price for the hostages, including the return of the dying shah.

Against the advice of Vance, who resigned, Carter tried to rescue the hostages using an airborne force. The attempt ended disastrously, when two helicopters crashed in the desert and killed eight Americans. Carter's humiliation, coupled with economic pain from rising energy prices, generated a landslide election victory for the conservative Republican Ronald Reagan. Diplomacy eventually secured the hostages' release, but only on the very last day of Carter's presidency, after 444 days of captivity, each one recorded by hostile media.[24]

The hostage crisis was a national trauma for the American people, who were already shocked by the replacement of their 'friend' the shah with an outlandish enemy, the Ayatollah Khomeini. During the 1980s, Carter's sunny successor Reagan showed himself no more able to protect Americans from Middle Eastern violence. His intervention in Lebanon brought about the deaths of 241 US servicemen by a single suicide bomber – the deadliest single attack on Americans until 9/11. (Unlike George W. Bush, Reagan promptly liquidated his Middle East adventure. He turned to high-visibility operations with no risk of major casualties, such as the invasion of Grenada, and the use of non-American proxies, such as the Nicaraguan contras.)

Reagan was also largely impotent when confronted by a new wave of hijackings and murders by Middle Eastern terror groups. Particularly horrific was the takeover of the Italian cruise ship *Achille Lauro* and the calculated murder of a helpless elderly American-Jewish passenger. In the dying days of his presidency, the blowing-up of Pan Am flight 103 over Lockerbie in Scotland killed thirty-seven American college students.

More important than any of these was the rise of Christian Zionism in shaping the American vision of the Middle East. This is a massively consequential subject that cannot be ignored or explained away. The origins of this movement lie deep in the American psyche. The next chapter is devoted to explaining how it emerged as the most dynamic force in contemporary US foreign policy.

APOCALYPSE IMMINENT: GOD'S PLAN FOR ISRAEL

These opening chapters have noted the influence of religion, particularly Protestant Christianity, in shaping American policy towards the Muslim world overseas. In the absence of any politically and culturally significant Muslim presence at home, and with no responsibilities for a large Muslim population in any of its colonies or satellites, the United States was free to regard Islam as an inferior, backward religion which served as a drag on progress towards American civilisation.

In this chapter I am going to look at how what was once a small and often mocked sector of American religion, Evangelical Protestantism, became a mighty cultural and political force. In the process, it not only acquired a stranglehold on US policy towards Israel and Palestine, but made the whole world a playground for its apocalyptic fantasies. In this process, all non-believers in its doctrines lost any right to assert their interests and wishes or even their identity. This applied not only to Muslims but to other Christians, and even the Jews with whom the Evangelicals were locked in alliance. In the Evangelical vision, all non-believers were fated to suffer torment and destruction in an imminent apocalypse foretold and ordained in biblical prophecy – unless they recanted and accepted Jesus Christ as their personal saviour.

Some popular Evangelical leaders cast Muslims into the armies of the Antichrist who would rule the earth until finally being vanquished by the Second Coming of Jesus. But even those who had other candidates for the Antichrist showed no respect for the Islamic faith. Muslims who remained Muslims would be annihilated by God's will.

Christian Zionism and the end of the world

There has been a special relationship between the United States and Israel since the Pilgrim Fathers. These original American settlers identified themselves strongly with the Israelites of the Old Testament and gave their settlements Hebrew names.

Most importantly, the Pilgrim Fathers modelled their governance on the Old Testament, particularly the concept that their prosperity or misery depended on their obedience to God's commandments. They saw themselves as a chosen people, like the Jews of ancient Israel, in a direct covenant with God, fulfilling a mission (and occupying territory) given to them.[1] These concepts recur regularly in US history: most recently, Evangelicals have reinforced them with the idea that the country's relationship with God requires an absolute commitment to present-day Israel.

In the early republic, it was commonplace to cite the US as a second Israel. Herman Melville declared boldly: 'We Americans are the peculiar, chosen people – the Israel of our time; we bear the ark of the liberties of the world.'[2] Even Abraham Lincoln thought Americans were God's 'almost chosen people'.[3] This identification had the incidental benefit of legitimising conquests of peoples that the Americans perceived to be inferior, Spaniards, Mexicans and, above all, those they still referred to as Indians, even when the latter's territories had been guaranteed by formal treaties. The Old Testament narratives of Israelites displacing the Canaanites at God's command gave the US the authority to displace the inhabitants of its own Promised Land.[4]

The early US experienced a profound and multifaceted religious revival that was in some ways similar in structure to Islam with its plethora of mosques and imams. There was no established

Church, even in colonial times, to lay down doctrine; there were long distances between communities and an expanding population almost constantly in motion to settle in new territories. In such conditions, it was natural for separate religious communities to form: many were based on an itinerant charismatic preacher achieving mass conversions of ecstatic followers in a revival tent. Even if they failed to achieve converts, such preachers were a free and unique source of local entertainment.[5]

At the same time, the entire English-speaking world saw a huge upsurge of interest in biblical prophecy, prompted by the dramatic upheavals of the French Revolution and Napoleon, especially by his foray into the Middle East and the crumbling of Ottoman power in the Holy Land, which appeared to presage the restoration of the Jews, which in turn presaged the end of the known world. No fewer than fifty books on the latter were published between 1796 and 1800.[6]

One of the most influential in the United States was that of the religious scholar Professor George Bush, a direct ancestor of both the presidents who share his name. Bush's 1844 book *The Valley of Vision, or The Dry Bones of Israel Revived* called for a revived Jewish state in Palestine, not only to restore the Holy Land to plenty but also to form 'a link of communication' between man and God. Such a state, said Bush, would 'blaze in notoriety. It will flash a splendid demonstration upon all kindreds and tongues of the truth.' Bush had another rather less elevated motive: he hoped that a Jewish state in the Holy Land would deflect Jewish migration to the US. He hoped that the Jews would be offered 'the same carnal inducements to remove to Syria as now promote them to emigrate to this country'.[7]

In the US, the leading prophetic movement, with at least 50,000 followers, was the Millerites, named after William Miller, a former Baptist who had conducted exhaustive research into all the prophetic verses of the Bible and linked them to current and historic events. He told them, on that basis, that the Second

Coming of Christ would occur on 22 October 1844, a day ever afterwards known to his followers as the Great Disappointment.[8] They regrouped, settled in Michigan and formed the Seventh-day Adventist Church. Under the influence of its biblically inspired dietary laws, one of its adherents, Dr Frank Kellogg, invented cornflakes and with his brother founded the breakfast cereal industry.[9]

The Great Disappointment reveals a mindset which can be detected in later Evangelical prophetic movements: rather than rejoicing that the world did not end, a small elite of believers is disappointed that they will not be saved. Since Miller, there have been a host of prophecies by Evangelical preachers of imminent apocalypse[10] but few have committed Miller's error of naming a specific date. The most decisive and lasting influence on American prophetic evangelism was a highly unlikely one: the English preacher, John Darby, a member of the Plymouth Brethren, the breakaway non-conformist sect who emphasised the Bible as the sole source of scriptural knowledge. Even his co-religionists had little regard for him as a preacher or as a writer. His reception on a speaking tour of the US in the 1860s was lukewarm and he grumbled to his brother that 'the condition of the States spiritually – indeed in every way except money-making – is frightful'.[11]

But Darby contributed three distinctive ideas to Evangelical thought. First, he had his own version of pre-millennialism. Based on detailed analysis of the Scriptures, he taught that God had divided the world into seven epochs known as 'dispensations'. The seventh and last would soon end with the Second Coming of Christ, followed by a short and terrible period of rule by the Antichrist, in which those left in the world would undergo torment and tribulation. Christ would then reappear to destroy the Antichrist at the battle of Armageddon. Only then would the millennium begin – a thousand-year reign of universal peace and perfection under Christ.

Darby's was therefore a pessimistic position compared to

his more numerous Evangelical postmillennialist opponents. They believed that Christ would reappear *after* the millennium. They believed that the world was getting better, and that Man, following God's guidance, could perfect it. Darby, like other Evangelicals, believed that the return of the Jews to Palestine was a clear sign that the end times were under way. He differed from them in his assumption that God had not transferred his promises from Jews to Christians, but had made separate promises to each. The Jews would enjoy their restored kingdom for only a short time, before succumbing to the rule of the Antichrist, but Darby's scheme still made them a chosen people, elevated beyond Muslims and heathens, and it gave Christians a clear duty to support unconditionally their claims to the land of Israel.

Thirdly, based on two obscure lines from St Paul's First Epistle to the Thessalonians, Darby propagated the idea of Rapture: before the horrific rule of the Antichrist, all those dead *and* alive who had made a personal decision to commit to Christ would be suddenly and without warning elevated to meet him somewhere above the earth. This is Darby's most powerful legacy. It has generated a billion-dollar industry today of multimedia presentations of Rapture, with people being sucked out of buildings and automobiles and aeroplanes. There is a 'Rapture Ready' index loosely modeled on the financial markets in the US, which tracks a series of world events to show the world moving closer to Rapture or further from it.[12] There is even an agency which provides non-believing carers for pets who will be left behind when their owners are Raptured. It began as a joke and is now a successful business.[13]

Darby's ideas gained traction in the late-nineteenth-century United States, an era of great economic and intellectual turbulence. Although the American economy hugely expanded, there were regular financial panics, bank crashes and natural disasters which struck hardest at vulnerable groups, particularly small farmers. There were wide disparities in income and wealth. American cities teemed with unfamiliar immigrants, not only from overseas but from the internal migration of ruined rural populations. Political leadership was either missing or corrupt. There was no president of any distinction between Lincoln, assassinated in 1865, and Theodore Roosevelt, sworn in in 1901.

Intellectually, the authority of the Bible was threatened both by Darwinism and the so-called higher criticism which challenged biblical chronology and history, and offered new meanings of sacred texts by treating them as allegory or moral guidance rather than literal fact. Worse still, higher criticism suggested that the Bible held no monopoly over such key ideas as the Flood or the Ten Commandments. Perhaps worst of all, the higher criticism was German and foreign. In this climate, Darby's ideas appealed to the many who wanted to believe again in the absolute authority of the Bible – by far the best-known book in the US. Even more appealing was the promise of selective eternal bliss to believers being tossed by a turbulent society and to rich people haunted by guilt over their success.

The latter group did much to popularise Darby's ideas. One of them was William Blackstone, who had made a fortune from Chicago real estate. His book *Jesus Is Coming*, published in 1878, carried a helpful diagram of the dispensations, the Rapture and the Tribulation. He emphasised Darby's idea that the return of the Jews to Palestine was a sign of the end times: he called them 'God's sundial' (Blackstone was a much more vivid writer than Darby). He lobbied energetically on their behalf to a succession of presidents. By the time of his death in 1934, Blackstone's book had sold more than a million copies in forty-eight languages.[14]

Even more important was a born-again reformed reprobate businessman, Cyrus Scofield. He formed a partnership with a leading preacher, Dwight Moody, who had founded the Moody

Bible Institute, which promoted rote-learning of each book of the Bible. Under Scofield's influence, Moody started to advocate Darby's ideas. Then Scofield, having awarded himself a non-existent doctorate, produced the *Scofield Reference Bible*. It had his own millennial dispensationist annotations (often plagiarised directly from Darby) on every page, some so mingled with the texts as to be indistinguishable from Holy Writ. From 1909 to 1937, it sold more than three million copies. Revised in 1967, it remains in print and in regular use.

Before the First World War, Darby's messages were also promoted by a number of well-attended and respectfully reported 'prophecy conferences' and successful prophetic magazines. Preachers took on celebrity status. A former baseball star turned preacher with the appropriate name of Billy Sunday delivered sermons in a punchy style to packed houses. Another popular Evangelical preacher, with her own magazine, was Aimée Semple McPherson, caricatured later by Evelyn Waugh as Mrs Ape in *Vile Bodies*.[15]

Christian Zionism and the Second World War

The threats arising from Mussolini, Hitler, Japanese militarism and Stalin were all seen as signs of the end times and created a new demand for prophetic forecasting. Since the Antichrist's kingdom was often depicted as a new universal Roman Empire, the fundamentalists thought that Mussolini's imperial ambitions made him a good candidate for the Antichrist. Characteristically, Mussolini was flattered to be informed of this by two visiting American Evangelicals.[16] Several prominent fundamentalists had a curious double standard on Hitler: although God would punish him for persecuting the Jews, he was nonetheless part of God's plan for the Jews by encouraging them to leave Europe and return to Palestine.[17]

American fundamentalist leaders had an ambivalent attitude

to Jews: like Blackstone, many wanted them in Palestine not the United States. Some followed Henry Ford in propagating the forged *Protocols of the Elders of Zion* and its accounts of universal Jewish conspiracy. When Ford was forced to apologise, they took this as evidence of the power of the *Protocols* conspirators. The most notorious fundamentalist anti-Semite was a popular preacher, William Bell Riley, who published two books defending the *Protocols* and denouncing 'the atheistic and international Jew [as] a world menace'. Some fundamentalists urged him unsuccessfully to dial down this rhetoric, not on grounds of morality or taste but for the special reason that God's plan required some Jews to be left to convert to Christianity after the Rapture.[18]

Fundamentalists had renewed difficulties 'fitting' the Second World War into biblical prophecy. At the war's outbreak in Europe, the *Sunday School Times* promoted a series of prophetic articles of imminent developments. Every one proved to be wrong, notably the prophecy that Mussolini would abandon Hitler and join Britain.[19] From a broader prophetic prospective, Hitler could not be the Antichrist because Germany was not part of the Roman Empire, nor could any of the great battles of the war be Armageddon, which had to be in Palestine. As the scale of the Holocaust became apparent, its timing seemed to be wrong: prophecy suggested that the Jews would be tormented *after* the Rapture, which had not yet happened. One of Riley's followers actually suggested that the Holocaust was only a rehearsal for the punishment which Jews would face from the Antichrist.[20]

A leading fundamentalist thinker, Harold J. Ockenga, offered the most coherent answers. The United States had been charged by God to defer the world's collapse into barbarism. If it turned back to God's teaching, it could defer the still-imminent apocalypse and allow more people time to save themselves by accepting Jesus as their saviour. In preparation for this role, he supported a strong military build-up and dampened his support for American isolationism and the Neutrality Acts, which prevented the United

States from supplying the beleaguered British. This position was adopted by other fundamentalist leaders. After Pearl Harbor, fundamentalists gave virtually unlimited support to Roosevelt's prosecution of the war, in contrast to their predecessors' divisions and equivocations over American entry into the First World War. Nearly all of them denounced conscientious objectors and told their followers to obey Roosevelt as commander-in-chief while continuing to reject his peacetime policies and his apparent indifference to God. None objected to the savage internment of Japanese-Americans, nor to the massive bombing of German civilians, nor, finally, to the dropping of the atom bombs on Japan.[21]

The war saw a noteworthy initiative, when some of the most prominent fundamentalists, led by Ockenga, formed the National Association of Evangelicals for United Action (NAE) in 1942. It was the first attempt to form a single representative organisation, and Ockenga hoped to mobilise the 'unvoiced multitudes' in the United States – a precursor to Nixon's conservative 'silent majority'. Some Evangelicals held aloof, and the NAE itself made no effort to include women or non-white Americans. But it established a permanent presence in American political life for an economic liberal agenda and a socially conservative one. Although the NAE soft-pedalled its members' prophetic beliefs, these remained the ultimate moral authority for its agenda.[22]

Christian Zionism in the post-war United States

Evangelical leaders readopted an isolationist stance when the war was over, particularly in resisting the League of Nations' successor, the United Nations, which they denounced as a godless body promoting a pro-Soviet agenda.[23] However, they rejoiced when the new UN recommended the creation of a Jewish state in Palestine, ignoring the fact that the UN had also called for an

Arab state. For many years, they had treated the Palestinian Arabs as virtually a non-people, with no rights at all, an attitude fed by their assumption that all of them were Muslims. To this day, Evangelical leaders rarely refer to Palestinian Arab Christians, of whom very few have adopted their brand of Christianity.

During the interwar period, the preacher Frank Norris, known as the 'Texas Tornado', visited the Holy Land and predicted that Jews would soon replace Arabs just as 'the white man' had displaced 'the American Indian'. He added that 'the Jew is industrious, the Arab lazy; the Jew is progressive, the Arab is only half-civilized'. His colleague Keith Brooks announced that 'the Arab and the Moslem world is not only anti-Semitic but is out and out anti-Christ'. More refined Evangelical thinkers like Ockenga acknowledged that Palestinian Arabs might have some claim to the land, but they must yield to the biblical settlement. 'God did not give it to the Arabs but gave it to Israel.'[24]

This remains the bedrock of Evangelical support for Israel. God made a covenant with Abraham, recorded in Genesis chapter 12: whoever fails to support Abraham's descendants unconditionally offends God and will be punished. However, the Evangelical Zionists identified only the Jews as descendants of Abraham. They excluded the Arabs who, whether Muslim or Christian, are also descendants of Abraham.[25]

Needless to say, Evangelical leaders were wildly excited by the foundation of the state of Israel and its recognition by President Truman. Professor Louis Talbot spoke for many in his regular radio programme: 'This could be the beginning of that train of events which will not end until the Lord Jesus Christ returns and sets up the everlasting Kingdom.'[26]

At this point, one should emphasise that American Evangelicals had no influence over Truman's decision. Truman was the most single-minded president of the modern age (he rejoiced in the name of his birthplace: Independence, Missouri) and the least likely to be influenced by lobbyists of any kind. He enjoyed denouncing them, always pungently, often profanely. He was also an autodidact who had read every verse of the Bible several times over by the time he was ten and who carried with him his own detailed maps of Palestine in biblical times. Truman's decision to recognise Israel was based on his personal conviction that he was destined to deliver the biblical promise of a Jewish state in Palestine, and that only such a state could provide a refuge for the survivors of the Holocaust. Such was his conviction that he was ready to lose George Marshall, his great Secretary of State, over this issue.[27]

Evangelical leaders gave eager support to the anti-communist campaigners of the 1950s.[28] One effect of this was to bring them closer to their traditional enemy, the Roman Catholic Church. Senator Joe McCarthy in particular was strongly supported by the Catholic hierarchy and the Kennedy dynasty, while Evangelicals had much more influence over the Eisenhower administration than over Truman's. Eisenhower and his vice-president, Richard Nixon, signed up to an NAE 'Declaration of Seven Divine Freedoms'.[29] The administration made many more direct references to God than its immediate predecessors, added the phrase 'under God' to the Pledge of Allegiance recited by naturalised immigrants and millions of school children, and made 'In God We Trust' the nation's motto, printed on its currency.

Eisenhower annexed religion generally as a guiding principle of the state in its resistance to Soviet Communism. He told the American Legion in 1955 that 'without God there can be no American form of government nor any American way of life'.[30] Americans seemed to agree with him: during the 1950s, Church membership rose from 49 per cent to 69 per cent of the population.

Above all, as president-elect in December 1952, Eisenhower called into being a Judaeo-Christian foundation for the American state. Speaking ex tempore, he announced that 'our form of government has no sense unless it is founded in a deeply-felt religious faith, and I don't care what it is. With us it is *of course* [my emphasis] the Judaeo-Christian concept but it must be a religion with all men are [*sic*] created equal.'[31] As already noted, the Eisenhower era saw the apogee of American relations with the Islamic world and almost certainly Eisenhower intended to endorse religion in general. However, Evangelical leaders and their favourite politicians have used his speech to suggest, first, that Jews and Christians are really the same and, secondly, that all other faiths are un-American. The latest is Donald Trump, who boasted in October 2017 that his administration was 'stopping cold the attacks on Judaeo-Christian values'.[32]

Billy Graham and his influence

The seminal figure in American evangelism in the Eisenhower era and after was Billy Graham. As a young minister among many, he came to national prominence in 1949 when his first great evangelical campaign, the Los Angeles crusade, was taken up by the anti-communist Hearst press. Graham remained a staunch anti-communist during his long life, but there was much more to him. He mastered the art of preaching in all media: live, radio, television, film, books, newspapers and magazines (he founded and edited a successful new one, *Christianity Today*), and latterly satellite broadcasting and the internet. He cultivated personal relationships with every president from Eisenhower to Obama[33] but was astute enough to avoid partisan politics (apart from a mis-step with Nixon) and remain a national figure. Long ahead of most other Evangelical preachers, he crusaded to desegregated audiences and reached out to Martin Luther King.

Graham believed in an imminent apocalypse. The prosperous Eisenhower era was not a favourable time for apocalyptic prophecy, but in his book *World Aflame*, Graham managed to identify portents which resonated with middle-class Americans, including hydrogen bombs, the launch of the Russian Sputnik, crime, sexual permissiveness and growing dependency on alcohol and drugs.

But Graham shrewdly avoided giving a date for the apocalypse. Responding to the general relaxation in attitudes among post-war Americans, he gradually shifted his main message from the fear of hellfire to the hope of being saved through the love of God. In the late 1960s, Graham started to reach out to young people caught up in the US counter-culture, applauding their rejection of materialism. In 1971, he produced a book for them, *The Jesus Generation*, referencing the Beatles, Bob Dylan and other youth heroes, placing Jesus Christ as 'the greatest revolutionary of all times', and recasting his apocalyptic message to appeal to the ragged youthful charismatic 'Jesus people' who were becoming a common sight in American communities.[34]

Graham was crucial in cementing the bond between Evangelicals and Israel, taking one of his theatrical Evangelical crusades to Israel in 1960. The government asked him not to preach to Jews – and he agreed. Instead he made a film, *His Land*, anchored by Cliff Richard, which lavished praise on Israel. For the rest of his life, he stood aside from efforts to convert Jews to Christianity or even to warn them about their fate in the end times if they did not accept Jesus. Instead, he gave unconditional support for the Jewish state, and lobbied for it with all the presidents he knew, especially Nixon during the Yom Kippur War which threatened its existence. He gave his followers the message that it was God's will to support Israel and that failure would be punished.[35] Later Evangelical leaders have pushed the same message, ever more stridently.

For all his support for Israel, Billy Graham never, in his long ministry, attacked Muslims. His son and chosen successor Franklin has taken a very different line and has been far more politically partisan. After 9/11, Franklin Graham denounced Islam as 'a very wicked and evil religion', and since then has consistently identified it with hatred, personal cruelty, terrorism and war. Franklin Graham was ahead of Donald Trump in calling for a ban on Muslim immigration.[36]

Bestselling apocalyptic visions

In 1967, Evangelicals gathered fresh strength from Israel's victory in the Six-Day War and conquest of Jerusalem, which presaged the restoration of the Temple, a key sign of the end times. No one was more excited than the preacher Hal Lindsey, who told his followers to prepare for the Rapture within a generation (nodding to the drug culture of the times, he called it 'the ultimate trip'). With the aid of a ghostwriter, C. C. Carlson, Lindsey produced *The Late Great Planet Earth*, a massive bestselling account of the apocalypse (which would take place in 1988), preceded by famines, earthquakes, communist subversion in the United States, Iran and the Soviet Union combining to attack Israel, and nuclear strikes on major Western cities. Lindsey also identified the European Economic Community as the new Roman Empire foreshadowed in prophecy and the source of the Antichrist.

Lindsey's was the first prophetic book to be brought out by a mainstream publisher (Bantam) and sold more than 7.5 million copies within ten years. Ronald Reagan recommended it. So did Menachem Begin. In 1979, it was made into a film narrated by Orson Welles; the great man by then was very short of money and forced to make television commercials for sherry. It grossed nearly $20 million – a remarkable sum then for a film purporting to be a documentary.[37] Lindsey followed it with a stream of other apocalyptic bestsellers, notably *The 1980s: Countdown to Armageddon* in 1981, and *The Rapture* in 1983.

In 2002, he published *The Everlasting Hatred*, purporting to show that, since its inception, Islam has been dedicated to the violent destruction of Judaeo-Christian civilisation and that Islamic terrorists are not an aberration but true followers of Muhammad. Lindsey's rhetoric was so anti-Muslim that his regular television show on the Trinity Broadcasting Network was cancelled – although it was soon restored.[38]

In 2004, a *Newsweek* poll suggested that 55 per cent of Americans believed in the Rapture.[39] In 2010, the respected Pew Research Center found that 58 per cent of survey respondents expected another world war within the next forty years, and 53 per cent a terrorist attack with nuclear weapons on the United States.[40]

At least two presidents, Ronald Reagan and George W. Bush, are known to have taken an interest in apocalyptic prophecy, and acknowledged this, at least unconsciously, in their rhetoric. The United States was locked into a global conflict between good and evil. Although good would ultimately triumph, evil would prevail for long enough to inflict terrible torment on the world. The only escape for individual believers was total commitment to God and his son, Jesus Christ. The only escape for nations was to align all their policies, domestic and international, to God's will. God might then defer the apocalypse to allow more people to be saved. In the international sphere, Israel was the only reliable ally of the United States, also founded on a covenant with God. Anything less than total commitment to Israel represented defiance of God and would be punished. Within these narratives, Muslims were either active agents of evil, or, at best, non-people with no rights under God's plan and no hope of being saved.

The Evangelicals organise politically

I've got ahead of the political narrative. It's time to look now at the ways in which Evangelicals organised themselves as a permanent political force in the United States, and how Israel, somewhat opportunistically, formed a deep alliance with them.

During the immediate post-war period, the Evangelical prophetic vision of Israel's future – a brief period of success, followed by tribulation and death unless they converted to Christianity – had been understandably unappealing to Israel. This changed after the Camp David peace agreement of 1978, in which President Carter had brokered a peace treaty between Israel and Egypt. The treaty offered little to the Palestinians beyond an ultimate promise of 'full autonomy' for them in the West Bank and Gaza. However, when Carter showed signs of taking this promise seriously, the right-wing Israeli government of Menachem Begin started to take alarm.

Begin therefore began a serious courtship of Evangelical leaders in the United States, based on unabashed political expediency. A spokesman for AIPAC, Israel's main lobbying organisation, explained the new strategy during the early Reagan years. 'We want to broaden Israel's support to the right – with the people who do not care what is happening on the West Bank but care a lot about [fending off] the Soviet Union.'

The Israelis especially courted the newly influential preacher Jerry Falwell, with Begin's government giving him an all-expenses-paid visit to Israel in 1978. Falwell obliged them by being photographed in a helicopter over the Golan Heights and then praying on bended knee in a newly planted forest named after him.[41] Falwell had first become famous in 1964 for a sermon opposing civil rights for African Americans; he labelled them 'civil wrongs' and called for preachers generally to keep out of politics and win souls for Jesus Christ instead. In a subsequent career built mainly on his long-running television show *The Old-Time Gospel Hour*, Falwell had consistently declined to get involved in national politics.

However, in the late 1970s, he was persuaded, for a combination of prophetic and political motives, to join neo-conservative leaders in forming the Moral Majority movement, uniting political and religious objectives. He enlisted his supporters on a threefold mission to get people saved, baptised and registered to vote.[42] He was notably successful: Jimmy Carter blamed him for his election defeat in 1980, claiming that Moral Majority had spent $10 million on radio and television commercials branding him a traitor to the South and no longer a Christian.[43] Moral Majority was primarily focused on traditional domestic issues – such as abortion, school prayer and homosexuality – but its sixth plank demanded that members commit 'to support the state of Israel in its battle for survival'. In a television interview, Falwell declared that 'you can't belong to Moral Majority without being a Zionist'.[44]

Falwell went back to Israel as a VIP many times during the 1980s, often leading a large group of other Evangelical pastors. The tours were totally focused on support for Israel. They actually avoided going to Bethlehem, despite its biblical significance, as Christ's birthplace is in Palestine, and Falwell's groups rarely met any Palestinian Christians. In 1981, before the Israelis attacked the Iraqi nuclear installation at Osirik, they did not tip off President Reagan – but they did tip off Falwell. He supported them enthusiastically, as he did the following year when Israel invaded Lebanon. Falwell mouthed Israeli propaganda in denying Israeli involvement in the massacres by Lebanese Christian militias at the Palestinian refugee camps at Sabra and Shatila.[45] The United States' other leading televangelist, Pat Robertson, went even further, ostentatiously joining General Sharon's invasion force in a jeep.[46]

Apart from political support, the Israelis saw Evangelicals as a profitable source of tourism, reviving the example of the pious American travellers to the Holy Land in the nineteenth century. Their ministry of tourism funded hundreds of free trips for pastors during the early 1980s, encouraging them to bring their congregations with them.[47] These pastors quickly repaid the Israelis' attention, creating a wide variety of political and charitable organisations which offered uncritical support and are still in existence today.

One of the earliest was the National Christian Leadership Conference for Israel, founded by Pentecostal preacher David Lewis. It continues to support Israel by scheduling conferences, organising letter-writing campaigns, placing advertisements in newspapers and putting on large public rallies. One in 2002 was attended by former New York mayor Rudolph Giuliani (now an attorney defending Donald Trump) and the then deputy defense secretary Paul Wolfowitz. Another such group, Christians for Israel, was active in helping Jews from the former Soviet Union immigrate to Israel. Its 'exodus' programme claimed to assist 1,200 people each month.[48]

The National Unity Coalition for Israel opposed 'the establishment of a Palestinian state within the borders of Israel'. The organisation distributed an array of newsletters and 'chutzpah action alerts' to keep its members informed and involved, and claimed that it could mount a 'virtual March on the White House' at a moment's notice if necessary. It offered a daily news service tracking stories in support of Israel and against all its enemies, especially Muslim ones. It asked for tax-deductible donations 'to help us continue to bring you more in-depth information on Israel and global jihad'.[49] Meanwhile, Christian Friends of Israeli Communities matched individual Evangelical congregations in the US with Israeli settlements on the West Bank.

No organisation has done more to cement relations between Evangelicals and Israel than the International Fellowship of Christians and Jews, founded in 1983 and still run by an Orthodox Jewish rabbi, Yechiel Eckstein, who has raised more than $250 million for Israel. Beginning with supporting Jewish immigrants from the Soviet Union, the IFCJ also funded a wide variety of welfare programmes within Israel – and a police anti-terror unit. With close connections to the Israeli government, the Bush Jr administration and Republican leaders in Congress, Eckstein was appointed 'a goodwill ambassador to the Christian world' by the Sharon government. In alliance with the Christian ideologue Ralph Reed, Eckstein set up the Stand For Israel lobbying group which organised an annual day of prayer for Israel by more than 100,000 American churches.

Rabbi Eckstein was always accommodating to the Evangelical pastors who were still seeking to convert all Jews with threats of torment and annihilation. According to the writer Victoria Clark, he echoed their belief that Israel's successes were a sign of the end times and proclaimed that the world was seeing 'the birth pangs' of a new moment in history.[50]

In 1996, the Evangelical–Israeli alliance gained new impetus when Benjamin Netanyahu became Israel's premier. Previously, as its UN representative, he had become a regular and popular speaker at prayer breakfasts, and organised his own tours of Israel for favoured Evangelical pastors. In 1998, Netanyahu ostentatiously decided to call on Falwell before meeting Bill Clinton, calculating that the president, beleaguered by the Monica Lewinsky scandal, would be powerless to react. Falwell obliged Netanyahu by promising a lobby of 200,000 pastors against the recent Oslo Accords, which promised a gradual Israeli withdrawal from its occupied territories. Falwell was successful: when Clinton finally met Netanyahu, he soft-pedalled demands for Israel to concede territory in the West Bank.[51]

Netanyahu's action demonstrated Falwell's enduring influence, even though he had stepped down from the leadership of Moral Majority and the organisation itself had dissolved in 1989. It had been hit by financial and sexual scandals, and membership was falling. Falwell claimed that it was a victim of its own success: after the two Reagan administrations 'the religious right is solidly in place and religious conservatives in America are now in for the duration'.[52]

The Christian Coalition of America's stated aim was to 'preserve, protect and defend the Judaeo-Christian values that made this the greatest country in the world'. Integral to this was unconditional support for Israel, without which the United States would not be blessed by God. Its leading light was Pat Robertson. In addition to his gifts as a television preacher, Robertson built a large-scale media empire around his Christian Broadcasting Network. He was far more politically active than Falwell and made a serious bid for the Republican presidential nomination in 1988, raising more money than any candidate, including the eventual winner George Bush Sr. In the 1994 midterm elections, the

Christian Coalition distributed 30 million leaflets for Christian voters, showing them how local candidates had voted on abortion, homosexuality, the teaching of Creationism in public schools – and Israel. It also gave lessons in political campaigning and fundraising. In 2000, the Christian Coalition printed 70 million voter guides which helped to propel white Evangelical voters towards George W. Bush. Christian Zionism was making a significant proportion of the American population virulently anti-Muslim (and anti-Arab and anti-Palestinian). The effect of this both domestically and in terms of foreign policy will be explored in the next chapter. The forces were in motion that would lead to Evangelical endorsement for Donald Trump in 2016.

6

THE IMPACT OF 9/11

There is a persistent myth in the United States that American Muslims failed to condemn the 9/11 attacks, and even celebrated them. The myth was fed by Donald Trump's repeated false claim that thousands of Muslims in New Jersey poured into the streets to cheer them.[1] But it has also been promoted by people who ought to know better, such as Thomas Friedman, author of the bestselling paean to global capitalism *The World Is Flat*. Writing in the *New York Times* as its foreign affairs columnist after the London bombings of July 2005, he claimed that 'to this day – to this day – no major Muslim cleric or religious body has ever issued a fatwa condemning Osama bin Laden'.[2]

In fact, immediately after 9/11 Friedman's own newspaper published an unequivocal condemnation of the attacks, which killed at least 28 Muslims in the World Trade Center, by dozens of Islamic leaders and scholars.[3] In the weeks after, it was followed by denunciations from Muslim leaders, clerics and organisations all over the world, including the Muslim Brotherhood and President Khatami of Iran.[4] On 27 September 2001, a fatwa by American and overseas clerics not only condemned the attacks, but also authorised Muslims to take part in the US-led actions against al-Qaeda in Afghanistan. The London bombings, which provoked Friedman's false statement, were condemned forcefully by Hamas and Hezbollah.[5]

Muslims across the United States responded immediately to the 9/11 attacks with charitable donations and sponsored blood drives. Muslim families and businesses bought and displayed thousands of US flags. Hundreds of Muslim children joined the Boy Scouts and Girl Scouts, a quintessentially American movement. In a public interview, a Texan Muslim Boy Scout emphasised that 'the values of scouting are so similar to what we learn in Islam'.[6]

Muslim organisations repeatedly professed their loyalty to the United States and its values,[7] with surveys of American Muslims never showing any significant support for extremism. In the 2011 Pew Research Center survey, 60 per cent of Muslim respondents expressed concern about the rise in Islamic extremism and 48 per cent thought that Muslim leaders should do more to attack it.

Islamophobia in American media

Fox News pumped out a stream of anti-Muslim news, real and fake. According to the journalist Jonathan Alter, the network's president, Roger Ailes, was personally terrified of Muslims, and barricaded his office and homes against them. He allegedly put the network's offices into lockdown on seeing a dark-skinned man 'in Muslim garb' in an elevator. The man turned out to be a janitor.[8]

Fox's commentators showed no restraint in projecting the idea that all Muslims, abroad and at home, were permanent enemies of the United States and its values. The most notorious was Andrea Tantaros, who told viewers of the popular programme *Outnumbered* that Muslims:

have been doing this for hundreds and hundreds of years. If you study the history of Islam, our ship captains were getting murdered. The French had to tip us off. I mean these were the days of Thomas Jefferson. They've been doing the same thing. This isn't a surprise. You can't solve it with a dialogue. You can't solve it with a summit. You solve it with a bullet to the head. It's the only thing these people understand.

(I have cited this at length, because it is an interesting revival of the fears of the Barbary pirates that we encountered in Chapter 1.)[9]

Tantaros was far from alone. Her colleague Bill O'Reilly questioned whether Islam was in general a destructive force and suggested that some Islamic groups were engaged in a holy war against the United States. Jeanine Pirro called on the United States to arm death squads and set them to work throughout the Muslim world to kill all members of Islamist organisations. O'Reilly gave a favourable showcase to a right-wing group which claimed that American Muslims were setting up secret paramilitary camps.[10] Meanwhile on CNN, Chris Cuomo called Muslims 'unusually violent' and 'unusually barbaric'. In an interview, the popular CNN anchor Don Lemon abruptly asked a respected Muslim human rights lawyer, 'Do you support Isis?'[11]

Most significantly, Muslim terror attacks in the United States were covered far more frequently than those by other perpetrators, despite the fact that the latter considerably outnumbered them. Research by the University of Alabama showed that terrorist attacks by non-Muslims (or people of unknown religion) between 2006 and 2015 received an average of 15 headlines, against 105 for those committed by Muslims.[12]

In April 2017, the US government's Accountability Office reported to Congress that between 12 September 2001 and the end of 2016, 73 per cent of terrorist incidents resulting in deaths were the work of far-right groups, compared to 27 per cent by Islamists.[13] However, it is not surprising that such statistics counted for little compared to the psychological impact of four major incidents which were the work of Muslims: the Fort Hood shootings of soldiers in November 2009, the Boston Marathon bombings of April 2013, the San Bernardino killings of December 2015 and the Orlando gay nightclub shootings in June 2016.

More influential in stereotyping Muslims than any news medium was the blockbuster 2014 movie *American Sniper*, directed by Clint Eastwood. It was based on the real-life story of Chris Kyle, an American sniper in the Iraq War who killed 255 Iraqis. All the victims in the movie were anonymised as evil Muslim killers who deserved to die – including a mother and child who were revealed to be carrying explosives. The movie took $350 million in North America and nearly $550 million worldwide.[14]

American Sniper drew a different power – its depiction of Muslims apart – from a gripping story and well-acted performances. Another important influence on American perceptions of Muslims was the television series *Homeland*. The central character Nicholas Brody (also well acted) is racked by conflict between his supposed Muslim identity, as a terrorist, and his supposed American identity as a model family man. All the enemies in the first five seasons are Muslims. Meanwhile, this period saw an attempted reality television series called *All-American Muslim*, with a sympathetic portrayal of an American Muslim family. It had to be cancelled when conservatives pressured advertisers to shun the programme.[15]

Islam and the intellectuals

After 9/11, what might be called the traditional enemies of Islam in the United States – neo-conservatives, Zionists and Evangelicals – multiplied their efforts, especially through online media. They were well financed; indeed, there were lucrative careers built on denouncing Islam, especially by 'moderate' Muslims and self-described 'reformed Islamists'.

They were supported by academics who, although mostly totally ignorant about Islam themselves, gave prejudice against it the appearance of intellectual repute. Perhaps surprisingly, this period also saw Islam come under fierce assault from liberal atheists who were normally defenders of free expression and tolerance.

We have already looked at the two intellectuals, Bernard Lewis and Samuel Huntington, whose (disputed) invention of the 'clash of civilisations' theory took hold of both public opinion and senior policy-makers. Two other intellectual gurus of anti-Muslim sentiment still around today are Daniel Pipes and David Horowitz, both fervent Zionists. In 1990, Pipes had told the *National Review* that Western European societies were 'unprepared for the massive immigration of brown-skinned peoples cooking strange foods and maintaining different standards of hygiene . . . Muslim immigrants bring with them a chauvinism that augurs badly for their integration into the mainstream of the European societies.'[16] He later regretted not putting quotation marks around 'brown-skinned peoples' and 'strange foods' to distance himself from the racist attitudes he attributed to European leaders.[17]

In 1994, Pipes founded the pro-Israeli think tank Middle East Forum. In the wake of 9/11, he founded an offshoot, Campus Watch, which set out to identify unduly pro-Palestinian academics, followed by Islamist Watch in 2006, which promoted the myth of 'creeping Sharia' – a stealthy conspiracy to replace the American justice system with Sharia law. In October 2001, Pipes told the American Jewish Congress that he feared 'the presence and increased stature and affluence and enfranchisement of American Muslims, because they are so much led by an Islamist leadership'.[18]

Pipes appears to have distinguished between traditional Islam (backward but non-violent), militant Islamism ('a totalitarian ideology less than a century old') and moderate Islam (largely underground, and greatly inferior in numbers, organisation and influence compared to the militants).[19] Pipes called for government intervention to bolster the moderates against the militants and, as we will see, Barack Obama attempted such a policy with his Countering Violent Extremism programme. In 2008, Pipes added his voice to those claiming that Obama had been a Muslim.[20]

Pipes's long-time associate David Horowitz has a left-wing past, having worked in the 1960s and 1970s with the Bertrand Russell Peace Foundation and the Black Panthers. During the 1980s he recanted,[21] and reinvented himself as a conservative gadfly attacking liberal bias in higher education. This was the main focus of his think tank, the David Horowitz Freedom Center, and its offshoot, Discover the Networks, although the latter's targets included people and groups accused of enabling Islamism and undermining American values. It also employed Robert Spencer, author of more than twenty anti-Muslim books, whom we will meet in Chapter 7 as the creator of the Jihad Watch blog which claimed to track Islamic conspiracies.[22]

Horowitz received generous funding from the secretive pro-Zionist Fairbrook Foundation.[23] He was, in a sense, an incidental Islamophobe. Unlike Pipes, who had studied Islam in some depth in Cairo, Horowitz had no background in Islam or the Middle East. His main personal contribution to Islamophobia came in 2007 and 2008 with a series of false claims on university campuses that the Muslim Students Association of the US and Canada had links with extremist organisations and 'supported a second Holocaust of Jews'.[24]

Horowitz also claimed, in his event Islamo-Fascism Awareness Week, held on 22–26 October 2007, that '150 million out of 750 million Muslims support a holy war against Christians, Jews and other Muslims'.[25] In February 2010, he went even further when he told the University of Massachusetts Amherst that 'Islamists are worse than the Nazis, because even the Nazis did not tell the world that they want to exterminate the Jews'.[26] Horowitz continues to operate his Freedom Center. Lately he has turned his invective against Black Lives Matter, and his latest book is titled *I Can't Breathe: How a Racial Hoax is Killing America*, defending the police who killed George Floyd from the charge of racial bias.

The '9/11 Monster Mosque' hysteria

Pamela Geller was a right-wing blogger whose speciality was to induce hysteria about the establishment of Arabic or Muslim institutions in New York. Geller was obsessive about Muslims, at one point even involving herself in an obscure controversy over the halal status of Campbell's Soup.[27] She achieved national prominence with her campaign against the so-called Park51 mosque in Lower Manhattan.

This project had been under way for more than a year with the minimum of fuss and the support of the local community board, the mayor of New York and – importantly – families of 9/11 victims. It was never intended to be a mosque, which means a large space for public congregational prayers, but designed to be a community centre (the developers likened it to the YMCA), with some private prayer space for Muslims.

But, in May 2010, Geller turned on it with a piece titled 'Monster Mosque Pushes Ahead in Shadow of World Trade Center Islamic Death and Destruction'. With astute online promotion, she managed to double the usual readership for this piece to 200,000. Helped by allies – especially the Rupert Murdoch-owned Fox News and the *New York Post* – Geller managed to link the proposed community centre to contemporary campaigns against 'Sharia by stealth' and allege that it would become an engine of Islamist propaganda.

Geller chose the anniversary of D-Day to stage a huge rally against the '9/11 Mosque', co-promoted by other right-wing bloggers in a coalition called Stop Islamization of America. The most powerful speaker was a 9/11 fireman, Tim Brown, who, with the help of Pat Robertson's Christian conservative law firm, mounted an unsuccessful legal challenge against the plans. Politicians, who had ignored the issue, now piled into it. They included not only the usual suspects, such as Newt Gingrich, John McCain, Sarah Palin and the future Republican presidential candidate Mitt Romney, but also Democrats, including the ex-governor of Vermont Howard Dean, who had campaigned for his party's presidential nomination in 2004 as an anti-war liberal.[28] Some Muslim voices were also raised against the project, not all of whom were in the category of 'professional good Muslims'. One was Neda Bolourchi, who had lost her mother on 9/11, who feared that the planned centre 'would become a symbol of victory for militant Muslims around the world'.[29]

It is fair to say that all this controversy stemmed from Geller, and that everyone involved followed her false agenda that the Park51 project was intended to create a giant mosque. In the end, the plans were drastically modified. At the time of writing, the site will be used for a luxury condominium building, without a mosque but including an 'Islamic cultural museum' with, as originally intended, some private prayer space.[30]

It would be ironic if, through the museum, the Islamic content of the centre actually increased as the result of Geller's efforts.

One of her key allies was a fervently pro-Israeli Muslim, Youssef M. Ibrahim. They joined forces at the right-wing Hudson Institute,[31] whose leading lights included John Bolton, formerly Bush's super-hawkish ambassador to the UN and Donald Trump's national security adviser. Bolton was something of a collector of right-wing think tanks and served as chairman of the Gatestone Institute, which produced baseless accounts of a violent takeover of European countries by Muslim immigrants.[32]

Islam and Evangelicals

As usual with national catastrophes, 9/11 was seen by Evangelical leaders as a warning of the imminent apocalypse – and a sign of God's displeasure with the United States. Jerry Falwell peddled this line on Pat Robertson's television programme *The 700 Club*, a few days later. He blamed 'the pagans, and the abortionists, and the feminists, and the gays and the lesbians who are actively trying to make that an alternative lifestyle . . . all of them who have tried to secularise America' for making God angry and withdrawing his protection from his second chosen people, as he periodically withdrew it from his first in the Old Testament.[33] These remarks caused a national outcry, and both Falwell and Robertson shifted the blame for the attacks to the pure evil of Islam – which of course had far fewer American supporters than the other enemies on Falwell's list. Robertson attacked the Prophet Muhammad as 'an absolute wild-eyed fanatic, a robber, a brigand, a killer', and Falwell called him simply a terrorist.[34]

Although Falwell and Robertson kept their following (and the incomes they derived from it), they were outdone in attacking Islam – and supporting Israel – by a new set of Evangelical leaders. Billy Graham's son Franklin had been chosen to give the inaugural religious invocation by George W. Bush. He compared Bush, at length, to King David, whose successes came from submitting himself to God's will, and he rarely cited anything from the New Testament.[35] A far more abrasive figure than his father, Graham responded to 9/11 thus: 'Islam has attacked us. The God of Islam is not the same God . . . [Islam] is a very evil and wicked religion.'[36]

Another successor was Bill Keller, who had discovered God – or at least Jerry Falwell's version – while serving a jail sentence for fraud in the 1990s. After a spell as a travelling evangelist, Keller had success on the internet, where he established LivePrayer.com, in which relays of preachers answered emails requesting guidance or prayers twenty-four hours a day from two and a half million subscribers. Keller had begun mainly with conventional attacks on homosexuals, liberals and abortionists but, after 9/11, he found Muslims a more profitable target. The attacks, he claimed, were part of God's plan for a holy war against Islam, which he called a false religion 'dreamed up' by a 'pedophile murderer'. The latter charge against the Prophet Muhammad was especially popular among Islamophobes, and Keller repeated it on his late-night television programme *Live*

Prayer with Bill Keller, where he described Islam as a '1,400-year-old lie from the pits of Hell'. Keller's programme was briefly cancelled after a wave of protests, but it was soon revived for him to attack Mitt Romney's Mormonism and call Obama a fulfilment of Islamic prophecy.[37]

Ergun Caner carved a profitable niche for himself by claiming to be an ex-jihadist converted to Christianity. Most of this narrative was invented: when Caner claimed to have been trained as a jihadi, he was aged between nine and twelve, and living in the un-militant milieu of Columbus, Ohio. Caner gave out sermons in an outrageous, shock-jock style which appealed to young people more than the standard tropes of established preachers. He published a series of commercially successful books, starting with *Unveiling Islam*, which asserted that although violent Christians were acting against the Bible, 'the Muslim who commits acts of violence in jihad does so with the approval of Muhammad'. Caner was adopted as an expert on Islam by the Ankerberg Theological Research Institute, a Christian media empire whose networks had 147 million viewers. Caner fed the Sharia conspiracy myth by telling them that American Muslims were aiming – with Saudi funding – to proselytise every American family and offer them a choice between Sharia and slaughter.[38]

Rod Parsley was another to acquire a major following after 9/11. He warned in his 2005 book *Silent No More* that the United States was caught in a 'war between Islam and Christian civilisation'. He called Islam 'an anti-Christ religion based on deception' that 'fully intends to conquer the world'. The Prophet Muhammad 'received revelations from demons and not from the true God' – a position echoed by many other Christian fundamentalists, which of course renders interfaith dialogue not only impossible but immoral. Parsley became active in the political arena in 2008 when he became spiritual adviser to the Republican presidential candidate John McCain.[39]

A major Evangelical political initiative was the formation of the Family Research Council. Commanding an annual budget of $12 million, it quickly established itself as a successor to Moral Majority and the Christian Coalition. Importantly, it drew support from the hitherto largely secular Tea Party movement. Its president Tony Perkins, who had links to the Ku Klux Klan and other ultra-right groups, demanded a loyalty test for Muslims and said prayers for their conversion. He said, 'The only thing that's going to stop radical Islam – the love of Jesus Christ and the Gospel that sets people free'.[40]

Evangelicals were also active in the Voter Values Summits of 2010 and 2011. Republican presidential hopeful Gary Bauer told them that 'Islamic culture keeps hundreds of millions of people on the verge of violence and mayhem twenty-four hours a day'. At the 2011 summit, Bryan Fischer, leader of the Evangelically aligned American Family Association, told those gathered that 'the threat is not radical Islam but Islam itself. This is not Islamophobia, this is Islamorealism.' Reaching far back into American history, he claimed that Christians had a right to supplant Muslims as exponents of a superior faith, just as the early colonists had the right to supplant Indigenous Americans who refused to convert to Christianity.[41]

In an unguarded first response to 9/11, Benjamin Netanyahu described its effect as 'very good'. He hastily walked back the comment and said he meant to refer to American–Israeli relations.[42] But he was totally right in predicting that it would consolidate Israel's hold on public opinion in the United States, especially the opportunist alliance between Israel and Evangelical voters.

No one did more for this alliance after 9/11 than the pastor John Hagee. A genial, portly Texan, Hagee had grown a congregation of twenty-five in 1980 to several thousand at his Cornerstone Church in Castle Hills, Texas, to which he had added a global following in the millions by telecasting his sermons. Immediately after 9/11, Hagee burst into print with the book *Attack on America: New York, Jerusalem and the Role of Terrorism in the Last Days*, which contained his version of the familiar message that the attacks were a prelude to Armageddon.[43] He followed it with a series of books of which the most successful was *Jerusalem Countdown* in 2006. There he claimed that 'Islam not only condones violence, it commands it'. He reinforced this in a radio interview at the time, claiming that the Holy Quran gave all Muslims 'a mandate to kill Christians and Jews'.

However, the book's main message was to recommend an immediate all-out Israeli–American strike on Iran. This would forestall an imminent strike by Iran which would be the start of Armageddon. Like others, Hagee foresaw a period of rule by the Antichrist, whom he identified as the 'President of the European Union' (a revelation that would startle even the most ardent Brexiteer).[44] In a crowded field, Hagee was the most fervent Zionist supporter, boasting of his many visits to Israel and his many highly placed contacts there. The relationship with Israel survived fury at his frequent suggestions that the Jews had invited persecution through the centuries by rebelling against God's covenant with them.[45] Such remarks – coupled with a wild attack on the 'Roman Church . . . the Great Whore of Babylon' as an inspiration for Hitler – led to his dismissal as a spiritual adviser by John McCain in 2008.[46]

However, Hagee had already achieved lasting political leverage in 2006 when he co-founded Christians United for Israel, a pressure group which quickly achieved phenomenal success in lobbying the Bush administration to give Israel a free hand against Hezbollah in Lebanon and, in Hagee's own words, to 'stop pressuring Israel to give up land for peace'. It amplified his previous message about Muslims with the claim that 'radical sects, which include about 200 million Islamics, believe they have a command from God to kill Christians and Jews . . . This is a religious war. If we lose the war to Islamic fascism it will change the world as we know it . . . They are waiting to respond as terrorist cells against this nation.'[47]

This would be the high-water mark of Christian Zionist influence over any administration – until, as we shall see shortly, Evangelicals captured that of Donald Trump.

The New Atheist attack on Islam

Those mentioned thus far were familiar sources of hostility, but in the post 9/11 era, Muslims also came under assault from a number of celebrated atheists. They went further than conventional atheists, because they not only rejected religion but actively despised it. Being a highly and overtly religious country, the United States has usually been a hard territory for atheists. I am tempted to believe that when one of the world's great religions was almost universally unpopular among Americans, the New Atheists took the chance to attack Islam as a proxy for all religions.

The attack on Islam was spearheaded by two of the United States' leading public intellectuals, Sam Harris and Christopher Hitchens. (I mean no condescension by this term. Although a regular target for British snobbery, the American public has always had more respect for intellect than the British. Take, for example, the flock of Britons, from Dickens onwards, who have profited from lecture tours of the US.)

Harris, a philosopher with qualifications in neuroscience, found a rich seam in his first book *The End of Faith* in 2004, a general attack on religion as a source of bad ideas and evil actions. He called for its extinction, not through persecution but through collective mental intolerance and rejection. But he had a special problem with Islam. In 2005, he wrote: 'There are gradations to the evil that is done in the name of God, and these gradations must be honestly observed.' He called on readers to acknowledge the obvious: 'There is a direct link between the doctrine of Islam and Muslim terrorism . . . Islam contains specific notions of martyrdom and jihad that fully explain the character of Muslim violence . . . The doctrine of Islam poses unique problems for the emergence of a global civilisation.'[48]

Harris never justified why there should be a single global civilisation at all, and why its creation should require the elimination of a faith believed by over a fifth of the inhabitants of the globe. A supporter of the Iraq War, Harris explained all the resistance to the (in his view benign) American intervention as derived from Islamic fanaticism.

> We are now mired in a religious war in Iraq, and elsewhere. Our enemies, as witnessed by their astonishing willingness to slaughter themselves, are not principally motivated by political or economic grievances . . . It is time we admitted that we are not at war with "terrorism". We are at war with Islam. This is not to say that we are at war with all Muslims, but we are absolutely at war with the vision of life that is prescribed to all Muslims in the Koran . . . The idea that Islam is a "peaceful religion hijacked by extremists" is a dangerous fantasy – and it is a particularly dangerous fantasy for Muslims to indulge.[49]

Later, Harris would call for the targeting of Muslims at airport security.

> We should profile Muslims, or anyone who looks like he or she could conceivably be Muslim, and we should be honest about it . . . Needless to say, a devout Muslim should be free to show up at the airport dressed like Osama bin Laden, and his wives should be free to wear burqas. But if their goal is simply to travel safely and efficiently, wouldn't they too want a system that notices people like themselves?[50]

Harris thus managed to outdo Lewis and Huntington in expressing the 'clash of civilisations' theory and in presenting Islam as a single monolithic enemy. He did as well as anyone on the ultra-right in stereotyping all Muslims by their appearance.

Like Harris, Christopher Hitchens had a general antipathy to religion, reflected in his attempted demolition of Mother Teresa, *The Missionary Position*, published in 1995, and *Letters to a Young Contrarian* in 2001, and fully expressed in his 2007 bestseller *God Is Not Great*. His style was more orotund than Harris's: calling organised religion 'the main source of hatred in the world', before adding 'violent, irrational, intolerant, allied to racism, tribalism and bigotry, invested in ignorance and hostile to free inquiry, contemptuous of women and coercive toward children'.[51]

Like Harris, Hitchens had a special animus against Islam, although it was a little more nuanced. In 2004, he wrote: 'All faiths are not always equally demented in the same way. Islam, which was once a civilising and creative force in many societies, is now undergoing a civil war. One faction in this civil war is explicitly totalitarian and wedded to a cult of death.'[52] Hitchens did not describe the other faction. In 2007 he wrote:

Islamic belief, however simply or modestly it may be stated, is an extreme position to begin with. No human being can possibly claim to know that there is a God at all, or that there are, or were, any other gods to be repudiated. And when these ontological claims have collided, as they must, with their logical limits, it is even further beyond the cognitive capacity of any person to claim without embarrassment that the lord of creation spoke his ultimate words to an unlettered merchant in seventh-century Arabia. Those who utter such fantastic brag-gings, however many times a day they do so, can by definition have no idea what they are talking about . . .

Why, then, should we be commanded to 'respect' those who insist that they alone know something that is both unknowable and unfalsifiable? Something, furthermore, that can turn in an instant into a license for murder and rape? . . . The plain fact is that the believable threat of violence undergirds the Muslim demand for 'respect'.[53]

Like Harris but more stridently, Hitchens supported George W. Bush's wars against Islamic nations, praising prematurely how 'the demolition of the Taliban, the huge damage inflicted on the al-Qaeda network and the confrontation with theocratic saboteurs in Iraq represent huge advances for the non-fundamentalist forces in many countries'.[54]

In a long series of articles, books, and film and video appearances, Hitchens never had a good word to say about Islam. Some Muslims were better than others, but *all* of them needed to abandon Islam to achieve full membership of the civilised world.

The British academic Richard Dawkins wrote an even bigger bestseller that attacked religion in general — 2006's *The God Delusion*. He promoted himself worldwide with methods remarkably similar to many Evangelical preachers, with grateful tributes from readers whose lives he had saved.[55] Dawkins told his disciples that he regarded Islam as 'the greatest force for evil today' while admitting that he had never read the Holy Quran.[56]

Harris, Hitchens and Dawkins knew little or nothing about Islam. Ayaan Hirsi Ali carried more authority. Her backstory, although disputed and partly invented, qualified her as an expert. Originally from Somalia, raised as a Muslim and a victim of genital mutilation, she came to the United States in 2006 and her initial message amplified the familiar 'clash of civilisations' rhetoric around Islam. She told *Reason* magazine: 'We are at war with Islam. And there is no middle ground in wars. Once [Islam] is defeated it can mutate into something peaceful. It's very difficult to talk about peace now. They're not interested in peace . . . There comes a moment when you crush your enemy.'[57] She told the London *Evening Standard*: 'Sharia law is as inimical to liberal democracy as Nazism . . . Violence is inherent in Islam. It's a destructive, nihilistic cult of death. It legitimates murder.'[58]

Hirsi Ali delighted enemies of Islam even more by denouncing Muslim immigration into Europe,[59] supporting Israel against Palestine and endorsing Netanyahu's crackdown in Gaza in 2014 (she recommended him for a Nobel Peace Prize). She also praised General Sisi, the military man who ousted the elected Muslim Brotherhood government in Egypt, as a 'reformer'.[60] In recent years, she has called for an Islamic reformation, saying at the Richmond Forum in 2013 that 'Muslim leaders who are serious about achieving true and enduring peace, need to revise the Quran and the Hadith, so that there is a consistency between what the peace-loving Muslims want and what their religion says'.[61] Hirsi Ali, along with thinkers like Hitchens and Dawkins, played a distinctive role in creating the intellectual environment for a vicious and sustained assault on Islam, the subject of the next chapter.

THE ASSAULT ON ISLAM

Facing attack from Evangelical and atheist leaders, stereotyping in the media and popular culture, and hysteria on social media, with almost no one ready to defend or even describe them accurately, Muslims predictably met disfavour in public opinion surveys. In a 2005 Gallup poll, 57 per cent of respondents said 'nothing' or 'don't know' when asked to say what they admired about Muslims.[1]

It's also not surprising that after 9/11 Muslims were targeted for discrimination in government policy and were subject to aggressive rhetoric from domestic politicians. In his initial response to 9/11, President George W. Bush was careful to distinguish Islam in general from the perpetrators, whom he identified with 'a fringe form of Islamic extremism that has been rejected by Muslim scholars and the vast majority of Muslim clerics'. However, his administration was dominated by neo-conservative ideologues who followed Samuel Huntington's 'clash of civilisations' theory. In fact, one of its key advisers was Bernard Lewis, who indignantly claimed that Huntington had purloined the phrase from his 1990 article 'The Roots of Muslim Rage'. Lewis had written a series of books since the 1960s, all arguing his thesis that *all* the Islamic world resented the global success of the West, based on its Judaeo-Christian heritage. Lewis advocated the imposition of a new culture on the Islamic world, by force if necessary, modelled on Atatürk's transformation of Turkey.

Other key Bush personnel were strongly aligned with the Evangelicals. Lieutenant General William G. Boykin, his under-secretary of defence for intelligence, repeatedly presented the war on terror in religious terms.[2] In the wake of 9/11, Bush created the new, Cabinet-level Department of Homeland Security (DHS), which was headed by a Republican politician called Tom Ridge. It presided over a massive extension and centralisation of surveillance, immigration and counter-terrorist policing.[3] Its efforts were focused on Muslims, although Ridge himself was frequently at odds with Vice President Dick Cheney and Defense Secretary Donald Rumsfeld who wanted to use his office for partisan purposes.[4]

The Bush administration introduced a new National Security Entry-Exit Registration System. It foreshadowed Trump by targeting US male residents or intending residents aged 16 to 64 from 25 countries, of which 23 were Muslim-majority. Such people were to be interviewed under oath, fingerprinted and identified as a potential threat to national security by the DHS. More than 200,000 people were specially registered under this system. *None* were found to be terrorists, but more than 13,000 were subjected to removal proceedings.[5]

The administration remodelled and expanded the so-called no-fly list of people denied the right to fly because they were thought to be a threat to aviation. At the time of 9/11, this stood at just sixteen. By April 2005, there were two lists: one of people denied outright and the other a wider group of people subject to – often humiliating – enhanced searches at airports. Combined, the names on these two lists numbered around 70,000. Muslims and 'Muslim-looking people' were the main victims.[6]

Bush's Attorney-General John Ashcroft – who had lost a Senate election in 2000 to a dead candidate[7] – adopted a new 'paradigm of prevention' against supposed Muslim terrorists. He weakened FBI guidelines to allow intrusive investigation without reasonable suspicion of criminal intent.[8] With suspicious promptitude and minimal Congressional resistance after 9/11, the administration introduced the sweeping and complex Patriot Act. It introduced indefinite detention of immigrants, rights for law enforcement officers to search homes and businesses without a warrant, and greatly expanded powers for the FBI to search written, telephone and email records (even borrowings from libraries) without having to prove suspicion of terrorism to a court. Revealingly, the Act actually declared that 'Arab Americans, Muslim Americans, and Americans from South Asia are . . . entitled to nothing less than the full rights of every American' – a clear signal of its intended targets.[9]

In the five years after 9/11, nearly 6,500 people, mostly Muslim, were held under the new laws. Some were detained for non-terrorist causes, such as alleged tax, immigration or welfare offences. Of these people, 64 per cent were not prosecuted. Of those prosecuted, a quarter were found not guilty. The great majority drew no jail time or a sentence of less than a year. In February 2005, a leaked FBI memo revealed that the agency had failed to find a single domestic al-Qaeda sleeper cell. The administration was embarrassed by the detention of two high-profile Muslim visitors: musician Yusuf Islam (formerly Cat Stevens) and Shahid Malik, a minister in Gordon Brown's Labour government.[10]

By 2008, the last year of the Bush administration, the FBI had more than 15,000 paid informants, mostly Muslims. Special 'snitch' green cards were introduced by the FBI, allowing immigrants to work if they were willing to become informants. Another important incentive for Muslims to inform was their removal from the no-fly list.[11] It is worth noting that the FBI made no comparable effort to infiltrate white supremacist or extreme right groups, although in the twenty years from 1990, they were responsible for 348 deaths by politically motivated violence, compared to twenty by *domestic* American Muslims (i.e. either American Muslim citizens or long-term US residents). In several high-profile cases, the FBI discovered large stocks of weapons in the hands of right-wing extremists – all by accident, rather than intelligence. When the DHS produced a report on the far right in 2009, it provoked such outrage from conservatives that they were forced to disavow it.[12]

Barack Obama and Muslims

Largely in response to the Bush administration's methods, American Muslims voted en masse for Barack Obama in 2008. He secured 92 per cent of their vote against 4 per cent for his rival, John McCain, who had tried to court doubtful Evangelical voters by aligning with anti-Muslim Zionist pastors.[13] But Obama proved a false dawn for American Muslims. The son of a Muslim father, with the middle name of Hussein, he was beset by allegations that he was himself a secret Muslim. Donald Trump would later make obsessive use of this myth, but he was not the first. It stemmed from a group of Islamophobic bloggers.

Obama's response was less than robust. His staff airbrushed the image of two Muslim women in hijabs from a campaign appearance, while also denouncing the allegations as 'smears' – implying, of course, that to be called a Muslim was an insult.[14] Once in office, Obama made an early visit to Cairo, where in an eloquent speech he tried to mend fences with the Muslim world and disavowed the Huntington (or Lewis) thesis of an inevitable 'clash of civilisations' between the West and Islam. 'America and Islam are not exclusive and need not be in competition,' he declared. 'Instead they overlap and share common principles – principles of justice and progress, tolerance and the dignity of all human beings.'

But the following year, 2010, on a visit to India, Obama was unable to visit the Sikh Golden Temple at Amritsar because he was afraid that the required head covering would make him look like a Muslim to voters at home. (Farcically, his aides suggested a modified baseball cap, but this was unacceptable to his hosts.)[15] Obama stayed away from any mosque or Islamic site in the United States until the penultimate year of his second, lame-duck term. These tactics did little good: too many white voters found the Muslim accusations a convenient excuse for hating the first African American president. In a survey in 2011 by the Public Religion Research Institute, 38 per cent of respondents identified him as Christian (as he indeed self-identifies), 18 per cent as Muslim and the rest did not know.[16]

Obama maintained Bush's DHS and the key provisions of the Patriot Act. When eventually he visited an Islamic centre, in Baltimore, his purpose was to enlist Muslims in support of his administration's new anti-terror strategy called Countering Violent Extremism (CVE). It essentially divided American Muslims into 'good' citizens, who stood up for American values, and 'bad' ones who drifted into supporting so-called Islamic extremism. 'Good' Muslims were expected not only to inform on the 'bad' ones (as under the Bush administration), but to help them actively resist the drift. In Obama's words at Baltimore, 'Muslims around the world have a responsibility to reject extremist ideologies that are trying to penetrate within Muslim communities'.[17]

As with Prevent and other European counter-terrorism strategies, CVE relied on identifying signs of 'radicalisation' of domestic Muslims. The Americans resisted this concept for a long time. In 2007, the DHS suggested – accurately – that domestic Muslims were *not* being radicalised, and cited this as 'a tribute to American society, which values free expression and encourages all to engage politically and economically'. This comforting belief was undermined by a series of Islamist attacks, notably the shootings by a US army major, Nidal Hasan, at the military base at Fort Hood, Texas, in 2009. As always, these attacks had a higher media profile than those perpetrated by, for example, white supremacists or anti-abortionists.[18]

CVE policing was piloted in the city of Minneapolis, which housed a large Somali population of refugees from the devastating conflicts in their native land. It was feared that younger Somalis were being enlisted for domestic terrorism by the rebel group al-Shabaab. This was almost certainly wrong: al-Shabaab had no ambitions or capability of operating outside their base in the horn of Africa. The FBI launched Operation Rhino, its biggest counter-terrorism operation since 9/11, in the city. It took no account of Somali politics and its impact on the exiles: if al-Shabaab had any admirers among them, it was for their resistance to a brutal invasion by (Christian) Ethiopia in support of Somali warlords backed by the United States.

Since al-Shabaab was a proscribed organisation, Somalis in the US could be charged with material support for terrorism not only for travelling to Somalia on its behalf, but also for helping anyone to travel there, or even distributing its literature. Operation Rhino enlisted Somali community leaders in Minneapolis (mostly self-appointed) to report on young Somalis; the FBI were especially interested in those who suddenly became pious Muslims and gave up alcohol, drugs, gambling and petty crime.[19] The leaders urged the young people to co-operate with the FBI and, most importantly, to accept interviews with the FBI without a lawyer. The FBI acquired information on thousands of local Somalis who wanted only to make a better life in the US and be able to help relatives still at home in the grip of war and famine. This was denied to them, however, because banks, in fear of counter-terrorist action, refused to transmit money to Somalia.[20]

CVE policing was rolled out nationally in August 2011. The DHS was charged with co-operating with local law enforcement agencies to identify local Muslims in danger of being radicalised and head them off. It separated four stages: pre-radicalisation, identification, indoctrination and action. Agencies and local Muslim leaders were urged to intervene at the first two stages, when the subject was showing general signs of discontent with the American way of life, but before he took an interest in any particular extremist group – and certainly before he took part in any action on their behalf. Most of the interventions were familiar responses to disaffected youth: clubs, sports, training, motivational speakers. CVE relied heavily on informants in mosques, community centres, cafés and, especially, student associations. The State Department helped the DHS to enlist 'moderate and liberal Muslims' to support CVE, and local Muslim institutions were promised federal funding to collaborate. CVE relied strongly on divisions within Islam.

The Lebanese American Heritage Club (LAHC), a mostly Shia organisation within the long-established Muslim community of Dearborn, Michigan, changed its name to Leaders Advancing and Helping Communities (keeping its acronym but losing its ethnic reference) when it accepted half a million dollars from the DHS. It claimed that the funding would support its existing programmes, but the DHS revealed the real agenda in a press release: 'In this age of self-radicalisation and terrorist-inspired acts of violence, domestic-based efforts to counter violent extremism have become a homeland security imperative.' The LAHC refused the grant, saying 'It's a continued slap in the face for communities that are suffering from terrorist acts and violent behaviour of these right-wing extremist groups, showing them that the administration does not care about the negative impact of white supremacy'. But other 'loyal' Muslim organisations in Boston, Los Angeles, Minneapolis and many university campuses quietly benefited from CVE funding.[21]

It should be emphasised that all these efforts were expended only on American Muslims. There were no matching programmes to prevent the radicalisation of white Christian extremists, or anti-abortion campaigners, or other groups who were major instigators of domestic terrorism. In many high-profile cases against Muslims in this period, the FBI relied blatantly on agents provocateurs. There have been hundreds of

Muslims driven towards terrorism by the FBI. The FBI would entrap these (usually poor) Muslims and encourage them towards acts of terrorism (often by offering them money), before then arresting and prosecuting them.* One example was that of the Newburgh Four, a gang so dysfunctional that their trial judge, Colleen McMahon, remarked 'only the government could have made a terrorist out of Mr Cromitie [the gang leader], a man whose buffoonery is positively Shakespearean in its scope . . . There would have been no crime here except that the government instigated it, planned it and brought it to fruition.' But they were still found guilty, and she handed them twenty-five-year jail sentences.[22]

In 2013, as Obama started his second term, senators Dianne Feinstein and Saxby Chambliss of the Senate Intelligence Committee told a press conference that the FBI had 10,000 intelligence analysts and 15,000 paid informants in the field of counter-terrorism.[23] On a conservative estimate that two-thirds were working on Muslims, that would mean one FBI agent or informant for every ninety-four American Muslims. Adding in the staff and informants of other counter-terrorism agencies and local police departments would bring the proportion down to one for every sixty-six – the same ratio of the hated Stasi to the former population of East Germany.[24]

In summary, both the Bush and the Obama administrations treated *all* American Muslims as a single, suspect community, subject to discriminatory measures of surveillance and detention. They were asked constantly, as no other group of the population were, to prove their loyalty to American values, all too frequently by acting as spies and informers on their own communities.

---

* The case of the Liberty City Seven is particularly interesting, as set out in the illuminating article by Adrian Horton: '. . . a tragic case study of the FBI's post-9/11 shift toward the controversial tactic of entrapment – paid informants, increasingly complex sting operations, fake terror plots leading to dubious, dramatic arrests.' 'When the FBI entraps: the forgotten case of the Liberty City Seven', Adrian Horton, *Guardian*, 9 August 2021.

The Sharia anti-Muslim panics

Anti-Muslim sentiment came to a head with the Sharia panic created by bloggers and politicians, which formed perhaps the most significant source of public debate on Islam in the years after 9/11. Fears of Sharia law originated with the ultra-Zionist David Yerushalmi, an American Hasidic Jew who had lived in Israel for some years, earning a reputation for outright resistance to any concessions to Palestinians.[25]

Returning to the United States, he founded a conservative pressure group called the Society of Americans for National Existence. This claimed the existence of a Muslim plot to overthrow the US government and impose Sharia law. He received backing from a prominent neo-conservative, Frank Gaffney, founder of the Center for Security Policy, to establish a research project called 'Mapping Sharia', led by a notorious Islamophobe called David Gaubatz. Gaubatz and two other Muslim impersonators donned 'Sharia costumes' (robes cut above the ankle with black stitching) and grew beards of one inch in length – but no moustaches – in order to infiltrate mosques. There they noted the length of the imam's beard and other significant information, such as the percentage of men wearing hats. They also collected samples of literature.

On the basis of such rigorous research collected over eighteen months, they concluded that more than 80 per cent of American mosques were promoting jihad and Islamic supremacy. Yerushalmi and Gaffney joined General Boykin – whom we met earlier as Bush's ultra-Evangelical undersecretary for defence promoting a 'holy war' between the US and Islamic fanaticism – and the three jointly published this conclusion in a report 'Shariah: a threat to America'. The 80 per cent figure was eagerly promoted by two other prominent anti-Muslim bloggers, Pamela Geller and Robert Spencer.[26]

We have already met Pamela Geller, the anti-Muslim blogger

who had built a strong following for her anti-Muslim blog Atlas
Shrugs, named after the immense didactic novel by the neo-
conservative guru Ayn Rand. Spencer had more academic
pretensions. In the wake of 9/11, despite a very sketchy knowledge of Islam, he published the book *Islam Unveiled* (anti-Muslim
writers were fond of this attempted pun), prophesying future
terrorist attacks on the United States as a precursor to its conquest and conversion into an Islamic empire. He founded two
online organisations, Jihad Watch and Dhimmi Watch, to pump
out anti-Muslim propaganda and rebut any favourable mentions of
Islam, especially in the media and academia. Spencer was backed
by Daniel Pipes and David Horowitz who, as already noted, were
America's two leading anti-Muslim academics. Spencer soon
added a new strand to his message: Muslims were targeting journalists, doctors and other professions in a campaign to introduce
'creeping Sharia' by subversion.[27]

Helped along by Geller and Spencer, the 80 per cent figure of
mosques engaged in the Sharia conspiracy gained traction in neo-
conservative circles. In 2011, Congressman Peter King, a hitherto
obscure New York Republican, endorsed the figure in a series of
hearings which achieved national prominence. As chairman of the
House Committee on Homeland Security (a worthy successor to
the anti-communist House Un-American Activities Committee
of the 1950s), he held the packed hearings on the 'homegrown
radicalisation' of Muslims targeted by al-Qaeda.

In 2007, a formal pressure group, ACT For America, was
formed to unite conservative Tea Party members with Evangelicals
and Zionists. The Tea Party, with their anti-government attitude,
were not natural allies of the Evangelicals, who wanted to use
government power to enforce their moral judgements. Many
were isolationist and had little enthusiasm for adventures in the
Middle East based on unconditional support for Zionism. But
all three groups were united by fear and hatred of Islam. The
founder of ACT!, Brigitte Gabriel, told her followers that Islam

had added nothing to human civilisation (all the learning nourished in the medieval Islamic states was presumably the work of the non-Muslims they had conquered) and that Muslim women had nothing to offer society except child bearing, childcare and cooking. She saw an Islamic conspiracy behind almost everything done by the Obama administration, especially the decision to give Osama bin Laden an Islamic burial at sea.[28] ACT was modelled on the National Rifle Association as a political pressure group and within a few years it had branches in all 50 states and 170,000 members worldwide. Its most successful activities were lobbies against the building of new mosques – and a push for a formal ban on Sharia law in every state.[29]

Adding to the new fear of an insidious global Islamic conspiracy, the secretive Clarion Fund contributed $17 million ahead of the presidential election campaign of 2008 to distribute twenty-eight million copies of a tendentious documentary called *Obsession: Radical Islam's War Against the West*. Ultra-Zionist in its message, the documentary equated Palestinians with the Nazis and predicted a new Holocaust of Jews if they achieved any of their demands. This message was backed up by a man called Walid Shoebat (one of many fake reformed jihadists who made successful careers in this period) and, more seriously, with input from Sir Martin Gilbert, the British historian and biographer of Winston Churchill – and soon to be a member of the UK's long-running inquiry into the Iraq War. *Obsession* told viewers not to trust any American Muslims or mosques or other organisations: all were 'fronts' for the intended Islamic theocracy.[30]

A persistent problem for the anti-Sharia coalition was the complete lack of evidence for any attempt by American Muslims to substitute Sharia for domestic American law. However, in 2009 a judge in New Jersey gave them a helping hand when he refused a restraining order to the wife of a Muslim husband on the grounds that he might reasonably believe, under Sharia law, that he was entitled to conjugal sex on demand. The judge's decision was wrong in domestic law and almost certainly under most inter-pretations of the Sharia as well, and was quickly overturned,[31] but it gave the coalition a pretext for a nationwide campaign to outlaw the Sharia. Model bills to achieve this were introduced in twenty-three states; they referred to 'foreign' law rather than Sharia, but everyone knew the real target. They were successful in Alabama, Arizona, Kansas, Louisiana, North Carolina, South Dakota, Tennessee and Texas. In Missouri the law was blocked by the governor (because it might have interfered with international adoptions) and in Oklahoma, it was blocked by a federal court on a suit from CAIR, the country's leading Muslim advocacy organisation.[32]

The coalition's biggest political capture was former House speaker Newt Gingrich. Long past his 1990s heyday, and out of favour with Evangelical voters over his personal life, Gingrich was persuaded by Spencer and Gaffney to use the anti-Sharia campaign to revive his political career. In July 2010, as keynote speaker, he told the neo-conservative American Enterprise Institute that the Sharia was 'a mortal threat to the survival of freedom in the United States and in the world as we know it'. He promised a total purge of alleged followers of Sharia from any part of US politics, government, education and justice. He was followed quickly by other Republican presidential contenders. Herman Cain promised (if elected) a loyalty test for all Muslims in government service, while Michele Bachmann demanded a National Security investigation of the Muslim Brotherhood infil-tration of the US.[33] In August 2011, a published survey suggested that 30 per cent of American voters believed that Muslims were indeed trying to replace the American Constitution with Sharia. The proportion doubled among those who followed Fox News.[34]

Meanwhile, both Spencer and Gaffney took the anti-Sharia message to the FBI, the armed services, the intelligence commu-nity and local police forces. In 2011, intelligence chiefs attended the launch of another tendentious report by Gaffney entitled

Shariah: The Threat to America. This claimed that jihadist violence was 'rooted in the Islamic texts, teachings and interpretations that constitute Shariah'. Gaffney claimed that, alongside terrorist violence, Islamists, especially the Muslim Brotherhood, were engaged in 'stealthy jihad tactics [to] impose a totalitarian régime [through] multi-layered cultural subversion'. Gaffney called for a total ban from public employment and the armed forces for anyone who 'espouses or supports Shariah' and for charging 'imams and mosques that advocate Shariah in America' with sedition.

No one, not even Donald Trump, has followed that recommendation, but it is striking enough that anyone in the US political system took it seriously. Given that the Sharia is contained in thousands of texts which are studied and expounded (and disputed) throughout the Muslim world,* it would have had the effect of making Islam itself a crime in the US.[35]

Counter-terrorism as an industry after 9/11

After 9/11, Islamophobia became far more commercially lucrative in the United States. It would go on to shape a massive public and private counter-terrorism industry.[36] It also established a self-admiring, self-promoting and self-populating network of research institutes, foundations, pressure groups and bloggers. Many previously obscure individuals became important and wealthy public figures, some as supposed experts on the Islamic threat, others just for being loudmouths.

In May 2018, the respected Stimson Center published an in-depth analysis of federal spending on counter-terrorism at home and abroad by a panel of genuine non-partisan experts on the subject.[37] Its task was complicated because departments and agencies

---

* The Sharia is also transmitted orally and operates in communal ways in local contexts (and a plurality of opinion among jurists on any given point is expected). That there is not one single interpretation of the Sharia is accepted by most Muslims. Moreover, the Sharia is embedded in the everyday practice of Muslims.

were less than transparent about their spending and its purposes. This problem became more acute after 2011, when the Budget Control Act of that year set limits on discretionary government spending. To avoid these, departments smuggled considerable spending at home into the non-controlled budgets for overseas contingency operations.

The Stimson figures may therefore be an underestimate, but their analysis was rigorous and conveys how much counter-terrorism spending might mean to its beneficiaries in the private sector. A very high proportion of this spending was derived from the wars in two Muslim-majority nations and countering the threat of terrorist attacks at home. As we have already seen, domestic terrorism threats were disproportionately ascribed to Muslims. Fear of Islam in general was therefore very valuable to a great number of contractors.

The Stimson panel found that between the fiscal years of 2002 and 2017, the government spent $2.8 *trillion* on counter-terrorism, representing nearly 15 per cent of total discretionary expenditure. Before 9/11, that proportion was less than 2 per cent. (Discretionary expenditure is distinguished from man-datory expenditure, such as Social Security payments, which depends on the number of claimants entitled to it.)

The panel remarked that 'since September 11, 2001, terrorist attacks by Muslim extremists or jihadis have killed 100 people in the United States or about six per year. In comparison, the opioid fentanyl was responsible for more than 20,000 deaths in the United States during 2016 alone.' Over the entire period, principally due to the wars, counter-terrorism spending rose much faster than overall discretionary spending – by 154 per cent compared to 102 per cent. Barack Obama taking office in 2009 did not make a substantial difference to this trend.

The panel estimated total spending in this period on home-land security at $979 billion,[38] thus creating far and away the biggest homeland security market in the world.[39] The Bush administration's 'war on terror' at home and abroad was especially valuable to defence contractors. The remuneration for CEOs in the industry rose by 108 per cent between 2001 and 2005, compared to 6 per cent for CEOs in other sectors. Many architects of the 'war on terror' privatised themselves profitably as consultants in the security business, including Tom Ridge and his successor as secretary of homeland security Michael Chertoff, as well as Bush's Attorney General John Ashcroft, and his Secretary of State Condoleezza Rice, with her deputy Stephen Hadley.[40]

It would be wrong to say that all these special interests created Islamophobia in the US for their own ends. It is fair to say that they found it profitable to maintain the fear of terrorism among the American people; as we have seen, this meant principally the fear of *Islamic* terrorism. The ground was well prepared for Donald Trump to be the first major presidential candidate to run on a platform of overt prejudice against one religious faith.*

---

* This title might be disputed by Millard Fillmore, the former president who was the candidate of the so-called Know Nothing Party in 1856, a significant political movement built on opposition to Roman Catholicism.

DONALD TRUMP AND ISLAM

Donald Trump's first specific pledge against Muslims came after the November 2015 Paris bombings when he called for a database to track Muslims in the US and surveillance of mosques. He also, for the first time, made his false claim that American Muslims in New Jersey had cheered 9/11.[1] A month later he responded to the mass shootings by a Muslim couple in San Bernardino, California, with the first commitment to 'a total and complete shutdown of Muslims entering the United States', adding the vague qualifying clause 'until our country's representatives can figure out what is going on'.[2]

Trump's Republican rivals for the presidency attacked the proposal instantly – but carefully. None declared outright that it was unconstitutional to discriminate against an entire faith or immoral to hold it up for hatred. Jeb Bush said that Trump was 'unhinged' and his policy proposals were 'not serious' (perhaps implying that if he had thought them through in more detail they would have been fine with him). John Kasich attacked Trump's 'outrageous divisiveness', while Carly Fiorina called Trump's 'over-reaction as dangerous as President Obama's under-reaction'. Ted Cruz simply said that he had a different policy. John McCain, the Republican presidential candidate in 2008, said that Trump's policy was 'foolish'. For the Democrats, Hillary Clinton seems to have made no immediate response and even the progressive candidate Bernie Sanders, despite showing some bravery on the issue, did not go far enough.[3] No one who condemned Trump offered any proposals to combat Islamophobia in the US, either then or at any time in the campaign.

When they found that Trump's proposal was actually popular with most Republican voters, his rivals turned up their own anti-Muslim rhetoric. Jeb Bush sought a ban on Muslim refugees from Syria, while Ben Carson compared the admission of Syrian Muslim refugees to taking risks with a rabid dog. Marco Rubio compared Muslim extremists to Nazis, while Ted Cruz, who had been a prominent supporter of the anti-Sharia law campaign, called for Muslim neighbourhoods to be tightly patrolled and secured before they could become radicalised.[4] The Pew Research Center detected a new rise in anti-Muslim sentiment and there was a new spike in crime against Muslims.[5]

Trump repeated the pledge several times but by June the following year, he had retreated from the idea of a blanket ban. Instead it would apply to people originating from countries with a proven history of terrorism against the US or its allies.[6] He never named these countries, but they were evidently all Muslim-majority countries (although not including Saudi Arabia, which spawned al-Qaeda). By then, Trump was the almost-certain nominee of his party and had no more need of the Muslim issue – or any other – to score off his Republican rivals.

Trump's use of Islamophobia throughout the presidential campaign was always casual and opportunistic: on one occasion he made up policy on his Scottish golf course.[7] It was never part of his main message to American voters. It is interesting to see how little it appears in his favourite medium of Twitter. Trump issued more than 36,000 tweets from the opening of his account in 2011 to February 2019. Just sixty mentioned the word 'Muslim' and another sixty-six 'Islam' or 'Islamic'.[8]

Trump rarely used Islam in his campaign against Hillary Clinton, except in support of his claims that she or Barack Obama were weak. He did not raise any of his proposals against Muslims in his three television debates with her, although in the second debate both candidates had to respond to a question about Islamophobia from a Muslim voter, Gorbah Hamed. Trump gave a rambling response in which he described Islamophobia as 'a shame', but then immediately denounced political correctness (and Obama) for refusing to express the problem as 'radical Islamic terrorists'. He accused Clinton of planning a huge increase in immigration of Muslim refugees and announced a new version of his Muslim ban as 'an extreme vetting from certain areas of the world'. Characteristically, he failed to define 'extreme vetting'.[9]

In many ways, Clinton's response was more telling. She denounced the 'very divisive, dark things said about Muslims' before, after a lengthy platitude, claiming that Trump's 'demagogic rhetoric' was 'very short-sighted and even dangerous'. But she then completely echoed Trump's call for Muslims to inform on each other – which, as we have seen, was also the policy of the Obama administration. 'We need American Muslims to be part of our eyes and ears on our front lawns,' she said. 'I've worked with a lot of different Muslim groups around America . . . I've heard how important it is for them to feel that they are wanted and included and part of our country, *part of our homeland security* [my emphasis].' Clinton seems to have expected American Muslim voters to fall into her lap in view of Trump's rhetoric, although she had received a warning not to take them for granted when they turned out for her Democratic rival Bernie Sanders in the Michigan primary, which he won by the narrow margin of 1.4 per cent, defying every opinion poll.

The Democrat party made considerable outreach efforts to Muslim voters, particularly through Clinton's chief adviser, Huma Abedin (who was falsely accused of being part of the Muslim Brotherhood). Clinton herself, however, was always guarded in her approach to them. Like Obama, she never appeared at a mosque during the campaign.[10] In *What Happened*, her long book about the election campaign, she did not mention a single meeting between herself and Muslim voters. Perhaps it never struck her that Muslim voters might resent her insistence that they must prove their loyalty by co-operating against extremism with the authorities: she did not make this demand to other communities whose extremists were responsible for more domestic terrorism in the United States.

Clinton may have paid a penalty for her lukewarm tactics, because Trump secured a surprisingly high share of Muslim votes. Nationally, an exit poll by the leading Muslim advocacy group CAIR suggested that he won 13 per cent of them – well ahead of his Republican predecessors Mitt Romney and John McCain.[11] As with voters generally, Trump's greatest appeal was to older Muslim voters. The survey indicated the ethnic and social diversity of American Muslims: it suggested that some actually agreed with his treatment of radical Islam and that many others were willing to ignore his anti-Muslim rhetoric because they liked other parts of his programme (or disliked Hillary Clinton).

Trump enacts the Muslim ban

In office, Trump needed three attempts to enact his anti-Muslim immigration policy. The first two succumbed to legal challenge because they discriminated on the basis of religion. The final version squeezed through the Supreme Court with five Republican votes to four Democrat votes in June 2018 as the justices divided on party lines.[12] Trump's original plans to ban all entry of Syrian refugees were abandoned; instead, Obama's target of 110,000 was cut by half. Similarly, the decision to include Iraq on the list of prohibited countries – to which his own Defense Department had objected, since it would have barred American allies in the war against Islamic State – was also dropped. The new order virtually shut down ordinary travel to the United States from five Muslim-majority countries – Syria, Iran, Libya, Somalia and Yemen – and two non-Muslim ones, North Korea and Venezuela. (The latter was an oddity in this context. Venezuela had an anti-American socialist government, but was not a terrorist state.)

Unhelpfully from Trump's point of view, the majority opinion authored by Chief Justice Roberts noted that the final version would affect only 8 per cent of the world's Muslims; the remaining 92 per cent would be able to seek entry into the US as if nothing had happened. He also refused to take into account any of Trump's statements and tweets as evidence that it was intended to ban Muslims. Instead, he looked at the order as it stood and determined that it was a lawful use, on national security grounds, of the president's executive power, citing the grim precedent of President Roosevelt's wartime internment of the Japanese-American population. In dissent, Justice Sonia Sotomayor said that the final version 'leaves undisturbed a policy first advertised openly and equivocally as a "total and complete shutdown of Muslims entering the United States" because the policy now masquerades behind a façade of national-security concerns'.

Although Trump greeted his victory in the Supreme Court with a characteristic tweet – 'Wow!' – his Muslim ban was largely a symbolic policy except for refugees in the US hoping to be joined by family members. As an executive decision, it was not debated in Congress. It was not a factor in the intense battle over the confirmation of Brett Kavanaugh, Trump's controversial choice for the Supreme Court.

Trump pays his debt to Evangelical voters

Trump's greatest gift to the Evangelical voters was the unconditional recognition of Jerusalem as the capital of the state of Israel. Again, this action can be traced to his campaign, forming part of the debt he paid to his Evangelical support, which was instrumental to his success. At first sight, it seems ironic that Evangelical leaders such as John Hagee and Franklin Graham should have given such early and consistent support to Trump, whose actions in his private life are far removed from their teaching. But, as Franklin Graham remarked at the height of Trump's woes with the Stormy Daniels sex scandal, 'we certainly don't hold him up as the pastor of the nation and he is not. But . . . the President does have a concern for Christian values, he does have a concern to protect Christians whether it's here at home or around the world and I appreciate the fact that he protects religious liberty and freedom.'[13]

Politically, Trump offered a lot to Evangelical leaders. They liked his commitment to American exceptionalism (which matched their own) and his economic mix of mercantilism, tax cutting and deregulation. They liked even more his stance as an outsider, fighting their hated enemy, the United States' liberal-secular elite.

As noted earlier, Evangelical Christians were the most important element of Trump's voter support. Although in relative decline (against rising numbers of atheists and non-affiliated religious people), they represented the largest religious demographic in the US. The Pew survey estimated them at 26 per cent of the population, ahead of Roman Catholics at 20 per cent.[14] Evangelicals had a strong interest in promoting Trump's anti-Mexican immigration policy – excluding young Roman Catholics who might create large families and thus overtake them.

But most important of all, Trump was committed to a Zionist policy. For Evangelical leaders, this made him an agent of God's will, not just for Israel but also for the United States. No one did more to cement Trump's alliance with Evangelical Zionists than his vice president, Mike Pence. It is fair to say that this was the major reason for Trump's choice of running mate. Originally a Catholic Democrat, Pence was converted to Evangelical Christianity as a young man at a Christian rock festival, and then to conservatism by Ronald Reagan. He embraced his two new faiths with the fervour of many converts. Two decades of down-the-line Evangelical conservative politics, coupled with an affable

personality, propelled him first into Congress and then into the
governor's mansion in his home state of Indiana. The Evangelical
leader Ralph Reed saw him as a potential presidential candidate
in 2016. But then disaster struck and his political career seemed
to be doomed.

As governor of Indiana, he had earned massive hostility right
across the political spectrum, and from vital commercial interests, for supporting a bill to allow local businesses to turn away
gay customers. He then defended himself very badly on television.
In mid-2016, almost no one saw him as a vice-presidential candidate. He appeared to add nothing to any Republican ticket. He
was certainly not Donald Trump's first choice: he wanted either
Newt Gingrich or the New Jersey governor Chris Christie – a
confrontational character like himself. But his campaign manager
Paul Manafort knew that Trump needed an Evangelical running
mate with an emollient style. He engineered a meeting between
Trump and Pence, and Trump gave him the job after a golf match,
which Pence astutely lost.[15]

During the presidential campaign, Pence did the usual tasks
of the number two on the ticket in shoring up his party's core
support, although he had the special task of making Trump more
palatable to Evangelical voters. During the vice-presidential televised debate, he said how proud he was to be standing with a
pro-life candidate.[16] At Trump's lowest ebb, when his so-called
'locker room' remarks about grabbing women almost forced him
out of the race, there was a brief window when it seemed that
Pence would replace him, with Condoleezza Rice as his running
mate. Pence disavowed Trump's remarks, but then said that he
and his family were praying for him and were looking forward to
his appearance the next day to explain himself.[17]

When Trump fought back, Pence stuck by him, resuming his
title as Trump's 'apologizer-in-chief'.[18] With Pence's help, Trump
overcame doubts among Evangelical voters over his character and
lifestyle. The Pew Research Center, surveying the exit polls on

the presidential election, suggested that he had taken 81 per cent of the votes of white born-again or Evangelical voters, slightly more than his three immediate Republican predecessors.[19] This group of voters was the one most likely to switch from Democrat to Republican in the crucial swing states which Trump won.[20] He paid back his political debts quickly. A year into his administration, both supporters and opponents hailed a long list of 'wins' for Evangelicals – on abortion, welfare payments for large families, faith agencies dispensing aid to Christian refugees, Trump's first appointment to the Supreme Court (the conservative judge Neil Gorsuch) and extending disaster relief to rebuilding churches. Pence received a considerable degree of credit for these policies from his admirers.[21]

However, nothing was more important to Evangelical supporters than Trump's unconditional recognition of undivided Jerusalem as the capital of Israel. The decision was widely disputed. It seemed to serve no immediate American interest, set the country at odds with its allies and exposed its troops and civilians to even greater hatred and danger overseas. It effectively gave the Netanyahu government a free hand over Palestine and in the Middle East generally, with guaranteed American support for any of his policies. Significantly, when Trump's daughter Ivanka and son-in-law Jared Kushner opened the new US embassy in Jerusalem in May 2018, the American delegation included Robert Jeffress, the megachurch pastor who gave such hyperbolic support to Trump during the campaign. His presence added religious significance to an ostensibly political and diplomatic decision.[22]

Pence was a key promoter of recognising Jerusalem as the capital of Israel and when he visited Israel at the end of 2017, he actually accelerated Trump's timetable for moving the embassy to the city. Pence identified US support for Israel with God's promise to the Jews. 'Down through the generations, the American people became fierce advocates of the Jewish people's aspiration to return to the land of your forefathers, to claim your own new birth of freedom in your beloved homeland,' he said to applause. 'The Jewish people held fast to a promise through all the ages, written so long ago, that "even if you have been banished to the most distant land under the heavens", from there He would gather and bring you back to the land which your fathers possessed.'[23]

Pence and Trump's other Evangelical supporters were predictably unconcerned with the rights of Muslims in Jerusalem and Palestine. The administration did disappoint Palestine's many Christians, but these were nearly all Catholic or Orthodox – barely Christian in Evangelical eyes.[24]

The 2020 American election and the advent of Joe Biden

Given his record in office, it is interesting that Trump made no use of Islamophobic themes in 2020, even when he was persistently lagging in the polls. On his favourite campaign medium, Twitter, he made only four references to Muslims or Islam in the whole of 2020. In the same year, Trump hailed 'good Muslim' states at the White House ceremony when the UAE and Bahrain signed US-brokered agreements recognising Israel.[25] His constant search for existential enemies switched to China overseas and a coalition of radical forces at home, especially those that allowed him to appeal to racist white voters. During his four years in office, China was certainly a far more convincing threat than any Muslims to 'the American way of life'. The Trump administration actually appealed to Muslim sentiment with powerful public attacks on China's treatment of its Muslim Uighur minority, and it may have won some American Muslim votes for this.[26]

His opponent Joe Biden certainly tried harder to win Muslim American votes than Hillary Clinton. Appealing to them with general economic and social policies, primarily as members of the American middle class or those aspiring to join it, he made a number of key pledges specifically for Muslims. He promised to end, on the first day of his administration, Trump's flagship anti-Muslim measure: the ban on entry into the United States for travellers from a group of Muslim-dominated countries. He promised high-level Muslim American representation in the administration, an attack on hate crime against Muslims (and a ban on gun possession for anyone convicted) and measures against bullying of Muslim children. On foreign policy, he attacked China's treatment of the Uighurs as 'unconscionable', along with Indian policies in Kashmir and Assam and its new anti-Muslim citizenship laws. He made a familiar noncommittal pledge on Israel and the Palestinians.

Biden did indeed end the Trump travel ban on his first day in office.[27] He gave a senior appointment to an American Muslim, Sameera Fazili, as deputy director of the National Economic Council.[28] However, in foreign policy, Biden alarmed not only Muslims but human rights campaigners worldwide with some remarks which resiled from his earlier attacks on China's treatment of the Uighurs. He appeared to rationalise it as 'a different norm' from Western values.[29] However, his new Secretary of State, Antony Blinken, maintained Trump's description of it – on his last day in office – as 'genocide'.[30] While not actually using the term, Biden made no concessions on the Uighurs in his first conversation as president with Xi Jinping.[31] On Israel, initial hopes (or fears) that Biden had snubbed Netanyahu were laid to rest by reports that the two had had a long friendly conversation.[32] He also discounted any fear that the United States would cut military aid to Israel, or indeed apply any deterrent to further Israeli annexations or repression of Palestinians.[33]

The Biden administration

The election of 2020 restored normality to US relations with Muslims at home and in international affairs. The Biden administration will not demonise them, but it will not show them any favours: Muslim states and Muslim people will be judged against American interests. The keystone of Biden's political career is his identification with the American middle class. That is why he was always the most dangerous Democratic opponent for Donald Trump, and the one Trump tried hardest to eliminate. Biden was born during the presidency of Franklin Roosevelt, who built a political coalition that made the Democratic Party the first choice of most of the skilled working class and lower middle class. Biden's overwhelming political ambition is to restore that coalition. That ambition will take priority over all minority interests: that will include, by definition, all foreign policy issues. Only a minority of Americans are actually interested in these issues at all.

The United States' Muslims remain a small minority of American voters – around 1 per cent of the total. As mentioned above, they do not form a concentrated voting bloc, politically or geographically. In the 2020 elections, three Muslim members of Congress (from 438) were re-elected, and fifty-seven other Muslim candidates (from 110) were elected to statewide offices.[34] In some states, they were the first-ever Muslims to win office. While that is a sign of progress, it leaves American Muslims a long way from collective influence over national or even local politics in the United States. But the religious and ideological forces which hate Islam within the country remain, as do the money and media outlets which sustain them. They are a massive – but not necessarily insurmountable – barrier to American understanding of Islam.

CONCLUSION TO PART ONE

In the chapters above, I have described the striking continuities which link the attitudes towards Islam from the start of the American republic to the present day. The first is the Holy Bible. It has been read by more Americans than any other document. From the time of the Pilgrim Fathers, it has caused them to identify with Israel, while feeling embedded hostility to Islam. The second continuity is ignorance. The vast majority of Americans throughout history have never met a Muslim and know nothing about Islam. This has made them especially vulnerable to preachers, popular politicians, TV show pundits and any other imposters posing as experts on Islam.

The next continuity is hostility towards Islam itself. The origins of this history date back to the Barbary Wars at the beginning of the American republic. Muslims came to occupy the same section of the American consciousness as the Native Americans who fought federal troops in conflicts throughout the nineteenth century. Like them, Muslims were identified as a backward alien people: at best, an obstacle to the advance of American civilisation and, at worst, an existential threat to it.

It is reasonable to suppose that the Heritage Foundation, Gatestone Institute and other so-called US think tanks are in part successors to the religious and other organisations which provoked hostility towards Islam in the nineteenth century and earlier. At the time of writing, all of the wars the

US acknowledges being engaged in are in Muslim-majority countries.[1]

Above all, Islam came to replace the USSR as the enemy of choice. This transformation took place at the moment when the United States needed to fill a vacancy in the aftermath of the fall of the Berlin Wall in 1989. However, the Islam against which the United States has organised itself so expensively for the last thirty years is in many respects a modern reimagining of a more ancient assailant. Islam is portrayed with exactly the same barbaric, merciless characteristics as the Barbary pirates 200 years ago, or the Moro against whom United States troops fought at the end of the nineteenth century. In reality, the idea of an existential clash between Islam and the United States is a fantasy, yet so far no mainstream American politician has found the language to comprehensively challenge the country's debased national conversation about Muslims. Joe Biden has come closest. The emergence of a new generation of Muslim leaders – including two Democratic members of Congress, Ilhan Omar and Rashida Tlaib, who both took office at the start of 2019 – perhaps gives ground for hope.

I will now turn my attention to the United Kingdom, which throughout the post-war period has claimed to be the closest ally of the United States. In the UK, where hostility to Islam dates back to the beginning of Islam itself, there is a modest tradition of engagement and understanding. Unlike the United States, British soldiers and merchants came into close contact with Islam. At a very early stage, they entered into treaties with Islamic powers, forming alliances and often conquering them. By the aftermath of the First World War, the UK had become the greatest Muslim power in the world, holding sovereignty over approximately half the global Muslim population.

The UK, along with France, played midwife to many modern Muslim states, including Saudi Arabia, Iraq, Jordan, Syria and Lebanon. It is also host to a much larger domestic Muslim population than the United States. Just over three million Muslims are today thought to live in the UK, representing around 5 per cent of the population.[2] By contrast, the 3.45 million Muslims who live in the United States represent barely 1 per cent of the US population.[3]

In the chapters that follow, I will show how the UK's richer understanding of the Islamic world has been lost. I will set out the structural factors that are leading the UK to adopt the same dangerous and simplistic discourse as the United States, one of the most significant of which is the direct influence of Britain's close relationship with America itself. Big money and patterns of media ownership and control have helped create the conditions for the return to earlier epochs of hostility and incomprehension.

As we shall see, the UK has also suffered a rash of bogus experts and pressure groups that have helped to inject Islamophobia into mainstream British politics. Until the emergence of Boris Johnson's Conservative government, they had not found a vehicle to fully articulate it and link Islamophobia lethally to the discontents of those who feel they have been failed by the country's ruling class.

PART TWO

Britain and Islam

'It is too often forgotten that we are the greatest Mahomedan power in the world and one-fourth of the population of the British Empire is Mahomedan. There have been no more loyal adherents to the throne and no more effective and loyal supporters of the Empire in its hour of trial.'

BRITISH PRIME MINISTER
DAVID LLOYD GEORGE,
to the representatives of the other
Big Four powers at the Paris Peace
Conference in May 1919

FROM BEDE TO ELIZABETH I

The venerable Bede is regarded as the father of English history. He is also the father of English propaganda against Islam. Like many later propagandists, Bede condemned Islam without any first-hand knowledge of it, or without meeting a single Muslim. Writing a century after the death of the Prophet Muhammad, he may have heard in his monastery at Jarrow of the frighteningly rapid Muslim conquests of North Africa and Spain, and the threatened conquest of France which was checked only by the Frankish victory at Poitiers in 732 (and the decision by Muslims to seek easier and more profitable conquests in present-day Iraq).

Bede called the Muslims 'Saracens', a term coined by the Greeks to describe the supposedly 'savage' inhabitants of Arabia. In this he followed his inspiration, St Jerome, who died 150 years before the Prophet Muhammad was even born. Regardless of what they believed, Bede described Muslims as 'shiftless, hateful, and violent'.[1] This would set the tone for Western descriptions of Islam until the Lewis–Huntington 'clash of civilisations' discourse thirteen centuries later.

Although he described Saracens in this way, there is evidence that Bede was a beneficiary from trade with them. When he bequeathed his 'treasure box' to his fellow monks (although not allowed personal possessions, monks received gifts from pious followers which were kept in trust), it contained two priceless ingredients – pepper and incense, which could have been obtained only from Muslim-controlled sources. A further early indication of Christian England's early trade with Muslims is a coin minted by the Saxon king Offa of Mercia, a few decades after Bede's death in 735. It is a direct copy of a coin minted by the Abbasid caliph Al-Mansur and is the first British artefact to bear an Islamic inscription, albeit upside-down.[2]

Onward Christian soldiers!

The European Christian perception of Islam began in military conflict and has been shaped by centuries of conflict afterwards.* There has rarely, if ever, been a period when some Christian polity somewhere in the world has not fought some kind of war against some Muslim polity. This is as true today as it was in the seventh century of the Christian era.

That observation may seem to be a platitude, but it is worth contrasting the Christian encounter with Islam with its encounters with all the world's other major faith groups. Islam alone has successfully contested important territories with Christianity. Islam alone developed the ideology, military technology and administrative capacity to conquer Christian societies and rule them.[3]

Their early conquests were all the more shocking to Christians because Muslims hailed from what they considered to be a barbaric place outside the limits of the civilised world. This was especially true of their seizure of the Levant (including Jerusalem) from the Byzantine Empire, successor to Rome and the greatest organised Christian power in the world. The Muslims had seized not only the spiritual centre of the Christian faith, but also control of a highly profitable industry based on the discovery and

---

* Wider Christianity is a different matter. According to the Muslim historical narrative, the Prophet was friends with Waraqah ibn Nawfal, a Christian priest in Mecca. During the early days of the Prophet's preaching of Islam, Muslims migrated from Mecca, where they faced persecution, to Abyssinia (present-day Ethiopia). They were welcomed by the Christian king Negus and given refuge.

preservation of relics, and the provisioning and protection of pilgrims.[4] Christian pilgrimage to Jerusalem therefore became rare and difficult for three centuries, but revived in the eleventh century after the Christian conversion of Hungary and the Balkans, and the reconquest of Asia Minor by the Byzantines. Their capital, Byzantium or Constantinople, became known as the New Jerusalem. It creamed off from the old city much of the profit from the restored pilgrimage industry, especially the discovery, preservation and, in many cases, invention of holy relics.

The new Muslim rulers were in fact generally tolerant of Jews and Christians in the old city of Jerusalem, allowing them to continue to practise their faiths on payment of tribute.[*] They were even welcomed by the minority Christian groups who had been oppressed by the Orthodox clergy of the Byzantine state. Many Christianised Arabs in and around Jerusalem converted to Islam, but it is an early and enduring Christian myth that all these conversions were driven by conquest and terror. The new faith of Islam had many features more likely to appeal to seventh-century (and later) agricultural and nomadic communities than organised Christianity. It had one God and one Prophet, not a puzzling three-in-one and a multitude of saints. The five pillars of Islam were – and are – simple to understand and apply, and could put the faithful in a direct relationship with God without the intervention of a specialised priesthood. They could be easily integrated into ordinary daily life, compared to the increasingly demanding rituals and lifestyles of seventh-century Christianity. Islam required fewer dedicated buildings, artefacts and hierarchies than Christianity, and was in that sense a precursor to the austere Protestantism which emerged eight centuries later in the West.[5]

---

[*] Caliph Umar permitted Jews to return to Jerusalem after nearly 500 years of exile. Many Christians also saw his arrival as a liberation. Abu-Munshar, *Islamic Jerusalem And Its Christians: A History of Tolerance and Tensions* (I. B. Taurus & Co., 2007), pp. 1, 55.

The Orthodox hierarchy shaped the Christian response to their Muslim conquerors. In 638 the Patriarch of Jerusalem accepted the protection of Caliph Umar, while muttering that he represented 'the abomination of desolation' prophesied by the prophet Daniel and Jesus Christ, a time of false Christs and false prophets which would deceive the very elect. A few decades later, John of Damascus condemned Muslims as infidels and denounced the Prophet Muhammad as the Antichrist. However, he was criticised as excessively kind to Islam by a synod in 754, when Nicetas Byzantios called Islam a 'bad and noxious religion . . . a destruction and a ruin' and described the Prophet as 'the son of the father of lies'. One member of the synod even described Muslims as subhuman, depicting them with dogs' heads.[6] Bishop Sebeos, who wrote the only contemporary account of the Byzantine defeats, went further still, identifying Muslims with the horrific Fourth Beast of the Apocalypse, an eagle riding the pale horse of Death.[7]

In this way, Muslims were given two contradictory roles in the early Christian world, of which Britain was a distant and peripheral part. They were an existential threat to Christianity, but at the same time, seen through the lens of biblical prophecy, they were agents of God's plan, a punishment for rulers and societies which did not obey his commandments. As we have seen, this interpretation of Muslims is still very much alive within the Christian world centuries later, especially in the United States.

In the eleventh century, the generally tolerant Muslim rule in the Christian Holy Land was ended by the eccentric Caliph Al-Hakim, who initiated the destruction of the Holy Sepulchre and other churches in Jerusalem, and imposed severe penalties on both Christians and Jews.* Even after his death, the Holy Land became

---

* Al-Hakim did not confine himself to the destructions of churches and synagogues. He also persecuted Muslims; for instance, forbidding women from appearing in public at all. To ensure this, he banned craftsmen from making women's shoes. He also campaigned against alcohol and outlawed the playing of chess. Paul Walker, *Caliph of Cairo: Al-Hakim bi-Amr Allah 996–1021* (American University in Cairo Press, 2011) p. 5.

more and more dangerous for local Christians and pilgrims alike: the latter returned to Christian Europe with tales of attacks and extortion by local Muslims and their leaders (ignoring those who continued to protect them). These tales inspired the most terrifying anti-Muslim propagandist in history: Pope Urban II.

There are several accounts of Urban's speech at the Council of Clermont in 1095 which launched the First Crusade (although that term did not become established until long after the defeat of the last one). But they all suggest his skill at describing and inventing Muslim atrocities. Robert the Monk's report of Urban's denunciation (composed two decades later) is the most vivid. 'An accursed race, a race utterly alienated from God . . . has invaded the lands of those Christians and has depopulated them by the sword, pillage and fire.' Local Christians were, according to Urban, enduring enforced circumcision, with the resulting blood used to defile altars and baptismal fonts. Urban then terrified his audience with tales of flogging, impalement, piercing with arrows and blows with naked swords. He added: 'What shall I say of the abominable rape of the women? To speak of it is worse than to be silent.'[8]

In spite of the example set by Richard the Lionheart and the future Edward I, few Englishmen joined any of the Crusades. Their biggest impact on most English people was financial, in the form of special taxes to pay for the Crusades, and the extra demands of paying ransoms to deliver crusading landowners from captivity. But they had a lasting effect on the psychology of English responses to Islam.

Men attracted not only honour but spiritual and legal privileges from taking the cross. Spiritually, this attracted an indulgence: automatic forgiveness of sins and reduced time in Purgatory. Legally, it brought the forgiveness of debts, relief from taxation and protection of their property from rapacious neighbours. Crusaders could even seek trial for any domestic criminal acts in special courts. The basis for these privileges was twofold: making a pilgrimage to Jerusalem *and* killing Muslims as God's enemies. When the Latin kingdoms in the Holy Land were extinguished in 1291, Jerusalem was out of reach, but the second objective was still achievable. Removing Muslims from the Holy Land represented virtue.

The Crusades were more important to England in memory or imagined memory than they were at the time. Chroniclers, artists, novelists (above all Walter Scott) and children's history books (especially the vivid Victorian narrative of H. E. Marshall's *Our Island Story*) presented gallant English knights beating off hordes of Muslim warriors, who were by turns cruel, treacherous and surprisingly effete. British sources had a problem with Richard the Lionheart's great adversary, the Kurdish Muslim Salahuddin Ayubi, whose chivalry was universally acknowledged. In his own time, he attracted rumours that he was not really a Muslim at all, but had made a secret conversion to Christianity.[9] Dante made him an example of a 'good pagan', while Walter Scott in *The Talisman* turns him an honorary European.[10] Saladin, as he became anglicised, is a very early example of the 'good Muslim' identified in our earlier discussion of Islam and the United States – a Muslim redeemed by his willingness to behave like a Western Christian. In Britain especially, Saladin became the archetype of the 'right sort of Muslim'. He was so popular there that when Stanley Lane-Poole wrote a bestselling account of his life in 1898, he confidently stated that the character of the Muslim leader was so well known that he needed no introduction.[11] During the Cold War, the British army appropriated Saladin's name for its standard model armoured car. However, he was an exception. For the most part, the Crusades consolidated the image of Muslims as an enemy, later inspiring generations of hymns and iconography of Christians as a disciplined army of holy warriors 'marching as to war'.*

---

* The idea of a disciplined army was sometimes at odds with the reality. The First Crusade was described as a 'passage of migration' in which many poor travellers were 'weighed down by wives, children and all their domestic goods'. Jonathan Riley-Smith (ed.), *Oxford Illustrated History of the Crusades* (Oxford University Press, 1995), p. 66.

As mentioned, the word 'crusade' did not arrive in the English language until long after the end of the seventh century. It was an import, via the French *croisade* and the Spanish *cruzado*, and was first used in 1706, in a literal sense of 'military expedition under the banner of the cross', specifically referring to those against the Muslims for defence or recovery of the Holy Land. Eighty years later, it acquired its figurative and complimentary sense of 'an aggressive action or enterprise against some public evil'.[12] The latter definition has flourished, to the degree that 'crusade' and the Islamic term 'jihad' have become cultural antonyms. To Westerners, especially Judaeo-Christians, a crusade is a worthy cause, whereas jihad denotes fanatical aggression; to Muslims, the overtones can be completely reversed.[*] Like many Muslim terms, the words 'jihad' and 'jihadi' have been misunderstood and put to mischievous use. As such, they need to be treated with care and respect.

Trading with the enemy

The fervour of Pope Urban's call for holy war never prevented contacts with the Islamic world through trade, diplomacy and cultural exchange.[†] Even during the Crusades, there were frequent ad hoc alliances between Christian and Muslim leaders.

---

[*] The term 'jihad' has been appropriated in the West, and the word 'jihadi' has become synonymous with a fighter or killer driven by militant Islam. This meaning is a distortion. Some apologists assert that jihad truly means a personal struggle to do right in the eyes of God, to which any war-fighting connotations are subsidiary. But this is not entirely correct either. According to the scholar Michael Bonner, 'it is possible to draw meaningful parallels between . . . Western doctrines of just war and the classical doctrine of jihad expressed by Muslim jurists. However, there are also differences.' See Michael Bonner, *Jihad in Islamic History* (Princeton University Press, 2006) p. 5.

[†] 'Islamic Civilisation' is neatly defined by the distinguished Georgetown scholar Jonathan Brown as 'that network of peoples, states, cultures and societies bound together by the institutions of the Shariah and the infrastructure, symbols and sentiments that were developed roughly between the death of the Prophet Muhammad and the thirteenth century' Jonathan A.C. Brown, *Slavery and Islam*, (Oneworld Acedemic, 2019), p. 102.

At the time of the First Crusade, the Muslim lands were locked in a bitter dispute between the Sunni Seljuks and Shia Fatimids. The Fatimids actually co-operated with the invading Crusaders. Muslims and Christians alike employed the services of the deadly Nizari Assassins.[13] Christian rulers in medieval Spain and Italy regularly employed Muslim soldiers in local conflicts, and in the great sieges of Constantinople and later Vienna, there were Muslim and Christian soldiers on both sides.[14]

In 1213, Richard the Lionheart's brother King John sent England's first diplomatic mission to a Muslim power – the Sultanate of Morocco. King John had been excommunicated by the Pope, was quarrelling with his barons and his bishops, and faced a threat from France – and was not too proud to seek an alliance with a Muslim ruler against his Christian enemies. According to the medieval chronicler (and Benedictine monk) Matthew Paris, he offered to convert to Islam and turn his kingdom into a Muslim state, but the churchmen who wrote history then were John's enemies and this may be an early piece of fake news.[15]

The most important Briton to visit Syria and Palestine in the twelfth century was not a Crusader but a scholar, Adelard of Bath. He spoke Arabic and translated Arabic works of astronomy and mathematics, which were far more accurate and advanced than their Western European counterparts. Through Adelard, the Arabic number system reached England.[16] Hugely superior to Roman numerals previously in use, and equipped with the vital concept of zero, the new system facilitated multiplication, division and more complex calculations. Over time, it would revolutionise private and public finance.

Adelard also introduced England to Muslim ideas about the role of learning and scholarship, and the importance of reason, logic and precise textual analysis alongside faith in divine revelation and reverence for religious authority. He openly admired Arabic learning and, in his major work *Quaestiones Naturales*, he ascribed to the Arabs any especially daring advanced idea.[17] Adelard was a strong influence on scholars such as Albertus Magnus and Roger Bacon.[18]

In the late fourteenth century, Geoffrey Chaucer, who was primarily a royal civil servant rather than a scholar, was familiar enough with Arabic learning to introduce several Arabic words into the English language, especially in his works on chess and astronomy. They included 'almanac', 'nadir', 'tartar' (the chemical not the ethnic group), 'satin' – and 'checkmate', derived from the Arabic for 'the king is dead'.[19] In the Prologue to *The Canterbury Tales*, through the figure of the learned Doctour of Phisyk, he writes with admiration of the great Muslim scholars Ibn Sina (Avicenna), Ibn Rushd (Averroes) and Muhammad Ibn Zakariya al-Razi (Rhazes). 'The Man of Law's Tale' has an Islamic plot taken from the earlier Anglo-Norman *Chronicle*. Chaucer gives a relatively sympathetic account of Islam itself, noting that it is a monotheistic faith, taught by 'Mahoun our prophete' through 'the holy lawes of our Alkoran'.[20]

Chaucer's language gives some indication of the extent of trade between Christian kingdoms and the Muslim world. Muslim merchants supplied Christian Europe with an extensive range of rare and highly valued goods, either sourced locally or as intermediaries for goods from China and the Indies. They included foodstuffs such as rice, oranges, apricots, figs, raisins and the spices so essential in disguising the flavours of medieval food, medicines and perfumes, and fabrics such as silk and cotton – along with those whose names suggested their Muslim origins: damask, gauze (from Gaza) and most obviously muslin. Muslim made rock crystal glassware was especially prized.[21]

The Ottomans: a new Islamic enemy

In the early thirteenth century, the Ottoman Turks, originally a band of mercenaries for the Sunni Seljuk Empire, established a small state of their own in Anatolia.[22] From there, they built a military machine which combined discipline, motivation and exceptional mobility (by medieval standards) to make them the principal Islamic power in the Near East.[23] In the latter half of the century, they turned the decayed Byzantine Empire into a vassal, crossed into Europe and expanded into the Balkans.[24]

Over the next 200 years, a series of victories over Christian opponents announced their arrival as a new and dominant Islamic superpower. In 1389, they broke Serbian power at Kosovo – a defeat which still resonates in Balkan politics.[25] In 1396, they annihilated a powerful Crusader army at Nicopolis, from which the few survivors returned home with stories of new organised torments for their prisoners, even noblemen, for whom, in medieval warfare, captivity while awaiting ransom was normally comfortable.[26] In 1448, again at Kosovo, the Ottomans defeated the last Crusader army (led by Hungary): each side was horrified by the other's atrocities.[27]

In 1453, the Ottomans captured Constantinople.[28] Although they disagree on how he died, contemporary accounts tend to accept that the last Byzantine emperor, Constantine, was killed in the conflict, possibly while fighting as a common soldier.* The loss of the 'second Jerusalem' created special horror and despair in the Christian world. Byzantine survivors relayed stories of the desecration of holy sites, and rapes and murders carried out by the conquerors. One of them, the scholar Bessarion, wrote to the Doge of Venice shortly after, describing the city as:

---

* A Florentine merchant called Jacopo Tedaldi, reported that the emperor had been killed and added: 'Some say that his head was cut off; others that he perished in the crush at the gate. Both stories may well be true.' According to Nicola Sagundino, a Venetian, the Byzantine emperor – not wanting to be captured alive – cast aside his regalia so that he would be undistinguishable from a private soldier and charged into the fray with his sword in his hands, dying like a common soldier. Despite all of these conflicting reports, the evidence that Constantine was killed in the fighting was strong and his corpse was probably found and decapitated. Donald M. Nicol, *The Immortal Emperor: The Life and Legend of Constantine Palaiologos, Last Emperor of the Romans* (Cambridge University Press, 1992), pp. 77–82.

sacked by the most inhuman barbarism and the most savage enemies of the Christian faith, by the fiercest of wild beasts. The public treasure has been consumed . . . the temples have been stripped of gold, silver, jewels, the relics of the saints and other most precious ornaments. Men have been butchered like cattle, women abducted, virgins ravished and children snatched from the arms of their parents.[29]

In the volley of propaganda, no one pointed out that similar deeds had been perpetrated by the Latin Christian Crusaders who sacked the city in 1204, or that Christian soldiers were a strong component of Sultan Mehmet's successful forces, still less that all armies, Christian as well as Muslim, were by convention allowed three days to loot a captured city. Mehmet was so horrified by the results that he ordered special protection for the city's buildings and people. The city enjoyed a mighty revival in which Christians played a full part, not only as worshippers but as traders and administrators.[30] This did nothing to relieve the Muslim conquerors' reputation for cruelty and terror, but added to it a new reputation for luxury, decadence and illicit sex.

Queen Elizabeth I and Islam

The Ottoman Empire reached its apex in three continents in the early sixteenth century under Suleiman the Magnificent, as he was known to Europeans (or the Lawgiver as he was known to the Ottomans), whose armies captured Belgrade, destroyed the Hungarians at Mohacs and twice laid siege to Vienna.[31] However fearsome to Christendom in general, Suleiman's victories had little impact on England, out on the outer edge of the Christian world. The English exploited the Ottomans' impact on European power politics. For instance, Henry VIII found it much easier to divorce Catherine of Aragon because her nephew, Emperor Charles V, was too busy protecting Vienna from the Turks to intervene on her behalf. Later, as Henry established the Church of England and confronted the Papacy, the Ottomans helped him again by entering an alliance with France against Charles V. It was the first time a Christian state had allied with a Muslim one against another Christian state, and the Pope turned on the French monarch, Francis I, rather than Henry.[32] Henry himself used to enjoy dressing in Turkish costume (or what he imagined it to be) and he himself had contemplated joining the Franco–Ottoman alliance.* His daughter Elizabeth made a more active effort to court Suleiman and indeed other Islamic powers.

As so often in the history of English diplomacy, Elizabeth's efforts began with commercial relations. Before her ascent to the throne, English merchants were trading regularly in Aleppo at the end of the Silk Road (the town was familiar enough to audiences for Shakespeare to mention it in both *Macbeth* and *Othello*). One merchant, Anthony Jenkinson, was in Aleppo as early as 1553, where he met Suleiman the Magnificent and was granted permission to trade on an equal footing with the Venetians and the French.[33] Elizabeth sent Jenkinson to make contact with another Islamic monarch, Shah Tahmasp of Persia, as representative of the new Muscovy Trading Company, in which she had an interest. Jenkinson reached Persia, saw the shah and was able to understand the differences between his Shia form of Islam and that of the Ottoman Sunnis, describing how 'either party regarded the other as worse than heretics'.[34] But Persia was too distant to sustain successful trade for long and, in 1578, Elizabeth's all-powerful secret service chief, Sir Francis Walsingham, urged her to refocus on the Ottomans, and to seek both a commercial and political alliance with Suleiman's successor Murad III.[35]

---

* As England imported more and more goods from the Ottoman Empire and Persia, including Turkish carpets, wall coverings with Islamic designs, silks, sugar, cotton, wine and such novelties as rhubarb, English fashions began to change. At court, it became fashionable for men (and the king) to wear Turkish silk and velvet clothing. They even wore turbans and scimitars. Pugh *Britain and Islam* (Yale University Press, 2019), p. 40.

Elizabeth had good reason to take the advice. In 1570, she had been excommunicated by Pope Pius. Every Roman Catholic power was invited, even commanded, to depose the Queen in favour of her Catholic cousin Mary, Queen of Scots. England was already fighting an undeclared naval war with the leading Catholic monarch, Philip II of Spain.* Against this desperate background, Elizabeth sent another merchant, William Harborne, to Constantinople as agent of a new trading organisation, the Levant Company. The Ottomans welcomed Harborne as a guest, and he organised a profitable contraband trade supplying them with scrap metal to be used for munitions in their wars with the Spanish. To infuriate the Spanish and the Pope still further, much of this came from the roofs and bells stripped from former Catholic monasteries and churches.[36]

The threats to Elizabeth multiplied in the 1580s, not only externally from Spain, but internally from Catholic plotters, although most of the latter were penetrated or even provoked by Walsingham. It is intriguing to see now how Roman Catholics then were treated as an enemy within and faced many of the accusations now levelled against British Muslims: extremism, direction by foreign terrorists, religiously sanctioned violence.[37] The threats led Elizabeth to exchange ambassadors, gifts and gushing letters with Sultan Mehmet III and his mother, Safiye. On one occasion, she sent Safiye 'a jewel of her majesties picture, set with some rubies and diamants, 3 great pieces of gilt plate, 10 garments of cloth of gold, a very fine case of glasse bottles silver & gilt with 2 pieces of fine Holland'.[38] Other gifts included a carriage and a clockwork organ. In response, Safiye wrote a letter flecked with gold in which she called Elizabeth's own writing paper 'more fragrant than pure

---

* Francis Drake began his own private war with Spain in 1569–71 through his expeditions in the West Indies. He returned with a profit of £100,000 but there is no evidence of royal investment or even permission, though that was likely granted. Since 1569, Mary Stuart had been held at Sheffield Castle and many of the Spanish plots were focused upon her. David Loades, *Elizabeth I* (Bloomsbury, 2003), pp. 184, 199, 220.

camphor and ambergris and its ink than finest musk'.[39] Elizabeth
also reached out to Ahmad al-Mansur, ruler of Marrakesh, through
yet another trading enterprise, the Barbary Company.*

Harborne continued his mission in Constantinople more inten-
sively in the late 1580s as the Spanish prepared the Armada to
invade England and depose Elizabeth. Harborne was unable to
fulfil Walsingham's instructions to induce the Ottomans to attack
the Spanish, but he did negotiate a comprehensive commercial
agreement for English merchants, with consuls to protect their
interests in Cairo, Alexandria, Damascus, Tripoli, Jerusalem and
Aleppo.[40] Known as the Capitulations, these arrangements lasted
until the end of the Ottoman Empire in 1922.[41]

Elizabeth I was even more successful at charming the
Moroccans and in 1600 she received an envoy from the sultan
with great ceremony in order to negotiate a military alliance
against Spain (one quickly abandoned by her successor, James
I). The Tudors occasionally saw the Moroccans as 'virtually
Protestant' and this frame of mind was shared by the Ottomans.
In 1574, their government told the Lutherans:

> You for your part do not worship idols, you have banished the
> idols and portraits and bells from churches, and declared your
> faith by stating that God almighty is One and Holy Jesus is his
> Prophet . . . but the faithless one they call [the pope] does not
> recognise his Creator as One, ascribing Divinity to Holy Jesus,
> and worshipping idols and pictures which he has made with his
> own hands.[42]

---

* In July 1585, Elizabeth I granted the letters patent for establishing the Barbary Company
to co-ordinate trade to the North African coast. After the execution of Mary, Queen of Scots
in 1587, Philip's enmity was certain and Elizabeth dispatched the Portuguese agent, Matias
Becudo, to Marrakesh to convince Al-Mansur to co-operate with her. While he initially refused
her request to grant the English a seaport in Morocco from which they might divert Spanish
ships away from England, in March 1588 he issued a royal edict protecting all English traders,
travellers and residents in his kingdom. Gerald MacLean and Nabil Matar, *Britain and the Islamic
World, 1558–1713* (Oxford University Press, 2011) pp. 51–52.

As part of her charm offensive, Elizabeth returned Turkish and North African slaves, rescued from Spanish galleys by Francis Drake and other privateers, to the sultan, but not before they had set foot on British soil.[43] Prisoner releases generated a scattering of conversions from Christianity to Islam, and a smaller number the opposite way. The first of these seems to have been Sinan, a Turk released from slavery in Cartagena by Francis Drake in 1586. He was taken to London, staged a public conversion to the Protestant faith and then disappeared into a small population of other Turks and Moors. The probable first convert to Islam was much more colourful. Samson Rowlie, an East Anglian merchant, was captured by Muslim pirates off Algiers, and castrated. Perhaps to avoid further injury he converted to Islam and, as Hassan Aga, prospered as chief eunuch and a high official in the Ottoman government of Algiers.[44]

Multiple identities of England's early Muslims

In the reign of the first Elizabeth, the number of Muslims in Britain was too small to elicit much religious hostility. In the reign of the second Elizabeth, this would change as Muslims became visible in British cities – as their faith appeared to preserve their separate identity and as domestic and international events allowed their domestic British enemies to cast doubt on their loyalty as Muslims to the British state. It was at this point that Islamophobia took over from xenophobia.

But in the time of the first Queen Elizabeth, Muslims were identified by their supposed origin as 'Moors' or 'Turks', rather than as adherents of a religion. They were also identified by race: Black. This can be seen from Elizabeth's proclamation in 1601 directed against 'Negroes and Blackamoores ... the most of them being infidels'. This could suggest they were to be expelled on racial grounds, even if they had adopted Christianity.[45] The proclamation had complex origins. It was partly a commercial venture: the Black people were to be rounded up by a merchant and exchanged for English prisoners in the hands of England's enemies, Spain and Portugal. This would be achieved either directly or by selling the Black people as slaves and ransoming the prisoners. But it was also an attempt, after years of bad harvests, to focus economic discontent on an unpopular minority.[46] This proclamation is therefore an early example of the double hostility which Muslims have faced in British society in modern times: first as part of the general population of foreign immigrants and, secondly, as adherents of a 'hostile' faith.

The *Oxford English Dictionary* records the first use of 'Mahometan' in sixteenth-century English by Thomas More in 1529: 'the Mahometanys beyng a sensual sect did in a few yeres draw the great part of the world unto it'. More may have meant 'sensual' as now in its pleasure-loving sense, or, as it sometimes meant then, without intellectual or spiritual content. John Foxe, an Elizabethan literary celebrity who created the bestselling *Book of Martyrs*, used the term 'Musulman' in 1583, inaccurately defining it as 'a Turkish priest'. The term 'Muslim' did not appear until 1615. It came from William Bedwell who, although a strong critic of Islam, is often described as the father of Arabic scholarship in Britain. He wrote that 'Muslim or Musulman is one that is instructed in the beleefe of the Mohamettanes'. Although first recorded in 1613, 'Islam' was not commonly used in the English language to describe the religious beliefs of Muslims until the early nineteenth century. Until roughly the Second World War, English speakers still commonly referred to Muslims as Mohammedans, and their faith as Mohammedanism, even though that is insulting to Muslims by assuming that they worship the Prophet as well as Allah.

One sees the same kind of confusion in modern English discourse about Muslims, particularly British Muslims, who may be identified by religion, by ethnicity (Asian) and by family origin (however remote), particularly if this is Pakistani. British Muslims are now asked to identify themselves in these ways in the census. The census of 1851 was the first to ask for place of birth; 1911's asked for 'Nationality of any Person born in a Foreign Country'. In 1961, the census introduced questions on migration, 1991's was the first to ask about ethnicity, while religion was introduced in 2001.*

England and Muslims: early experience and enquiry

In the early seventeenth century, England started to acquire permanent Muslim settlers. By 1627, there were almost forty living in London, working as weavers, tailors, shoemakers and button makers; one was even a solicitor. In 1641, an official document noted that London harboured a sect 'with a certaine foolish beliefe of Mahomet'. In addition, inhabitants of London and other seaports were accustomed to see visiting Ottoman merchants and the ships' crews that carried them.[47] As we shall see, many coastal towns, especially in south-west England, saw regular incursions from Muslim pirates.

The most significant Muslim visitor was the Turkish servant of a Levant merchant, who came to England in 1650 and introduced the Turkish art of coffee-making. In 1652, London's first coffee house opened and, within a decade, more than eighty imitations had opened and were thriving. The emergence of this culture – with mosque, coffee house and merchant activities clustered – was identified by the celebrated German philosopher and sociologist Jürgen Habermas in his book *The Structural Transformation of the Public Sphere*, without any mention of its Islamic parallel.

It is getting a little ahead of the narrative to note that these coffee houses would become the sites of England's first stock exchange, insurance companies and organised political parties.

---

* The 1851 census had a voluntary section on religious observance to be completed by places of worship. All the categories were for Christians, except that of synagogues.

At the time, their first great effect on society was the country's introduction to caffeine as a stimulant. Its unaccustomed effect on imbibers more used to the numbing effect of alcohol in taverns led some campaigners to denounce coffee as 'Mahometan gruel' sent from Satan. Uncannily foreshadowing the modern conspiracy theorists who imagine Muslims plotting to install Sharia law by stealth, the caffephobes identified coffee as an Ottoman plot to make Englishmen too weak to resist conversion to Islam.*

And British travellers were also venturing further afield and in greater numbers. George Sandys wrote a popular account of a long journey in 1610 through the Levant, the Holy Land and Egypt. Although he attacked the Prophet and the Quran, he wrote accurately about the Muslim societies he encountered and had praise for some Muslim philosophers.[48]

Charles I's chaplain, Alexander Ross, was the first to attempt an English translation of the Quran. Published in 1648, his effort was mediocre and full of omissions. It was not even translated directly from Arabic, but from a French translation. The news of his intended translation caused considerable agitation in an England now engulfed in civil war. The printers were arrested for encouraging apostasy and Ross had to defend himself in the Council of State, controlled by the Parliament that was fighting Ross's king. Ross told them that 'there have been continual wars [against Islamic powers] and will be still between us',[49] which once again foreshadows the Lewis–Huntington 'clash of civilisations' discourse. The first Arabic dictionary was produced in the 1590s and, in 1632, a chair in Arabic studies was established at Cambridge University.[50]

Perhaps in consequence of greater contacts with real Muslims, the seventeenth century saw the first serious English enquiries into

---

* Public house names, such as the Saracen's Head, the Turk's Head and the Trip To Jerusalem, often date from this period. Pugh *op. cit.*, p. 49 and Sophie Gilliat-Ray, *Muslims In Britain* (Cambridge University Press, 2010) pp. 14–15.

their faith. In 1603, Richard Knolles produced a *Generall Historie of the Turkes*. It was a second-hand work of propaganda, drawn from continental European sources, showing Christian communities terrorised by Muslim conquerors.[51] In 1663, Henry Marsh adapted a continental European work – *A New Survey of the Turkish Empire*. He asked a question later put by many modern Evangelical leaders: since Christianity was clearly a superior faith to Islam, why were Muslims capable of doing so much harm? He came up with the same answer: 'We have a God most great, most good: but alienated from us so far.' Christians had abandoned God's ways and he held up the Muslim enemy as an example to them: 'Turks leave their vices in their houses, from whence we carry ours . . . What wonder then if they conquer who are preserved by sobriety, parsimony, diligence, fidelity and obedience?'[52]

In total contrast was the remarkable Henry Stubbe. A much better scholar than Ross, conversant with Hebrew and Arabic, he wrote *An Account of the Rise and Progress of Mahometanism*. It was too daring to publish in his time after the Restoration of Charles II, and portions were circulated only among trusted friends. The full text was published only in 1911, when it was discovered by some Ottoman Muslims living in London.

Stubbe saw the Prophet and Islam as actually restoring Christianity to its purest original form: a monotheistic faith, with simple rules of personal conduct. He referred to Mahomet as a 'great Prophet', his son-in-law Ali as a 'gallant advocate' and the Quran as a 'standing miracle'. Daringly for his time, Stubbe rejected the doctrine of the Trinity. Already suspect to Charles II's government as a supporter of Cromwell, Stubbe was wise to suppress this view and his support for Islam, so the field was left to Ross and his successors to denounce Muslims wrongly as superstitious idolaters and perpetuate the myth that they worshipped the Prophet.[53]

THE FIRST MUSLIM COLONIES

In the early seventeenth century, the south-western coast of England was regularly terrorised by Barbary pirates in search of captives for the slave markets of North Africa. They seized Lundy Island, in the Bristol Channel, as a base for raids on merchant ships and towns on the Devon and Cornwall coasts, although they also penetrated as far as Scotland, Ireland and even Iceland. James I's government reacted almost as helplessly as would the early American governments: a state paper of May 1625 recorded that 'the Turks are upon our coasts. They take ships only to take the men to make slaves of them.'

It was unfair to blame the Turks. At that time, as already noted, any Muslim was identified as a Turk or a Moor. The Ottoman Empire, whom Queen Elizabeth had courted, had no effective control over the Maghreb states which sponsored the pirates. There was a general problem with piracy which went way beyond the Maghreb, although the Elizabethan navy probably had greater control over the activities of English pirates.[1]

The pirate raids gave James's successor, Charles I, a pretext to demand ship money, a special tax to rebuild England's decayed navy, without the consent of Parliament. Landowners, led by John Hampden, resisted it and when the king was finally forced to meet Parliament in 1640, he was obliged to abandon it. In this way, the Barbary pirates lit a fuse for the English Civil War.[2]

Like the Americans later, the English oscillated between

attempted force and payment of tribute. Parliament took charge of policy in the 1640s, but no more effectively than the Royalist administrations. In December 1640, Parliament set up a Committee for Algiers to ransom the British captives there who were numbered at between 3,000–5,000.[3] In 1645, a single, particularly aggressive raid on the Cornish coast seized 240 men, women and children. Parliament sent an experienced negotiator, Edmund Cason, to Algiers with ransom money. Spending the huge sum of thirty pounds per man (women cost more, because they were sought after as concubines), Cason procured the release of about 250 people but ran out of money. He spent the remaining eight years of his life trying without success to secure funds for the release of another 400.[4] At least the prisoners could count themselves in distinguished company. Miguel de Cervantes was held in Algiers between 1575 and 1580. His masterpiece, *Don Quixote*, was written twenty-five years later.

The raids threatened to paralyse England's fishing industry, and the new Lord Protector, Oliver Cromwell, ordered a naval bombardment of Lundy Island, as well as violent reprisals on any captured pirate corsair. This failed to deter the pirates and Samuel Pepys, in February 1661, recorded in his diary that he 'went to the Fleece Tavern to drink, and there we spent until four o'clock, telling stories of Algiers and the manner of slaves there ... as how they eat nothing but bread and water ... how they are beat upon the soles of their feet and bellies at the liberty of their padron'.[5]

There were frequent conversions from Christianity to Islam among the captives. It is impossible to tell how many, and what proportion were forced, opportunistic or genuine. But the Barbary rulers were able to form entire armies of converted men, and, significantly, the word 'renegade' entered the English language as a pejorative description of them, from the Spanish *renegado* (apostate).[6]

Finally, in 1675, Charles II's government sent a negotiator, Sir John Narborough, with a powerful naval squadron to bombard the North African coast.[7] He secured a peace treaty with the Barbary states, although, as already noted, Barbary pirates continued to prey on British and European ships, as well as American vessels, until they were finally suppressed by the French conquest of Algeria in the 1830s.

Trade and tolerance: the message of John Locke

The terrors of the Barbary pirates did not prevent English people from trading profitably with North Africa and the Ottoman Empire, and forming a network of commercial, political and even cultural relationships with Muslim rulers and their subjects. In the Dutch War of 1666, the English actually welcomed Turkish fleets to protect their coastline.[8] Travellers, merchants and sometimes even captives brought back a much more favourable picture of Muslim societies than the standard propaganda against the terrible Turks. One aspect was especially attractive in an era of religious persecution and conflict: freedom of worship for all the monotheistic religions. Successive writers noted that the Quran honoured Moses and Jesus as well as Muhammad, and one Englishman who settled in Constantinople noted enthusiastically that 'all men are to be saved by their own religion, so that neither Christian, Turk nor Jew can curse each other's faith, but, upon complaint to the magistrate, you may have them punished'.[9]

John Locke was the first major English writer to call publicly for such tolerance at home. He had acquired some knowledge of Arabic and his library contained the French translation of the Quran which Ross had rendered tendentiously into English. Locke was no admirer of Islam, but he acknowledged the value of trade and military co-operation with Muslim rulers, and of the protection they offered to a growing band of English set-tlers.* He therefore urged that 'neither pagan nor Mahometan nor Jew ought to be excluded from the civil rights of the com-monwealth because of his religion'.[10]

Locke was writing in a pivotal moment of English history when the Stuart dynasty had embarked on the last stages of its doomed project to establish absolute rule along the lines of the Bourbon monarchy in France. As part of this, the Stuarts needed to restore Catholicism. Locke, the founder of English liberalism, ruled out tolerance for Roman Catholics, whom he viewed as enemies of the English state.[†] There are some striking comparisons between Locke's view of Catholicism and official British attitudes towards Muslims today. In his famous 'A Letter Concerning Toleration', Locke warned that Catholics were disloyal: 'That church can have no right to be tolerated by the magistrate, which is so constituted that all who enter it *ipso facto* pass into the allegiance and service of another prince.' Locke thought Catholics did not seek toleration for its own sake, and ultimately would exploit tolerance in order to deny it to others. They did not accept the grand bargain set out by the founder of

---

* He was deeply influenced in his ideas about tolerance by his reading on the Ottoman Empire. In his theorising on religious tolerance, Locke explicitly drew on the Muslim example and exhorted his fellow Englishmen to 'admire how Muslims tolerated Christian and Jewish worship and did not persecute on theological nor on denominational bases.' Was it not absurd, Locke asked, that both Calvinists and Armenians could practise their faiths unmolested in Constantinople but not in London? Did not, he mused, 'the Turks meanwhile silently stand by and laugh to see with what inhuman cruelty Christians thus rage against Christians?' (Nabil Matar, 'John Locke and the "Turbanned Nations"' *Journal of Islamic Studies* 2:1 (1991) pp 67–77.)

† In 2019, however, a previously unpublished manuscript titled 'Reasons for Tolerating Papists Equally with Others' written in Locke's hand in 1667 or 1688 was published in *The Historical Journal* of Cambridge University Press. In the manuscript he writes, 'if all subjects should be equally countenanced, and imployed by the Prince, the Papist[s] have an equall title'. According to J. C. Walmsley, 'all his published work suggested that he would never even consider this as a possibility. This manuscript shows him taking an initial position that's startling for him and for thinkers of his time – next to no one suggested this at this point. It shows him to be much more tolerant in certain respects than was ever previously supposed.' J. C. Walmsley and Felix Waldmann, 'John Locke and the Toleration of Catholics: a new manuscript', *The Historical Journal*, 62, 4 (2019), pp. 1093–1115.

English (and American) liberalism, namely that religions should
be tolerated so long as they confined themselves to the private
sphere, and kept out of public affairs.

Catholics were the object of slander and ostracism for many
years, and excluded from public life. The Test Acts, which
required that all peers and members of the House of Commons
should make a declaration against transubstantiation, invocation
of saints and the sacrament of Mass, were not repealed until 1828.
Even then, Catholics remained vulnerable to public suspicion.
Britain did not get a Catholic prime minister until Tony Blair's
election in 1997, and tellingly he did not risk converting until
after leaving office.[11] Boris Johnson, prime minister at the time
of writing, was baptised a Catholic but confirmed in the Church
of England.[12]

The United States did not get a Catholic president until John
F. Kennedy became the thirty-fifth president in 1960.[13] The long
delay is more striking than the British experience because of the
large populations of Irish Catholic and Italian immigrants in the
United States. Joe Biden, like Kennedy of Irish heritage, is only
the second Catholic president, having served as the first ever
Catholic vice president under Barack Obama.[14]

England's first Muslim colonies

In 1662, Charles II married the Portuguese princess, Catherine of
Braganza. As part of her dowry, she brought with her two territories with a Muslim population.[15] One was the island of Bombay,
which was immediately leased to the East India Company in 1667.
The other was the port of Tangier, then considered far more
valuable. Charles himself called it 'a jewell of immense value in
the royal diadem'.[16] The Portuguese had struggled to maintain
their possession for 200 years against hostile natives, despite their
fine navy and the short supply route. But the English confidently
expected to maintain it as a base to suppress the Barbary pirates

who were continuing to raid English coasts and take English slaves. Because of its location, they also expected it to dominate all the trade of the Mediterranean. To this end, Charles's government set up the colony as a free city under a governor reporting to the Tangier Committee in London. One of its leading members was Samuel Pepys.

The English wasted huge sums of seventeenth-century money on Tangier, and ran their new colony almost as badly as possible.[17] Despite local hostility, the Portuguese settlers had managed to secure a reliable water supply and feed themselves on abundant local produce. The English offended the Portuguese, and nearly all of the latter returned home taking their local knowledge with them. They left behind a map of the water supply but the English managed to lose it. The English could get water only from a place under constant attack by tribesmen, and relied on ships supplying preserved foods – especially salt pork, the worst possible choice for a hot climate.[18] The lone British achievement was the construction of the Mole, a gigantic sea wall which was a stupendous feat of contemporary engineering.

Above all, the English could not cope with the hostile local population. They failed equally to bribe or conciliate them, or to subdue them, and lived under siege conditions, in constant fear of raids and ambushes. They were unlucky to encounter two highly successful local Muslim warlords. The first, Aḥmad al-Khādir ibn 'Alī Ghaylān (anglicised to Guyland), inflicted the first defeat of an English force by a Muslim army since the Crusades, in the Battle of Tangier in 1664. The English governor, Lord Teviot, was killed, as were hundreds of his troops. As was customary, their corpses were mutilated.[19]

In modern times, this kind of outrage by Muslim natives would have provoked demands for revenge and a punitive expedition. In the age of Charles II, there was no such response. Except for a very few like Pepys, who derived money from the place, the English population had limited interest in Tangier, no wish to pay taxes to maintain it and — at a time of renewed fear of Roman Catholicism — no wish to allow Charles (a suspected Catholic) and his heir (an open one) to raise a papist army.

The English made a series of truces with Guyland. Their lone riposte was to expel the local Jews from Tangier, again under the wrongful suspicion that they were allies of the local Muslims.[20] Guyland was defeated and killed by a local rival, Sultan Moulay Ismail, but it brought no relief to the English. Moulay Ismail was an even better organiser who managed to unite the local tribes[21] and mount continuous successful hit-and-run raids on English fortifications. Parliament had had enough of Tangier and the king was forced to send a fleet there with secret orders to destroy everything of value, evacuate the remaining English and hand the place over to Moulay Ismail, whose dynasty survives to this day.[22]

The fleet under Lord Dartmouth carried out its instructions and, after several attempts, managed to blow up the expensive Mole. This provided a glorious display for Samuel Pepys who had travelled out with the fleet with a mission to compensate the remaining Portuguese settlers for the loss of their property. Pepys resumed his diary. It is full of complaints — against the Moors, the mosquitoes, the price of milk and the local whores. Worst of all to Pepys was the last English governor Colonel Percy Kirke, corrupt and cynical, who set an example of louche behaviour followed by many later British residents and remittance men in Tangier.

Pepys was much more complimentary about the most important Muslim he encountered, Moulay Ismail's representative, the alcalde. He wrote: 'The Alcade and his company appeared like very grave and sober men. His discourse and manner were very good, and, I thought, with more presence of mind than our master's . . . My Lord moved the Alcade, and he readilly, and very civilly, shook hands with Kirke.'[23]

Catherine's dowry of the port of Tangier had only further entrenched the misunderstanding and ill will between the West and Islam, largely as a result of English incompetence. Her other gift of Bombay, however, would give England a much deeper and more profitable involvement with the Muslim world, as we shall see when tracing the impact of the East India Company.

Britain's initial encounter with Islam in India

Through the East India Company, the English would develop a new and very different experience of Islam. Its servants became privileged interlopers in rich and complex societies with Muslim rulers who, both by personal choice and for reasons of state, accommodated a majority of non-Muslim subjects. Far from imposing a rigid form of Islam, both the Mughal emperors and lesser Muslim rulers tended to leave their non-Muslim populations alone. Their courts encouraged scholarship, culture, poetry and science, although fatally for them, with one or two notable exceptions, they neglected technology.

The company's agents and servants, particularly in the lower ranks, enjoyed a far superior lifestyle to anything which was possible for them in England. Those with military or technical skills could progress even further by leaving the company and serving local rulers directly. In either case, Englishmen quickly adopted local habits which were clearly better adapted to local conditions than English ones: clothing, food, medicine, hours of activity, smoking hookahs. Local sexual mores were gratifying and guiltless. It is no surprise that some who chose an Indian life-style should also have chosen an Indian religion. Of those on offer, Islam as a monotheistic faith which respected Jesus was an easier step to take than Hinduism with its pantheon of unfamiliar gods,[24] although this would also gain some notable adherents. Elsewhere, other Englishmen had converted to Islam – but often as captives. In India, the converts were by choice or ambition.

From its beginnings the company sent out Protestant chaplains on its trading missions to India and they were established in its first permanent settlements in Surat and Madras. They had no mission to convert the native population – only to police the English. Like India's Muslim rulers, they found that a policy of religious tolerance avoided friction. When the company's Portuguese rivals introduced the Inquisition in the late sixteenth century, this policy secured it the loyalty of Hindu and Muslim refugees.[25]

Nonetheless, the company chaplains expected its personnel to set a Christian example to the natives, and fretted constantly that the natives seemed to be setting an example to the Christians. In 1618, one chaplain, the Reverend Mr Copland, complained that his colleague, the Reverend Mr Goulding, was enjoying the local night life so much that he would 'harden [the natives] in their idolatry'.[26] The company's chaplains and senior secular leaders were especially concerned with the threat of apostasy among its Christian employees. The Reverend Mr Terry particularly noted the appeal of Islamic marriage law to men with little or no opportunity in India to marry a Christian. The next two centuries proved him right, as Englishmen went through forms of Islamic marriage with local women.[27]

The first apostate at the company seems to have been a Portuguese working for the company at Agra. This was bearable because he brought no shame on Protestant England, only on Catholic Portugal (and, no doubt, because his productivity increased dramatically after his conversion, much to the company's benefit).[28] But the company was deeply shocked by the conversion to Islam of William Blackwell. As the son of King James I's grocer, he was well connected and held an important post representing the company at the Mughal court. Reporting the news to London, the company's senior official Francis Breton referred to 'the dishonour of our nation and (which is incomparably worse) of our Christian profession'. Since Breton could not imagine that a man would convert from Protestant Christianity to Islam for genuine religious reasons, the company's reports on Blackwell suggested that he was prompted by 'idle hopes of worldly preferments [from the Mughals] and the vaine suggestions of the Devill'.[29] They could have ascribed such motives more plausibly to the hundreds of men who accepted enticing offers from the Mughals and other Islamic rulers and deserted the company.[30]

Nabobs, Ayahs and lascars

During the eighteenth century, the East India Company eliminated commercial competition from the Dutch and military competition from the French in the Indian subcontinent. A military genius, Robert Clive, transformed himself from a company scribe to its proconsul, seizing de facto control of Bengal, India's richest province, from the declining Mughal Empire. It greatly expanded its trading bases not only in India but along the sea routes to India. As the English (and the American colonists) became addicted to tea, the company's monopoly over the tea trade with China became hugely valuable. Above all, it gave ambitious and enterprising men, even its teenage recruits, the opportunity to make fortunes which would have been far beyond them in England. These derived primarily from unregulated private trading with local suppliers and merchants, often mixed with bribery and corruption.[31]

The company's operations and lifestyle gave Britain new contacts with Muslim people, culture, art and architecture. Britain acquired a small but noticeable population of Muslims (and Hindus) as sailors on the company's ships.[32] These became known as lascars, a corruption of the term *lashkar*, for a soldier of the Mughal Empire. This term first appeared, in a neutral sense, in the seventeenth century.[33] By the nineteenth century, it had acquired a pejorative note. In a novel of 1832 by Captain Marryat (the author of *The Coral Island*), a ship's officer complains: 'if only we had *all* English seamen on board, instead of these Lascars and Chinamen, who look so blank.'[34]

Beginning as early as the seventeenth century but with more frequency later, lascars were conscripted by the East India Company at its coastal trading stations. Their conditions were terrible and many jumped ship at English ports. Their numbers surged during the Napoleonic Wars so that there were reportedly 1,336 in Britain by 1813. Numbers rose by as many as 1,600 each year. Penniless and vulnerable to biting winters, an estimated 100 perished each year, with one estimate before 1810 suggesting that 130 died annually. During the winter of 1813, nine died in a single day.[35] They lived in small communities at the margins of English society, occasionally shocking their respectable neighbours, as in 1805 when the *Gentleman's Magazine* reported a 'Mahommedan Jubilee' in the East End of London, with drumming, dancing and pantomime.[36] Some lascars were sucked into the criminal underworld of London's East End, as demonstrated by trial records at the Old Bailey.[37] As we shall see, the advent of steam ships and, even more, the opening of the Suez Canal led to an even greater increase in the lascar population. As a result, they became more visible and slightly more integrated into local society as the century wore on. Another new Muslim population in the eighteenth century arrived as household servants of the company men who came home with their newfound wealth. A few even came back with Muslim wives and half-Indian children.

The best known was General William Palmer, married to a high-born Muslim of Persian origins, Begum Fyse Baksh, who presented him with six children – to add to the five by his first wife, a Creole beauty from the West Indies, to whom he was still legally married. Palmer, his second wife and their first three children were captured in a beautiful painting by the Court painter Johan Zoffany, which picks out not only Begum and her sisters but also the children's nannies – ayahs – and a wet nurse. Only the general is in English costume.[38]

These children – and others with a Muslim parent or ancestor – made their path in English upper-class society, the best-known being Lord Liverpool, the long-serving Tory prime minister of the early nineteenth century. Heathcliff, the tortured anti-hero in Emily Brontë's *Wuthering Heights*, may be another case in point.[39] But a series of racially discriminating measures by the company from the 1780s denied the best places in its service to Anglo-Indian children. Their fathers or carers often faced an invidious decision: 'fair' children who could pass for white in British society would be sent to England and given an English upbringing and education, while 'swarthy' ones stayed in India and were prepared for the increasingly inferior posts available to them from the company.[40]

The families of successful Britons in India brought a Muslim population with them in the form of servants, particularly ayahs (nannies).[41] Some were adored in their families and properly cared for, but many others were cut adrift in a strange country where they were totally unequipped to cope. They had no rights and, although the famous Mansfield judgement in 1769 had formally outlawed the status of slavery in England, they could in effect be bought and sold. Those dismissed as servants, or who absconded, often ended up on British streets living in destitution as street herbalists or vendors of goods such as spices and printed religious tracts. In 1890, the Ayahs' Home, accommodating about a hundred maidservants each year, was founded in East London.[42] *The Servants Pocket Book*, published in 1761, referred to the 'wonted haunts of Moormen and Gentoos' in London as places where destitute Indian Hindus and Muslims congregated.[43]

The money and lifestyles of returning company men earned them a mocking nickname: nabob, derived from a Muslim source, *nawab*, a title given by the Mughal emperors to their regional governors and viceroys. The nabobs were the subjects of savage caricatures, primarily as vulgar arrivistes, but also as a source of financial and political corruption. Pitt the Elder unleashed a bitter attack on them, primarily for inflating the price of 'rotten boroughs' in Parliament:

The riches of Asia have been poured in upon us and have brought with them not only Asiatic Luxury, but, I fear, Asiatic principles of government. Without connections, without any natural interest in the soil, the importers of foreign gold have forced their way into Parliament by such a torrent of private corruption as no hereditary fortune could resist.[44]

Two 'evil' Muslims

The company's clashes with local powers supplied the British people with two archetypes of evil Muslim despots. The first was the last independent ruler of Bengal, Siraj ud-Daulah, the man held responsible for the atrocity which has passed permanently into the English language: the Black Hole of Calcutta. After capturing the English post at Fort William in Calcutta, the Bengalis incarcerated an unknown quantity of military and civilian survivors in a dungeon intended for at most three prisoners. The initial account spoke of 146 captives (and 123 deaths) and was written by a survivor, John Zephaniah Holwell, leader of the captives who had negotiated the surrender of the city against overwhelming force. It went through several editions in 1756, and inspired demands for a punitive expedition. The latter generated Clive's overwhelming victory at Plassey, which gave the British control over Bengal. Even Holwell did not believe that Siraj ud-Daulah intended so many captives to die in the Black Hole (which had actually been the guardroom of the company's garrison in Calcutta), but he created a legend which justified the virtual annexation of Bengal, the execution of Siraj ud-Daulah and his replacement – at British behest – by a puppet ruler.[45]

Siraj ud-Daulah and the Black Hole were then largely forgotten until the legend was revived in the next century by a mighty propagandist: Thomas Babington Macaulay. In a brilliant essay which turned Clive for ever into an imperial hero, Macaulay embellished Holwell's account of what he called 'that great crime, memorable for its singular atrocity'. Significantly, he calls Siraj 'the Nabob', the insulting and anglicised form of *nawab*. He cannot blame Siraj directly for the captives' deaths, but invents the detail of him sleeping off a debauch, unheeding their pleas for mercy.[46] This version passed into the education of generations of English and British Empire schoolchildren. Indeed, I was taught it at prep school.

In the 1790s, the company faced a much more dangerous opponent: Tipu Sultan, the ruler of Mysore. He was a first-rate military commander, daring and innovative (he used rockets against the British long before they adopted the version designed by William Congreve), an economic reformer and an active diplomat who courted the French Revolutionary government by styling himself Citizen Tipu. When Napoleon conquered Egypt, there was serious alarm that he would achieve his aim of linking with Tipu and driving the company out of India.

Tipu was therefore demonised by the British governor general Richard Wellesley, the elder brother of the future Duke of Wellington. Like most rulers at war, he had provided copious examples of cruelty and crime. Like those of Saddam Hussein years later, these were worked up into a narrative of existential evil. His reputation would be worsened still in novels by Rider Haggard and G. A. Henty, and schoolboy comics such as *Boy's Own* in which plucky white English boys would inspire outnumbered British soldiers to stand firm against Tipu's dark hordes.[47] Tipu was killed at Seringapatam in 1799 during the Second Mysore War, a victory over Islamic 'tyranny' which the British and French celebrated without reserve.

ISLAM AND EMPIRE

The nineteenth century brought an increased Muslim population to the United Kingdom. The major factor in this was Britain's dominance of international seaborne trade, which depended on Muslim sailors; others came as servants of British families returning from India.[1] These two groups of Muslims generally had a deprived and marginal existence, their conditions not far removed from those of runaway slaves in the United States. However, British imperialism, particularly in the later part of the century, also brought regular visits from wealthy and powerful Muslims from princely dynasties to the great benefit of luxury hotels and estate agents for expensive properties. Of more lasting significance was the growing population of Muslim students, following the call of reform-minded Muslim leaders to master Western learning and professions.

We have already noted the increasing number of Muslim seamen recruited to fight the Napoleonic Wars, and the pitiable conditions they faced in England after jumping ship. As steam replaced sail in the nineteenth century, it created a new demand for stokers and other dirty, exhausting jobs which had little appeal to white European workers attracted by new opportunities created by the Industrial Revolution or emigration to the United States. So the steamships came to rely heavily on Muslim seafarers, not only from India but also Somalis, Yemenis and Malays, ready to work as firemen and stokers for a third or less of the wages of a British seaman. In 1855 alone, there were an estimated 12,000 lascars in

British ports, mostly Muslims, and their number expanded after the opening of the Suez Canal in 1869.[2]

These workers created the first relatively permanent, large-scale British Muslim communities in the mid-nineteenth century in places such as Cardiff, South Shields and Liverpool.[3] They lived in boarding houses in poor isolated communities, as recorded in rare accounts, such as Christian missionary Joseph Salter's *The Asiatic in England: Sketches of Sixteen Years' Work Among Orientals*, published in 1868. In British society, their class status was more important than their race or religion. Most scraped a living in casual labour or as hawkers or street entertainers, while others inevitably depended on begging or petty crime. Some had relationships, including legal marriages, with poor white women, who could interpret for them and help them adapt to British society. Like other poor people in Victorian times, they were often found dead on the streets of London in winter.

The nineteenth century saw frequent attempts to convert destitute Muslims to Christianity by well-meaning philanthropists such as Salter. These attempts were almost universal failures, and to the indignation of the missions, the few conversions were done for practical reasons of survival.[4] Nearly all tried to cling to their diverse Muslim traditions. For example, Yemenis of the Shāfi'ī school of Sunni Islam living on Tyneside prayed and celebrated the festival of Eid, while struggling to develop mosques.[5]

At the other end of the social scale, a few princely Muslims delighted late Victorian magazines and journals with their opulent lifestyles and generous spending. One was the Nawab Nazim of Bengal, who arrived in 1870 with an impressive entourage. He became a favourite of Queen Victoria, but not with her government in India, who frowned on his 'life of debauchery' and, even more, on his marriage to 'an English woman of low extraction'. Much more acceptable were Mir Jaffer Ali, from Surat, who boosted house prices in London's Paddington district, and 'the Mohammedan Queen of Oudh' who brought 130 followers with her.[6]

More importantly, a growing number of Indian Muslims came to study and teach. Scottish universities and technical institutes were especially popular, because Scottish teachers and technicians had a high reputation in India. The Edinburgh Indian Association was founded in 1883 by six students and membership grew to 200 by the end of the century. The law attracted many students, especially those with family means. Three who achieved notable success were Syed Ameer Ali, who advanced in the British establishment to become a privy councillor, and Muhammad Iqbal and M. A. Jinnah, the founding fathers of Pakistan.

Trade and administration created a demand in Britain for teachers of Oriental languages, along with experts in Islamic law and practice. The most famous teacher, or munshi, was Abdul Karim, who formed a deep relationship with his employer, Queen Victoria. She tried to learn Hindustani from him, but more importantly he taught her much about Indian society, as she took seriously her new, largely self-created role as empress-mother of all her Indian peoples. She had halal meals served to him and his family, and built them a cottage at Balmoral.[7] He was named Indian secretary in 1894 and awarded a Companion of the Order of the Indian Empire. Abdul Karim struggled against the racism of the queen's family and entourage though, and came under suspicion from her government for his association with a radical law student, Rafiuddin Ahmed. On Victoria's death, he and his family were shipped back to India forthwith and nearly all his papers and souvenirs from her were burned.[8]

The rise of manufacturing also brought Muslim workers to other cities – such as Birmingham, Bradford and Manchester – where, by the end of the nineteenth century, the textile industry had attracted a dozen Moroccan families and where there were 150 Arab merchant houses.[9] These were still minuscule numbers, and it is very difficult to guess how many Muslims there were in

Britain at this time.[10] But the patterns of migration that would shape the later twentieth century had begun.

The 'Indian Mutiny': British fury against Muslims

The Indian uprising of 1857 unnerved mid-Victorian society. Beginning with a mutiny by native troops of the East India Company's army in the garrison town of Meerut, it spread into a series of uprisings across central and northern India. The British lost several major cities, including Delhi where the Indian soldiers tried to restore the rule of the aged client Mughal emperor. Hundreds of British people were victims, for whom savage vengeance was taken, even though the British took over a year to suppress all the local uprisings. The company's rule was replaced by the British Crown, amid promises to Her Majesty's new Indian subjects which went unfulfilled.

The uprisings were generally described at the time, and for generations after, as the Indian Mutiny, in order to suggest that its origins were local and particular. Although many contemporaries, led by future British prime minister Benjamin Disraeli, acknowledged the widespread grievances which had provoked the uprising, there was almost universal agreement that its suppression was essential for the survival of British civilisation.[11] Stories of atrocities committed by the rebels created a demand for punitive reprisals.

Charles Dickens – so compassionate towards the underclass at home – was one of the most vocal in demanding retribution against it in India. He had some indirect experience of the country through two of his children who pursued careers there – Walter was a lieutenant in the East India Company's army while Francis served in the Bengal Mounted Police. Neither was a success and Walter died in India aged only twenty-two, burdened with debts which his father refused to meet. Dickens's one fictional excursion into India is a standing embarrassment to his followers, especially in India. Co-written with Wilkie Collins, *The Perils of Certain English Prisoners* is based on a crude and inaccurate account of the Cawnpore Massacre during the 1857 Indian uprising. The chief character is 'the native Sambo, a double-dyed traitor and a most infernal villain'. In real life, Dickens toyed with the idea of genocide, writing to the philanthropist Emile de la Rue that:

> I wish I were Commander in Chief over there! I would address that Oriental character which must be powerfully spoken to, in something like the following placard, which should be vigorously translated into all native dialects, 'I, The Inimitable, holding this office of mine, and firmly believing that I hold it by the permission of Heaven and not by the appointment of Satan, have the honor to inform you Hindoo gentry that it is my intention, with all possible avoidance of unnecessary cruelty and with all merciful swiftness of execution, to exterminate the Race from the face of the earth, which disfigured the earth with the late abominable atrocities'.[12]

Dickens seems to have hated all the rebels indiscriminately, but many of his contemporaries regarded Muslims as darker villains than the rest. Many of the initial responses to the uprising played down its significance on the assumption that it was led by Hindus. For example, *The Times* quoted a senior local British officer as saying that 'the Sepoy army [specifically identified as Hindu] is hopelessly effete'. But when Muslims were clearly involved, especially the helpless but demonised Mughal emperor, the newspaper changed course with a strong editorial: 'This mutiny has assumed a very serious character. The moment has arrived for action – sharp, stern and decisive. An imperial interest is at stake – nothing less than our dominion in British India.'[13] The response was part of an established colonial pattern – that of exemplary violence.

Writing a year after the 'mutiny', a British judge in India,

C. L. Raikes, squarely blamed the Muslims for the uprising. 'They have behaved in the part of India where I had jurisdiction very ill; so ill indeed that if the rest of the population had sympathised with them, instead of antagonised, I should despair of governing India for the future.' Other contemporaries followed this line. The future Lord Roberts of Kandahar promised that he would 'show these rascally Musalmans that, with God's help, Englishmen will still be masters of India'.[14]

At home, the Evangelical William Muir wrote the anti-Islamic *Life of Mahomet* at the height of the uprising. Anticipating the Lewis–Huntington thesis by more than a hundred years, he claimed that 'the sword of Mahomet and the Coran during this period of crisis are the most fatal enemies of Civilisation, Liberty and the Truth which the world has yet known'. Islam, he stated, was a false religion which had trapped its adherents 'in a backward and in some respects barbarous state'.[15]

Like Jerry Falwell and Pat Robertson on 9/11, some Evangelical leaders, particularly from the Clapham Sect which had a strong influence on the leadership of the East India Company, rationalised the mutiny as a judgement of God for failure to obey his commandments. In this case, the punishment was due for failing to evangelise India and leaving native religions intact. The missionary Mrs Weitbrecht accused the government of India of being 'intolerant of its own religion' and actually striving 'to hold India a preserve for heathenism'. Many of the leading military figures who suppressed the rising had a Calvinistic or Evangelical background, which may partly account for the violence of their reprisals.[16]

The war produced one villain especially grim to British eyes – the rebel commander Nana Sahib, characterised as 'arch fiend . . . treacherous and cowardly assassin . . . that unhung miscreant . . . that now famous monster . . .'[17] As we shall see, he would be held up to generations of children as an archetype of native evil. He was blamed for a widely publicised atrocity, the massacre of more than a hundred British women and children held captive at Cawnpore, although his precise degree of responsibility has never been established. In reputation, he was virtually the Osama bin Laden of his time, but unlike Bin Laden, he escaped retribution and there were regular sightings of him in hiding for the next forty years.

Nana Sahib was a high-caste Hindu, but many popular accounts converted him into a Muslim. One such was the first popular stage drama about the uprising, Dion Boucicault's *Jessie Brown, or The Relief of Lucknow*, which turned Nana Sahib into a cruel Muslim ruler. This anti-Muslim narrative transferred itself to France which, despite its recent conquest of Algeria, was then far less engaged in the Muslim world than it later became. The journalist T. N. Bernard wrote in the influential *Le Siècle*: 'We will regret the triumph of Nana Sahib and his Muslims because instead of opening up India to European civilisation . . . his triumph could only see the population of the Ganges and the Indus being plunged back into an age-old barbarism . . . under the yoke of Muslim rule.'[18]

The English would in due course learn to differentiate between 'good' loyal Indian Muslims and 'bad' seditious, treacherous, savage ones. But the distinction between 'warlike' Muslims and loquacious, unsoldierly Hindus lasted much longer, and would hold a lifelong influence over Winston Churchill.[19]

Two authors who gave British children an image of Muslims

Since so few Britons had any first-hand contact with Islam and Muslims until the late 1950s, the second-hand perceptions that they received through their education and other cultural influences were hugely important. G. A. Henty published more than a hundred boys' adventure stories between 1870 and his death in 1902. He developed a following of collectors, young and old, who purchased his latest work as eagerly as later generations snapped up the latest Harry Potter. His books also enjoyed a long afterlife in lending and school libraries, and for school prize-giving days. They were still there during my schooldays in the late 1960s when I devoured every Henty novel, before fading away for about forty years. They are now, though, enjoying a revival in Christian institutions and in the home-schooling movement.[20]

Henty's stories have an almost unvaried basic structure: a teen-age boy (usually British, and always endowed with identifiably British qualities of pluck and modesty) takes part in some historic conflict and triumphs against desperate odds. Henty was a war correspondent and had served in the Crimean War. His frequent battle scenes were detailed and convincing, and accompanied by maps. They inspired some famous historians, including A. J. P. Taylor and Arthur Schlesinger Jr[21] – and, most importantly, the young Winston Churchill. The first book known to be inscribed by him was a gift of a G. A. Henty novel to his younger brother, Jack, and he used the title of a Henty novel, *A Roving Commission,* as the subtitle to his reminiscences in the memoir *My Early Life.*[22]

Henty's political outlook could be described as liberal imperialist. The British Empire was earned not only by the pluck of his heroes but through their ability to provide civilised leadership to inferior races. This attitude is expressed clearly by one of his young heroes, Peters, in his 1884 novel *With Clive in India* (a novel Henty thought important enough to revisit twice in later editions). Acknowledging that native Indian troops had fought well in the decisive victories against the French, Peters notes that 'it is singular that, contemptible as are these natives of India when officered by men of their own race and religion, they will fight to the death when led by us'.[23]

Nonetheless, Henty offered his readers a view of Muslims based on a frequently stated belief that Christians, Jews and Muslims all at heart believe in the same God. He puts this thought into two of his novels about Sudan, in sharp counterpart to the general late Victorian narrative of British heroes confronting a fanatical Muslim leader. In *With Kitchener in the Soudan*, published posthumously, the young hero's father tells a Muslim that 'we Christians feel no enmity against the followers of Mahomet – the hatred is all on your side. And yet, 'tis strange, the Allah that you worship and the God of the Christians is one and the same. Mahomet himself had no enmity against the Christians, and regarded our Christ as a great prophet like himself.'[24]

In *With Clive in India*, Henty creates a major character, Hossein, who is an archetype of the loyal, 'good' Muslim who devotes himself to his British master and his master's empire. Hossein is the cook to the young hero, Charlie Marryat. Early in the novel, Hossein is suborned into entering a plot to poison Charlie. The Muslim ruler, in alliance with the British, offers to torture him. Charlie refuses this and earns the undying gratitude of Hossein. Apart from being brave and loyal, Hossein is quick-witted and capable of independent thought, in contrast to Charlie's other devoted follower, Tim, a caricature comic Irishman. In fact, Hossein is able to mastermind two escapes for Charlie in desperate circumstances, including imprisonment in the Black Hole of Calcutta. In a significant passage, Tim learns to respect Hossein *as a Muslim*.

> He had come to the conclusion that a man who at stated times in the day would leave his employment, whatever it might be, spread his carpet and be for some minutes lost in prayer, could not altogether be a heathen, especially when he learned from Charlie that the Mahommedans, like ourselves, worship one God. For the sake of his friend, then, he now generally excluded the Mahommedans from the general designation of heathen, which he still applied to the Hindoos.[25]

Henty's character of Hossein receives the ultimate reward for being a 'good Muslim': admission to English society. He not only accompanies Charlie back to England as part of his household, but he actually marries a white woman: 'the pretty cook of Charlie's establishment made no objection to his swarthy hue'. They raise a large brood of mixed-race children – although Henty is silent on their religious upbringing.[26]

As to non-fiction, generations of British children had their first experience of history through a book called *Our Island Story*. In 2010, David Cameron revealed that it was his favourite childhood book, explaining that 'it is written in a way that really captured my imagination and which nurtured my interest in the history of our great nation'.[27] The author was a reticent Scottish-born writer, Henrietta Elizabeth Marshall, who concealed her gender with initials. Her prime motive was to connect children to their 'home' country. It quickly became a bestseller throughout the British Empire and went through many editions. A centenary edition was reprinted in 2005, significantly with sponsorship from the *Daily Telegraph*.

Marshall portrays Islam as barbaric. Her main treatment of Muslims is in three chapters on India. She barely distinguishes them from Hindus, but subsumes them in a general narrative of cruel and treacherous Indian native rulers and disloyal sepoys. The first such chapter is 'George II – the story of the Black Hole of Calcutta'; like most school histories of her time, she linked all significant events to reigns even if the sovereign had nothing to do with them. In this chapter, Marshall describes how a Muslim prince attacks the British in Calcutta, destroying their houses and factories, and killing many. Some 146 survivors are shut up in 'a horrible prison called the Black Hole', airless and with barely enough room for them all to stand. 'When the prisoners were told that they were all to go into this dreadful place, they could not believe it. They thought at first that the prince meant it as a jest. But they soon found that it was no jest but horrible sinful earnest.' I vividly remember shuddering with horror and indignation when I read this passage as a 10-year-old schoolboy.

The wicked prince ignores their pleas and drives them into the prison, where 'cruel Indians held torches to the windows and, looking in, laughed at the terrible sufferings of the poor prisoners'. Only twenty-three survive their hellish ordeal. When Robert Clive hears of 'this horrible deed', he marches against the wicked prince, routs him at Plassey and replaces him with 'another prince, who was friendly towards the British'.[28] This happy ending to Marshall's account is in sharp contrast to that of Henty, who treats the installation of the British puppet ruler ('Meer Jaffier, our creature') as one of the blackest transactions in the annals of English history.[29] These books, with their sensationalised and contradictory narratives, were essential to creating the popular understanding of Islam at the height of the British Empire. Good and bad narratives circulated about Muslims, though neither were nuanced or accurate.

Muslims as beneficiaries of British divide and rule

In the immediate aftermath of the so-called Indian Mutiny, Muslims and Hindus alike suffered from a ferocious backlash by their British rulers. The Mughal Empire was extinguished, Muslim culture and artefacts were pillaged or destroyed, and thousands of individual Muslims suffered financial and social ruin and vicious reprisals. However, in the longer term, Muslims were treated more favourably than Hindus by their British conquerors. Some Muslim rulers and their armies had played an essential role in British success by staying out of the uprising, if not actually helping to suppress it.

The two main Muslim responses to the failed uprising represented no threat to the British. The Deobandi movement looked backwards to a purer form of Islam, purged of Western influences, which meant that it could not challenge the technology and finance that underpinned British rule. By contrast, the Aligarh movement, led by Sir Sayyid Ahmed Khan, sought to master

Western science and learning, but assumed that British rule in India would be necessary to teach them, either permanently or for a very long time.[30]

The British came to regard Indian Muslims as a loyal bulwark against the unreliable, seditious and much larger Hindu population. Army and police recruitment favoured Muslims, especially those identified as part of the so-called 'warrior races', and the British lavished money, honours and educational opportunities on favoured Muslims. In 1888, Sir John Strachey, a prominent civil servant in India, wrote that 'the better classes of Mohammedans are already a source to us of strength and not of weakness . . . They constitute a small but energetic minority of the population, whose political interests are identical with our own.'

The British fostered differences between Muslims and Hindus in India. Lord George Hamilton, who was a long-serving India secretary under the Marquess of Salisbury and Arthur Balfour, asked the viceroy, George Curzon, to ensure that textbooks played up differences between Muslims and Hindus. 'If we could break educated Indians into two sections holding widely different views, we should . . . strengthen our position against the subtle and continuous attack which the spread of education must make upon our system of government.'[31] Today, the Conservative Party has adapted this practice of divide and rule for domestic use. This time Hindus are favoured, while the victims of this strategy are Muslim.

BRITAIN AND ISLAM, 1914–45

In the years leading up to the First World War, the importance of the Suez Canal as the artery to India led Britain to turn Egypt, nominally ruled by an independent monarch as a vassal of the Ottoman Sultan, into a virtual colony. The British revenged themselves savagely after the Muslim uprising in Sudan which had claimed the life of General Gordon. Its leader, the Mahdi, and his successor, the Khalifa, were demonised like the 'evil' Indian Muslims who had fought the British. School textbooks presented them and their followers as fanatical Dervishes and enemies of civilisation, ignoring their appeal to local nationalism and the leadership skills that allowed them to defy British power for fifteen years.*

The route of the Suez Canal also led the British to take an interest in all the harbours of the Red Sea, including those used by pilgrims completing the hajj. In a development pregnant with future significance, the conversion of the British navy from steam to oil power led Britain to extend its power into Persia. Britain continued its role as an alternating protector and bully of the decaying Ottoman Empire. In general, Conservatives were determined to preserve the empire as a bulwark against Russian expansionism in the Straits of Constantinople and against India.

---

* G. A. Henty's novel *With Kitchener In the Soudan* (Blackie & Son, 1903), was an example, although it pays tribute to the bravery of the Dervish army, and of the Egyptians when led by British officers.

Liberals, particularly Gladstonians and Evangelicals, continued to denounce Turkish oppression of Christian peoples, especially in Crete and Armenia.[1]

But from about 1900 onwards, both parties had to react to a new competitor for influence over the Ottoman Empire. Kaiser Wilhelm II visited Sultan Abdul Hamid II and theatrically proclaimed himself a protector of Muslims. More practically, the Germans planned a railway from Berlin to Baghdad.[2] Few sections were actually built, but it threatened to take a hostile power nearer to India and nearer still to Britain's new oil supply in Persia. In response, the British mended fences with Russia. In effect, each power gave the other a free hand in dealing with its Muslim subject races and they agreed on zones of influence in the nominally independent Muslim state of Persia.

In 1908, the Young Turk coup promised a new era of reform, tolerance and constitutional government in the decayed Ottoman Empire.[3] Most of this promise was soon dissipated, but the Young Turks continued to enjoy a favourable image overseas and their uprising led to the abdication of the much-reviled Sultan Abdul Hamid II, 'Abdul the Damned'.[4] His successor as Sultan and Caliph, Mehmet V, was a corpulent nonentity, but he gave Islam a more benign image in the West.

The Young Turks wrestled with debt, internal uprisings and heavy defeats in wars which cost the empire Libya and nearly all its remaining territory in Europe.[5] Germany and Britain now began an intense struggle for influence over the empire. The Germans offered to modernise its army,[6] while Britain did the same for its navy and offered to sell it two powerful dreadnaughts at a cut price.[7] The Germans entertained serious hopes of persuading the Sultan and the Young Turks to proclaim jihad against the British in a coming war, to break the loyalty of Britain's Indian Muslim soldiers, and to induce Egypt's Muslims to eject the British from the Suez Canal. The British took this threat seriously and it inspired John Buchan's thrilling wartime novel *Greenmantle*.[8]

When war broke out in August 1914, the Germans had more to offer the Turks than the British, who were now in alliance with the Ottoman Empire's bitterest enemy, Russia. The Young Turks held out for better terms for joining either alliance, or a guarantee of its possessions (and a Greek island or two) in exchange for neutrality. Their fate was sealed by four ships. The British sequestered the two warships they built for the Turks, the *Sultan Osman* and the *Reshadieh*, a decision which caused popular anguish in the Ottoman Empire since much of their price had been met by voluntary contributions, including schoolchildren's pocket money. Then two German warships, the *Goeben* and the *Breslau*, eluded the British and French fleets in the Mediterranean and appeared miraculously at the straits as potential replacements. The most pro-German Young Turk leader, Enver Pasha, admitted them to Constantinople. Nominally sold to the Turks, they stayed under German control, bringing the Sultan and his government under the kaiser's guns.[9] The Young Turks joined the war on the German side in November 1914. In this somewhat accidental way, the British Empire, a self-proclaimed great 'Mohammedan' power, found itself in a struggle against the military and spiritual leader of the Islamic world.

The first British response was to shore up Egypt. They deposed its ruler, Abbas II, who had been at odds with their pro consuls Cromer and Kitchener, installed a more pliable relative and severed the country's links with its overlord, the Ottoman Sultan. Abbas was actually visiting the Sultan in August 1914. He remained his guest – and 'a king over the water' – for the duration of the war. The British commander, General Maxwell, promised that the British would do all the fighting. But he could not manage without Egyptian manpower, and thousands of Egyptians were unwillingly conscripted into British service as labourers and providers of supplies.[10] The British repulsed Turkish attacks on the Suez Canal without much difficulty, but with good reason they feared a general Egyptian uprising and decided to push the Turks away from the canal by advancing beyond Sinai into Palestine, with consequences which have lasted until this day.

The British became especially unpopular in Egypt during the war through the drunken womanising of some Australian soldiers stationed there, and even more so when the Egyptians were not allowed to present their case as an independent country at the Paris Peace Conference.[11] Meanwhile, Sultan Mehmet V declared jihad against the Entente Powers.[12] It made little impact on Britain's Muslim Indian soldiers. The king-emperor, George V, immediately promised that he and his allies would protect all the holy cities of Islam under Ottoman control. This was quickly followed by pledges of allegiance from Indian Muslim notables, led by the Aga Khan, spiritual leader of the Ismaili Muslims, who actually repudiated the authority of the Ottoman Sultan and Caliph.[13]

The Indian army sent some 1.5 million men to fight for the British Empire in all theatres. All were volunteers (although recruitment campaigns became more aggressive as the war continued), of which at least 400,000 were Muslims. Thousands more were seamen or labourers.[14] Their casualty rates were very high, not only in battle but from sickness, especially during the influenza pandemic at the end of the war.

In spite of British fears about their loyalties, Muslim soldiers did most of their service *against* the Ottoman Sultan – at Gallipoli, and in Egypt, Aden and the Persian Gulf, Palestine and Mesopotamia. Eighty per cent of all Indian soldiers served in these theatres.[15] Both the Turks and the Germans attempted to recruit Muslim prisoners of war. There are no reliable records of their success, but the upper limit seems to be a few hundred, mostly French colonials from North Africa.[16]

The use of Muslim troops against the Ottoman Empire had a strong influence on British strategy. It led the British to continue many operations for the sake of prestige – notably Gallipoli, where they feared that an Ottoman victory might revive the appeal of jihad.[17] It also led them to build up the Hashemite Arab Sharif of Mecca and his sons as alternative sources of Islamic authority. Over time, the exposure of poor British generalship (one Indian army operation in German East Africa was routed by bees[18]) may have weakened Indian Muslims' belief in British superiority, as it did for other British Empire contingents.

At the end of the war, Indians as a whole realised that they had obtained very little in exchange for their sacrifices. Their interests and demands were ignored at the Paris Peace Conference. Indian Muslims also had to acknowledge that they had helped to destroy the leading independent Muslim power in the world. Within a few years, the Sultan and the caliphate would disappear, leaving no spiritual leadership for a global Muslim community controlled by foreigners and their puppets.

Britain's 'invisible' Muslim empire

Britain's control over the Muslim world reached its greatest extent in the interwar period, yet I am continually struck by how little interest most British people took in their empire. Its fate hardly figures in the domestic politics of the interwar period, except in the economic sphere when the press barons, lords Beaverbrook and Rothermere, tried to revive the cause of Empire Free Trade in 1930. Even then, its main impact was on the internal politics of the Conservative Party. By far the biggest imperial news story in this period was the impact of the 'Bodyline' cricket tour of Australia from 1932–33, which also eclipsed news of the rise of Adolf Hitler.

Those with a real interest in the empire were often right-wingers such as Enfield MP Colonel Applin, a veteran of the Boer War who had served as a policeman in Borneo. In 1928, he opposed lowering the age of voting for women from thirty to twenty-one because of its impact on 'Mohammedans' in the empire. Applin told the House of Commons:

We are governing a great empire – and we forget it very often – and that empire comprises not only our great self-governing Dominions, but the largest Mohammedan population in the world. We are the greatest Mohammedan power in the world. Among the Mohammedans, women not only have no voice, but are not seen. What will be the effect on the great Mohammedan population of the world of granting, the franchise in this country – the governing country – to a majority of 2,200,000 women over men? [*Laughter*] Apparently hon. Members have not lived, as I have, among Mohammedans, or they would know that it will create a serious impression.[19]

The governance of Britain's formal and informal empire consumed much government and parliamentary time during the 1920s and 1930s. The decisions the British government took during this interwar period, particularly in regard to India, Palestine, Iraq, Egypt and Arabia, would have a lasting impact on the world. And yet they meant little to the general public; they did not involve the great mass of the population, nor give them any additional contact with or understanding of Islam. The future of India, and the empire generally, is hardly mentioned in any party election manifesto of this period.[20]

However, one development is relevant to this history.

The British discovered that aerial bombardment was a cheap way of subduing enemies of its rule over Muslim territories in Iraq, Afghanistan and the north-west frontier of India, which were to be three of the most bloody centres of the so-called 'war on terror' launched by the United States and her allies eighty years later.[21] For this reason, Britain consistently resisted international calls for a ban on bombing during the 1920s and early 1930s.[22] In fairness, the British took care to minimise casualties (and to avoid hitting mosques), and the policy was presented as a humane alternative to the traditional punitive expeditions. The British were not the first colonial power to use air strikes in this way. The Italians bombed their opponents in the Italian–Turkish War in 1911, and the French used aircraft for reconnaissance and bombing during their 1912–14 conquest of Morocco.[23] The British also used aircraft for reconnaissance in Egypt in 1916. But it is worth noting that the first casualties of a form of warfare which would maim and kill millions of civilians worldwide were Muslims. The progenitors of this policy, including Winston Churchill as secretary for war and air in Lloyd George's post-war coalition government, openly hailed the success of air power in enthralling Muslim people they regarded as backward, stubborn and recalcitrant tribesmen.[24]

Muslims in interwar Britain

The First World War hugely increased the demand for Muslims (mainly of Arabic and Somali rather than Indian extraction) on British ships, and some were able to settle in British ports, particularly Cardiff, Liverpool and South Shields in the post-war boom. In the subsequent slump, many lost their jobs to returning British seamen and dock workers, and were forced to leave, but there were still about 3,000 Muslims living in Cardiff alone at the outbreak of the Second World War.[25] This small population faced a strikingly modern mix of official and popular racism.

The Home Office, led by the ultra-reactionary Sir William Joynson-Hicks from 1924 to 1929, ignored their status as subjects of the Crown and their service in the Great War, and introduced a series of orders reducing their status to aliens, virtually without rights.[26] Shamefully, the National Union of Seamen and the Labour movement generally supported this, with the NUS demanding jobs for its 'white' members in preference to Muslims. Like many others, Labour's newspaper, the *Daily Herald*, fretted about the mixed-race marriages and relationships of the Muslim settlers in seaports, producing this headline in 1929: 'Black men and white girls – seaport problems of mixed marriage – café menace'. In 1935, a detailed report by a Captain Richardson for the British Social Hygiene Council received widespread respectful coverage by describing Arabs among people of colour generally as a 'social problem', with a culture which made them predisposed to immorality. They did not share England's standards of civilisation or 'assimilated our conventions of life'. Richardson fulminated especially against those who came into 'intimate contact with white women of loose character' and produced mixed-race children who inherited their flaws, especially girls who were 'disinclined to discipline and routine work'. A letter from a female reader to *The Spectator* in 1931 has many contemporary echoes. She wrote: 'When I see a veiled woman, it is as if she shouted at me "My menfolk are barbarians".'*

Muslims in the Second World War

By the end of the Second World War, around 3 million Britons had served in its armed forces. The British Empire contributed a further 3.5 million. Of these, 2.5 million came from India, the largest volunteer army ever assembled, and of these around 40 per cent were Muslim.[27] To them can be added millions of Muslims who served as merchant seamen, and labourers who produced foodstuffs and munitions for the Allied war effort. By the end of the war, Britain's debt to India stood at £1.3 billion.[28]

One effect of the war and Britain's desperate need for manpower was the end of the discriminatory citizenship provisions against Muslim seamen to make them eligible for conscription. The war also encouraged the country's scattered Muslim communities to congregate in cities such as Birmingham, Leeds and Bradford to take up new factory jobs.[29]

---

* However, these attitudes did not go entirely unchallenged. In South Shields, rebuttals came from the Arabs themselves, their wives and some liberals within the white population. Ali Said, who was a leader of the Arab community in the area, refuted charges from the councillors that the Arabs in the town were a 'menace'. See Humayun Ansari, *The Infidel Within: Muslims in Britain Since 1800* (Hurst & Co., 2004) pp. 42–44, 93–95.

India entered the war in September 1939 on a bare declaration by the viceroy, Lord Linlithgow, made without consulting Indian political parties. This resulted in the resignation of all the Congress-run provincial ministries, but the Muslim-led provincial ones in Bengal and Punjab agreed to support the war, as did M. A. Jinnah, the leader of the All-India Muslim League – although, in March 1940, he named the price of his support: an independent Muslim entity at the end of the war.[30]

Muslim Indian support for the war was shaken badly by the poor performance of British administrators and officers in defeat in Malaya and Burma, and even more so by the British handling of the wartime famine in Bengal, which led to the deaths of up to three million.[31] But none of these events affected the flow of Muslim volunteers to the forces. As in the Great War, enlistment gave many Muslim men an opportunity to achieve higher earnings and local respect, and to travel. For the bulk of the Muslim leadership in India, co-operation with the British war effort strengthened their chances of gaining concessions both from the British and the Hindu-dominated Congress in the future settlement of India.[32] This motive was strengthened after the Lahore Resolution of 1940 which first expressed the ambition for a separate nation for India's Muslims, to be known as Pakistan. To this day, Pakistani official narratives celebrate the impact of the Second World War in destroying British plans for a federal Hindu-dominated India.[33]

As in the First World War, Britain's enemies tried to turn Muslims against her. They had even less success, primarily because the Nazis and the Japanese were racists who despised Indians and Arabs, and had no understanding of Muslim culture or aspirations. When the Germans first captured Muslims fighting for the Soviet Union, they thought they were Jews because they were circumcised, and murdered them out of hand. Eventually they enlisted thousands as auxiliaries and labourers, particularly from the Crimean Tatars who were deported wholesale by Stalin after the war and are still being punished by Vladimir Putin.[34] The Nazis were unable to exploit the one great opportunity presented to them in the Muslim world: the short-lived coup in Iraq in 1941 which briefly ousted the pro-British government.[35] The Italians pumped some effective propaganda at Muslim Arabs, and Mussolini posed, like the kaiser before him, as a protector of Islam. But the Italians were committed to colonialism and therefore had no appeal to Arab nationalists. Contrary to widespread myth, Egyptian middle- and upper-class society showed little support for the Axis powers when they invaded Egypt.[36]

If one adds to the British Empire's Muslims the service of thousands of Muslims to French and Dutch forces, and the Bosnian and Albanian Muslim resistance to the Axis in the Balkans, the Moro resistance to the Japanese in the Philippines, and countless others as seamen, farmers and labourers, the Muslim world was a huge net contributor to the Allied victory against fascism. There were some Muslims who allied themselves with Axis powers, and the biggest Muslim thorn in the British side was the troublesome Fakir of Ipi, whose campaigns preceded the war and were almost totally independent of the Axis. He tied down tens of thousands of British troops in the North-West Frontier.[37]

At its peak, around 30,000 Indian prisoners of war joined the second so-called Indian National Army formed by the Indian National Congress leader Subbash Chandra Bose under Japanese tutelage. They included an unknown quantity of Muslims. Since the alternative to joining Bose was death or slave labour, one cannot say how many were genuine volunteers. Unlike the British, Bose tried to integrate his forces rather than maintain them in communal units.[38] His army caused some alarm in the British authorities and was able to spread confusion in British defences when the Japanese made their final thrust into India at Kohima–Imphal in June 1944. The Japanese never gave it the supplies nor the respect it needed to achieve anything more.

Winston Churchill and Islam

I shall now examine Winston Churchill's complex and evolving attitude to Islam and the Islamic world. It began when Churchill was a soldier, helping to suppress groups of 'savage' Muslims threatening the outer edge of the British Empire. It ended as a global statesman, coming to terms with a world in which the empire had disappeared and good relations with Muslim states, especially in the Middle East, had become vital to Britain's economic life and the remains of its international power and influence.

As one might expect of the greatest Briton of his age, Churchill formed his own opinions of Islam, often, though by no means always, managing to escape contemporary prejudices. Although at times romantic or wrong-headed, he showed respect for Muslims – be it as partners or enemies. Churchill's first known opinion on Islam was expressed as a young subaltern in India. He told his former schoolmaster, Rev. J. E. C. Welldon, that it was futile to attempt to convert Muslims to Christianity, because 'providence has given each man the form of worship best suited to his environment'.[39] Even when fighting, or later bombing, particular groups of Muslims, Churchill recognised that their faith was deeply rooted in local conditions.

Over the course of five decades of dealing with Islam as a politician, he sought 'liberal' local Muslim leaders who would co-operate with Britain in what it saw as its civilising mission. His first direct encounters with Islam took him to the North-West Frontier on a punitive expedition with the Malakand Field Force in 1897. In his letters home, and his later writings on the expedition, one can trace a distinction between 'bad' and 'good' Muslims which is familiar today. Bad Muslims were the reactionary clerics who made local tribesmen believe in 'the most miserable fanaticism, in which cruelty, credulity and immorality are all equally represented'. But he admired the bravery and stoicism of his tribal enemies, and even more so the loyal Muslim Punjab soldiers with whom he played polo.[40]

Churchill encountered another group of 'bad' Muslims during Kitchener's suppression of the Mahdist State in Sudan. There is a much-quoted passage in the first edition of his book about it, *The River War*. 'How dreadful are the curses which Mohammedanism lays on its votaries! Besides the fanatical frenzy, which is as dangerous in man as hydrophobia in a dog, there is this fearful fatalistic apathy.' The effects of apathy included slovenly agriculture (a theme to which Churchill would repeatedly return in relation to Arabs in Palestine), sluggish methods of commerce and insecurity of property. Citations of this passage usually omit the fact that Churchill's comments related to the Sudan rather than the Islamic world as a whole, that he praised the 'splendid qualities' of the thousands of brave and loyal Muslim soldiers of the Queen – and that he cut the passage altogether in the second edition.[41]

Churchill praised the Mahdi himself as a soldier and a leader of a state, and recognised, unlike most of his contemporaries, that the Mahdist movement was primarily an expression of nationalism rather than of religious fanaticism. He was profoundly moved by the last stand of the Dervish warriors against the British cavalry and wrote: '"Mad fanaticism" is the depreciating comment of their conquerors. I hold this to be a cruel injustice . . . Why should we regard as madness in the savage what would be sublime in civilised men?'[42]

As a newly elected Conservative MP, Churchill stood out against his party and most of the country by attacking the national hero, Kitchener, for bloody reprisals against the Dervishes and for desecrating the Mahdi's tomb and even his corpse. He voted against an award for Kitchener from public funds, a decision that Kitchener never forgot.[43]

Churchill's stance won the admiration of his father's friend Wilfrid Scawen Blunt, a man who would influence his attitude to Muslims for the next two decades. In particular, Churchill would learn to share Blunt's respect for the life and culture of the desert Bedouin. The two men enjoyed convivial evenings in Bedouin costume: this, of course, predated any modern concept of 'cultural appropriation'. Churchill's future sister-in-law, Lady Gwendoline Bertie, fretted that he might even convert to Islam, and begged him not to give in to his disposition to 'orientalism and pasha-like tendencies'.[44]

When Churchill first took office, in the Liberal government of Henry Campbell-Bannerman, Blunt strengthened his resistance to punitive expeditions against Muslims in northern Nigeria and Somaliland, and his reform of education for Muslims in the Sudan.[45] More importantly, Blunt alerted Churchill to the force of Pan-Islamism. In 1910, as Home Secretary, Churchill made a private visit to Constantinople, hoping to counter the well-organised German attempt to win over the Ottoman Empire. Unlike most of the Liberal government, who despised the decaying Ottomans, Churchill saw it as a strategic asset (particularly after oil became vital for the British navy) and as a crucial influence on the loyalty of the British Empire's Muslim subjects. He was not impressed by the actual Sultan and Caliph, the fat and apathetic Mehmet V, but had warm feelings for the ambitious Young Turks who had seized control of his empire.[46] Churchill was especially attracted by the Napoleonic Young Turk leader Enver Pasha, and never lost his hope that he might become a British ally.

Churchill followed up his personal diplomacy when he became First Lord of the Admiralty. He acutely sought to prevent any religious incident by ordering the Royal Navy not to fire on vessels taking pilgrims on the hajj and was furious when the order was disobeyed.[47] He was, nonetheless, characteristically determined to demonstrate British power over the Muslim world and force the Ottoman Empire to abandon the Germans. This was a major motive for the Dardanelles Campaign, a naval invasion of the Gallipoli peninsula in Ottoman territory which Churchill, disastrously, considered might induce Enver to change sides.[48] As the campaign foundered and the Turks showed unexpected resistance, he and his old enemy Kitchener feared that a British withdrawal would revive Islamic threats to the British Empire. The French marshal Joseph Gallieni, the saviour of Paris, believed that it might cost his country Algeria and Morocco.[49]

The Turkish victories at Gallipoli and later in Mesopotamia were the most resonant by any Islamic force against a major Western power since the British were expelled from Afghanistan with great loss of life in 1842. The Gallipoli fiasco forced Churchill out of government and he had no further responsibility for the Muslim world until he became Secretary of State for war and air, and then for the colonies, in Lloyd George's post-war coalition. In the latter post, he became effectively a proconsul for the area which was starting to be known as the Middle East, housing millions of Muslims asserting new national claims within the conquered Ottoman Empire.

British control over these occupied areas depended heavily on Indian Muslim troops, and Churchill worried about their loyalty. The Sultan and Caliph (Mehmet VI had replaced his half-brother in the last months of the war) was a British prisoner in his capital and his empire was being dismembered and humiliated. The Muslim world rallied against the threat to the caliphate, a cause which briefly united Indian Muslims with Mahatma Gandhi in protests throughout India. Churchill saw opportunities for his hated Bolsheviks to foment local Islamist risings; in a revival of the Great Game, he fought a short war against the Amir of Afghanistan.[50]

Churchill therefore struggled hard in Cabinet against Lloyd George's anti-Turkish policies, especially the latter's support for the Greeks. Churchill urged him instead to seek an alliance with the Sultan's government in post-war Turkey to create a Muslim barrier against the Bolsheviks. Publicly and privately, he repeated his description of the British Empire as 'the greatest

Mohammedan power in the world' and sought to conciliate global Islam.[51] But Churchill had initially completely misread Kemal Atatürk as a religious fanatic in league with Bolshevism and was agreeably surprised when he turned out to be a secular national-ist.[52] Although Atatürk abolished the sultanate and the caliphate, this did not cause the feared upheaval in the Muslim world; over time, Churchill revived his hopes that a Turkish alliance would help to safeguard the British Empire. During the war, he made a productive personal visit to Atatürk's successor Ismet Inönü.[53]

However, as colonial secretary in the early 1920s, Churchill turned away from Turkey and pinned his hopes on other figure-heads to give leadership to the Muslim world. He left an enduring legacy at the Cairo Conference by creating the Arab states of Iraq and Transjordan, under two brothers of the Hashemite dynasty. Still influenced by Wilfrid Blunt, and latterly by his new friend T. E. Lawrence, Churchill adopted the Hashemites as represent-atives of the best type of Muslim: desert Bedouins willing to co-operate with the British Empire and accept its tutelage. He contrasted them with the Palestinian Arab fellahin, backward and disloyal (they had fought for the Ottomans, although they had little choice).

Churchill is often described as a Zionist, though he did not believe that the Jews should extinguish the rights and ultimate sovereignty of the Arab majority of Palestine. He regarded Jewish settlement as a force for the economic and social develop-ment of Palestine, bringing 'general prosperity and wealth to all Palestinians'. Some scholars have noted racism in this. The historian Michael Cohen says that Churchill could adopt 'an arro-gant and scolding tone' with Arabs, and accuses him of treating the Palestinian Arabs as if he were 'explaining the benefits of white civilisation at the African natives'.[54] Churchill expected the Arabs to welcome them and, for two decades, pursued the hope that an Arab sovereign over Palestine would give them a protected status.[55]

In due course, Churchill invested this hope in Ibn Saud. Even though Saud had driven his favoured Hashemite dynasty out of Arabia, Churchill developed virtually a schoolboy crush on him. In 1941, he called him 'the greatest living Arab' and imagined fondly that he might become the overlord of Syria, Iraq, Transjordan and Palestine, *and* that he would accept a Jewish state within Palestine.[56] Echoes of Churchill's doomed vision are to be found in the dark alliance between Donald Trump and Ibn Saud's bloodthirsty grandson, Mohammed bin Salman. There is room for many books about British and American illusions about the Saudi dynasty, which has an almost unbroken record of reaction, cruelty, self-indulgence and corruption stretching back nearly a century.

It is noteworthy that, as colonial secretary, Churchill asked to be given a crash course in Islamic geography, nomenclature and doctrinal differences. After fifteen years of dealing with the Islamic world, he learned about the schism between Sunni and Shia for the first time, although it did not prevent him from putting a Sunni king into Shia-majority Iraq.[57]

Churchill and India's Muslims

Churchill's relationship with the Muslims of India helped shape his political activity in opposition in the early 1930s. The relationship was deeply personal. He liked and respected Muslims, he disliked and distrusted Hindus, and he detested Gandhi. Islam was a monotheistic faith, sharing a heritage with Christianity, while Hinduism was polytheistic and took nothing from Christianity. Muslims were strong and silent, loyal to the British Empire and potential partners in its civilising mission. Hindus were unreliable, loquacious and self-centred: their religion encouraged sybaritism and sexual depravity. Apart from his own selective memories, Churchill was strongly influenced by Katherine Mayo's popular anti-Hindu tract, *Mother India*.[58]

More seriously, Churchill hated the caste system. He identified the Indian Congress with a narrow section of Brahmins and rich vested interests, and suggested constantly that if it took power over India, it would institute 'caste rule', oppressing not only Muslims but the millions of low-caste Hindu untouchables.[59] He ignored Gandhi's attempt to rename them *harijan* – children of God.

During the 1930s, Churchill developed a network of Muslim informants and sympathisers led by the Aga Khan and the aristocratic convert Lord Headley, an Irish peer who had written a book identifying Islam with the basic tenets of early Christianity. The latter drew him into the British Muslim Society and reinforced Churchill's belief that Muslims in general were opposed to sedition and secession from the British Empire.[60] Indeed, the Second World War reinforced Churchill's perception of Muslims as loyal and Hindus as disruptive. At the height of Britain's troubles in Burma and Egypt, Churchill was exasperated by the Quit India agitation promoted by Congress, which the viceroy described as the greatest threat to British rule since the 1857 uprising. But Churchill was gratified that Muslims kept aloof from it and continued to volunteer for the Indian army.[61] He was equally exasperated by President Roosevelt's antipathy to the British Empire in general and its Indian empire in particular, and American efforts to influence India by the control of essential supplies. He told Roosevelt repeatedly – to no avail – that the Congress was unrepresentative of India as a whole. In March 1942, he wrote the president a long letter, explaining that he could not deny '100 million Muslims' the right to representative government, and that they formed 'the main army elements on which we must rely for immediate fighting'.[62]

In opposition after the war, Churchill reluctantly accepted partition as a means of protecting loyal Muslims from oppression and maintaining some British influence (and military bases) on the Indian subcontinent. He later acquired a new reason for favouring Pakistan: it was anti-communist while India was unreliably neutralist.[63]

When Churchill returned to office in 1951, the British Empire was formally at an end. But Britain still retained huge colonial possessions and remained a power in the Middle East. Churchill believed that this state of affairs would endure, giving Britain power status despite its diminished military and economic resources. He held on to his view that the right kind of Muslim leaders could help Britain hold on to this informal empire and act as junior partners in British civilisation. By the time he left office in 1955, aged eighty, this view of the world was still remarkably intact. He was furious with his Foreign Secretary, Anthony Eden, for losing British influence in the Sudan and Egypt, but he had exulted in the overthrow of the nationalist Mohammad Mosaddegh in Iran, whom he had regarded as a communist sympathiser. Persia, under the young shah, could be counted a British ally again. Like Pakistan, it had joined CENTO, the Asian anti-communist counterpart to NATO. The two Hashemite monarchies were still ruling Iraq and Jordan,[64] while the Saudi monarchy had renamed the whole country after itself. Britain maintained Muslim client states in the Red Sea and the Gulf.

At the very end of his premiership, Churchill suddenly turned against Britain's Commonwealth immigrants, using language later much quoted by the far right. According to reports, Churchill wanted to use the racist election slogan 'Keep Britain White'.[65] He made other racist statements which cannot be ignored, including the insistence that Britain and the United States shared 'Anglo-Saxon superiority', and his description of anti-colonial campaigners as 'savages armed with ideas'.[66] One can say, however, that over the course of his long and intensely active life, Churchill usually had some admiration for Islam. He classed Muslims among the most loyal subjects of the British Empire; even when they fought against the empire, he often admired them.

Churchill was a mass of contradictions. His rhetoric justified armed resistance to any threats, perceived or otherwise, to the British (or any other) Empire. In the first instalment of his four-volume *A History of the English-Speaking Peoples*, published after his retirement as prime minister, he wrote of Boadicea's tribal uprising against the Roman Empire that 'it is the primary right of men to die and kill for the land they live in, and to punish with exceptional severity all members of their own race who have warmed their hands at the invaders' hearth'.[67] Such a remark from a British politician today would mark him down as a terrorist sympathiser and spell the end of his career.

CONCLUSION TO PART TWO

In the first part of this book, I explored the American involvement with Islam from the earliest settlers to the present day. I showed how the American attitude to Islam has, with few exceptions, been based on hostility, ignorance and violence. I also demonstrated the ways in which it was and is influenced by an obscurantist version of biblical theology. The British relationship with Islam is richer, more interesting and more complex. As with the United States, there is plenty of prejudice and violence. Indeed, from Bede to the Crusades and beyond, the two countries shared a common history rooted in bloodshed, bigotry and ignorance. However, in later centuries, trade and (later) empire brought the British state into a deeper relationship with Muslim countries.

Scholars, merchants and soldiers often acquired an astonishing knowledge of Muslim culture and Islamic learning, along with a deep understanding of the societies where they were based. While historic conflicts with Christian powers did partly influence British understanding, there were other instances where the religions were seen to share key principles. Unlike the United States, the British comprehension of Islam is based on more than a caricature, although it is certainly the case that caricatures of Islam existed, particularly among British people who never met a Muslim. As we have seen, writers who appealed to a domestic British audience often painted simplistic images of Islam, which were often both obscene and hostile, and left a stubborn legacy.

This kind of approach to Islam was balanced, however, by serious scholars who were profoundly influenced by Islam and, in some cases, converted to it.

Despite Britain's richer and more varied contact with Islam, negative propaganda about Islam from Bede through to Churchill managed to colour opinion for centuries. This has become an especially noxious problem in recent years, as I will explain in the fourth part of the book. But that process cannot be understood without an understanding of the experience of France, Britain's closest continental neighbour. France followed a dramatically different and tragic path. As we have seen, Britain pursued a multicultural empire which allowed different religions and local traditions to continue and flourish. By contrast, France sought to integrate Muslims into the republic, inflicting unspeakable savagery and bloodshed in the process.

PART THREE

France and Islam

'The first year of great apocalyptic battles, weighty events, unfortunate occurrences, shocking misfortunes, the multiplication of evils, one thing following another, continuous trials, the rapture of the age, the upheaval of the natural order and the overturning of custom, successive horrors, the change of conditions, the corruption of the administration, the arrival of destruction, the generalization of devastation, and the unsettling of effects.'

HISTORIAN AL-JABARTI[1]

FRANCE AS A COLONIAL POWER

This and the next chapter will examine the history of French encounters with Muslims to point up some instructive contrasts with those of the United Kingdom and the United States. Essentially, the French were far more deeply engaged in their formal and informal Muslim empires than either the British or the Americans, crucially absorbing their most significant possession, Algeria, as a department of mainland France. France remains engaged as an ex-colonial power economically, politically, militarily and culturally. Largely as a result of this, it has the highest proportion of Muslims in its population of any European country today, although precise figures are unobtainable because French public policy bars the identification of religion in official figures.

Nevertheless, the Pew Research Center cited France's Muslim population being a proportion of 8.8 per cent in 2016, compared to 6.3 per cent for the UK and 4.9 per cent for the EU plus Norway and Switzerland.[2] The French Institute for Demographic Studies indicated that in 2005 some 3.5 million French people could trace their heritage to France's former empire of Algeria, Morocco and Tunisia, equating to 5.8 per cent of the total population.[3] That would suggest that more than two-thirds of France's Muslim population originate from these countries.

Unlike the UK and the US, France in its earliest days had to beat back a serious Muslim incursion. Charles Martel – grandfather of Charlemagne and victor of the Battle of Tours (or

Poitiers) in 732 – is still presented to French and indeed European schoolchildren as a hero who saved France and, with it, Western Christianity from Muslim conquest. As always, myth is more important than reality. Martel spent far more time fighting rival Christian nobles than Muslims, and the losers at Tours were almost certainly more interested in looting than in a full-scale invasion.[4] Martel's name has lately been stolen by ultra-right nationalists and white supremacists.[5]

Like the British, the French had commercial relations and occasional alliances with Muslim rulers during the medieval and Renaissance eras. However, the French were more involved than the British in the protection of Roman Catholic Christians in the Muslim Near East,* and in asserting their rights against Orthodox Christians. These twin tasks became a distinctly French mission after the Reformation. The British achieved a constitutional settlement for their state, including a Church which was given privileges but little influence over public policy. In England, religious issues rarely figured in frontline politics – although they remained significant in Wales, Scotland and, of course, Ireland.

By contrast, the French had a revolution against an absolutist state with which the Roman Catholic Church was closely identified. Religion thereafter became one of the battlefields of French politics. Left-of-centre France was anti-clerical while conservative France was pro-clerical (although also nationalist and accepting no governance from the Pope).[6] Above all, left-of-centre France established the idea of a secular republic in which all religion was excluded from the public realm and established patriotism in terms of loyalty to secular values. Conservative France remained loyal to traditional values, of which the Catholic

---

* Over the course of the nineteenth century, Europeans and Americans increasingly divided what had previously been referred to as the 'Orient' into two sections: a 'Near East' comprising south-eastern Europe, the Levant and other parts of western Asia nearer to Europe; and a 'Far East' encompassing India, south-east Asia, China and Japan. Zachary Lockman, *Contending Visions of the Middle East: The History and Politics of Orientalism* (Cambridge University Press, 2004).

religion was part. The cultural and political battles they fought, especially over education, had no place for non-Christian faiths. Both sides regarded first Jews, and later Muslims, as a potential threat to the republic. Under Napoleon, the Jews were forced to renounce the Mosaic Law if they were to be 'French', foreshadowing what is happening to Muslims in France today.

With a brief interlude for the wartime Vichy regime,* the idea of a secular republic has dominated French political discourse for more than a hundred years. It demands far more loyalty from French citizens than the British are expected to give 'British values' (a bizarre twenty-first-century invention) and even Americans to the 'American' way of life. It is expressed in the French term *laïcité,* and precludes the pursuit of autonomy by any community within the French state.

It is important to pause the narrative here to explore the concept of *laïcité*: it is central to the predicament facing Muslims in contemporary France. There is no English equivalent of the term. Secularism, the closest equivalent, describes a social phenomenon. There are no laws enforcing secularism in the UK. By contrast, *laïcité* is political, setting out in legal terms the role of religion in the public sphere. Paradoxically for a movement which has its origins in anti-clericalism, it is the nearest thing that France now has to a state religion, in certain respects assuming the role of the Catholic Church before 1789.

The Separation of the Churches and the State law of 1905 laid the foundation stone for the modern idea. It forbade the French state from recognising any religion, imposing neutrality on civil servants in order to protect freedom of conscience. Nevertheless, it did not police religious belief. A Roman Catholic priest could

---

* Many of the clerics of Vichy France had lived through the anti-clericalism of the Third Republic (1870 to 1940) and they had bitterly resented the Front Populaire. At the beginning of the Vichy regime, many Catholics were hopeful that Marshal Pétain would raise the status of the Church. Frank Tallett, *Religion, Society and Politics in France Since 1789* (Bloomsbury, 2003), chapter 10.

preach from the pulpit that abortion was a mortal sin,[7] but if the same priest encouraged attacks on abortion clinics, that was a criminal offence. This principle was further entrenched in the Constitution of the Fifth Republic, established by Charles de Gaulle in 1958, which embraced the principles of the 1789 Declaration of the Rights of Man, including the famous assertion that 'No one should be worried about his opinions, even religious, provided that their manifestation does not disturb the public order established by law.'[8]

In other words, the 1905 law – while resented by the Catholic Church, which took two decades to come to terms with it – was about protecting religion, as well as controlling it. That is why the French Council of State (in some ways comparable to the Supreme Court in the United States) will not allow the state to involve itself with religion. In 1989, the council ruled that *laïcité* was consistent with Muslim schoolgirls wearing headscarves, unless the practice threatened public order. More recently, the council ruled against bans on burkinis (Muslim swimsuits covering the full body) on the same basis that they infringed the 'basic liberties protected by the French constitution' and that 'an alleged disturbance of public order was not proven'.[9] Today, this scrupulous legal interpretation of *laïcité* is coming under massive pressure not just from the far right, but from mainstream politicians including President Macron.

Two groups that were bitterly opposed ahead of the 1905 Act have now come together in a common struggle against Islam. French conservatives are deploying *laïcité* in protection of what they see as the country's Christian (or Judaeo-Christian[10]) values in order to argue that Muslims do not belong in France.[11] Meanwhile, the secular left asserts that Muslim identity is a threat to the universalist traditions of the Enlightenment. Both have stretched the original conception of *laïcité* beyond recognition to include criminalisation of beliefs and ideas. This two-pronged assault has created an existential crisis for French Muslims.

France and its Islamic empire

The French African colonial empire began in 1830 and ended formally with Algerian independence in 1962. France's three main African possessions – Algeria, Morocco and Tunisia – were almost exclusively Muslim. There was no question of trying to make Muslims a favoured minority, as the British attempted in their Indian empire, although the French sometimes tried to cultivate particular ethnic groups within Islam, especially the Berbers. For example, in Morocco the French sought to preserve Berber customary law, believing that the unveiled Berber woman was inherently more liberated than the sequestered urban Arab woman.[12] To maintain their rule in North Africa, the French were, quite simply, committed to suppressing those Muslims who failed to accept the French '*mission civilisatrice*'.[13]

The British never sent many people to their empire. Settlers acquired extensive land and property in South Africa and its northern neighbour Rhodesia, but these were exceptions and lacked the scale of French settlement in North Africa. As long as they were loyal, peaceable and served the needs of British commerce (with memorable exceptions such as the elimination of widow-burning in India, still cited as a moral vindication of British imperialism), the British arrivals left local cultures, including religion, largely alone. They created little pockets of British life in settlements and clubs, and in some schools imitated British public schools in order to inculcate loyalty in prominent families. The French, however, were much closer to their Muslim possessions than the British – literally so, especially after steamship travel. Many more French people visited Algeria than Britons visited India, including artists and writers who imported into France their ideas of Muslim 'Oriental' styles and culture.[14] Well-to-do people could live in both France and Algeria during the space of a year.

The French sent many more permanent settlers (often known

as *colons*) to Algeria and, in lesser numbers to Tunisia and Morocco, than the British sent to India.[15] They took over, without compensation, far more of the best land.[16] Many of the settlers were not born French, and those who were tended to come from poorer backgrounds.[17] Their own status as French people therefore depended on French possessions, especially Algeria, being regarded as part of France. A hierarchy established itself among the *colons*, with the Spanish, Italian and Maltese sometimes referred to as *le petit peuple* or as *Français du deuxième zone*. The Maltese ranked lowest, but regarded themselves as superior to Algerians.[18]

Unlike the British in India, the *colons* had votes in French elections and could send deputies to the National Assembly. Rather like 'poor whites' in the antebellum United States, their status in the French Empire required a class below them to 'keep down' – Algerian Muslims. They also despised Jews. In the mid-1890s, anti-Jewish 'leagues' flourished and rioters attacked Jewish homes. In January 1898 in central Algiers, a crowd burned and pillaged for five days, killing two people, destroying the synagogue and several homes, and ransacking eighty-seven businesses.[19] Anti-Jewish activity continued into the twentieth century and Dr Jules Molle – the founder of Unions Latines, an anti-Semitic popular movement – became mayor of Oran in 1925 and deputy in 1928. This result was repeated in other elections and there were more riots in the interwar period.[20]

The French tried far harder than the British to make all their colonies replicas of the home country. They established a French secular education system which instructed local children in French patriotic history, including Gallic resistance to the Romans.[21] Those children were offered far more access to French society than Indian children were given to British society – *if* they were ready to accept French authority, values and behaviours. They were allowed to keep their Islamic faith, as long as they treated it as a private matter. Paradoxically, the teaching of French history and values in Algerian schools ultimately helped to shape Algerian nationalism, with many drawing on the gap between French egalitarian principles and the reality of segregation. For example, the Algerian nationalist Jean el-Mouhouve Amrouche attacked French colonial hypocrisy for betraying its own republican traditions.[22]

In the First World War the French used far more African Muslim manpower in their home armed forces than the British used Muslim Indian manpower at home.[23] Of course, the French were relying on a conscript army to defend themselves against an enemy (Germany) with a higher population. The British never wanted a large peacetime standing army at home, and had no need to put colonial forces into it, Muslim or otherwise. Some 600,000 Muslims are estimated to have fought for France on the Western Front in the Great War.[24] They took high casualties and were generally given worse treatment.[*]

Later on, the sacrifices made by Muslim troops helped to feed into the rising tide of nationalism in French overseas territories. Georges Clemenceau, the celebrated wartime leader, had promised that the 80,000 Tunisians who signed up to fight in the First World War would be rewarded for their heroism. However, after the war, economic problems meant that this promise went unfulfilled and led many Tunisians to believe that their relationship with the metropole (the common term for mainland France, tellingly still in use today) was one-sided.[25]

Hundreds of thousands of North African Muslims were again part of the French army in 1939, and were often said to have offered stiffer resistance than native French units. Muslim soldiers were the backbone of de Gaulle's Free French army, with many *colons* supporting Vichy. Large numbers of Muslim soldiers fought in Italy and for the liberation of France. They were denigrated by

---

[*] However, the Germans had little success in recruiting them to fight for their ally, the Ottoman Sultan and Caliph, when they tried to recruit them as prisoners of war.

their white officers, frequently went unpaid and unfed, and were overlooked in official French celebrations.[26] Philippe Masson, historian of the French army, nevertheless states that 233,000 out of 600,000 soldiers in the liberation army by the end of 1944 were Muslim – more than a third of the total.[27] A wholly convincing explanation for this paradox is hard to find. One theory is that they continued to enlist partly in the hope that France would reward their communities with independence or at least autonomy. Another is that the army, however perilous, offered a potential escape from grinding poverty. Some may even have entertained an ambition to rise up through the ranks. Whatever the reason, the British abandoned their empire in the post-war period with few casualties to themselves and with surprisingly little impact on British politics. By contrast, the French fought devastating wars to retain control of Indochina and Algeria. Both left deep scars on French politics and society.

The Indochina War[28] was fought largely by conventional means and was ended by a conventional military defeat. As with the British in India, few French people had any connection with Indochina.[29] The decisive defeat of French forces by the Viet Minh at Dien Bien Phu in 1954 caused great bitterness among veterans and shook the army's faith in the Fourth Republic,[30] but the subsequent 'loss' of Indochina was generally accepted with equanimity by the French population. This national bereavement, alongside the losses of Tunisia and Morocco, nevertheless contributed to the French determination to hold on to Algeria, which briefly, through France, was a subordinate member of the emerging European Union. Relinquishing Algeria risked denting France's international prestige.[31] The socialist daily *Le Populaire* warned in December 1954 that 'to lose North Africa . . . would be to lose in quick succession all of Africa, then the French union, it would make France fall to the level of a second-rate power and even a vassal power. It is not only our prestige that is at stake, but also our national independence.'[32]

The Algerian War of Independence began in 1954, the same year that the French were driven out of Vietnam. It is estimated to have claimed more than 300,000 lives, of whom approximately half were combatants.[33] It was a 'dirty war' fought largely in secret by the French state and its forces outside public scrutiny and accountability.[34] Resistance to Algerian independence by French settlers – and their sympathisers in the armed forces and paramilitary organisations – destroyed the Fourth Republic and came near to ending the Fifth. Those who fought in Algeria, such as the French nationalist politician Jean-Marie Le Pen, had a training in hatred against Muslims which was far more poisonous even than that of Tommy Robinson and the British far right.[35]

Conversely, the independence struggle left bitter memories of the French state with the millions of North African Muslims who settled in France during its thirty years of post-war expansion. This made Muslim immigration into France fundamentally different from the British experience during the same period. When the expansion came to an end, France's Muslims were the first to feel its impact as they faced discrimination in competing for the jobs and opportunities which remained. Dumped in purpose-built ghettoes, largely excluded from the mainstream of French life (except in sport and entertainment), they were expected to show absolute loyalty to French values.

When the British quit India, they were almost totally unaffected by its post-independence history and the conflicts between India and Pakistan. This remained so even when the United Kingdom received large-scale immigration from both countries, including disputed Kashmir – an issue which has barely figured in British politics. France, in contrast, has been strongly marked by the post-independence history of Algeria, Morocco and Tunisia. The independence struggles in these countries had fierce internal conflicts, which endured and multiplied after independence was achieved. The French state, including the security and intelligence arms, remained deeply involved in all three, especially with favoured client governments or rich, privileged elites. France was a land of opportunity for enterprising Algerian, Tunisian and Moroccan citizens who travelled to France in huge numbers after the war to fill labour shortages, but it also became the natural enemy of marginalised Muslims from these countries, whether living in North Africa or in France. This background has made the relationship between French Muslims and the French state far more fraught than that between British Muslims and the British state.

Bonaparte's Muslim conquest

Although short-lived, Napoleon's invasion of Egypt in 1798 antici-pated many of the themes of French colonial rule over Muslim territories. Indeed, he foresaw the doctrine of liberal imperial-ism, according to which advanced Western states modernised and elevated reactionary Oriental despotisms. Napoleon and his soldiers claimed to be exporting French civilisation – especially the new republic's cult of liberty – to an oppressed, backward land. His expedition contained an unusually high number of sci-entists and savants to advance this mission. (One lasting result of the expedition was the decoding of the Rosetta Stone.)[36]

Napoleon was the first modern master of propaganda, which ena-bled him to turn the ultimate failure of his expedition into part of his legend. He established a lasting myth of Egypt as a failed Muslim society that was in massive decline from its former (pre-Muslim) population and success. In fact, Ottoman Egypt was an economic powerhouse in the early eighteenth century, thanks to its control of the coffee trade, and remained a functioning state and society even after later years of depression, plague and civil skirmishes.[37]

Napoleon differed from nearly all his successors (excepting his nephew Napoleon III) in professing respect for Islam.[38] He styled himself the Great Sultan, celebrated the Festival of the Nile (dominated by Egyptian folk Islam) and the Prophet's birthday, and even suggested that he and the French were ready to convert to Islam.[*][39] He made great efforts to find clerical sympathisers. Remarkably, given current Western attitudes to Iran's clerical government, Napoleon was the first ruler to allow clerical influence in colonial administration.[40] He appears to have believed in these efforts, but they were vitiated by French brutality, especially reprisals for attacks on French soldiers, heavy official taxation and private rapacity, and a lack of respect for local women – all factors which would reappear in French colonial rule over Muslims just a few decades later. All these grew worse after the loss of the French fleet to the English commanded by Horatio Nelson at Abū Qīr Bay in 1798.[41] The French never enjoyed the security and permanence in Egypt which would later in Algeria encourage the emergence of reliable Muslim intermediaries.

French colonial rule in Algeria

Many Napoleonic veterans were part of the French conquest of Algeria in 1830 and were accompanied by upper-class French sightseers.[42] Like many such adventures, it was prompted in part by internal politics.[†] The ultra-reactionary French king, Charles X, may have wanted a cheap colourful victory to head off discontent at home, but it did him no good. Within weeks, he was displaced by his cousin Louis-Philippe.[43]

---

* There is, however, evidence that Napoleon was being disingenuous. To quote the historian Tom Holland: 'In private, however, or when addressing his soldiers, Napoleon was contemptuous of the Islamic word. "You have come to this country," he told his army before the Battle of the Pyramids, "to save the inhabitants from barbarism, and to bring civilisation to the Orient."' 'The age-old tension between Islam and France', *UnHerd*, 2 November 2020.

† But also by disputes over grain. In the 1790s, the Livorno-based Jewish merchant houses Busnac and Bacri, backed by a group of creditors including the Algerian dey's treasury, gave revolutionary France and its armies grain supplies. The subsequent liquidation of the French state's debts to Bacri (a source of litigation into the 1820s) systematically ignored the claims of the Algerian state on sums due to Bacri but which Bacri owed the dey. After the famous 'fly-whisk' incident of April 1827 – when Husayn Dey struck the French consul, Pierre Deval, with a fly whisk – war was declared by both sides and French ships blockaded Algiers for three years. In 1830, 37,000 troops landed in Algiers and the conquest began. James McDougall, *A History of Algeria* (Cambridge, 2017), pp. 50–51.

The new thrifty, bourgeois monarch resented the cost of the war he inherited, but could not afford to look weak by abandoning it. Instead, he ordered the conquest of the Algerian hinterland and imposed colonial status – and the new name of Algeria – on the whole territory.[44] Invented by a French academic, Fontenelle, this name had never been used by its inhabitants. A local leader, Abdel Kader, united Muslim resistance against the French and secured a ceasefire. Pressure from the French media, infuriated by attacks on settlers, induced Louis-Philippe to abrogate the ceasefire and send in two strong generals, Bugeaud and Cavaignac. Their scorched-earth tactics and ethnic cleansing succeeded in subduing the area and bringing it under French control.[*45] Abdel Kader went into exile, having won some admiration in French high society. As for Bugeaud, he later recanted, opposed the continued occupation of Algeria and told the French Parliament that 'great nations must make their mistakes with greatness [*grandeur*]'.[46]

The conquest of Algeria (today Africa's largest country by land mass) led tens of thousands of white European settlers to grab land, property and other assets from Muslims.[47] Some were from poor parts of France, but the majority came from Spain, Malta, Sardinia and Sicily; they actually became French only through Algeria.[48] This explains the scale of the bloodshed. Unlike the British conquest of India (but akin to the British in Ireland or the United States' treatment of American Indians), the colonisation of Algeria was about the dispossession of natives and seizure of land. The facts speak for themselves. Some 2 per cent of the colonial population of Delhi was European in 1921 and 5 per cent of colonial Cairo in 1897. By contrast, between

---

* The tactic of *les enfumades* (smoking out) was employed and led to the deaths of thousands of Algerians. The first such *enfumade* was ordered by General Cavaignac, who got his men to wall up caves and set fires at the entrances, leading the people inside to choke to death. And Abdel Kader later went into exile in Damascus after his surrender to the army of Bugeaud in 1946. Edmond Pellissier de Reynaud, *Annales Algériennes* (1854), vol. 3, pp. 165–169.

75 and 80 per cent of colonial Algiers was European during the period 1881–1926.[49]

Within a generation, the Algerian *colons* were beyond the control of the French government. They openly mocked the new emperor, Napoleon III, who seized power in late 1851 and who feted Abdel Kader (as an heir to the Gauls who had resisted the Romans!) and had a sentimental fondness for his Muslim Arab subjects, who furnished him with the Zouaves, the most colourful and loyal soldiers in his Crimean army. In a well-meant but misguided decree in 1865, Napoleon III offered Algerian Arabs a pathway into French citizenship.[50] The 'indigenous Muslim' was declared French, but paradoxically wasn't a citizen. While he was obliged to carry out military service and could join the civil service, he did not gain the rights of full French citizenship unless he renounced his 'Muslim personal status' in matters of family law. It is worth recalling that French women did not receive the vote until 1944 and, at the time, their civil rights were also restricted. Under the 1804 Napoleonic Code, married women were entirely subject to their husbands. They had no share in the acquisition and disposal of property, and their husbands alone possessed authority over their children.[51] Algerian Jews were offered the same kind of deal: citizenship in exchange for renouncing many aspects of Jewish family law (by contrast, under the Ottoman Empire they had had the right to their own laws and religious customs).*

The late nineteenth century saw the most self-confident expression of French colonialism in Algeria. In 1881, the prime minister, Jules Ferry, one of the architects of *laïcité*, defined

---

* Jewish family law proved to be a hurdle when it came to assimilating the Algerian Jews. However, by 1870 it was decreed that Jews would be required to abandon their personal status and would now have to conform with the guidelines of the French *status personnel* and the *état civil*. However, they did not rush to do this and sources indicate that they had to be reminded of the new requirement to contract civil marriages. Joshua Schreier, *Arabs of the Jewish Faith: The Civilizing Mission in Colonial Algeria* (Rutgers University Press, 2010), pp. 174–175.

France's civilising mission by the 'superior notions of which we are the guardians' and in terms of modernism over Islam. The liberal philosopher Ernest Renan called Islam 'the complete negation of Europe . . . Islam is contempt for science, the suppression of civil society, it is the shocking simplicity of the Semitic mind.'[52] The Algerians were French subjects, not citizens; according to the Indigénat of 1881 (Indigenous Code), they were subject to measures which were not applied to French citizens. Ferry banned Algerians from making anti-French remarks and insulting colonial officials. Meeting without authorisation, showing disrespect to an agent of authority (even when off duty) and travelling without official permission were all punishable by fine or imprisonment. Collective punishments, such as the burning down of a local forest, were applied when a single Algerian was deemed to have breached these laws.[53] Meanwhile, the colons completed their grip on the country, grabbing the best land and ruling huge tracts indirectly through friendly Muslim officials (cadis). While insisting on their status as French, the colons developed their own distinct culture, cuisine, lifestyle and vernacular language, and political connections with the mainland parties of the French ultra-right.

As already mentioned, more than 100,000 Algerian Muslims fought or laboured for France in the Great War.[54] Their treatment helped to fuel the first political resistance to French rule by Algerian Muslims, divided between young francophone intellectuals seeking integration into a French Algeria and a socialist-nationalist faction (the Étoile Nord-Africaine) led by Messali Hadj.[55] Resistance was also expressed through the Wahabist Islamic ulema and, at a popular level, through displays at football matches. The colons fiercely resisted all attempts at liberalisation and blocked a modest reform by the leftist Popular Front government which took power in France in 1936.[56]

The fall of France was a massive shock to Algerian Muslims. Although it represented the collapse of the colonial oppression, it threatened a worse racial tyranny through Nazi occupation. In the event, the Nazis left Algeria in Vichy hands, and many *colons* rallied to the right-wing, authoritarian state under Marshal Pétain.[57]

The Allied occupation of Algeria after Operation Torch encouraged Muslim and nationalist hopes of an end to French rule. These were disappointed when the Americans installed first François Darlan, an admiral who had been de facto leader of the Vichy government, to administer the country.[58] After Darlan's assassination, they put the military hero Henri Giraud in his place. The American army itself sent mixed messages – of a hugely prosperous society dispensing chewing gum, nylons and Hollywood movies, but also one which was still racially segregated.

As mentioned, hundreds of thousands of Muslim soldiers joined the battles to liberate Italy and France.[59] Towards the end of the war, Charles de Gaulle replaced Giraud and promised major reforms to head off nationalist demands.[60] However, it was too late to stop the Algerian factions from uniting in a demand for independence. On VE Day itself – and therefore ignored by the French and the world's media – pro-independence demonstrators at the town of Sétif were massacred by units of the French army and the survivors publicly humiliated. This brutal policy was set in motion by de Gaulle who instructed: 'Take all necessary measures to repress all anti-French acts by a minority of agitators.'[61] This repression – first by settler militia, then by regular troops and artillery – killed many thousands and, in many ways, was a prelude to the War of Independence.[62] In the short term, however, it paved the way for the restoration of *colon* power, backed by repression, corruption and fraud, with support from a succession of French mainland governments.

After almost a decade of sporadic skirmishes within and between nationalist factions, and attacks on and against *colons*, one faction – the Front de Libération Nationale (FLN) – escalated the struggle with the savage murder of a French teacher, Guy Monnerot, in a remote area of north-eastern Algeria, and a wave of attacks on other French civilians. Most Algerian Muslims repudiated these tactics and their call for a mass uprising, but the FLN succeeded in its objective of provoking the French mainland government. Monnerot, whose wife Jeanine was also injured in the attack, is often cited as the first French victim of the Algerian War of Independence. This event helped to convince European opinion that a criminal band of 'rebels' had imported terrorism from Tunisia.[63]

The French prime minister declared in November 1954 that 'one does not compromise when it comes to defending the internal peace of the nation, the unity and the integrity of the Republic. The Algerian departments are part of the French Republic . . . Ici, c'est la France.'[64] Significantly, that prime minister was the reforming socialist Pierre Mendès-France – the man who had ended France's war in Vietnam and conceded independence to Morocco and Tunisia. He was supported by his interior minister, François Mitterrand, the future president, who sent crack riot police to Algeria. The choice of the interior minister and the riot police rather than the army was a signal in itself that Algeria was considered an integral part of France.[65]

The war can be divided into three phases. In the first, the FLN tried to oust its rival, the Mouvement National Algérien (MNA), and take full control of the nationalist movement. Its main targets were other Muslims, who were defined as collaborators simply for not joining the FLN.[66] Their attacks in the coastal town of Philippeville were so savage as to shatter any hope of reconciliation between Europeans and Muslims. The great writer Albert Camus, who was born in Algeria, failed to broker a truce and warned Jean-Paul Sartre and other left-wing intellectuals sympathetic with the Algerian independence movement that the FLN had no respect for liberal enlightenment and instead was bent on installing an Islamic tyranny.[67]

In the second phase, across eighteen months from January 1956, the FLN launched terrorist attacks against Algiers, provoking the

government to send in the army under one of its toughest generals, Jacques Massu. He crushed the FLN in Algiers, but alienated
world opinion.[68] The third phase saw a general uprising of *colons* in
Algiers, who feared abandonment by the French government leading to independence. They inflicted savage violence on Muslims,
including women and children. The Fourth Republic collapsed
as the civil war in Algeria threatened to spread to the mainland,
where the *colons* had organised a secret army, the Organisation
Armée Secrète (OAS). Sympathetic elements of the regular army
and senior officers were unwilling to act against them. De Gaulle
was summoned out of retirement to take up position as head of
government with a commitment to a new constitution to replace
the unstable Fourth Republic. He too tried for a truce with the
FLN. When this was unsuccessful, he started a new military
crackdown to crush them.

The war now mutated into a brutal triangular conflict, with
the FLN, the OAS and the French army all fighting each other.
The OAS staged a short-lived putsch in Algiers which only
narrowly failed to ignite across France.[69] It instigated random
killings of Muslims in Algeria and terrorist attacks on Algeria
and the mainland. The Paris prefect, Maurice Papon, responded
on 17 October 1961 with a crackdown not against the OAS but
against the Algerian population of Paris, having already imposed
a curfew on 'French Muslims from Algeria'.[70] A peaceful public
demonstration against this turned into a bloodbath, demonstrators were massacred, some gunned down by armed police and
dozens of dead victims were thrown into the Seine.[71] To this
day, no one knows exactly how many died. The official record
for the day and night of 17 October, published the following
day, was three fatalities – two Algerians and one Frenchman –
and sixty-four police wounded, but today, estimates of the
dead range up to 300. Police pressure on French media ensured
almost no reporting of the massacre at the time, and for many
decades afterwards.

Papon was a notorious Vichyard and Nazi collaborator who, as police general secretary in Bordeaux, had taken part in round-ups of Jews.[72] He resorted to the use of torture on many occasions. One victim described being:

> stripped naked, some held my hands while others attached an electrically charged wire to my feet, my penis, my anus, and my back. Then, still naked, they had me drop to my knees. I stayed in this position for several hours, holding a chair above my head. If I dropped the chair, I was beaten with a billy club. This treatment made me vomit all night. Then they collected my vomit and made me drink it.[73]

Some policemen were *harkis* – the term for Algerians who were considered traitors by the independence movement for joining the French security services or assisting the French authorities.[74] During this period, policemen were often subject to violence at the hands of the FLN, which had begun to carry out its own attacks on French soil. Eleven police officers were killed between late August and early October 1961 before attacks were called off by the French Federation of the FLN. Bodies were found in canals with atrocities committed by both sides and the air thick with a desire for revenge. Speaking at the funeral of one police victim of the FLN, Papon told his troops: 'For every blow received, we'll give them ten more!'[75]

Nobody has ever been brought to justice for that October atrocity. Papon was finally convicted for crimes against humanity in 1998, but this was in relation to his conduct during the Holocaust.[76] Forty years were to pass before the authorities began to admit that far more Algerians had been killed by his forces on 17 October than previously acknowledged. In 2012, François Hollande became the first president to pay tribute to the memory of the victims, recognising a 'bloody repression'.[77] Five years later, Emmanuel Macron conceded there had been 'a violent crackdown'.[78] There has been no official apology.

New secret negotiations between de Gaulle and the Algerian FLN independence movement finally produced a ceasefire agreement and a referendum on Algerian independence in both France and Algeria, where it passed in March 1962 with heavy majorities. There were more months of terrorism by the OAS in Algeria – and atrocities against Europeans and *harkis* by Muslims who had kept out of the independence struggle but were anxious to demonstrate their loyalty to the FLN.[79]

Algeria became independent in July 1962 and, within weeks, some 350,000 embittered *colons* fled to France.[80] They were only allowed to take two suitcases with them, so many smashed anything they could not take with them to prevent it falling into 'enemy' Muslim hands and destroyed their remaining property.[81] They were followed by a million more – the nucleus of a right-wing movement which hated all Muslims.[82] The *harkis* were abandoned by the French government they had served and given no general right to go to France. Tens of thousands were victimised after independence, mutilated or murdered; those who did get to France were interned. The *harkis* and their descendants were even more socially isolated than Muslim immigrants in general, and the term has become an all-purpose insult to this day.[83]

The eight-year war (technically a civil war within Europe, bearing comparison with the American Civil War in its consequences for how history is understood and told) was the most destructive ever waged by any state against Muslim enemies. Algerian official sources put the death toll in Algeria at 1.5 million and French casualties at 400,000.[84] A more conservative recent estimate from Martin Thomas has suggested that at least 300,000 Algerians died in the eight years of conflict between 1954 and 1962.[85] Alistair Horne, the British military historian, made a calculation of 700,000 for his book *A Savage War of Peace*, published in 1977.[86] Algerian nationalists may have exaggerated to make the figures seem more heroic, while the chaos of war at a time when people were fleeing the country presents insurmountable difficulties to anything better than guesswork. The three main participants – the French state, the FLN and the *colons* – fought without rules or restraint, using terror and torture, unsparing of civilians and innocent bystanders, and treating their victims as inhuman. Its legacy endures and continues to influence France's relationship not only with Muslim nations overseas but with its own Muslim population at home.

Morocco and Tunisia

France's engagement in its other Muslim North African possessions, Morocco and Tunisia, was never as deep as in Algeria, and mercifully withdrawal was achieved with far less bloodshed. But the same basic French narrative applied: Muslims were a backward people expected to show gratitude for the blessings of French civilisation – and to be punished if they did not.

Neither Morocco nor Tunisia were formally French possessions, let alone part of metropolitan France, like Algeria. They were protectorates in which France acquired the dominant share through unrepayable loans and diplomatic horse-trading.[87] In each case, the French had to compete with a rival European power. They partitioned Morocco with Spain and sent a punitive expeditionary force to Tunisia on a flimsy pretext to forestall Italy, whose settlers outnumbered their own.[88] Against this background the Italian premier, Francesco Crispi, described Tunisia as 'an Italian colony occupied by France.'

In both countries, French rule followed a pattern of using a client ruler to mask French control of all essential government functions, especially taxation and defence. As in Algeria, European settlers grabbed land and businesses. Reprisals followed resistance, as in Casablanca in 1907 when the French took fierce revenge for the murder of some of their railway workers in a dispute which had started over the impious sound of a train whistle as it passed local Muslim graveyards.[89]

In Morocco, the French found an exceptionally able administrator, Marshal Lyautey,[90] who believed that Morocco, unlike Algeria, should not be annexed. He promised to 'offend no tradition, change no custom, and remind ourselves that in all human society there is a ruling class, born to rule, without which nothing can be done', meaning that his task was to 'enlist the ruling class in our service'. This vision was close to the British system of 'indirect rule', which Lyautey admired. Speculated by some to be a model for Marcel Proust's Baron de Charlus, Lyautey had genuine empathy with Moroccan culture – reputedly including the opportunities it gave him as a closeted gay man.

In the First World War, some 34,000 Moroccan Muslims enlisted for France, suffering terrible casualties out of all proportion with the numbers due to their use as shock troops in the front line.[91] After the war, a local Berber leader Abd al-Karim launched a revolt which ejected the Spanish from their zone and almost ended French rule as well. Eventually – and bloodily – the revolt was suppressed by joint action from France and Spain, led by the future Nazi puppet Marshal Pétain and the future Spanish dictator General Franco. Modern weaponry – such as aerial bombardment, poison gas, armoured tanks and cars – was used against the inhabitants of the Rif mountains in northern Morocco.[92] Bearing in mind that brutal background, it is surprising that when the Second World War broke out, 47,000 Moroccans joined the French army.[93]

After the fall of France, Morocco's severe French resident-general, Charles Noguès, remained in control for the Vichy regime, on whose behalf he sought to implement anti-Semitic race laws. The sultan, Mohammed V, aligned himself more and more with Moroccan nationalism and, through an ingenious legal stratagem, protected Morocco's Jews. He refused to sign off on the regime's plan to ghettoise and deport Morocco's quarter of a million Jews to the death and concentration camps of Europe. Despite his opposition, partial race laws were still imposed which pushed Morocco's Jews to the edge of society.[94]

The sultan and his people had high hopes from the Anglo-American invasion in 1943, which quickly overcame slight resistance by Vichy forces. As in Algeria, the Americans brought previously unheard of luxuries, together with the image of a successful (albeit still segregated) society. When Roosevelt travelled to the Casablanca Conference, he was thought to be a secret sympathiser with Moroccan independence, but Moroccan hopes were dashed when the Allies restored French control to their former zone in Morocco, displacing Franco's Spanish, who had taken advantage of the French collapse to annexe some territory.

The French presence in Tunisia was sparked by the catastrophe of the Franco-Prussian War of 1871, after which France looked for ways of restoring its shattered international standing. The French occupation in 1881 was initiated in part by determination to get ahead of the British and Italians. It provoked resistance, and 100,000 people fled to Libya (then called Tripolitania and still under Ottoman control) to continue the struggle, until they were distracted by the need to return home to harvest their crops.[95] A treaty signed in 1883 made the sultan little more than a French puppet.

At first, the French were more concerned with the challenge from Italy than from local Muslims.[96] Before the Great War, a group of young Tunisian intellectuals sought integration into French society, but they became more independently minded after clashes with the Italians and riots over the desecration of Muslim cemeteries by a French-built railway. Some went into exile in Turkey (which became an enemy power in the Great War) and the situation became tense enough for the French to maintain a sizeable army in Tunisia despite their losses in the war.[97]

During the 1930s, the small group of Tunisian intellectuals was split between nationalists, socialists and trade unionists, but local protestors united in 1930 against a tactless Catholic Congress in Carthage (wide open to interpretation as a Christian attempt to evangelise the country) and the following year against an even more tactless French celebration of fifty years of colonial rule. The French responded by exiling the leading nationalist leader, Habib Bourguiba. The arrival of the short-lived Popular Front government saw a brief thaw – and official talks with Bourguiba – but its fall in 1937 led to renewed repression. A general strike in Tunis the following year, plus a student demonstration, were met with a state of emergency, renewed banishment for Bourguiba and dozens of shootings.[98] Tunisia had to endure an Axis occupation and was the theatre of heavy fighting.[99] Some Tunisian nationalists collaborated but Bourguiba, in exile in Cairo, kept faith with the Allies. Like Mohammed V, he had no reward from them as French rule was restored in Tunisia on pre-war terms.[100]

The post-war path to independence in both countries followed a similar trajectory: brutal crackdowns by the French against protests which they attributed falsely to communism; the use of terrorism by French settlers and local nationalists; exile for Mohammed V and Bourguiba.[101] Eventual independence left the new states with specific grievances. Tunisians resented the continued French naval base at Bizerte and in July 1961, five years after independence, Tunisia attempted to reclaim it by force. Six hundred and thirty Tunisians and twenty-four French were killed in a brutal three-day battle. Though France's overwhelmingly superior firepower won the day, the port was handed back to Tunisia after the end of the Algerian war in 1963. Moroccans, especially Mohammed V, had to deal with the enduring status of Tangier as an 'international zone' and a seedy playground for remittance men and rich foreigners in search of drugs and Moroccan boys.

More important, the new states were poor, faction-ridden and were unable to fulfil the expectations of their peoples for a better life. Half a century after Tunisian independence, on 4 January 2011, Mohamed Bouazizi, a street vendor, bought a can of petrol and burned himself to death outside the governor's office in the rural town of Sidi Bouzid. This despairing protest against corruption, hopelessness and economic stagnation ignited the Arab

Spring. I paid a pilgrimage to Sidi Bouzid four years ago, and stood on the spot where Bouazizi immolated himself. Local people told me that nothing had changed and the outlook was even more desperate than before.

14

FRANCE'S COLONIAL LEGACY

France's colonial legacy is the backdrop to its entire relationship with Muslims. It explains the intensity with which the country's ruling class has demanded proof of conformity from French Muslims to the ideology and culture – and even dress codes – of the republic. It explains why a mainstream political movement, the Rassemblement National (RN), could openly promote an anti-Muslim agenda of a virulence so far confined to fringe parties in the United Kingdom.

With local variations, Algeria, Morocco and Tunisia followed a similar trajectory after independence. The hopes of their peoples for economic advance and representative democracy were especially frustrated; instead they endured large-scale corruption and repression. Wealth and power remained concentrated among francophone elites, who helped France to establish neo-colonial dominance over the new states economically, militarily and culturally. In Morocco and Tunisia, tourism brought new wealth but largely to foreign interests and the local elites, and turned thousands of people into servants, or colourful spectacles, or sexual playthings for foreigners. These humiliating conditions understandably increased the attraction of Salafist forms of Islam and militant movements to disillusioned people.

The rulers of all three states identified protests with an Islamist threat, in some cases accurately, but also as a means to enlist French and wider Western support, particularly after 9/11. Algeria, Tunisia and Morocco all experienced and exported terrorism, and their governments took fierce counter-measures.

North African Muslim immigration into France

In the aftermath of independence, hundreds of thousands of North African Muslims went to work in France, especially during its long expansion in the 1960s and early 1970s. Unlike in the UK, such immigration was not a new phenomenon: France had regularly imported North African workers to relieve labour shortages during the twentieth century.[1] As with British immigrants, many took low-paid jobs abandoned by native workers. Tunisians, like Indians in the UK, acquired a special reputation for opening shops and small businesses.[2]

In several important ways, however, the experience of North African Muslim immigrants to France was different. One was citizenship. In the UK, every Muslim immigrant was automatically a citizen, as a subject of the Queen. He or she became eligible to vote and take part in civic society after six months' lawful residence. This remained the position even after immigration itself was restricted. It is still the position today. In France, Muslim immigrants from North Africa were given the status of subjects but not citizens, even those who were born in pre-independence Algeria, which was legally considered part of metropolitan France. In fairness, this situation was encouraged by the post-independence governments of Algeria and Morocco, where floods in 1963 prompted large-scale migration. Both countries were glad to benefit from migrants' remittances but anxious not to lose their most dynamic and productive workers to permanent settlement in France.[3]

Secondly, France's Muslim immigrants had far fewer opportunities and incentives to acquire property than those in the UK. The first waves of immigration, almost exclusively men in low-wage jobs trying to send money back to their families, usually lived in *bidonvilles* (shanty towns) on the outskirts of French cities.[4] As France's need for labour increased during the 1960s and 1970s, French Muslims were generally able to move up to *banlieues* – purpose-built developments also on the fringes of large cities. As in the UK, these developments were thought attractive in the 1960s, but soon deteriorated in status, and became housing of last resort for people who could find nowhere else to live. The usual English translation for *banlieue* is 'suburb', but 'ghetto' might be a better term for conveying their physical and social distance from the main hubs of French life.[5]

Thirdly, the legacy of Algeria's independence struggle has endured, particularly hatred directed at the so-called *harkis* – Muslims deemed to have collaborated with the French. They found themselves doubly isolated, with many living in makeshift camps, accepted by neither the majority Algerian community nor the French state which had claimed their service.[6] As recently as 2021 Macron has asked the *harkis* for forgiveness and vowed recognition of their contribution.[7] These memories remain fresh and is a theme that will be returned to later when discussing Emmanuel Macron's interior minister, Gérald Darmanin, in the context of the Macron government's deep hostility to Muslims.

Islam as a threat to the French state

During the boom years of the 1960s, many French employers, especially coalmines, displayed considerable paternalism towards their Muslim workers, accommodating their shifts and working days to their religious needs. A manual for mine directors and managers warned them that 'religion is sacred to the Muslim. Do not make fun of it and while you may discuss it, do so only with workers whom you know well, for the Muslim . . . cannot bear any outside interference with it.' Some schools even allowed Muslim prayers, contravening the long-standing separation of

Church and State. This accommodating attitude disappeared in the 1970s and 1980s when the French boom ended and the labour market slackened.[8]

By the mid-1960s, there were more than half a million Algerians living in France[9] and about 200,000 Moroccans.[10] They were nearly all men, better off and better housed than they would have been in Algeria and Morocco, but poorly integrated into French society and dependent on their own social networks. The largest Algerian community in Paris was in the Saint-Séverin quarter in the 5th arrondissement.[11] Some benefitted from benign employers, but many more were often supervised locally by former colonial officials whose attitudes had been formed in the bitter War of Independence.[12] The term 'Maghrebian' (originally a neutral phrase to describe a person from the Maghreb region embracing Morocco, Algeria, Tunisia and Libya) came to be synonymous with 'delinquent'.

The 1970s saw a new pattern of immigration, of the arrival of entire families, but this started just at the moment when Muslim immigrants were hardest hit as the long post-war expansion of the French economy came to an end. Post-industrialisation left Muslim immigrants stranded without jobs and qualifications. Hundreds of thousands of them lived on welfare in the *banlieues*, isolated and generally despised by their French neighbours. Poorly schooled and with few outlets for economic advance, their children were unsurprisingly attracted to gangs, drugs and anti-social behaviour. Increasing crime provoked heavy-handed policing and filled France's jails with young Muslims.[13]

France's Muslim immigrants faced hostility and discrimination on ethnic and economic grounds. They were perceived as foreign strangers who were competing for jobs, housing and social provision with the majority white population. As in the UK, this gave way to hostility to them *as Muslims*. But this was expressed more deeply in France than in the UK, and across a wider political spectrum, such that any overt display of adherence to Islam can often be treated as an attack on the cherished secularism of the French state itself.

There were several contributory factors. Hostility to Islam was fomented deliberately by mainstream politicians, and not only of the right. It was fed by events overseas, beginning with the Iranian Revolution, and by regular outbreaks of Islamic-derived violence and terrorism, some from domestic sources and some exported to France from factions in its former North African possessions. In the late 1970s and early 1980s, the pent-up anger of immigrants in the ghettoes made its first impact on French politics. There were riots in the Vaulx-en-Velin and Vénissieux, both *banlieues* of Lyon, a notoriously right-wing city. In 1984, President François Mitterrand visited Vénissieux, promising that something would be done for them, even though the mostly young rioters had few specific demands and were expressing their general resentment at their place in the margins of French society.[14]

In March 1983, more than 100,000 North Africans marched from Marseilles to Paris to protest against labour discrimination, police brutality and hate crimes against Arabs and Africans. Formally known as the March for Equality and Against Racism, it was generally known by participants as the Marche des Beurs. *Beur* was a back-formation from *arabe*, formerly a white insult appropriated by its victims as a term of pride, rather as 'queer' was adopted by gay men. The French left generally assumed that the protesters were pursuing traditional 'progressive' goals. The right, although racist, were more accurate in identifying them with Arabs.[15]

The march was followed by violent car strikes led by Moroccan immigrants. The French right-wing press claimed that the strikers had been influenced by Iranian fundamentalists, but most of their demands were not faith-based and all had the endorsement of the Confédération Générale du Travail (CGT – the French equivalent of the TUC). French politicians played up the references to God in the strikers' demands, including three ministers in Mitterrand's Socialist government: Gaston Defferre (interior), Jean Auroux (labour) and Pierre Mauroy, the prime minister. Auroux said that 'when some workers pledge allegiance to the Quran, this stops being a trade union question', casting doubt on their loyalty to the French state.[16]

This was the period when Jean-Marie Le Pen's National Front began to shift from ethnic attacks on Arab immigrants to anti-Muslim rhetoric. Its first specifically anti-Muslim poster was used in 1987. It showed a minaret against a green background and an alleged Hezbollah quote saying that 'in twenty years, France will be an Islamic republic'.[17] This tactic had long-term consequences, opening the way to a coalition of left and right against Islam. The late 1980s saw a major rise in media and politicians' references to the principle of *laïcité* as the far right launched into a double attack on 'cultural Marxists'[18] and Muslims as fundamental enemies of France.

The year 1989 was a seminal one for anti-Muslim discourse from the right and some elements of the French left. It combined the bicentenary of the French Revolution, the fallout from the Salman Rushdie row in the UK and the 'headscarf affair'. Three Muslim girl students were suspended from their high school in Creil, north of Paris, for refusing to remove their headscarves,[19] provoking grandiloquent statements from two groups of mostly left-wing intellectuals, denouncing a 'Munich of Republican schools' and a 'Vichy' of concessions to multiculturalism.[20] In a crucial ruling, the Conseil d'État – the French administrative High Court – ruled that the wearing of the headscarf was compatible with the principle of *laïcité* unless it threatened public order.[21]

Thus began a protracted debate. Both right and left supported campaigns against veiling and Islamic dress for women, and in due course a new law against the display of religious symbols in schools.[22] Leading politicians on the left, including Manuel Valls who became prime minister, were as passionate in suppressing

Islamic identity (while simultaneously denying the very existence of Islamophobia[23]) as Le Pen and his successor, his daughter Marine.[24]

Civil war in Algeria

Back in Algeria, the FLN slowly squandered the political and moral capital it had gained during the independence struggle. Post-colonial Algeria was a one-party state, riddled with corruption and not helped by a political directorate out of touch with voters and hopeless at dealing with economic problems.[25] At length, liberal reforms led to the country's first free elections in June 1990. The winning party was one that had enjoyed legal existence for less than a year: the Front Islamique du Salut (FIS), in English, the Islamic Salvation Front. These were local elections where, as is often the case with Islamist movements, the FIS were admired by many Algerians for their honesty and competence when it came to running local government.[26]

Its co-founder Ali Belhadj[27] proclaimed his intention 'to ban France from Algeria intellectually and ideologically, and be done, once and for all, with those whom France has nursed with her poisoned milk'.[28] This meant shifting the language used in schools from French to Arabic. It also involved banning the sale of alcohol and insisting that women who worked for local government should wear the veil.[29] 'If the people vote against the law of God,' stated Benhadj, 'this is nothing other than blasphemy.'[30] The FIS comprehensively won the first round of national elections held on 26 December, 1991 and appeared to be on course to secure an absolute majority in parliament when the second round was held the following month.[31]

Two weeks later, the army cancelled the elections, installed the exiled independence fighter Mohamed Boudiaf as president of the council and dissolved the FIS.[32] This *coup d'état* condemned Algeria to a decade of conflict comparable in scale and barbarity to the War of Independence thirty years before. In France, the Algerian population in the *banlieues* began to divide on generational lines, as older people favoured the established order but younger ones were attracted to the FIS for its economic message and as a badge of identity and self-respect after years at the margins of French society.[33]

The FIS began to develop links with French mosques.[34] The Mitterrand government in France tried to head off the FIS both at home and in Algeria by a large-scale restructuring of Algeria's debt, but the benefits were largely wasted in corruption.[35] When Boudiaf began to deal with this, to tackle the Algerian army's control of the country's oil and gas, and in general to escape from the grip of the deep state, he was assassinated. Like so many such assassinations, it remains unsolved. Many pointed the finger at the army, although naturally they blamed the Islamists and used this claim as a pretext for further repression.[36] This in turn was met by a wave of terrorist attacks by a new Islamist coalition, the Groupe Islamique Armé (GIA), much more violent than the FIS and out of its control.

GIA violence spread to metropolitan France in 1994, with an air hijacking and the murder of a prominent imam who had acted as a go-between for the French government and the FIS.[37] The GIA planted bombs in the Latin Quarter in Paris (an area popular with tourists) and attacked public transport in Paris and Lyon, as well as a Jewish school in Villeurbanne. A terrorist mastermind, Khaled Kelkal, became a national figure when anti-terrorist police shot him dead on primetime television.[38] The arrival of terror in the heart of France had an enduring effect on the national psyche in many ways. In practical terms, it provoked a new security regime: the alert system, Vigipirate, remains in force to this day.[39]

When peace finally came, Algeria was numbed by horror and violence. Violent groups have pointed to the 1992 military take-over as proof that Western democracy is a sham; Western interests, say supporters of al-Qaeda, will never allow Islam to win an election, leaving violence as the only serious route to power.

Western policy-makers make an arrestingly similar case in reverse, as the US diplomat Edward Djerejian stated in a speech shortly after the Algerian coup. 'We are suspect of those who would use the democratic process to come to power, only to destroy that very process in order to retain power and political dominance.' Djerejian added that 'while we believe in the principle of "one person, one vote", we do not support "one person, one vote, one time".'[40] In fact, the 'one vote, one time' doctrine rule had been applied by Algeria's secular generals, not the FIS. The Western-backed coup which later deposed Mohamed Morsi, Egypt's first ever democratically elected president, added further credibility to the al-Qaeda argument. I will assess the Djerejian doctrine in more detail later, balancing it against al-Qaeda's analysis of Western democracy.

Back to mainland France

France's relationship with its Muslim population was poisoned further by 9/11, but even more so by the wave of domestic riots in fifteen French towns and cities in 2005, following the deaths of two Muslim boys in a police chase.[41] The riots' intensity shook France and provoked talk of a Sixth Republic. Future president Nicolas Sarkozy, still interior minister at this stage, promised to clean the 'racaille'[42] (the English translation is 'scum') and restored order with a heavy paramilitary response. Although politicians on both the right and the left blamed the riots on Islamic extremists, they had little to do with religion and were largely an expression of rage against the French state, especially the police.[43] Large numbers of rioters identified themselves with the Black struggle in the United States.[44]

Apart from heavy police and paramilitary responses to specific outbreaks, French governments went much further than the

British in attempting to regulate Islam itself. The first attempt was by Sarkozy who, in 2003, set up an official council charged with creating an 'Islam of France' (later, he would speak derisively of an 'Islam of basements and garages'[45]). This council foundered amid divisions over representation and disappeared in 2008.[46] In 2018, President Emmanuel Macron revived the plan, hoping to create a moderate domestic Islam to conquer adherents from 'foreign' versions. This also failed to gain traction among France's Muslims.[47]

In 2012, a rabbi, his small children and an 8-year-old girl were murdered in south-western France by an Algerian terrorist. The killer provoked special fear and hatred by his links to al-Qaeda and even more by his pride in his work as a 'soldier for God'.[48] The terrible year of 2015 produced the Charlie Hebdo killings, the Hypercacher supermarket siege, the attacks on the Stade de France (where the French national football team were playing against Germany) and mass shootings at the Bataclan theatre – all in and around Paris. On the very day of the *Charlie Hebdo* attacks, the writer Michel Houellebecq published his dystopian anti-Muslim novel *Submission*. It envisaged a national election in 2022 producing a coalition government led by an Islamist with ties to the Muslim Brotherhood. Despite the efforts of determined right-wingers fighting gun battles in the *banlieues* against Muslim Arabs and Africans, in the novel France submits to virile, determined Muslims imposing an Islamic society.

The French government responded to the real-life terrorist outbreaks in 2015 with a state of emergency that allowed the security forces to carry out raids, shut down private institutions and limit the movement of individuals. The new powers were used copiously but several thousand warrantless raids produced few charges. Despite this, most of the new powers were made permanent in 2017. The crisis also led to pressures on Muslim men in public service to become police informants or lose their security clearance.[49]

For all the violent history of France's relations with Muslim people, however, and inflammatory statements and policies from politicians of left and right, the French people have not shown themselves conspicuously anti-Muslim by comparison with other European peoples. Figures published by the Pew Research Center suggested that in 2016, 29 per cent of French people had an unfavourable view of Muslims – in line with the UK (28 per cent) and Germany (29 per cent), and well below Italy (69 per cent) and Hungary (72 per cent).[50] This may be why Marine Le Pen's sustained anti-Muslim campaign failed when her National Rally party performed well below its expectations in the French European parliamentary elections of 2019.[51]

In 2018, the Commission Nationale Consultative des Droits de l'Homme produced a chart suggesting that tolerance in France for Muslims had risen from 42 per cent to more than 60 per cent between 1990 and 2018.[52] The chart showed a sharp rise in 2001, despite 9/11, and sharp falls in 2005 and other years marked by Muslim-related violence in France, suggesting that the country's response to Muslims is governed by French events rather than world events.

Emmanuel Macron had campaigned for the French presidency as a champion of progress and diversity, and against racism, including Islamophobia.[53] He stated that colonies (including French colonies) were crimes against humanity,[54] and argued against the use of *laïceté* as a tool against Muslims.[55] Once he was in power, this changed. With Marine Le Pen looming as a threat in the 2022 French presidential elections, Macron ceased to fight her ideas. Instead, he adopted many of them, particularly after two murderous attacks by Muslims at the end of 2020.

On 16 October, a teacher, Samuel Paty, was beheaded outside the Collège de Conflans-Sainte-Honorine, in Paris's northern suburbs, where he worked. According to a report published by the L'Inspection Générale, Paty had shown his students the obscene caricature of the Prophet Muhammad published by *Charlie Hebdo*,

one of which had made the journal a terrorist target in 2015. Prior
to the class, which took place on 6 October, he had told students
that any student who did not wish to view the caricature was free
to leave. He was later the victim of an online campaign which
called for him to be punished. He was murdered by Abdoullakh
Anzorov, a Chechen born in Moscow in 2002.[56] A fortnight later,
three people were stabbed to death in a church in Nice by an
attacker who subsequently identified as Muslim.[57] The killer was a
Tunisian who had arrived in France a month earlier. Investigators
found on him a photo of the killer of Samuel Paty and Islamic
State material.

French Muslims were then caught in a crossfire as the Macron
government launched a crackdown against alleged Islamist
extremist organisations and strengthened existing laws against
any expression of Islamic identity in the public realm. The crackdown included deportations, bans on mosques and preachers,
and new powers to proscribe organisations for fostering Islamism
or separatism. The government also introduced jail sentences for
parents who home-schooled their children.[58] This was especially
directed at Muslim parents who sent their children to receive
religious instruction in private classes. Macron painted a picture of children arriving in windowless rooms where they are
welcomed by 'des femmes en niqab' who teach them prayer but
little else.[59]

Macron had previously described Islam as a 'religion in crisis',
one fundamentally at odds with freedom of expression and the
secular values of the French Republic. He revived his plan to give
France a state-recognised and state-licensed form of Islam.[60] This
was supposed to exclude foreign influence. No similar demand
was made on French Roman Catholics to repudiate the Vatican.
Macron insisted he was not hostile to ordinary Muslim citizens –
only Muslim separatism.[61] However, many felt that his definition
of Muslim separatism embraced normal characteristics of mainstream Islam. His government targeted well-accepted Islamic

practices, which included 'growing a beard' and 'attending congregational prayers during Ramadan'.[62]

The government asked the population to report suspicious behaviour to a 'Stop jihadism' call centre, including signs such as a new diet, a change of clothing, not listening to music or failure to watch TV.[63] This line became jammed with false reports on neighbours and colleagues.[64] Prominent French Muslims denounced Macron for stigmatising Muslims and predicted that his measures would increase Islamophobic attacks. Nagib Azergui, founder of the Union of French Muslim Democrats political party, accused Macron of making a direct link between all Muslims and terrorism. The atmosphere worsened further when the two leading campaign organisations, BarakaCity and the Collective Against Islamophobia in France (CCIF), were closed down.[65] There was no evidence either had broken the law, let alone advocated violence. However, they had been critical of the French government and had monitored French Islamophobia.

Marwan Muhammad, former director of the CCIF, accused France of 'weaponising its ideals and values as means of exclusion'.[66] He said that *laïcité* had mutated from a 'liberal framework for freedom of religion or belief, into a "neo-*laïcité*," an instrument for the demonisation and exclusion of any religious visibility'. Marwan explained that 'by placing under surveillance the whole infrastructure of Islamic institutions, including associations, mosques and sports clubs (with many Muslim members), Macron is seeking to strip Muslims of the possibility of genuine, grassroots and independent self-organisation outside the state's control'.[67]

The prime instrument of Macron's new hard-line policies was his interior minister Gérald Darmanin. From an Algerian-Maltese family, Darmanin's maternal grandfather Moussa Ouakid was a warrant officer in the French army, meaning that his grandson's background was *harki*, the Algerian term used for Muslims considered traitors for collaboration with the regime. Darminin was labelled a Judas in parliament by Marine Le Pen[68] for walking

out on Les Républicains (the current name for the Gaullist conservatives) to further his career under Macron. He returned the
compliment by accusing Le Pen of being too 'soft' towards Islam,
an accusation which shocked both Ms Le Pen and many political
commentators.[69] These remarks have opened up a competition
between Marine Le Pen and Emmanuel Macron over who could
be more hostile to Islam.

Clash of civilisations

The outlook of both Macron and Le Pen fitted like a glove with
the theories of Bernard Lewis and Samuel Huntington that there
is a clash of civilisations between Islam and the West, that the two
cannot peacefully coexist. For both Macron and Le Pen, French
citizenship means abandoning Muslim identity and embracing the
country's secular values. There is a dark contradiction at work
here. Freedom of expression (which encompasses, for example,
wearing a headscarf and praying in public), supposedly one of the
founding ideals of the French Republic, is increasingly denied to
French Muslims.[70]

Tellingly, Macron's assault on French Islamic organisations in
late 2020 was applauded by Arab dictatorships. The Saudi Council
of Senior Scholars and the UAE Fatwa Council issued rulings
stating that the Muslim Brotherhood 'does not have any link to
Islam. It is a stray group'.[71] Meanwhile, Macron awarded the
Grand Croix of the Légion d'Honneur to Abdel Fattah el-Sisi,
the Egyptian dictator who probably killed as many unarmed citizens at Rabaa Square as the Chinese authorities did at Tiananmen
Square, and who had locked up 60,000 political prisoners.[72] The
Saudi and the Egyptian dictatorships shared a common enemy
with France: political Islam. (This alliance between Middle
Eastern despots and Western critics of Islam, and their shared
analysis of political Islam, will be examined later.)

In Brexit Britain, Macron had long been an unpopular figure, owing to his post-Brexit position on fishing and other issues. But there was almost universal media and political praise for his approach to Islam, with *The Times* urging 'unqualified support'.[73] It declared the French government's plan to ban home-schooling and prevent foreign imams from training preachers in France to be a 'self-defence mechanism' for democracy. The *Guardian* accepted Macron's own dubious claims that he was introducing legislation 'against religious separatism'.

The *Financial Times* published a long, prominent letter from the French president which falsely claimed that there were French districts where 'small girls aged three or four' wear the full veil and are 'raised in hatred of France's values'.[74] Macron spoke of 'breeding grounds for terrorists in France'. This combination of inflammatory falsehoods and dehumanising terminology – which echoed the rhetoric of former US president Donald Trump – felt like the language of the far right rather than that of a respectable president in a Western liberal democracy.[75] Yet the *Financial Times* not only published Macron's inflammatory language, it then defended its decision to do so. Earlier it had published, then taken down from its website, an article criticising Macron by one of its own journalists, who was herself a Muslim.

There is no British tradition comparable to *laïcité*. The British Empire, unlike the French, broadly tolerated religious and cultural traditions, so British endorsement of President Macron's campaign against Islam demands explanation. The story of Islam in post-war Britain is the story of how, as in France, Muslims have become the enemy within.

PART FOUR

The Enemy Within

'Two new words have recently come into existence with regard to our politics, and they are Moderates and Extremists. These words have a specific relation to time, and they, therefore, will change with time. The Extremists of today will be Moderates tomorrow, Just as the Moderates of today were Extremists yesterday.'

INDIAN NATIONAL CONGRESS MEMBER
BAL GANGADHAR TILAK,
addressing the Indian National
Congress in 1907.[1]

THE COLD WAR ON ISLAM

Revisiting the end of the Second World War is crucial in order to understand contemporary Western policy towards Islam. The Soviet Union, the British Empire and the United States had won their great victory against fascism. It was a glorious moment for decency, democracy and freedom. But the coalition which defeated Hitler fell apart. As Winston Churchill declared in 1946, 'from Stettin in the Baltic to Trieste in the Adriatic, an iron curtain has descended across the continent' of Europe.[2]

This speech marked the beginning of the Cold War between the West and the Soviet Union, which endured for approximately forty years. With the fall of the Berlin Wall in 1989, liberal democracy appeared to have triumphed. The American political scientist Francis Fukuyama (a student of Samuel Huntington) proclaimed: 'What we may be witnessing is not just the end of the Cold War, or the passing of a particular period of post-war history, but the end of history.'[3]

Fukuyama was not quite saying that history in the sense of momentous events had suddenly come to an end. He was asserting that history understood as a conflict between the two clashing ideologies of individualism and collectivism had ended and that liberal democracy was set to dominate.[4] There were problems, however, in this analysis of the defeat of Soviet Communism as a triumph of Western modernity. Colonialism and empire had been at the heart of that modernity. For much of the world it felt less like a victory for freedom, and more as if one imperial power had defeated another. Within a few years, the West – in the sense of Fukuyama's Western liberal democracy – had found another enemy. Instead of a struggle between freedom and communism, it embarked on a struggle between secular liberalism and what intellectuals and politicians were beginning to call 'Islamism'. The new war started in earnest with the attack by al-Qaeda on the Twin Towers in New York City on 11 September 2001.

As with the post-war struggle against communism, only part of the war against Islamism has been disputed on the battlefield. The battle of ideas was at least as important. Western policy-makers were quick to realise that they could learn from the type of political warfare famously articulated at the outset of the Cold War by the US diplomat George Kennan:

> Political warfare is the logical application of Clausewitz's doctrine in time of peace. In the broadest definition, political warfare is the employment of all means at a nation's command, short of war, to achieve its national objectives. Such operations are both overt and covert. They range from such overt activities as political alliances, economic measures, and 'white' propaganda to such covert operations as clandestine support of 'friendly' foreign elements, 'black' psychological warfare and even encouragement of underground resistance in hostile states.[5]

Kennan was setting out, very effectively, a strategy of covert assistance to carefully chosen left-wing movements in Europe in the aftermath of the Second World War.

An important advocate of the view that the so-called Islamist threat should be fought with these methods of the Soviet era was the RAND Corporation, an American think tank with strong links to the US military and foreign policy establishment. RAND had started life after discussions in 1945 between the US Air Force, the Douglas Aircraft Company and scientists about the need to co-ordinate research and military strategy. It pioneered many of the programmes that powered the West's challenge to the Soviet Union. Its chief strategist in the 1950s, Herman Kahn, famously declared that a nuclear exchange between the US and the USSR was 'winnable'.[6] (Kahn is thought to be an inspiration for Stanley Kubrick's Dr Strangelove in his 1964 film.)[7]

Good and bad Muslims

In 2007, the RAND Corporation declared that 'at the beginning of the Cold War the threat was a global Communist movement led by a nuclear-armed Soviet Union; today it is a global jihadist movement striking against the West with acts of mass-casualty terrorism.'[8]

The corporation noted that the US had been regarded as a liberator in Europe after the Second World War, though not in the Middle East after the invasion of Iraq.[9] RAND nevertheless saw the necessity to counter the influence of 'radical Muslims' who 'have been successful in intimidating, marginalising, or silencing moderate Muslims – those who share the key dimensions of democratic culture – to varying degrees'.[10]

RAND despaired that 'liberal and moderate Muslims generally do not have the organisational tools to effectively counter the radicals'.[11] It concluded these 'moderates' should be given financial help and support. But it also emphasised secrecy:

> The concern that US backing would discredit democratic organisations was substantial during the Cold War, as it is today. Policymakers in the late 1940s and early 1950s attempted to avoid this pitfall by keeping their support secret. The United States funded the organisations through foundations, both real and fictional. Initially, only a limited number of individuals knew about the covert backing of the new democratic organisations, and thus they avoided the negative repercussions of US support for a time.[12]

The US would need to adopt the same techniques against 'radical Islam' by 'maintaining some distance between these organisations and the US government' and 'selecting prominent individuals with a great deal of personal credibility for leadership positions in the networks'.[13] This meant that the US would have to make delicate decisions about who to support. RAND explained that 'the potential partners of the West in the struggle against radical Islamism are moderate, liberal, and secular Muslims with political values congruent to the universal values underlying all modern liberal societies'.[14] Paradoxically, those very values celebrated by RAND were increasingly contested within the US across exactly the same period, as shown in Part One.

RAND recommended that the US should not focus its efforts on the Middle East, where it felt that limits to free speech and the strength of religious conservatism would make it difficult to influence discourse. Instead it advised targeting areas where 'the environment is more open to activism and influence, and success is more likely and more perceptible'.[15] RAND stressed that the US should support Muslim groups across North America and Europe, as well as in Muslim-majority democratic countries like Turkey and Indonesia. In other words, the US would help good (or 'moderate') Muslims and would oppose bad (or 'radical') Muslims. And much of this US support would be secret.

But which Muslims were bad and which were good? Who decided? In the post-war era, the decision had been relatively simple. The West supported left-wing movements unless they gave their allegiance to Soviet Communism. When it came to Islam, the decision was more complicated. The US and her allies were not fighting against a nation state, let alone a group of nation states. The enemy was al-Qaeda and like-minded terror groups. Yet Western strategists concluded after 9/11 that they were involved in a struggle comparable to the Cold War rather than conducting a counter-terrorism operation, such as the British had carried out in Northern Ireland.

This meant that, for the West, the category of 'bad' Muslims soon became very large. It did not simply include the tiny community of desperate men engaged in violent attacks on the West. Rather, it included any Muslim who did not subscribe to what RAND had called the 'political values congruent to the universal values underlying all modern liberal societies'. This had overtones of authoritarianism and turned countless non-violent Muslims into enemies. As a result, the US found itself leading a second war against collectivism. Liberal democracies had won their war against Soviet collectivism, but now secular liberalism was at war against religious collectivism. This had particular consequences for British Muslims.

Dusting down the Information Research Department

The RAND Corporation next asked how to conduct the propaganda struggle against so-called radical Islam. In its search for answers, its attention alighted on the Information Research Department (IRD), a creation of the British Foreign Office. Christopher Mayhew, a junior minister in Clement Attlee's post-war Labour government, wanted an organisation inside the Foreign Office that would use covert methods to dissuade nations from going communist. Ernest Bevin, the Foreign Secretary, was convinced. The Labour Cabinet approved the creation of the secret IRD on 4 January 1948. It would have close links to MI5 and MI6, and would promote 'the vital ideas of British social democracy and Western civilisation' and 'give a lead to our friends abroad and help them in the anti-communist struggle'.[16]

For almost thirty years, first from the Foreign Office and then from an anonymous address in Westminster, the IRD produced, promoted and distributed a huge range of material. IRD staff could not even tell their Foreign Office colleagues what they did. The IRD understood, in the words of the future British Cabinet minister Richard Crossman, that 'the way to carry out good propaganda is never to appear to be carrying it out at all'.[17]

The IRD fed stories to journalists from every major newspaper in the UK, as well as the BBC and BBC World Service.[18] It ran a network of artificial media agencies from North Africa to south-east Asia. It supplied briefs to ministers, MPs and British delegates to the United Nations,[19] and developed contacts with trade unions. It published magazines and literature through IRD-run publishing houses that could not be traced to the Foreign Office.[20] With the CIA – through the Congress for Cultural Freedom – it funded with some success the anti-Stalinist literary magazine *Encounter*, edited by former communists Irving Kristol and Stephen Spender.[21] By the 1960s, the IRD employed around 400 people in London and around the world.[22]

The Soviet Union had known about the IRD only months after it was launched since the traitor Guy Burgess had worked there before defecting to Russia.[23] Its existence was made public by the *Observer* in 1978, a year after it had closed.[24] In the 1960s, it contributed to one of the worst mass killings of the twentieth century when it circulated propaganda through the BBC and other media attacking the Indonesian Communist Party after a failed coup attempt. The Indonesian army then slaughtered up to a million political opponents in 1965 and 1966, atrocities partly fuelled by IRD propaganda.[25]

Half a century after the start of the Cold War, Western policy-makers concluded that Islam (or alternatively 'Islamism') posed a threat to the West as significant as the threat posed by the Soviet Union in the post-war era. They concluded that identical techniques to those used against the Soviets now needed to be deployed once more in defence of Western values. The Home Office approach to British Islam since 9/11 (and more especially the London bombings of July 2005) was based around an attempt to recreate a version of the IRD.

An officially approved discourse about Islam was constructed within Whitehall. Muslims were divided between 'moderates' and 'extremists', two deceptively simple and easy-to-understand words which have been used against Muslims to devastating effect. So-called moderate voices which amplified the government-approved message received funding and often access to mainstream media, above all the BBC. Those who challenged the official narrative were denied such access. Front organisations were created to promote government-approved doctrines.

All of this came from the textbook constructed by George Kennan for the struggle against Soviet Communism. There was, however, one important difference. Kennan's version of political warfare was patriotic combat on behalf of a unified nation (the United States) against a foreign enemy (the Soviet Union). Half a century later, his descendants in the British Home Office were devising covert political strategies that mobilised the idea of ideological struggle against those they considered internal enemies: namely British Muslims.

At the heart of these political strategies was Prevent, the counter-extremism programme introduced by Blair's government in 2003. It was not enough to target terrorists, the government believed. It was necessary to identify and seek to influence British Muslims who were vulnerable to radicalisation. Prevent served this purpose by targeting Muslim civil society, transforming the task of stopping terrorism into a broad social engineering project. Prevent was given a budget of hundreds of millions of pounds,[26] vast amounts of which were awarded to local authorities across England and Wales, with funding allocated based on the amount of Muslims in a given region.[27] A whole range of apparently grassroots Muslim organisations, meanwhile, were funded by Prevent to promote the government's narrative on terrorism.[28] Over the years, the Prevent programme has come to serve as the backdrop against which a cold war on British Islam has been waged.

The propaganda war against British Muslims

The UK's covert communication campaign was and is run by a unit inside the Home Office called the Research, Information and Communications Unit (RICU). It was deliberately modelled on the IRD. Like the IRD it uses bogus media groups to produce propaganda. Its output was (and remains) secret. However, painstaking work by the investigative journalist Ian Cobain at *Middle East Eye* has provided a glimpse of how state-backed organisations produce propaganda aimed at Muslims. Cobain has shown how RICU, set up in 2007, was initially little more than a shadow Home Office press department, providing Whitehall departments and UK high commissions and embassies with suggested reading material, such as press cuttings. Although the IRD has greatly diminished in Whitehall's 'folk memory', younger civil servants at the Home Office still read *Who Paid the Piper?*, Frances Stonor Saunders's thorough account of the cultural Cold War between Soviet Communism and the Western powers, which had become required reading in Whitehall. They realised that RICU could be remodelled on the IRD.[29]

This time around, social media was the preferred means of distributing propaganda, although film, radio, student freshers' fairs and house-to-house leafleting have also been employed. The underlying aim, according to documents leaked to Cobain, has been to bring about 'attitudinal and behavioural change' and 'measurable attitudinal change outcomes' among what are described as 'Prevent audiences', which we will come to below. Those Prevent audiences are defined in the documents as British Muslims, particularly males aged between sixteen and thirty-nine. The ultimate aim, according to the leaks, is to promote 'a reconciled British Muslim identity'.[30]

Previous information campaigns that were intended to change the behaviour of significant sections of the British public were usually acknowledged as being the work of government, and were no less successful as a result. In the 1970s, for example, advertising campaigns that were clearly attributed to government succeeded in persuading large numbers of people to desist from drinking and driving, and to wear seatbelts.

Within a few years of 9/11, however, the British government's relationship with its Muslim citizens was assumed to be in such a poor state of repair that subterfuge became the default way of doing such business. Employing psychologists, anthropologists, data analysts, intelligence officers, marketing consultants and digital media experts, RICU was soon producing some highly innovative messaging. This Is Woke, for example, described itself as a 'news/media company' engaged in 'critical discussions around Muslim identity, tradition and reform. It was in fact created by a London communications company, Breakthrough Media, under contract to RICU, as part of the covert element of the Prevent programme that seeks to influence the way in which Muslims think and act.[31]

A series of programmes were created for broadcast by local radio stations.[32] A documentary film about Muslim athletes was seen by around a million viewers in the UK and around 30 million globally. They were all under the impression that it was an independent production, when it was in fact a UK government attempt to reduce the chances of a terrorist attack on the 2012 London Olympics. Even the director, who filmed in Pakistan and Afghanistan, was unaware that he was working for the British government.[33]

RICU also infiltrated the charity sector. Help for Syria appeared to be an independent British campaign that was raising funds and aid for Syrian refugees during the civil war. It had a Twitter feed and Facebook page, and 760,000 UK households received their leaflets or, at least, within what RICU termed 'Prevent priority areas' – neighbourhoods with large Muslim populations.[34] Students manned Help for Syria stalls at freshers' fairs at dozens of universities, handing out merchandise that drew people to these social media feeds. Those students thought they were working for an independent campaign, but they were actually in the service of RICU, as part of a project designed to reduce young Muslims' desire to travel to Syria to deliver aid, as the government feared that some would return with terrorist intent.

There has been very little official acknowledgement of RICU's work, although in 2012, Theresa May, then the UK's Home Secretary, did allude to it when giving evidence to the Intelligence and Security Committee, the parliamentary body that provides oversight of the National Counter Terrorism Security Office. RICU, May said, was at that time 'road-testing some quite innovative approaches to counter-ideological messages'.[35]

The key to the success of this messaging has, of course, been secrecy. For propaganda to be effective, it must not be seen to be propaganda. And that has required an enormous amount of deception. RICU was performing a con-trick on the UK's Muslim population. One Home Office official privately justified this to a colleague of mine that 'all we're trying to do is stop people becoming suicide bombers'. But when the curtain was occasionally pulled aside a little thanks to investigative journalism, and the deception slowly became clear, the relationship between government and Muslim citizens became even more strained.[36]

Despite this, the British government is quietly very proud of RICU's work. It is a model that has been exported to dozens of countries that have taken steps to counter extremism, including Tunisia, Kenya, France and Belgium.[37] At one point, RICU was even attempting to persuade the United Nations to create programmes based upon its own work in the UK, telling officials in New York that it had begun delivering 'sophisticated communications campaigns that utilise audio-visual products on and at an industrial scale and pace'.[38]

The cold war on Islam has not just involved the state seeking to influence Muslim civil society. It has also turned Muslims into a suspect community. All Muslims are viewed as potential terrorists, and thus suspicious. This is best illustrated in the application of Schedule 7 of the Terrorism Act 2000, under which people can be stopped at the airport with no formal cause for suspicion.[39] In 2016, it was found that 78 per cent of people detained were ethnic minorities. Most of these people would have been Muslims. In 2013, the Equality and Human Rights Commission (EHRC) found that people of Pakistani heritage – who are almost all Muslim – were 52 times more likely to be stopped than white people and 135 times more likely to be questioned for over an hour.[40]

If you are stopped under Schedule 7, you can be held for up to nine hours and interrogated extensively. You may be required to hand over your digital devices, alongside the passwords to them.[41] And until a High Court ruling named the practice 'unlawful' in November 2013, you did not have the right to remain silent, nor did you have the right to a publicly funded lawyer.[42] In 2016, only 0.2 per cent of people stopped under Schedule 7 were actually arrested.[43] The number of people charged with a crime is even lower. Schedule 7 effectively functions as an intelligence-gathering operation which discriminates against Muslims and treats them as objects of suspicion. This is what the cold war on Islam has led to: the singling out of a minority within Britain and their subjection to high levels of scrutiny.

Careers for ex-Islamists

Just as the Cold War produced career opportunities for ex-communists, particularly through the IRD, the West's struggle against militant Islam produced similar opportunities. In the UK, the leading ex-Islamists were Ed Husain and Maajid Nawaz, former activists with the pan-Islamic organisation Hizb ut-Tahrir (HT), usually translated as 'Party of Liberation'. Founded in 1953, its central objective is to establish a unified Islamic state ruled by a restored caliphate, governed by Sharia law and eventually establishing Islam across the rest of the world.[44] It is hard to think of an organisation which more faithfully embodies Samuel Huntington's notion of Islam as set out in his 'clash of civilisations' thesis.

Banned in dozens of countries, mainly Muslim ones, the organisation operates in tight networks. Husain, Nawaz and others have described its methods of enlisting Muslims, especially students, in opportunistic confrontations with authority, thus mirroring student radical tactics of the late 1960s by engineering confrontations with college authorities. Hizb ut-Tahrir has frequently claimed to be a non-violent organisation, but critics have accused it of legitimising Islamic violence and terrorism, and serving as the first stage of the supposed 'conveyor belt' by which young Muslims are transported from radicalisation to jihadism.[45]

Husain first came to prominence in 2007 with the publication of a vivid and well-written memoir, *The Islamist*. It describes his life's journey into and out of political Islam. As a schoolboy misfit in East London, he was attracted to the local vanguard Young Muslim Organisation, but broke with it as a student at Tower Hamlets College in the 1990s over its neglect of the plight of Bosnian Muslims. He became an organiser for Hizb ut-Tahrir, which had a more universalist message of struggle for all oppressed Muslims, staging frequent confrontations with rival groups and the college authorities.[46] Husain broke with HT when such a confrontation resulted in the fatal stabbing of Ayotunde Obanubi, a Nigerian Christian student. He was appalled not only by the act itself but also by HT's denial of any responsibility.[47]

This concluded Husain's career as a radical political Islamist. The remainder of the book describes the rediscovery of the Islam he learned from his Bengali family: a personal relationship with God as distinct from identification with a global community in need of a universal government. The process was accelerated by living in Syria and, particularly, Saudi Arabia, where he saw

Muslims who were victims of racism and living in far worse conditions than in secular Britain.[48]

On return to England, Husain was horrified by the prevalence of forms of aggressive, political Islamism which he had rejected. The book concluded with a call for British Muslims to reject both political Islam and its attitudes to women, homosexuals and non-Muslims, and the prevalent British culture of aggressive hedonism by lads and ladettes.[49]

The book was so well received that it was a finalist for that year's Orwell Prize for political writing. The most favourable criticisms came from non-Muslim critics, including Melanie Phillips, author of the alarmist anti-Muslim tract *Londonistan*. In the *Guardian*, however, Riazat Butt suggested that Husain was 'happy to reinforce stereotypes' based on a very limited contact with Islamic groups whose methods had changed significantly since the 1990s.[50] The *Guardian*'s criticisms were unfair in that Husain could only write about his own experience and could not take responsibility for how others would interpret or exploit it. However, it is reasonable to suggest that Husain's subsequent career showed that he had more of a following as an ex-radical among the Western establishment than he ever gained within the Muslim communities he hoped to inspire. He became an adviser to former prime minister Tony Blair's Faith Foundation, then, in 2008, he founded the Quilliam think tank on extremism with Maajid Nawaz.

Nawaz was a more strident and assertive figure than Husain, both as a radical Islamist and an ex-radical Islamist. Like Husain, he published a successful account of his political journey, in 2012, titled *Radical: My Journey Out of Islamist Extremism*. It begins with him as a schoolboy lover of hip-hop culture, fighting back against 'Paki-bashing' and police prejudice. Like Ed Husain, whom he would soon meet at college, he was drawn to Hizb ut-Tahrir by its support for Bosnia's Muslims. Mentored by Husain, he became a successful HT organiser at Newham College and swept its slate to power in student elections. By his own account, he was far more deeply involved than Husain in the fatal stabbing of Ayotunde Obanubi, but it did not lead him to leave HT.[51]

Nawaz became an active recruiter and set up cells in the UK, Denmark, Pakistan and Egypt, where he was arrested by Hosni Mubarak's secret police and imprisoned for four years in harsh conditions with frequent solitary confinement and mental torture. He was adopted as an Amnesty International prisoner of conscience. Correspondence with an Amnesty International member, John Cornwall – and experience of the compassion of fellow prisoners of widely different politics and personality – led him to renounce HT and the entire notion of politicised Islam in favour of a personal Islam which allowed engagement in Western society.[52]

Nawaz publicly abjured HT not long after his final release and return to London in 2006. I first came across him around this time, shortly after he came back to the UK and was still a member of HT. He was good-looking, young and eloquent. I watched him speak at a public meeting to which I had been invited by HT's executive chairman Abdul Wahid, a doctor from North-west London.[53] Over dinner afterwards, he was amusing company. There was no hint, either then or during his fiery speech, of an impending change of heart.

His recantation resulted in estrangement from family and former personal friends – and even death threats.[54] Undeterred, Nawaz, reunited with his old friend Husain, set out to promulgate more liberal forms of Islam: 'we wanted less separation of communities and more involvement of Muslims in every aspect of society, to focus less on the differences and more on the similarities of cultures'.[55] It was Husain's idea to do this through a think tank and to attach the name of William Abdullah Quilliam, a nineteenth-century British Muslim convert, determined advocate for Islam and critic of British foreign policy who might have been horrified by some of the behaviour of the organisation set up in his name.

Even before the formal launch, Quilliam's founders were taken up by the then Labour government for their supposed insights into Islamic extremism and how to counter it. Later in 2007, the BBC news programme *Newsnight* one evening led with Maajid Nawaz's departure from Hizb ut-Tahrir.[56] This was quickly followed by a meeting of Nawaz and Husain with three of Gordon Brown's Cabinet: communities secretary Hazel Blears, Home Secretary Jacqui Smith and Foreign Secretary David Miliband.[57] The convener of the meeting would have a crucial influence over the fledgling organisation: Charles Farr, a former MI6 officer who was then director-general of the government's Office for Security and Counter Terrorism. (Farr, who died in 2019, was also responsible for setting up RICU.)[58]

When two early funders, from Kuwait and Egypt – the latter a surprising financial backer in the first place, given Maajid Nawaz's long incarceration – withdrew their support, Farr stepped in with money from the government's Preventing Violent Extremism programme. Maajid Nawaz was invited to testify before the US Senate and met President George W. Bush over lunch. He became a frequent panellist in public discussions in both Britain and the US.[59] Following the 2010 British general election, Nawaz was also invited to two meetings at Downing Street with the new prime minister, David Cameron, and claimed credit for much of the content of Cameron's speech at Munich in February 2011.[60] (He was not the only such claimant and my own strong impression is that a more important influence was the think tank Policy Exchange, of which more later.) This was the speech in which Cameron denounced 'state multiculturalism', distinguished between Islam the religion and political Islamism, and demanded a demonstration of loyalty to British values from Muslim organisations.[61] There were problems with the prime minister's speech. There was little evidence that multiculturalism had failed, while the distinction between Islam as a religion and political Islam had become unsustainable once

Cameron's government concluded that a new interest in religion was an indicator of extremism.

In 2011, the Quilliam Foundation was incorporated in the United States as a tax-exempt foundation.[62] The foundation's directors included Chad Sweet, who had been chief of staff to Bush's secretary of homeland security Michael Chertoff, not always a friend of Muslims. Sweet was also campaign director for Ted Cruz in his bid the following year for the presidency. Cruz's anti-Muslim stance has already been noted, and he was a regular supporter of the anti-Muslim activists David Horowitz and Robert Spencer, who was banned from the UK by Home Secretary Theresa May in 2013.[63]

The US Quilliam Foundation also formed eye-catching links with the Gen Next company, with whom it shared a California-registered address and the same principal officer – Michael P. Davidson.[64] Gen Next was founded by a billionaire, Paul Makarechian, whose family had amassed huge wealth in construction working on projects for the Shah of Iran and US military. He was a major Republican Party donor, particularly to candidates such as Mitt Romney, who took a tough stance against the shah's successors.

Under this patronage, Quilliam raised over over $800,000 from 2011 to 2013, much of which was transferred to Quilliam UK. Sweet, Davidson and Gen Next members also arranged for Quilliam to deliver 'radicalisation awareness training' and supply research to American government agencies, and for Maajid Nawaz to be showcased at a series of high-profile anti-extremist events.[65]

In 2012, Quilliam US formed an alliance with the right-wing Stuart Foundation, which had been donors to the anti-Muslim Frank Gaffney's Center for Security Policy. Quilliam US received close to a million dollars from the foundation over a period of four years and was its highest recipient of funds.[66] In 2013, Quilliam found another ultra-conservative donor, the Bradley Foundation, while the following year it achieved a notable coup in attracting funds from both the atheist Sam Harris and the Christian Zionist John Templeton Foundation.[67]

In 2012, Ed Husain was replaced as a director of American Quilliam, ending his formal links with the organisation in any country. His replacement was an investment banker, Darren Henderson, another senior member of Gen Next.[68] The following year, Chad Sweet was replaced by Courtney La Bau, another Gen Next member and a venture capitalist.

At the beginning of 2015, Nawaz and another Quilliam director, Usama Hasan, signed a statement published by the Gatestone Institute, calling on Muslims to 'reclaim' their religion from Islamists and extremists.[69] This earned a sarcastic commentary from Chuka Umunna, then still a Labour MP, during the Home Affairs Select Committee inquiry into counter-extremism.[70] Umunna suggested that aligning Quilliam with the notoriously anti-Muslim Gatestone Institute might explain why so many other Muslim organisations had lost faith in it. In reply, Haras Rafiq, managing director of UK Quilliam, professed ignorance of Gatestone's links to Spencer, Gaffney and Steve Emerson, the anti-terrorist 'expert' who had recently suggested that Birmingham had become a 'totally Muslim city', thus helping to launch the popular myth of no-go zones.[71] Rafiq claimed that Quilliam US and UK were separate organisations,[72] although Nawaz chaired both of them and Quilliam UK appears to have derived most of its funds from Quilliam US.[73]

The Gatestone statement was a sign of the journey Quilliam had made from a London-based Muslim organisation to one dependent on agenda-driven American money.[74] Criticism of such associations led to a windfall in 2018 after the progressive American organisation the Southern Poverty Law Center (SPLC) listed Nawaz as an 'anti-Muslim extremist'.[75] This went too far: he had, after all, remained a Muslim and continued to advocate for those Muslims who followed his recommendations. Appearing on the television show of the (seriously anti-Muslim[76]) liberal Bill Maher, he threatened the SPLC with a lawsuit. He elicited a public apology, an acknowledgement of his own and Quilliam's work 'to fight anti-Muslim bigotry and extremism', and a settlement of more than three million dollars.[77]

The SPLC had been slapdash. It could have asked instead whether the stance and methods of Nawaz, Quilliam UK and Quilliam US had contributed more to Muslims or to their detractors. Before that analysis, there are some important episodes to be explored.

Quilliam and Tommy Robinson

Back in the UK, Quilliam announced a notable coup at a well-attended press conference. Under its influence, the anti-Muslim campaigner Tommy Robinson (whose real name is Stephen Yaxley-Lennon) and his cousin Kevin Carroll had decided to leave their organisation, the English Defence League. (It described the EDL as an 'anti-Islamist' group, rather than anti-Muslim.) It quoted Robinson as saying, 'I acknowledge the dangers of far-right extremism and the ongoing need to counter Islamist ideology not with violence but with better democratic ideas'. It hailed his 'transition' as a 'huge success for community relations in the United Kingdom. We have previously identified the symbiotic relationship between far-right extremism and Islamism and think that this event can dismantle the underpinnings of one phenomenon while removing the need for the other phenomenon.'[78]

Robinson had made no such transition. He had abandoned the street-based EDL only to launch a more upmarket form of campaigning against Muslims, by forming a UK branch of the far-right German organisation PEGIDA, and campaigning for a halt to all Muslim immigration to the UK and the building of new mosques.[79] In this phase of his career, he became an icon of the international alt-right, if anything assisted rather than impeded by a series of prison sentences.[80]

Robinson embarrassed Quilliam in 2015 with the publication of his book *Enemy of the State*, by claiming that they had paid him and that the press conference was an elaborate stunt in the hope of eliciting a renewal of their government funding. Robinson took part in the Channel 4 documentary *When Tommy met Mo* with the political commentator Mohammed Ansar. At the time of filming the documentary, Robinson was thinking of leaving the EDL and Maajid Nawaz allegedly told him that, should he quit the group, he should let Quilliam know if he was interested in working for them. On this, Robinson said 'Quilliam wanted to be seen facilitating my exit from EDL and taking the credit for it'. According to Robinson, who was facing legal charges at the time, he struck a deal with the organisation: 'While I was inside, Quilliam would pay my wife's rent and help with the basic bills. In return, Tommy Robinson would be their poster boy.'[81] Quilliam conceded that it had indeed paid him several thousand pounds 'as an external actor, after invoicing us for costs associated with the outreach that he and Usama Hasan [Quilliam's Head of Islamic Studies] did to Muslim communities after Tommy's departure from the EDL'.[82] Retreating from its press conference claims, it said that 'Quilliam never claimed to "deradicalise" Tommy or "reform" him, only that we facilitated his departure from the EDL'.[83]

The episode reinforced suspicion and hostility to Quilliam among other Muslim organisations. Robinson himself cynically commented that Quilliam was even less popular among Muslims than himself.[84] Finally, from 2018 Quilliam and Maajid Nawaz attacked the concept of Islamophobia, particularly the version put forward, after long internal debate, by the All-Party Parliamentary Group on British Muslims.[85] Quilliam attacked the APPG definition for wrongly modelling itself on the International

Holocaust Remembrance Alliance definition of anti-Semitism, and for ignoring sectarian attacks by one body of Muslims against another. It ended – not for the first time – with some ad hominem attacks against its opponents. This might be considered a plea for a better definition, but elsewhere Quilliam argued against using the term 'Islamophobia' at all.[86]

Its prime arguments were that attacking Islamophobia precluded reasonable criticism of Islamic teaching (for example, on gays and women) or of Islam itself, and that it would give Muslim beliefs an immunity denied to others. Characteristically, it also suggested that recognising Islamophobia would encourage the wrong sort of Muslims to claim leadership of their communities.[87]

All of these arguments reinforced Quilliam's alignment with both secularist and neo-conservative critics of Islam.[88] Early in 2021, Maajid Nawaz courted more controversy with tweets suggesting support for conspiracy theories about the coronavirus pandemic and for Donald Trump's claims of fraud in the US presidential election.[89] Two months later, the Quilliam organisation folded in mysterious circumstances.[90]

A Cold War legacy

Quilliam reflects two aspects of the Cold War. Its founders, Ed Husain and Maajid Nawaz, illustrate the benefits of recantation. Both have enjoyed opportunities, especially in the US, which they were unlikely to have gained from a lifetime of moderation. Both were admired by Tony Blair, although by then this almost guaranteed that they would be rejected by a wide swathe of Muslims – 'moderates' as well as 'Islamists'.

Nawaz was adopted as a Liberal Democrat candidate in the 2015 general election and as a radio chat-show host by LBC. In 2016, the investigative journalists Nafeez Ahmed and Max Blumenthal challenged much of the narrative of *Radical*, especially on family issues, but this had little impact on the reputation of the book or its author.[91]

In 2015, Nawaz published a book jointly with the New Atheist and anti-Muslim polemicist Sam Harris called *Islam and the Future of Tolerance*. It was generally well received and reviewers accepted Nawaz's claim to represent liberal Islam, although *The Economist* was sceptical about his suggestion that liberal and conservative Muslims could find a common cause in defeating political Islamism.[92] At the end of 2018, the book became the basis for a television documentary in which the two men were joined by the anti-Muslim polemicist Douglas Murray and Ayaan Hirsi Ali.[93]

More importantly, Quilliam embodied a key practice from the Cold War: it was not enough to renounce ideas thought to threaten Western society. Renouncers were also expected to promote that society – and recruit others to its defence. Hannah Arendt had established a semantic distinction between 'former communists', who quietly abandoned their former faith, and 'ex-communists', who campaigned publicly against it.[94]

In due course, Quilliam became embarrassing for its government patrons. Too many British Muslims were repelled by the blatancy of its appeal for support from the British government and demand for recognition as its interlocutor with Muslim communities. After 2011, it received substantially less public funding.[95] In consequence, it became dependent on donors who lavishly supported anti-Muslim activities and activists. Understandably, this rendered Quilliam even less trusted by Muslims. Although Quilliam described itself as 'the world's first counter-extremism organisation'[96] it did nothing that I can discern to counter right-wing extremism in any country, barring the misfired stunt with Tommy Robinson. When I looked at the publications on its website (now closed), they were focused on aspects of Islamic teaching, or practice or culture, and not on combatting any manifestation of hatred against Muslims. Of course, if Quilliam had exposed and denounced far-right extremism, it would have been obliged to denounce some of its donors.

But a more sophisticated message was sent out by another organisation that paid attention to British Islam.

POLICY EXCHANGE: HOW A NEO-CONSERVATIVE THINK TANK DEFINED BRITISH MUSLIMS

In the wake of the calamity of the Iraq invasion of 2003, one might have supposed that the ideology which lay behind Tony Blair and George W. Bush's bloody misadventure would have been discredited. This has not happened. Neo-conservatism* has continued to set the parameters for a great deal of policy discourse, and its supporters have continued to occupy many of the most prominent positions in British (and American) public life.

There are a number of reasons for this resilience. In the UK, Policy Exchange, a London-based think tank, is one organisation which kept the neo-conservative flame burning. Though its public profile is small, it has exerted prodigious influence in political circles. In conventional politics, Policy Exchange was at first associated in particular with 'marketisation', an ugly word which describes how the disciplines of the private sector have

---

* There are many definitions of neo-conservatism. According to one authority, it is 'a school of political thought in the USA. Neoconservatism first emerged in the 1970s and is distinguished from other strands of conservatism by its approach to foreign policy, which holds that security is best attained by using US power to spread freedom and democracy, if necessary by force and without international cooperation. Many early neoconservatives were former liberals converted to conservatism by the perceived failures of liberal and multilateral foreign policies: as Irving Kristol (1920–2009), a prominent neoconservative thinker, famously phrased it, a neoconservative is "a liberal mugged by reality".' Edmund Wright (ed.), *A Dictionary of World History* (Oxford University Press, 2007).

been introduced into the education system and the wider civil service.[1] The think tank's most enduring achievement, however, has probably been the reshaping of government policy towards British Muslims.

To simplify a rather complicated story, the British government, police and intelligence services originally saw their job as enforcing the law rather than policing ideology or personal beliefs. Abu Hamza, the notorious one-eyed cleric who made no secret of his sympathies with al-Qaeda, provides a fascinating illustration of this approach. Hamza, who used his position as imam of the Finsbury Park mosque to preach violent jihad, was skilful at ensuring that his public pronouncements stayed just within the law. There was general amazement and surprise when his eviction was suddenly brought about not apparently by the British state, but by his own congregation, who locked the doors of the mosque against him. The Metropolitan Police were, however, involved in Abu Hamza's downfall. Its policemen built up close relations with the mosque's faithful and were unobtrusively stationed nearby on the day of the imam's eviction in case of trouble. This sensitive operation was a model of old-fashioned intelligence work and community policing.[2]

However, the Muslim congregation who threw out Abu Hamza themselves held views which many sections of British society would find offensive. The congregation included sympathisers with Hamas, the Palestinian resistance group. Probably without exception, they were hostile to the invasions of Afghanistan and Iraq, and were dismayed by the Israeli occupation of the West Bank and Gaza. Many worshippers at the Finsbury Park mosque held socially conservative views about homosexuality and women which, while by no means unknown among the Conservative Party membership, are no longer mainstream opinions in the modern UK.[3] None of these views bothered the Metropolitan Police. They were happy to work with the Muslim community for the removal of a figure who they rightly saw as a menace. They were eager to do so with the minimum of noise and disruption. The police saw their job as enforcing law and order, and not trying to enforce any special outlook or doctrine.

This kind of 'multicultural' approach lay at the heart of what was then the British way. As long as they obeyed the law (including the provisions of the 2010 Equality Act involving non-discrimination), immigrants were allowed to bring with them the traditions and customs of the countries they had left behind. This approach fitted in naturally with the national tradition of letting in dissidents and exiles from abroad, from the Huguenots expelled from France in the seventeenth century to the Jews who made their way to the UK as refugees from the Russian pogroms before the First World War, or later as refugees from National Socialism.

Karl Marx, scribbling away at *Das Kapital* in the reading room of the British Library in the middle of the nineteenth century, was one of the beneficiaries of this tolerance. So was Lenin, on the run from the Tsarist police at the start of the twentieth century. And so were many of a dazzling array of Jewish scientists, writers, artists, broadcasters and others who fled the shadow of Nazism before the Second World War to find sanctuary in the UK and make an enduring mark on the country's intellectual and cultural life.* This tradition of tolerance also embraced Irish Republicans during the Troubles. They were generally allowed to think or say what they wanted, as long as they did not get involved in violence.

From time to time, however, this tolerance has given rise to protest, with British Muslims today facing formidable criticism and authorities accused of being *too* tolerant. The influential book

---

* This group includes the philosopher Karl Popper, historians Eric Hobsbawm and Sir Geoffrey Elton, musician Hans Keller, biochemist Max Perutz and the architectural historian Sir Nikolaus Pevsner. Stephen Hearst, father of David Hearst, editor of *Middle East Eye* for which I write a column, is another among many. See Daniel Snowman, *The Hitler Emigrés: The Cultural Impact on Britain of Refugees from Nazism* (Chatto & Windus, 2002).

Londonistan,[4] by *The Times* columnist Melanie Phillips, painted a picture of London as a hotbed of jihadist agitation, the consequence of complacent domestic authorities who tolerated the presence of international terrorists, as long as they did not let off their bombs in the UK. Needless to say, many foreign regimes agreed with Phillips's depiction and complained that the UK was hosting trouble-makers who ought to be sent back home to face justice.

The think tank Policy Exchange dismantled the British approach of tolerance. Its analysts naturally agreed that the police should counter violence. But they disagreed profoundly with any tolerance of the ideas which (so they maintained) might become gateways to this violence. Policy Exchange's connections were second to none. It was set up in 2002, in the wake of heavy Conservative Party defeats in the 1997 and 2001 general elections, by a group of Conservatives who feared their party was destined to perpetual opposition. These were the self-proclaimed Tory 'modernisers'. They greatly admired Tony Blair, and had supported the Iraq War. These modernisers believed that their mission was to help the Conservatives copy Tony Blair's achievements in making the Labour Party electorally successful. Michael Gove, at the time of writing a senior member of the Boris Johnson government, was the first chairman of Policy Exchange. Later David Frum, the speechwriter who coined the term 'axis of evil' used by George W. Bush in his State of the Union speech in January 2002*, would hold that position.

When David Cameron ran for the Tory leadership after the 2005 general election defeat, he looked to Policy Exchange for ideas. The organisation – defined by the *Evening Standard* as 'the intellectual boot camp of the Tory modernisers' – helped shape

---

* Frum told me that he looked for inspiration to Franklin D. Roosevelt's famous 'date that will live in infamy' speech, made immediately after Pearl Harbor. He noted that Roosevelt used the attack from Japan to make the case for war against all the Axis powers of the Second World War. Private conversation.

his thinking.[5] At its heart, Policy Exchange spoke of a political philosophy which appeals almost as deeply to the Blairite or Starmer wing of the Labour Party as it does to David Cameron or Boris Johnson's Conservatives. Better than any comparable organisation, it has come to articulate what was rapidly becoming the philosophy of the British governing class in the early decades of the twenty-first century.

Policy Exchange and British Muslims

When the think tank was founded, it contained a 'Foreign Policy and Security Unit'. As far as can be ascertained, its publications focused on foreign policy, but displayed no interest in domestic 'extremism'. This changed overnight with the arrival of Dean Godson with the title of research director of international affairs in 2005. Godson, who had worked as chief leader writer for the *Daily Telegraph*, appeared to interpret his international brief as a mandate to generate domestic policy towards British Muslims. This should never cause surprise: the political right in the UK has a habit of discussing British Muslims as if they were a foreign policy issue.*

Godson came from a family with a tradition of interest in Cold War intelligence work, propaganda and covert action.[6] His father Joseph Godson was Labour attaché at the United States embassy in London in the 1950s and used his influence to promote the interest of the pro-US wing of the Labour Party. At one stage, he was part of a plot to expel Aneurin Bevan from the Labour Party.[7]

By contrast, Dean Godson's public profile is all but non-existent. At Policy Exchange, it was unclear who – if anyone – he

---

* For example, the backbench Tory MP Michael Fabricant used the phrase 'Anglo-Muslim relations' in a tweet, implying that Muslims are not English. When Labour's Naz Shah called for a debate on Islamophobia in the UK, Andrea Leadsom, then leader of the Commons, replied that Islamophobia was a matter for the Foreign Office. See Peter Oborne, 'Shawcross Prevent role is Tories' latest salvo in culture war against Muslims', *Middle East Eye*, 2 February 2021. https://www.middleeasteye.net/opinion/shawcross-prevent-role-tories-latest-salvo-cultur e-war-against-muslims

reported to. When Neil O'Brien (later to move to the Treasury as adviser to George Osborne and later still a Tory MP) became director of Policy Exchange in 2008, he told me that while he might have been officially in charge, Godson was outside his control, had separate sources of funding and that O'Brien left him alone, unable to influence what he did.

From 2005 onwards, Godson seems to have been on a mission to rip up the counter-terrorism strategy adopted by successive British governments. He promoted the new approach to Muslims through research papers, seminars and, not least, media muscle. In particular, he argued that methods used by the British state against terrorism – above all against the IRA during the Troubles – were no longer relevant. In Ireland, British ministers were happy to work with Catholic communities in order to isolate the gunmen and bring about reconciliation. They did not, as a whole, stigmatise all republicans as terrorists. Rather, their ultimate purpose was to bring all parties to the negotiating table and stop the killing.

Sometimes this approach was ignored, as when British troops shot dead thirteen unarmed demonstrators on Bloody Sunday, or when the Thatcher government prevented Sinn Féin spokespeople from appearing in the media. These were, however, exceptions to the fundamental strategy, one which sought to isolate the men of violence politically in order to encourage them to give up arms.

Confronted with the threat of terrorism in the aftermath of the 9/11 attack on the Twin Towers, the first instinct of the British state was to copy the Irish experience. The police identified leaders who they felt they could trust with links into local communities. They sought to draw these figures into British politics, inviting them on to public platforms and making public funds available. In this way, they hoped to single out and segregate those individuals with an inclination to violence while gaining intelligence about their activities.

Policy Exchange argued that this strategy was wrong because, so it claimed, the British government was not merely confronting terrorists. Something much bigger was afoot: a confrontation of ideologies. For Policy Exchange, the UK was one of a band of free states, led by the US, that were engaged in a mortal battle against a set of deadly foes dedicated to a project to destroy Western civilisation. These foes were called 'Islamists' and they subscribed to a murderous ideology called Islamism. Policy Exchange acknowledged that not every Islamist was violent. However, over the long term that was irrelevant: Islamism had to be fought and ultimately it had to be defeated.

Islamism, said Policy Exchange, is a worldview which teaches its adherents that Islam is a comprehensive political ideology and must be treated as such. According to Policy Exchange, its proponents believe that Islam must be placed at the centre of an individual's identity, as either the overriding or the only source of that identity. The Islamist outlook is one that essentially divides the world into two distinct spheres: 'Muslim' and 'the rest'.

Policy Exchange further argues that:

> it is this binary division of the world that makes accommodation between Islamism and liberal democracy so difficult. The individualism and pluralism that lie at the heart of the latter run counter to the notion of a discrete communal-faith bloc that must be preserved, and for this reason Islamists often reject liberal democratic principles. Muslims are therefore presumed to be members of a de-territorialised, globalised *ummah*, in which allegiance is defined through fraternity of faith alone. Islamists suggest that Muslims are under constant attack, and it is this perceived danger that drives the Islamist narrative of victimhood and grievance.[8]

There could therefore be no negotiation. Islamists could never accept democracy, the rule of law, political institutions or the nation state. They were governed by rival principles, which were derived from the Quran, the sacred text of Islam. There was therefore no point in bringing Muslims into politics unless they renounced Islamism, in which case they could be welcomed.

The above analysis explains why Policy Exchange rejected the counter-terrorism model used in Northern Ireland and elsewhere. The core aim was no longer just protecting British citizens against violence. It was also the assertion of what Policy Exchange claimed to be Western values against so-called Muslim 'extremism'. This grand battle of ideas demanded a return to the strategy of counter-subversion employed against the Soviet Union during the Cold War. My close reading of Policy Exchange publications has led me to conclude that Godson was, in essence, arguing that British Islamists should be isolated, never embraced and treated as suspect. Godson set about his work at Policy Exchange with relish, with a gift for organisation and was sometimes capable of unleashing tremendous charm.

A portrait of Dean Godson

Twenty years ago I would attend the *Telegraph* leader conference. Godson, as chief leader writer, held court. He was a good mimic, an art he used to mock or denigrate political opponents or, if feeling cheerful, merely to entertain. He welcomed acolytes, but I took the liberty of challenging Godson. That evening I received a message through a mutual friend, who had arranged a dinner so that we could get to know each other better ('You and Dean would get on so well'), that Godson was offended and no longer wanted to come across me socially.* He was as good as his word.

---

* Our intermediary was the late Frank Johnson. He was then *Telegraph* political sketch-writer and had been editor of *The Spectator*. I attended *Telegraph* leader conferences during and immediately after the 2001 general election campaign. Godson hailed the 2001 result, when the Blair government secured a majority of 167 seats, as a success for Tory leader William Hague. When I asked why, Godson pointed to the sole Tory gain of Andrew Rosindell, who campaigned with a Union Jack-clad bulldog, in Romford, as evidence. Godson did not relish my mockery.

Godson is, I suspect, devoid of personal ambition. He put his heart and mind into causes, ranking them ahead of careerist considerations. In this way, he exemplified the remark by President Ronald Reagan that there is no limit to what you can achieve as long as you don't mind who gets the credit.[9] After graduating from Cambridge University, Godson worked as a researcher for the Tory MP Ray Whitney, a former army officer and diplomat. Whitney remained in obscurity for most of his career as an MP. Before that, however, he held roles in a number of Cold War propaganda organisations, including being director of the Information Research Department, the secret Whitehall predecessor to RICU. While I have no idea whether or how directly Whitney influenced Godson, it seems likely, given Policy Exchange's position on counter-subversion techniques.

Godson reportedly then worked for the shadowy Institute for European Defence and Strategic Studies, another Cold War organisation with which Whitney was connected.[10] He was then reportedly employed as assistant to John Lehman, US navy secretary under Reagan, before joining business tycoon and Referendum Party creator Sir James Goldsmith as Librarian, a reassuringly old-fashioned title.[11]

Godson joined Conrad Black's *Daily Telegraph* in the early 1990s, a period spent mainly as chief leader writer, a position he occupied for almost a decade under the editorship of his friend Charles Moore. He was simultaneously, under the editorship of Boris Johnson, associate editor at *The Spectator*. Once again we found ourselves colleagues. At *The Spectator*, as at the *Daily Telegraph*, I found that Godson was sensitive to criticism. He departed one weekly leader conference early after I once again challenged his views, never to be seen again, at least not by me.

Godson left the *Daily Telegraph* soon after his patron Conrad Black was forced to resign as chairman of the holding company, Hollinger International, in the wake of the allegations of financial wrongdoing that later caused him to go to jail. The *Daily Telegraph*'s then editor Martin Newland told the *Guardian*:

> I soon came to recognise we were speaking a language on geopolitical events and even domestic events that was dictated too much from across the Atlantic. It's OK to be pro-Israel, but not to be unbelievably pro-Likud Israel; it's OK to be pro-American but not look as if you're taking instructions from Washington. Dean Godson and Barbara Amiel [Conrad Black's wife] were key departures.[12]

A survey of his work at Policy Exchange suggests Godson had three objectives. First, he sought to weaken – or, better still, wreck – the alliance between the British left and British Muslim organisations. This he did by portraying Islamism as an outlandish far-right movement, with features in common with fascism. Secondly, Policy Exchange sought to challenge multiculturalism both as an idea and, more especially, as a basis for government policy. Above all, Godson was determined to break the link between so-called Islamist movements and the British state.

Godson was successful in all these objectives. His excellent Whitehall and Westminster connections may well have helped. These connections endure. Policy Exchange can whistle up a Cabinet minister for an event, an op-ed in a newspaper or access to Downing Street, while its authors are sought as experts on Islam on radio and television. The organisation's reports tell the Conservative Party exactly what its leaders want to hear. At least six special advisers in the Boris Johnson government previously worked for Policy Exchange.[13]

Godson's first publication for Policy Exchange targeted British government collaboration with what was coming to be termed 'radical Islam'.[14] The author, Martin Bright, was a left-leaning journalist and then political editor of the *New Statesman*. This in itself sent out the important message that Policy Exchange worked with both political persuasions.[15] Bright's analysis was based on leaked material, courtesy of a Foreign Office source alarmed at the government's relationship with Muslim organisations both in the UK and overseas. 'It depresses me deeply,' wrote Bright, 'that a Labour government has been prepared to rush so easily into the arms of the representatives of a reactionary, authoritarian brand of Islam, rather than look to real grassroots moderates as allies.'[16]

Bright's document took aim at two targets: the Muslim Brotherhood and the Muslim Council of Britain. A detailed examination of the Muslim Brotherhood will follow when analysing British policy towards Islamic countries, showing that it is in the invidious position of being feared by Arab dictatorships across the Persian Gulf and North Africa, as well as being despised by terrorist movements such as al-Qaeda. The Muslim Brotherhood formed the nearest thing that existed to a democratic opposition in many countries, which explains why it needed to operate underground when confronting dictatorships. Policy Exchange (and Martin Bright) present the Muslim Brotherhood as an Islamist movement guilty of propagating a dangerous ideology at odds with the West.[17] As for the Muslim Council of Britain, that was condemned as guilty of being Islamist too. Bright's document was an important blow in a campaign which would eventually lead to the severing of relations between the British government and the MCB.[18] Policy Exchange can claim a large part of the credit.

Godson was an acute talent-spotter. Munira Mirza wrote his second publication and later worked with Boris Johnson when he was mayor of London, before moving to the crucial role of head of the Downing Street policy unit. Mirza demanded an end to 'institutional attacks on Britain and its culture',[19] arguing that 'the preoccupation with Muslim vulnerability and Islamophobia has skewered our understanding of why such problems exist, and in many ways, has made things worse for Muslims.'[20] Mirza asserted that this reflected a 'victim mentality' which was 'given social credence by institutions, politicians, the media and lobby groups'.[21] Her report also claimed Islamophobia has been 'exaggerated' by some British Muslims.[22] Policy Exchange has a long history of questioning the idea of Islamophobia and has a record of recruiting members of minority groups to do the questioning.*

One project went wrong. Godson commissioned Denis MacEoin, a writer of crime fiction and ghost stories, to examine literature sold in mosques and other Islamic institutions. The result was the publication *The Hijacking of British Islam: How Extremist Literature is Subverting Mosques in the UK*. Policy Exchange claimed to have sent researchers to scores of Muslim institutions 'to determine the extent to which literature inculcating Muslim separatism and hatred of nonbelievers was accessible in those institutions'. The results were splashed across the front pages of many national newspapers.[23]

However, when Policy Exchange gave *Newsnight* the receipts for this 'hate literature', rather than join in the media outcry, the programme examined them. Careful inspection suggested that some had been fabricated. Charles Moore, then chairman of Policy Exchange, responded with an article in the *Daily Telegraph*, writing: 'I find it repellent that the might of the BBC is deployed to threaten and bully a charity in this way.'[24] However, the former *Telegraph* editor showed no balancing concern for the reputation of the Muslim organisation which had been attacked. Eventually, Policy Exchange removed the report from its website and published the following statement:

> In this report, we state that Al-Manaar Muslim Cultural Heritage Centre is one of the Centres where extremist literature was found. Policy Exchange accepts the Centre's

---

* The broadcaster and former chair of the Equality and Human Rights Commission, Trevor Phillips, has published a number of reports for Policy Exchange attacking the term.

assurances that none of the literature cited in the Report has ever been sold or distributed at the Centre with the knowledge or consent of the Centre's trustees or staff, who condemn the extremist and intolerant views set out in such literature. We are happy to set the record straight.'[25]

The invention of non-violent extremism

In 2009, Policy Exchange published a report which explicitly presented the demand for the British state to apply to British Muslims the same counter-subversion regime used against trade unionists, socialists and others during the Cold War. This well-written and powerful polemic probably represents – more explicitly than any other Policy Exchange publication – the full Godson agenda. It was written by two Cambridge scholars. Martyn Frampton was a fellow of Peterhouse, the high Tory Cambridge college.[26] His co-author Shiraz Maher was a former member of Hizb ut-Tahrir, having worked for the organisation as a regional officer in the north-east of England.[27]

Maher therefore fitted – like Ed Husain and Maajid Nawaz, the two founders of Quilliam – into the category of former Islamist who had seen the light. In a personal article about his renunciation of Islamism in 2007, he acknowledged Husain's guidance: 'When I met him, Ed's first words, breaking their way through a beaming smile, were: "It feels like I've known you for years." Immediately our stories resonated with remarkable familiarity.'[28]

Frampton and Maher's report called for the government to reinstate the 1989 Security Service Act, which would give MI5 the power to investigate subversion. As far as the British government was concerned, this involved a giant conceptual leap. The 'Preventing Violent Extremism' initiative was rebranded as, simply, 'Preventing Extremism'.

This was also a profound change of policy because it implied that the state should target not just violence but opinion as well.

It criticised the government for 'stressing law enforcement and strict security concerns over and above everything else'. Instead, it should deal with 'non-violent radicals' who were 'indoctrinating young people with an ideology of hostility to Western values'. This was an explicit call for the British state to carry out political counter-subversion using the Cold War model. Policy Exchange in this way urged that with Islamists the UK should abandon the strategy of engagement used during the Troubles in Northern Ireland with republicans. Instead, it should learn from the Cold War: 'The intelligence services need to recover some of their intellectual inheritance in relation to developing a definition of "subversion" fit for the challenges of the twenty-first century.'[29]

In other words, Policy Exchange wanted to create a new relationship between the British state and Muslims. This project meant creating a different kind of British citizenship. It led to a new concept in British public discourse: non-violent extremism. Policy Exchange was urging that Muslims should be obliged to sign up to a set of beliefs that fell within a state prescribed remit. In order to become British, Muslims were being asked to deny, or at least modify, their own identity and heritage. Until that moment, British citizens had generally been allowed to think and conduct themselves as they wanted, as long as they stayed within the law. The invention of the concept of non-violent extremism meant citizens could now be harassed, put on secret lists or barred from public life for offences which they often did not even know they had committed. It lies at the heart of the Prevent doctrine.

We have seen how Prevent was used to fund organisations that would promote the government line on terrorism and extremism. But there was another component to the programme, which the Cameron government adapted to target 'non-violent extremism' rather than just violent extremism. In 2015, Prevent became a legal duty for public sector institutions – including hospitals, schools, and universities.[30] Under Prevent, public sector workers were and are (at the time of writing) expected to report anyone they suspect of extremism to the programme. If the person reported is then deemed by a 'Prevent Panel' to be an extremist, they are referred to 'Channel', a governmental deradicalisation programme.

Extremism, according to the government, constitutes 'vocal or active opposition to British values'.[31] This means that people whose views may be mainstream or illiberal, but certainly not illegal, can be targeted as a threat to British society.

In a school context, Prevent demands that any teacher who suspects a pupil of having been radicalised must report them to the programme. The policy has failed at the crucial test of effectiveness. From April 2020 to March 2021, 86 per cent of referrals to the programme were false positives – representing people who were wrongly referred.[32] Prevent only occasionally catches the people that it wants to. Even these individuals, however, have never committed a crime. There is, moreover, no evidence that they will ever commit a crime in the future, or that they would have committed a crime were it not for being identified by Prevent. Government statistics, meanwhile, do not illuminate the full picture: there are thousands of cases within schools, universities and hospitals where innocent people, often children, are needlessly interrogated and harassed over suspected extremism. Their cases are dismissed before being officially referred to Prevent and are left out of the official statistics.[33]

Muslims are disproportionately affected by the policy, which relies on profiling. Over 70 per cent of Muslims in England and Wales live in 'Prevent Priority Areas' (PPAs), compared with just over 30 per cent of the general population.[34] By requiring public sector workers to report people they find suspicious, moreover, Prevent effectively compels them to act on their prejudices.[35] It makes Muslims subject to majoritarian biases, with results that are often darkly comical.

In 2016, at a school in East London, an 8-year old boy wore

a T-shirt to school displaying the words 'I want to be like Abu Bakr al-Siddique', referring to the famous companion of the Prophet Muhammad. His schoolteachers mistook the slogan for a reference to Abu Bakr al-Baghdadi, at that time the notorious leader of the terrorist group Islamic State, and reported him to Prevent.[36] This is only one example of many. In 2015, a 14-year old Muslim pupil in North London who mentioned 'ecoterrorism' in a French lesson was pulled out of class a few days later and asked whether he was affiliated with Islamic State.[37] And in 2020, students at De Montfort University in Leicester had their academic essays read by counter-terror police without their knowledge.[38]

The development of the concept of extremism, pushed by think tanks like Policy Exchange, has had a material impact on the lives of ordinary British Muslims, pressuring them to assimilate by downplaying their distinctiveness from other Britons.

The idea of non-violent extremism thus brought with it a particular conception of national belonging: if foreigners wanted to become British, why shouldn't they be like Britons? But this wasn't a British logic. This country has always had a generous and capacious identity. You can be British at the same time as being Welsh, Jamaican, Cornish, Black, Jewish, Hindu, Muslim or Scottish.[39] You can be both British and a member of the Scottish National Party or Plaid Cymru, both of which advocate the break-up of the UK itself. The biggest problem is that nobody can be certain who is – or who is not – a non-violent extremist. That is why all attempts to establish a legally secure definition have so far failed. Ironically, though, opinion polls have shown that Muslims have a higher adherence to values deemed to be British than other sections of the population.[40]

Policy Exchange's proposals have shifted the UK towards an American model of citizenship where, as we have seen, new arrivals are expected to abandon old identities and join a common melting pot. Policy Exchange's project to save Britishness was therefore also an attempt to destroy it. Policy Exchange could not have won its argument without powerful allies. The most important of these was the Conservative Party, as we shall see in the next chapter.

THE CONSERVATIVE PARTY
AND BRITISH ISLAM

During the first two decades of the twenty-first century, the British Conservative Party mutated. I watched this happen first-hand. When I arrived at Westminster as a reporter in 1992, the Conservative Party could boast that it was the most successful and enduring political organisation in the Western world, having been a frequent party of government ever since its conception in the early nineteenth century. Caution, scepticism and pragmatism were the secret to its success. The party supported the British welfare state and membership of the European Union, though in neither case with much enthusiasm.

The then prime minister, John Major, and the Foreign Secretary, Douglas Hurd, were doctrinally opposed not so much to foreign intervention (as is sometimes asserted) as to grand schemes to change the world. Major and Hurd supported the first Gulf War, but were only ready to drive Saddam Hussein's army out of Kuwait. Thereafter, they refused to get involved in regime change in Iraq itself. One famous critic (Michael Gove) called the Major years the 'weightless decade'.[1] For example, he accused the government of failing to avert the bloodshed in the Balkans and of giving in to the IRA in the Northern Irish peace process.[2]

This type of conservatism slowly died, or at any rate went into abeyance, after the general election calamity of 1997. By the turn of the century, the Conservative Party appeared to have run out of steam. This reflected puzzling changes in society that it couldn't cope with. Above all, it was suffering a collapse in its membership base. After the Second World War, the party could boast 2.8 million members, or approximately one in ten of the British adult voting population. By the time David Cameron became prime minister in 2010, party membership had collapsed to less than 200,000.[3] This meant that the party had lost much of its connection to civil society and was increasingly controlled by donors and special interest groups, a process which was accepted and even welcomed by Cameron and the clique that surrounded him.

Cameron and his allies modelled themselves not on the traditional Tory leadership, but on Tony Blair and his fellow New Labour modernisers who had positioned themselves in opposition to the traditional Labour Party. Cameron's chief strategist and Chancellor, George Osborne, boasted to his friends 'how easily we have taken over the party'.[4] This phrase suggests that for Osborne there was nothing especially valuable in itself about the Conservative Party and its history, tradition and civic importance. It was a vehicle for his personal ambition.

This state of affairs was hidden, in part because of David Cameron. Educated at Eton, married into the landed aristocracy and a member of White's, the London gentlemen's club where his stockbroker father was chairman, he had the hallmarks of an old-fashioned establishment grandee along the lines of Harold Macmillan or Rab Butler. This background was not misleading and many of David Cameron's instincts were Tory. But he was simultaneously – thanks to one of those paradoxes which are admittedly entirely characteristic of the British governing class – a member of a fluid international and financial elite.

It's helpful to compare the young David Cameron to the emergent George W. Bush. Before he entered the White House, Bush rarely seemed troubled by thoughts about anything much. This may have been one of the reasons the US electorate warmed to him. Once in office, however, he was quickly captured by a clique led by his vice president Dick Cheney. It was the same with Cameron. His chief strategist, George Osborne, and his ideologist,

Michael Gove, intellectually dominated the young Tory leader. Their views came from the right wing of the Republican Party; in terms of power politics, this was logical. New Labour was dominant in the UK, while left-wing parties were ascendant in Europe. So it made sense for ambitious young Conservatives like Osborne and Gove to seek to emulate Republican success in the US. Certainly, they gave the impression that they thought things had been done better there. They had been supporters of the Iraq invasion, which they regarded as virtuous. Osborne dramatically told the Commons that Bush was 'an intelligent and thoughtful politician and is surrounded by some of the wisest advisers ever to be assembled in an American administration'.[5]

Political journalists labelled the Osborne Tories as 'modernisers'. It is true they were young, metropolitan, well connected and (for a while) fashionable. But this label did not tell the full story. These young Tories had become adherents to a new and influential world-view: neo-conservatism. This is a term which needs to be treated with caution because it sounds as if it is an up-to-date way of talking about conservatism. It is actually nothing of the sort. It is more accurate to think of neo-conservatism as the *opposite* of conservatism.

Traditional conservatives are suspicious of change. They like long-established ways of doing business and ancient institutions, which they view as embodying wisdom. They hold a pessimistic view of human attempts to influence world events, which makes them sceptical of dramatic or sweeping reform. Neo-conservatives, on the other hand, seek to transform the world. They believe human nature is malleable and can be created afresh. This optimistic view explains their disastrous belief that they can export their democratic ideals into foreign lands.[6]

For these reasons, neo-conservatism demands a completely different type of statecraft. Traditional conservatism puts special importance on due process. It cherishes the rule of law, truth-telling, accuracy. Neo-conservatives have no special respect for any of these things. They believe they are fighting for a great cause which justifies all kinds of rule-breaking, including deceit, assassination, torture and arbitrary arrest. This is the most important difference between conservatism as traditionally practised in Britain and expounded by Conservative philosophers from Burke to Oakeshott, and neo-conservatism as imported from the US.

It sounds paradoxical that neo-conservatism shares with Marxism the murderous dogma that the end justifies the means. This paradox can perhaps be explained in part by the fact that neo-conservatism sprang from Marxist origins and retains to this day a Marxist disdain for the compromises, pragmatism and bourgeois notions of decency.[7] Though neo-conservatives hail from the right, they nonetheless have a great deal in common with Marx in the sense that they want to tear up the world and begin again.

David Cameron evolved from traditional Tory to revolutionary neo-conservative over the course of his leadership. In his early years as Conservative leader, he worked closely with Muslims, took a generally optimistic view of Islam and spoke up for Muslim causes. He saw this as part of the modernising project. He claimed that the Israeli blockade had turned the Gaza Strip into a 'prison camp'.[8] His foreign affairs spokesman William Hague also criticised the Israeli attack on Lebanon in 2006 as 'disproportionate', arousing Israeli fury.[9]

Cameron identified Sayeeda Warsi, a Muslim woman then in her mid-thirties who had unsuccessfully fought the Dewsbury seat in the 2005 general election, as a new face for his Conservative Party.* He offered her a peerage and a place in his Shadow Cabinet. What's more, he gave her the sensitive role of shadow minister for community cohesion, which had responsibility for relations with Muslims and other minority groups.

The second of five daughters to Pakistani immigrant parents,

---

* Sayeeda Warsi was born in Dewsbury in 1971. In 2010, Cameron appointed her co-chairman of the Conservative Party and also a minister without portfolio in the Cabinet, making her the first female Muslim Cabinet minister. She acted as minister for faith and communities and senior minister for foreign and Commonwealth affairs before resigning from the government in 2014 over what she saw as its 'morally indefensible' failure to act on Israel's bombardment of Gaza.

Warsi had studied at Leeds University and qualified as a solicitor. She also helped run the family business, a furniture factory in Yorkshire. In due course, she was to be given a job as joint chairman of the party. For a few years, the entrepreneurial and family-minded Warsi appeared to be the future of Muslims in David Cameron's Conservative Party. But not for long, and the story of Warsi's downfall is instructive.

In 2007, two years after becoming leader of the party and on the advice of Warsi, Cameron stayed for a week with a Muslim family. This involved entering a mosque, something that, it seems, he had never done before. It was one of only a handful of times that he would do so in his twelve years as Conservative leader.[10]

He wrote about his experience for the *Guardian*.[11] Reading it today is like entering another world; at the time, he set out a series of positions about Islam which he would go on to diametrically oppose as prime minister, positions only a brave mainstream politician would dare utter today. He insisted that 'we cannot bully people into feeling British', adding that 'by using the word "Islamist" to describe the [terrorist] threat, we actually help do the terrorists' work for them'. Mr Cameron was adamant that 'those who say that faith-based schools hinder integration are wrong'. More remarkable still, he suggested that 'it is mainstream Britain which needs to integrate more with the British Asian way of life, not the other way around'. He added that 'if we want to remind ourselves of British values — hospitality, tolerance and generosity to name just three — there are plenty of British Muslims ready to show us what those really mean'.* Alarm bells started to ring.

---

* Later, once he had assumed the position of prime minister, Cameron attracted the wrath of the family who had put him up. In 2015, the father of the family, Abdullah Rehman, said that if Cameron ever came to stay again, his message to the prime minister would be simple: 'I love this country, my father loved it and my children love it. So don't take away our contribution.' See Homa Khaleeli, 'I welcomed Cameron into my home, but his talk on British Muslims saddens me', *Guardian*, 3 July 2015. https://www.theguardian.com/society/2015/jul/03/david-cameron-british-muslims-extremism-alienation

Warsi vs Gove

In 2007, Cameron's leadership hit a crisis point as the new Labour leader Gordon Brown pondered calling an election with the Tories sinking in the polls. It was only when he hired Andy Coulson – a former editor of the Rupert Murdoch-owned *News of the World*, who later went to jail in the wake of the phone-hacking scandal – as media handler that Cameron began to recover. One of Coulson's main jobs was to make sure the views of the Murdoch press were reflected in Cameron's policy announcements. The Murdoch press tended to adopt, with uncritical and even unbridled enthusiasm, the narrative about Muslims developed by Policy Exchange and the Quilliam Foundation.

Meanwhile, the neo-conservatives around David Cameron were engineering a conservatism which had no room for Sayeeda Warsi. The most famous protagonist – and beneficiary – of this project was Michael Gove, the Murdoch protégé who had given up a Fleet Street career to enter politics as a Tory MP in 2005.

We have already encountered Gove as the first chairman of Policy Exchange. In 2006, the year after David Cameron was elected leader, Michael Gove wrote a celebrated book. Titled *Celsius 7/7*, it was a call to action, and an attempt to reshape the UK and the world. Gove – and this came naturally to a founder of Policy Exchange – distinguished Islam from Islamism, asserting that the latter was a form of 'totalitarianism' that was fundamentally hostile to Western liberal values. While David Cameron had warned against abuse of the term 'Islamism', for Gove, the battle against Islamism lay at the heart of his political philosophy. 'Islamists', thundered Gove, 'are a self-conscious vanguard who look down on other Muslims and consider the majority of their co-religionists as sunk in barbarity or error.'[12]

He believed that Islamists were at war with the West, with Israel standing at the frontline of the battle. Gove announced his belief that 'a sizeable minority' of the UK's then 1.8 million

Muslims held 'rejectionist Islamist views' which, so he said, presented a threat comparable to Nazism or communism.[13] He declared that Islamists were on the march and that the West had collectively failed to act.

Gove's polemic has reportedly since been handed to every new member of the Conservative Friends of Israel group, to which an estimated 80 per cent of all Conservative MPs belong.[14] In a short space of time, Mr Gove's treatise created an enduring Tory narrative about Islam.

Like so much neo-conservative thinking, Gove's ideas came from the United States. He repeated various neo-conservative myths, including the dubious claim that Saddam Hussein had 'invited jihadists into Iraq to join him in his fight against the West'.[15] Gove's scant knowledge of Islamic history and theology meant he was obliged to rely heavily on the writings of the British-American orientalist Bernard Lewis who, as already seen, was the first proponent of the 'clash of civilisations' thesis which sees Western European civilisation and Islam at war. Gove's book thus marked the entry of this theory into mainstream Conservative political discourse.

The views of Gove and Warsi were impossible to reconcile. On the one hand, Warsi argued that Muslims were law-abiding, family-minded and naturally conservative. Gove and his allies painted a darker picture. For him, Policy Exchange was a constant source of intellectual support, as well as fresh ideas and material. Warsi had no comparable intellectual secretariat.

After the 2010 general election, I became chief political commentator on the *Daily Telegraph*, then the most important Tory-supporting paper. As such, I found myself in the perfect position to witness the clash between Michael Gove's neo-conservatism and Sayeeda Warsi's last-ditch defence of multiculturalism. At first, the coalition government looked promising for Warsi. She had natural allies and supporters in the shape of the Liberal Democrats and, above all, the deputy prime minister Nick Clegg.

Even with Clegg as an ally, however, Warsi was no match for her opponents. The Chancellor of the Exchequer George Osborne, defence secretary Liam Fox (before his resignation in October 2011), Cabinet office minister Oliver Letwin and Home Secretary Theresa May all leant towards the same side as Michael Gove. So did the mainstream Tory newspapers.

Furthermore, Gove was advised by the most effective backroom political operator of the modern era: Dominic Cummings. Cummings, who was an adviser at the Department for Education before being appointed as Gove's chief of staff, was at this point an almost unknown figure, and had none of the national recognition that followed several years later when Boris Johnson foolishly appointed him his senior adviser in July 2019. Nevertheless, Cummings had already brooded hard on techniques of campaign management, popular mobilisation and press manipulation, and was all the more effective for being unrecognised outside a small circle.

Before working for Gove, Cummings had been director of a think tank, the New Frontiers Foundation. Its website claimed that 'the consequences of economic stagnation coinciding with rising Muslim immigration cannot fill anyone familiar with European history with anything other than a sense of apprehension, at least, about the future of the Continent'.[16] Cummings's New Frontiers Foundation was an admirer of Samuel Huntington and his clash of civilisations theory. It favourably highlighted a *New York Times* article by the historian Niall Ferguson warning of 'a creeping Islamicization of a decadent Christendom'.[17] For Cummings, the threat to the West did not just come from Islamism, the term used by Michael Gove. The threat came from the religion of Islam itself, as became clear in an article written for his personal blog in 2014. Cummings lists some of Britain's 'biggest problems' which, due to scientific advancement, have 'ever greater destructive possibilities'. They include 'autonomous robotics, synthetic biology, the rise of China' and, finally, 'the collision of Islam with modernity'.[18]

Dominic Cummings was an important asset for Michael Gove as he fought his battles as Cabinet minister. But the support that the new education secretary could take for granted from the Murdoch press was beyond price. Gove had worked for the Murdoch-owned *Times* newspaper for nine years before moving into politics. By far the most powerful media owner in the UK, Murdoch's papers produced a relentless diatribe of fabrication, propaganda and bile aimed at Muslims.[19] The Murdoch press has been a powerful weapon in modern British politics, and it has always been on Gove's side.

Apart from Nick Clegg (whose office was just a few feet down the corridor from Warsi's inside the Cabinet Office in 70 Whitehall), Warsi could only rely on an incoherent group of One Nation Tories, of whom the most distinguished was probably the Attorney General, Dominic Grieve. Most of her supporters were on the back benches, a tiny group of elderly MPs who were going nowhere. She didn't have a hope. The Cabinet split first entered public view over the Global Peace and Unity Conference, the event described in the Prologue. Warsi was invited to speak, accepted and then withdrew at the last minute, acting under an instruction from Downing Street.

When I sought the reason for Baroness Warsi's humiliation, I was told about a secret memorandum that had been circulated round Whitehall at this time. This memorandum was said to make a sweeping division between 'good' and 'bad' Muslims. At the time I tried and failed to get hold of this memo, but in the course of researching this book, I finally did manage to find the briefing paper in an obscure corner of the internet. It had been sent by Ed Husain and Maajid Nawaz of the Quilliam Foundation to Charles Farr, then head of the Office for Security and Counter Terrorism.

The paper described a number of mosques and Muslim organisations – as well as the Muslim Contact Unit in the Metropolitan

Police – as being broadly sympathetic to Islamism. This statement was accompanied by the warning that 'local and central government should be wary of engagement with these groups as it risks empowering proponents of the ideology, if not the methodology, that is behind terrorism'.[20]

It is impossible to say what influence this paper had, if any, or to what extent it was responsible for Baroness Warsi's withdrawal from the conference. Nevertheless, it sets out with clarity the view that was by then taking hold in official and media circles: that Muslims sympathetic to 'Islamism' were part of a suspect community. Any politician who met them or attended a public event in their company risked being damned by association.

The new McCarthyism

Now let's return to the Cold War. During the 1950s, the United States was infected by a malaise called McCarthyism. The infection is seen today in retrospect as a form of national madness. McCarthyism describes a technique of making reckless and unsubstantiated allegations against individuals for political ends.[21] The essence of the technique was that the victims could not defend themselves by reason or evidence. If challenged, McCarthyites would invent new evidence or make a new allegation or simply move on to a new target, leaving the original victim still tarred by the original allegation. Anybody who had once been a communist, had ever expressed sympathy for communism, or had ever known a communist, was viewed as an object of suspicion.

Many decent men and women had their careers destroyed, or were obliged to emigrate. A number of unscrupulous politicians, like the hitherto obscure Senator McCarthy[22] and an ambitious young huckster named Richard Nixon,[23] used the anti-communist frenzy to make or to consolidate their reputations.

McCarthyism operated with the co-operation of the security services, and its most damaging weapon was the blacklist, with many victims never aware that charges had been levelled against them. McCarthyism was mainly (although not exclusively) a phenomenon of the right. Joseph McCarthy himself was a Republican, while a strong supporter was the right-wing newspaper editor William Buckley,[24] who called McCarthyism 'a movement around which men of good will and morality can close ranks'.[25]

It is important to bear in mind that Senator McCarthy had an elastic definition of communism, which went far beyond membership or support of the minuscule American Communist Party, or even membership of its many 'front organisations' in the 1930s and 1940s. This allowed him to target anyone as an ally, agent or dupe. McCarthy and his allies targeted communist sympathisers, subversives, left-wingers, liberals, homosexuals[26] – anyone whose conception of American society did not fit in with the mainstream.

One of the most potent expressions of McCarthyism – although the senator himself was not personally involved – was the House Committee on Un-American Activities.[27] As the name suggests, the business of this committee was the suppression of political dissent. It claimed to represent American values, while in practice rejected everything that the Founding Fathers had embodied. Above all, McCarthy promoted the idea of an enemy within, a secret nest of traitors or dupes, whose machinations had to be exposed.

Conclusion

The parallels between McCarthyism and the UK's own cold war on British Muslims, though far from exact, hit me hard soon after I started to research this book. Someone, somewhere, has made allegations against pretty well every senior British Muslim, with the exception of those who were officially sponsored or approved.

Like thousands in the 1950s, Muslims today are being asked to prove their loyalty to the American or British states: this, as the case of Quilliam suggests, includes 'naming names'. As in the 1950s, lawful movements and opinions held by Muslims are being identified as subversive and their adherents are being blacklisted. As in the 1950s with communism, there are special concerns over Islamist infiltration of schools and colleges, and about local cells seeking control over individual communities. As in the Cold War, there is a huge intellectual offensive against so-called radical Islam, with supposed independent organisations, journals and thinkers funded secretly from public sources. As in the 1950s for ex-communists, there are profitable careers to be made now for reformed radical Islamists as commentators and experts on detecting current radicals. There are tell-tale signs of potential radicalism as there were for potential communists in the 1950s (such as beards, in both eras).

As in the 1950s for anti-communism, anti-Islamism has nurtured, and been nurtured by, dozens of politicians who were otherwise mediocre (such as Joe McCarthy), journalists, intellectuals and religious leaders. It has become an industry creating jobs and profits for public servants and private contractors. As we have seen, the Godson dynasty actually links the two eras, with father and son adopting the same techniques in politics and opinion-forming against Islamism as were used against communism.

The anti-communist crusade wrecked lives. But it also had its successes. It made its contribution to the Cold War, which was a huge triumph for the Western world against a real enemy. The anti-Islamist crusade has already claimed many more victims. It risks plunging the Western world into a new and ultimately unwinnable cold war against millions of people who are not its enemies at all.

So I will now change my focus of attention. Until now, I have examined how politicians, think tanks and intellectuals have collaborated to impose a common narrative on British Islam. I am now going to examine what it's like in such circumstances to be a British Muslim.

18

THE TROJAN HORSE AFFAIR

Tahir Alam was born in Pakistan in 1971, the momentous year of secession and civil war when Bangladesh seized independence in a moment of humiliation and disaster for the newly formed state of Pakistan. Tahir spent the first eight years of his life in a Kashmiri village, the eldest of six brothers and sisters from a family of peasant farmers. There was no electricity. After dark, Tahir and his brothers and sisters lived by candlelight and went to bed at 8pm, rising with the sun.

Jobs were scarce. Tahir's father, Noor Alam, travelled for work far from home in factories in Dewsbury, Reading and Bradford. In 1978, he decided to bring his family to England with him. Seven-year-old Tahir could not speak English and knew only four Roman letters – F, O, R and D, the letters stuck to the vans that drove through his village. He'd been brought up speaking the local language, Mirpuri. He could also speak Urdu, the national language of Pakistan used at his school.

The Alams settled in Birmingham. To support his family, Noor Alam had two jobs. He would return home at the end of his shift at medical equipment manufacturers Smith & Nephew and knock out shalwar kameez (Pakistani suits) for local customers. Eight-year-old Tahir attended Nansen Primary School in the Alum Rock area of east Birmingham. After a couple of years, he moved on to Park View, the local comprehensive. Most of the children could boast Pakistani heritage, with the majority, like Tahir, coming from the Mirpuri community in Kashmir.

Most of the children spoke English as a second language – one of the main reasons educational standards were low. So Tahir did well to advance to higher education at Birmingham Polytechnic where he studied mechanical production engineering. This was enough to get a job as an engineer at Cable & Wireless. Then, in 1993, came the moment of revelation that was to change his life, and that of thousands of others, and would eventually lead him to become a notorious national figure.

He watched a BBC *Panorama* film called 'Underclass in Purdah'. It highlighted how dreadful education standards in east Birmingham (and in Bradford) had created an underclass of British Muslims. They were unemployable, uneducated, and many ended up in crime. Park View pupils had little chance of contributing to society. Today, Tahir recalls: 'I was watching black and white TV. I recognised the area, I recognised the neighbour's children. And then I saw the film was about the school I had attended – Park View.'[1]

Tahir considered he had done well for himself. He decided there and then that he wanted to give something back: 'I felt that this was not right. I felt that I should respond. I went to the school. I opened a tuition centre nearby to help children raise their performance.' Four years later, a group of parents invited Tahir to become chairman of the governors. He remembers the date: 7 January 1997. The first three times he visited the school, Alam witnessed fights. In one of the brawls, children fought and threw chairs in front of the school's staff. He thought to himself: 'There's something not right here.' He recalls that he 'became a governor knowing nothing about how education was run. So I went to every single course I could find on governance that was going. Systematically, I went through all these courses.'

Alam slowly turned the school around. Today he puts his success down to two linked methods. One was zero tolerance. Governors and staff realised that the first thing they needed to address was discipline. They expelled a number of children for abuse and assaults on teachers. 'We called it a "tough love approach". In other words, if we love these children then we have to be tough with them in order to ensure that they actually had an opportunity to succeed academically.'

The second method was to cause problems later. Throughout the entire time that Alam has been involved with Park View, at least 95 per cent of its pupils have been Muslim. 'We tried to make the school as friendly as we could, from a cultural and from a children's background point of view, so that they would see that this was a school which allowed them expression, which allowed them inclusion, and so that they felt that this was their school.' In 1997, they had applied for, and were granted, the statutory right to hold a daily act of worship of Islamic rather than Christian character. By law, British non-faith schools are required to provide a daily act of collective worship. This is normally Christian, but schools with a majority of non-Christian pupils can apply for a determination that allows this collective worship to be from another religious tradition.[2]

Alam says that the shift to Islamic worship improved academic performance. 'This was an important part of the ethos, because they felt that they belonged, and the parents felt that this was their school as well. If you were going to get parents really supporting their children, they had to have confidence in the school that we were doing the right thing. And they believed in it.'

The academic record Tahir inherited was terrible. Less than 5 per cent of children were achieving five or more GCSEs above a C grade. Ofsted judged the school to be failing. At first, Alam and his team decided to set out to raise that figure to 20 per cent. This involved a battle with union representatives on the governing body. They said the issues that these children carried around with them were simply too great.

Later, while interviewing for new senior staff, Alam and his team tested candidates by telling them they wanted to achieve 50 per cent. He recalls that one of the old guard, who had taught at

Park View throughout its ruinous period, responded that if they were going to achieve that target, they would have to bus children in from another part of the city. Alam responded by appointing more ambitious teachers. Over the years, results went up. In 2012 the GCSE figure that two decades earlier had been 5 per cent was now 76 per cent – well above the national average.

It's worth putting these figures into context. More than 70 per cent of Park View pupils were in receipt of free school meals, compared with a national average of 15.2 per cent. Only 7.5 per cent of the children spoke English as a first language, compared to a national figure of 82.7 per cent. Let's repeat that. Only 7.5 per cent of the children had English as a first language. Yet the school was in the top 14 per cent nationally by results. It is hard to exaggerate the magnitude of this achievement.

At the beginning of 2012, the new education secretary, Michael Gove, introduced a tougher framework for school inspection. Schools everywhere worried that they would be downgraded, but Ofsted inspectors declared Park View 'outstanding' in all areas.[3] And not just academically. The inspectors praised the role of Islam in promoting tolerance – what would become one of the government's 'fundamental British values' that the school allegedly neglected – and contributing to a harmonious school community. 'There is a wide range of opportunities for spiritual development, for example, through the well-attended voluntary Friday prayers meeting,' inspectors wrote. 'Assemblies and tutorials promote a very strong sense of pride in the school community. This contributes very well to students' keen understanding of their rights and responsibilities, and they are profoundly aware of how their actions can affect others.'[4]

An open letter from lead inspector Keith Brown to the pupils of Park View was included in the report. 'You told us that you are happy and feel exceptionally safe at school,' it said. 'At the same time, you are developing into very mature and aware citizens.'[5] Alam told me that he remembers a *Times Educational Supplement* reporter calling him up saying that he had never read such a glowing report.

Banned for life

In fewer than two decades, Tahir Alam's achievement was more than heart-warming. It was amazing. It showed the ability of human perseverance to transform even the most hopeless situation. There are thousands of young Muslims from Birmingham whose lives have been enriched thanks to the blessing of education by Alam and his team of teachers.

Alam was universally praised, and Prime Minister David Cameron singled out Park View as a school that was 'closing the achievement gap'.[6] But the greatest accolade came in March 2012 when the head of Ofsted himself, Sir Michael Wilshaw, visited Park View and declared that 'all schools should be like this'.[7]

And yet, in just a few months, everything went wrong for Tahir Alam and Park View school. In the months that followed, he was hounded from his job and turned into a hate figure by politicians and the press. He was banned for life from being a governor and accused of being an extremist dedicated to the destruction of British values. And as he faced these accusations, nobody of importance lifted a finger to help.

The sequence of events is as follows. In late November 2013, Sir Albert Bore, leader of Birmingham City Council, received an unsigned and undated letter. Accompanying the anonymous letter was a document, which the letter's author claimed to have 'found when I was clearing my bosses [sic] files'.[8] The document appeared to be addressed to an educator in Bradford. It set out the process whereby state schools could be taken over and run 'by strict Islamic principles' in what it called 'Operation Trojan Horse'. It described five steps necessary to infiltrate school governance and senior leadership. It claimed that this takeover had already been carried out successfully in Birmingham. It pointed the finger at Tahir Alam, claiming that he had 'fine-tuned the "Trojan Horse" so that it is totally invisible to the naked eye and allows us to operate under the radar'. Bore passed the letter on to the West Midlands counter-terrorism unit, which passed it on to the Home Office, which in turn forwarded it to the Department for Education (DfE).

On 23 February 2014, *Sunday Times* security correspondent Richard Kerbaj and his colleague Sian Griffiths became the first journalists to report on what swiftly became known as the Trojan Horse plot. They published a report based on an allegation from the year before that Park View school had (to use their words) 'in effect excluded female students from after-school tennis lessons because it had ruled that they could not be coached by male staff'.[9] The article quoted an anonymous Whitehall source saying that the DfE did not want Park View to 'become another Al-Madinah' – a Muslim school in Derby forced to close due to its policies on music and headscarves.

On 2 March, they broke news of the Trojan Horse letter itself, reporting that there was an apparent 'Islamist plot to take over schools'.[10] The BBC and other media followed suit. On 14 April, Birmingham City Council announced that a former head teacher – Ian Kershaw, CEO of Northern Education Trust, an academy chain in Newcastle – would lead an investigation into east Birmingham schools. Then, two days later, Michael Gove declared that it was necessary for 'wider, more comprehensive action' to be taken and appointed Peter Clarke to investigate whether there was evidence of 'extremist' infiltration both in academies and council-run schools.[11]

This was a turning point. Peter Clarke was the former head of counter-terrorism for the Metropolitan Police who had run the police response to the London bombings. His appointment signalled that the British government considered the Trojan Horse affair to be a security issue. Clarke's report was utterly devastating and destructive. He concluded that there were 'a number of people, associated with each other and in positions of influence in schools and governing bodies, who espouse, endorse or fail to challenge extremist views'.[12] He suggested there had been, in effect, an organised agreement to Islamicise Birmingham schools, and positioned Alam, as chair of governors at Park View, at the centre of a network of extremism. He went to the lengths of providing an intricate spider diagram depicting what he called the 'linkages between key members of the Park View Educational Trust, intolerant discussion groups and schools where an Islamising agenda has been evident'.[13]

Nicky Morgan, who replaced Gove as Secretary of State for education days before the publication of Clarke's report, presented its findings to Parliament on 22 July 2014. She told MPs that 'there is a clear account in the report of people in positions of influence in these schools, who have a restricted and narrow interpretation of their faith, not promoting British values and failing to challenge the extremist views of others'.[14]

Morgan issued a banning order on Alam in September 2015 which prevented him from having any further involvement in the school.[15] The education secretary said that he had engaged in conduct 'which is aimed at undermining fundamental British values of democracy, the rule of law, individual liberty, and mutual respect and tolerance of those with different faiths and beliefs'.[16] Alam thus became, as far as I can discover, the first British citizen to be declared guilty of breaching British values. As the supposed ringleader of the Trojan Horse affair, he was deemed an enemy of the state. He had apparently worked to Islamicise British state schools and, for that, he was unfit to go near them. He was utterly disgraced and his involvement in British schools was over.

The truth about Trojan Horse

Peter Clarke did identify troubling allegations by whistleblowers which cried out for investigation. But the report also contained errors, oversights and misunderstandings so serious, and so elementary, that they undermine the report itself. The first error concerns Clarke's failure to understand the role played by religion in the British education system. His report distinguishes between what he calls 'secular' state schools and 'faith' schools that are supported by the state. The report gives no indication that Clarke was aware that *all* schools, whether or not they are faith schools, have a legal duty to hold daily acts of collective worship and to teach religious education. There is no such thing as a 'secular' British state school. This led Clarke to a fundamental mistake. The former counter-terrorism police chief interpreted ordinary Muslim practices, such as the call to prayer, visits to Mecca and Arabic tuition as evidence of extremism.[17]

This is not so. The use of the call to prayer was no more sinister than the ringing of church bells in the Anglican school Clarke had attended in the 1970s, Arabic is a more useful language these days than French and there is no reason why a visit to Mecca should be regarded as any more suspicious than a trip to the Vatican in Rome.

This brings me to the most serious failure of Clarke's report. The 'takeover' of schools in Birmingham and their incorporation into the Park View Educational Trust (PVET) was not – as he suggested – a scheme dreamed up by a group of Islamist conspirators. The PVET came about as part of a schools improvement programme backed by Birmingham City Council – and authorised by the Department for Education. Indeed, as education secretary, Michael Gove himself pressed for Park View to sponsor Al-Furqan, a local primary school. Gove signed a letter on 11 July 2013 supporting this sponsorship.

The takeover did not go ahead. Tellingly, this was because Park View itself objected. Park View felt that Al-Furqan's strict religious codes (it was and is an Islamic faith school) would hold back academic progress. One would have thought that if Clarke was right and Tahir Alam was part of a conspiracy to 'Islamicise'

Birmingham schools, he would have jumped at the chance of getting his clutches on Al-Furqan. One would also have thought that the active involvement of the education secretary and the local council in the so-called takeover of Birmingham schools was an essential element in any serious understanding of whether or not an Islamist conspiracy took place. Yet Clarke's report made no mention of this at all.

These were not the only problems with the report. Another issue worth mentioning is the fact that Clarke accepted anonymous statements from witnesses. This was deeply unfair because it meant that those criticised in the report were unable to respond fully to the allegations made against them. For them, it was a Kafkaesque process, with accusations hurled at them which they had no way of fully assessing.

The Clarke Report exposed

In view of the shallowness of the Clarke Report, as well as the errors, it is little surprise that the claims of a Trojan Horse conspiracy were very rapidly found to be worthless. As early as March 2015, less than a year after the report was first commissioned, the Education Select Committee found that there was 'no evidence to support claims of an organised plot to take over English schools'.[18] Two years later came a yet more damaging blow. In the wake of the publication of the report, Nicky Morgan had ordered an investigation of the teachers criticised in the Clarke Inquiry. Professional disciplinary proceedings were duly instituted against a number of teachers, including five senior teachers associated with Park View, for 'undue religious influence'. Significantly, the teachers were not charged with extremism.

The case against the teachers collapsed on 30 May 2017. The original, unsourced claims about the existence of a so-called Trojan Horse plot had been given massive publicity over the summer of 2014. In comparison, the collapse of the tribunal case was granted minimal coverage. On the day the case was thrown out, there were stories across the UK media, but there was almost no follow-up.[19] The *Sunday Times* did revisit the story a few days later, in what appeared to be an attempt to discredit the National College for Teaching and Leadership (NCTL, since renamed the Teaching Regulation Agency), the arm of the Department for Education to which the case was brought. The article quoted the former head of Ofsted, Sir Michael Wilshaw, criticising the NCTL's 'incompetence'.[20]

The promoters of the myth of the so-called Trojan Horse plot said the failure of the case was of no importance. They claimed it was down to a technical issue of court procedure involving the failure of the prosecuting lawyers, acting for the NCTL, to disclose evidence. The journalist Andrew Gilligan, who had been at the forefront of reporting about Trojan Horse, dismissed the failure of the court case, sticking with the line that 'what really happened was that a group of hardline Muslims took over state schools in Birmingham'.[21]

But the collapse of the case against the teachers was more than merely technical. The prosecution had failed to meet their obligations for disclosure of evidence. The documents that had not been disclosed contained information supportive of the teachers' case[22] and contradicted the findings of the Clarke Report, calling the whole Trojan Horse affair into question.

Among the documents not disclosed were statements provided to Peter Clarke's inquiry. They included statements from Birmingham City Council officials and from officials at the Department for Education responsible for their academies programme. These statements included an interview with an official from the Birmingham Standing Advisory Council on Religious Education. She confirmed that Park View had been authorised to replace the daily act of Christian worship required by law with one that was Islamic in nature. She said that the school fully complied with its requirements in view of the religious education curriculum. Other statements highlighted the fact that the take-over of schools and subsequent incorporation into Park View Educational Trust was instigated and overseen by the Department for Education in London.

Lessons of the Trojan Horse affair

The case for the Trojan Horse plot now lies in ruins. Yet belief in the Trojan Horse persists, with intelligent and well-informed people continuing to insist that something sinister happened.

Nick Timothy, best known as chief adviser to former prime minister Theresa May, has repeatedly defended claims that the Trojan Horse plot was real. For Timothy, the idea that there was no plot is 'a fiction that has been contradicted by multiple inves-tigations' and that plays into the hands of extremists.[23]

But we are talking here of a tragedy which has had a dire effect on literally thousands of young people studying at schools in Birmingham, almost all of whom are Muslim. First of all, education standards in the schools involved have collapsed as a direct result of the Trojan Horse affair. From being an 'out-standing' school performing at well above the national average (notwithstanding the high number of pupils on free school meals and without English as a first language in the home), Park View is now 'good', performing at below both the national average and the average for Birmingham.[24]

Meanwhile, the lives of some of the teachers from these schools have been ruined. Although their suspensions from teaching have been lifted and they have escaped bans, their employment record at Park View, and the high visibility of the case, means that they can no longer find employment in teaching. Despite being gifted teachers, they have had to train for other careers; some have suf-fered long-term ill-health from stress. They have not been able to clear their names.[25]

Trojan Horse was a fabricated event which has nevertheless

been given a documented existence by state officials and acted upon by politicians. Journalists, whose trade it is to be sceptical, reported it as fact. In 2015, the government cited Clarke's report in its counter-extremism strategy.[26] In the wake of the affair, the Cameron government imposed on schools a duty to 'promote fundamental British values'.[27] Schools which fail to 'actively promote' these values can be admonished by the schools inspector and closed. Teachers and governors who fail to do so can be banned from teaching and deprived of their livelihoods.

As for Tahir Alam, he is stranded. He cannot move forward. He cannot move back. He has been banned from involvement in education – the vocation he loved, to which he dedicated his life and which enabled him to change and improve the lives of thousands.

The so-called Trojan Horse affair was a state-sanctioned attack on Muslims in east Birmingham, carried out in alliance with the mainstream media. In many ways this feels like a comparable miscarriage of justice to the judgment by the Coroner's Report into the Hillsborough disaster on 15 April 1989, stating that all ninety-six deaths were accidental. It took nearly three decades for the truth about Hillsborough to be recognised, a process that officially began with the Hillsorough Incident Panel in 2009. I believe that a similar body should be set up to examine the Trojan Horse enquiry. It would need to interrogate not just the conduct of the teachers involved, but also government ministers (above all Michael Gove), council officials and the role of the media.

In the next chapter, I examine the reporting of so-called Muslim 'grooming gangs'. It contains many of the same features as the Trojan Horse affair, including flawed and inflammatory reportage led by the Murdoch press with high-level political complicity. The 'grooming gang' myth was exploited by sinister far-right elements, and given credence through bogus research. As with the Trojan Horse affair, the grooming gang myth persists, even though it has been comprehensively disproved.

A FALSE NARRATIVE ABOUT
MUSLIM 'GROOMING GANGS'

Prejudice against Muslims in the UK received a powerful stimulus from the narrative of Muslim 'grooming gangs'.* This narrative had special power because it derived from facts – selectively reported and falsely analysed – but facts nonetheless, and horrific ones.

Local and national media reported, in over twenty British towns and cities, the convictions of groups of men with Asian origins and identifiably Muslim names for sexual offences including rape against girls under sixteen. The crimes were carried out in groups with varying degrees of organisation which were quickly given the sinister name of 'grooming gangs' – although, as we shall see, this was a highly inaccurate term.[1]

Offenders behaved with terrifying brutality towards their victims and with astonishing freedom. There are still profound unresolved questions about why such a pattern of crime should have become established in so many different places, but serious discussions of these had been sidelined and buried under the simplistic assumption that these crimes had their origins in supposed South Asian Muslim culture or indeed in Islam itself.

Many cases revealed scandalous failings by local authorities supposedly caring for vulnerable children, and by local police forces.

---

* This term has become commonplace, but I have not been able to trace its first use. I have kept it in inverted commas because it is not a legal or technical term.

These failings were attributed in part to a fear by those responsible of challenging and offending local Muslim populations, a factor noted in several official inquiries. There were many other reasons for the failures, but these too were buried under the simplistic assumption that local Muslims preferred to protect serious offenders in their community rather than bring them to justice.

Taken together, the reporting of the crimes themselves and the perceived delays in combatting them had an understandably toxic impact on public opinion. They allowed politicians, especially on the far right, and the media to treat all these cases as part of a pattern, rather than acts of individual evil. Thanks to the media, especially *The Times*, but also with some encouragement from Sajid Javid, the first Home Secretary of Muslim heritage,* 'grooming gangs' of predatory men were identified as a discrete category of crime especially associated with Muslims.

A myth was created and fostered that Muslim men were especially eager to rape vulnerable white English girls,[2] echoing the persistent racial myth that white women were in danger of rape from Black men, which sustained segregation for so long in the United States and South Africa. The 'grooming gang' narrative was used to validate familiar accusations that Islam itself encouraged paedophilia and child abuse. There is important evidence that the 'grooming gang' narrative inspired violence against Muslims. In August 2015, an 81-year-old Muslim pensioner, Mushin Ahmed, was murdered in a race hate attack in Rotherham, South Yorkshire. His killer, Dale Jones, was jailed for life, with a minimum term of thirty-two years, on 29 February 2016. He attacked Mr Ahmed after baselessly accusing him of being a 'groomer'.[3] In June 2017, Darren Osborne ran down worshippers outside the Finsbury Park mosque, killing one and injuring others severely.

---

* In Javid's words: 'My own family's heritage is Muslim. Myself and my four brothers were brought up to believe in God, but I do not practise any religion. My wife is a practising Christian and the only religion practised in my house is Christianity.' Harry Farley, 'Sajid Javid: What has the new home secretary said about faith?', *Christian Today*, 30 April 2018.

At his trial, he was said to have become obsessed with hatred of Muslims after watching the BBC television drama *Three Girls* about the 'grooming gang' events in Rochdale.[4] In distant New Zealand, the shooter at the mosques in Christchurch was found to have 'For Rotherham' written on his bullets.[5]

Certainly the narrative of delayed exposure of 'grooming gangs' (with the supposed cover-up of Muslim perpetrators) was a gift to the far right in the UK. It encouraged a mainstream British political party – UKIP – to reinvent itself as the country's first overtly Islamophobic party. Its colourless leader, Gerard Batten, recruited the Muslim-hating agitator Tommy Robinson as his 'special personal adviser on rape gangs'[6] while Robinson was feted in the House of Lords by UKIP's lone representative in Parliament, Lord Pearson of Rannoch. UKIP and its new far-right allies, who had not shown any previous interest in child abuse, tried to parasitise on the suffering of childhood victims and to pose as their champions. They cultivated survivors of child abuse and rape, and tried to recruit them into their anti-Muslim campaigns.[7]

Challengers of the 'grooming gang' narrative were ignored by the media in favour of those who endorsed it. They were often insulted. Worst of all, the 'grooming gang' narrative buried the suffering of the many thousands of children whose abuse and rape had nothing to do with grooming, nor with Muslims.

The Role of *The Times*

Andrew Norfolk, *The Times* investigative reporter,[8] won major awards for a series of reports of organised collective rape of teenage girls in British towns and cities.[9] Particularly in Rotherham and Rochdale, he exposed major failings by the police and local authorities, including the deliberate suppression of vital evidence from researchers and whistleblowers. Norfolk won the trust of some high-profile campaigners and victims, and is glowingly praised in the books by Jayne Senior (the leading campaigner against abuse in Rotherham) and Sammy Woodhouse, a victim of multiple abuse.[10]

Norfolk's reports, in some cases at least, accelerated the prosecution and conviction of evil men and the removal from office in the police service and local government of some who had totally failed in their duty to protect local children. But his reporting also introduced into the mainstream of British media and politics a new narrative previously confined to elements of the extreme right: an 'epidemic' of Muslim men preying on vulnerable white under-age British girls in organised gangs. This was the central idea of his four-page *Times* splash on 5 January 2011, 'Revealed: conspiracy of silence on UK sex gangs'.

Norfolk claimed that a 'culture of silence' had allowed the sexual exploitation of hundreds of young British girls. He said that unnamed 'child protection experts' had identified 'a repeated pattern of sex offending' in Northern and Midlands towns and cities, 'involving groups of older men who groom and abuse vulnerable girls aged eleven to sixteen after befriending them on the street'. He added: 'Most of the victims are white and most of the convicted offenders are of Pakistani heritage, unlike other known models of child-sex offending in Britain, including child abuse initiated by online grooming, in which the vast majority of perpetrators are white.'

Norfolk's article never identified the cases which sustained this conclusion, still less tried to relate them to any total of children abused or raped by people outside their homes. Instead, it said that '*The Times* has identified 17 court prosecutions since 1997, 14 of them during the past three years, involving the on-street grooming of girls aged 11 to 16 by groups of men', from 13 towns and cities. 'In total, 56 people, with an average age of 28, were found guilty of crimes including rape, child abduction, indecent assault and sex with a child. Three of the 56 were white, 53 were Asian. Of those, 50 were Muslim and a majority were members of the British Pakistani community.'

There were important weaknesses in Norfolk's analysis, to be repeated in later analyses which claimed academic rigour. He gave no explanation for the selection of his cases, or for the exclusion of those involving the sexual abuse of boys, omissions which raise questions about the double racial and religious narrative of Asian Muslim men preying on vulnerable white English girls. Newspaper reports of convictions were not a reliable database, being potentially biased towards those considered newsworthy because they were carried out in groups rather than single men or because they suggested a racial or religious element. The term 'on-street grooming' does not denote a criminal offence and is not recorded in police records: it derives from the cases selectively reported in the media. Above all, the numbers in Norfolk's article were never related to any totals for child rape and sexual abuse, and meant very little statistically. In general, the grooming gang narrative was an example of *post hoc, propter hoc* reasoning: the implication in much coverage was that if offenders were Muslim, they had offended *because* they were Muslims.[11]

Unleashing the far right

The Times claims proved explosive. They were quickly followed by other media, and politicians, and established the narrative of 'grooming gangs' as a major issue in public debate, framed as a Muslim phenomenon. This framing lacked any academic or research authority, but this was supplied – spuriously – by the Quilliam organisation, whose history and outlook as professional anti-extremist Muslims were described earlier. In December 2017, Quilliam published a report entitled 'Group-Based Child Sexual Exploitation: Dissecting Grooming Gangs'.[12] The two authors were Haras Rafiq, the organisation's Managing Director, and Muna Adil. They had no expertise in child protection, and if they did consult any person or organisation which did they did not acknowledge them. Their qualifications to write about the topic rested on their status as Muslims, as they themselves declared at the outset of the report. They claimed that their backgrounds, combined with their deep links to the Pakistani and Muslim community, 'have given us an adequate understanding of cultural context and the framework of Pakistani society which has allowed us to provide an informed opinion on the potential cultural under-pinnings of the data found in this report'.[13]

Their opinions had no value, except on the pre-assumption that the offenders committed vile crimes because they were Muslims. They would also have required a comprehensive analysis of all sexual offences against children, rather than the selective and opaque one which they offered. Their headline finding was that 84 per cent of convicted sexual offenders in 'grooming gangs' since 2005 were of Asian Muslim extraction. This was reported almost uncritically in British media. The *Daily Telegraph* used the finding to attribute 'grooming gang' violence to Muslim men who had failed to integrate into British society,[14] while *The Times* headlined the 84 per cent although initially misreported it as 84 per cent of all groomers rather than offenders in gangs. The newspaper quoted Quilliam's strident attack on its 'regressive left' critics.[15] The liberal *Independent* also led its story with the 84 per cent figure and quoted Haras Rafiq's call for a debate on it 'because the problem won't go away'.[16]

Although the authors claimed academic rigour, the report gave no indication that it had been peer-reviewed. They claimed to be illuminating a serious threat to vulnerable children, but there was no sign that they followed up their findings with any children's organisation, nor with the children's commissioner for England. They gave no satisfactory answer to basic questions about their methodology (including mine[17]). They responded to critics, espe-cially the criminologist Dr Ella Cockbain (whose research they misused), with attacks on their personal motives and accusations of being in league with extremism.[18]

Quilliam's 84 per cent figure derived from their selection of published newspaper reports of 58 cases resulting in 264 convictions *over a period of twelve years*.[19] The report did not list those cases, nor establish why they were representative of anything, nor explain how it had eliminated possible bias, in that newspapers were more likely to report high-profile trans-racial sexual convictions than others. Crucially it gave no information about their sources, search strategy or selection and rejection criteria. Above all, it did not relate these numbers (around twenty convictions annually) to the tens of thousands of reported sexual offences against children each year. It is quite simply meaningless to make any general statement about the characteristics of child sexual abusers from analysis of such a small proportion of them.

The Quilliam report's authorship made it particularly useful as a source for anti-Muslim commentators, think tanks, and pressure groups and politicians. In the *Daily Telegraph*, Allison Pearson hailed its findings and shut down any criticisms with a sarcastic split infinitive: 'Islamophobia! Up goes the cry to quickly shut down debate. Sorry, but that won't wash on this occasion. The Quilliam report is written by Haris Rafi [actually Haras Rafiq] and Muna Zainab*, both of Pakistani heritage, so it's pretty hard to accuse them of demonising Muslims.'[20] UKIP's spokesman, Alan Craig, used the Quilliam report at his party's conference to support an offensive reference to a 'holocaust' of rape by Muslims of 'our children'.[21] In the House of Lords, that lone UKIP peer, Lord Pearson of Rannoch, exploited it to extrapolate a figure of 250,000 victims of 'radical Muslim grooming gangs' and support a reference to millions of rapes of white and Sikh girls by Muslim men.[22]

Quilliam was also used as an authority in the United States, where Ayaan Hirsi Ali's AHA Foundation had strong links with Quilliam. On its website, AHA features an interview with the

---

* On the Quilliam report, Muna Zainab is credited under the name Muna Adil. Haras Rafiq and Muna Adil, 'Group-Based Child Sexual Exploitation: Dissecting "Grooming Gangs"' (London: Quilliam 2017).

organisation's US director and offers links to the 'grooming gang' report as a sample of its good work.[23] In addition, it is referenced five times by the Middle East Forum.[24]

Although he was not alone, the leading exploiter and beneficiary of the narrative was Tommy Robinson. It transformed his status from thuggish agitator to a 'serious' campaigner with an international following. He was invited to speak on sexual violence to the Czech parliament. The conservative author and commentator Douglas Murray hailed him as a 'citizen journalist' after his well-orchestrated imprisonment for contempt of court at a major 'grooming gang' trial in Huddersfield.[25]

Robinson, who took his pseudonym from a member of the 'Men In Gear' group of hooligan followers of his local football team, Luton Town, began his political career with the racist far-right British National Party.[26] He left and founded his own anti-Muslim street gang, the English Defence League (EDL). It staged a series of anti-Muslim demonstrations in British cities, regularly attracting thousands.[27] However, the organisation started to splinter into factions and Robinson made his highly publicised break, as we have seen, through the press conference with Quilliam.[28]

Robinson soon returned to anti-Islamic activity by forming a British chapter of PEGIDA, the German anti-migrant organisation. It gave him a European profile for the first time (as well as access to new finance) and he addressed one of its large rallies in the Netherlands on the infiltration of Islamist terrorists as refugees.[29] Robinson had yet to discover the power of the 'grooming gang' narrative. It received only one mention when he self-published his autobiography *Enemy of the State* in 2015. However, his focus changed when, in 2017, he joined the fringe-right media group Rebel Media, funded by a fellowship from the American billionaire Robert Shillman, a board member of the David Horowitz Freedom Center.[30] Robinson earned the first of his highly visible arrests for contempt of court, attempting to film 'Muslim paedophiles' at a rape trial in Canterbury.[31] Thus began a journey into mainstream-right politics, not just as a self-proclaimed campaigner against 'grooming gangs' but as a supposed expert on them.

In 2017, Robinson added his name to the self-published book *Mohammed's Koran: Why Muslims Kill for Islam*, which was promptly banned by Amazon, to his bitter protest.[32] The blurb claimed: 'This book provides you with a revolutionary way to understand Islam: you can understand the Koran within minutes instead of months. You will have concrete evidence that any part of the Koran which appears peaceful has been cancelled by a later command to be violent. You will see Islam's hatred and contempt for non-Muslims laid bare.' It attacked the 'Grand Lie' put out since 9/11 by Western leaders and Pope Francis that Islam was a religion of peace.[33]

The co-author was the mysterious Peter McLoughlin, author of *Easy Meat: Inside Britain's Grooming Gang Scandal*. The title was taken from a phrase used by Jack Straw in response to the original *Times* story.[34] McLoughlin, of whom no biographical details appeared either on his book or his website, claimed to have done exhaustive research on the 'grooming gang' phenomenon in both the UK and the Netherlands. He argued that it had gone on longer and on a far greater scale than previously imagined, thanks to 'the sinister power of political correctness' – and that its origins lay in Islam itself.[35] *Easy Meat* is almost entirely polemic and makes an unsubstantiated claim to have analysed the definitive list of cases of child sexual abuse by groups of men.

The 'grooming gang' narrative goes mainstream

In July 2018, the Home Secretary Sajid Javid intervened in the issue with a public letter promising special research into the problem.[36] The letter excluded all mention of ethnicity and religion, and the term 'grooming gang', but Andrew Norfolk in *The Times* on 24 July reported the letter under the headline 'Sajid Javid orders research into ethnic origins of sex grooming gangs'.[37] The *Daily Mail* did the same on 26 July.[38] The reporting made it appear as if the government had accepted, for the first time, the hypothesis that 'grooming gangs' were a discrete form of crime especially associated with Muslims of Asian extraction.

Javid powerfully reinforced that perception on 19 October when he hailed the conviction of twenty Asian men for child rapes in Huddersfield. In a tweet he said: 'These sick Asian paedophiles are finally facing justice. I want to commend the bravery of the victims. For too long, they were ignored. Not on my watch. There will be no no-go areas.'[39]

The tweet caused a storm, but he defended it strongly on BBC Radio 4 on 26 December, suggesting that it was wrong to ignore the ethnicity issue in 'grooming gangs'.[40] This was the only tweet Javid ever issued on child sexual abusers: it therefore ignored the multitude of non-Asian abusers and their victims, and the commitment in his original letter to address all forms of child sexual abuse. His silence on other forms of abuse was all the more striking since these were under investigation by the Independent Inquiry into Child Sexual Abuse which had made many horrendous revelations of abuse in other contexts, including schools and non-Muslim religious institutions.

In February 2020, the Home Office refused a Freedom of Information request by the *Independent* to publish the results of the research commissioned by Sajid Javid. It said that some of the information was based on police operational information and could not be released, and that ministers and officials needed time to deliberate the findings in preparation of a promised comprehensive strategy on *all* child sexual abuse.

Home Office officials expressed worry that the information could give a misleading impression if quoted out of context.[41] This almost invited suspicions of another official cover-up – not only from the far right – and a petition to make the findings

public soon attracted more than 50,000 signatories, well past the
threshold requiring a government response and on the way to
the 100,000 which would produce a debate in Parliament.[42] The
row was inflamed by Home Secretary Priti Patel, who gave out
the impression that she wanted to release the information and her
officials were blocking it.[43]

In December 2020, the Home Office finally published the
research originally commissioned by Sajid Javid. It concluded
that 'group-based child sexual exploitation offenders are most
commonly white. Some studies suggest an over-representation of
black and Asian offenders relative to the demographics of national
populations. However, it is not possible to conclude that this is
representative of all group-based CSE offending.'

The report cited data-quality problems in these studies, their
selection of samples, and their potential for bias and inaccuracy
in the collection of ethnicity data. Examining data from more
than seventy live investigations across the UK in June 2020, the
researchers found that the nationalities and ethnicities of suspects
varied considerably, and included British, American, Bulgarian,
Dutch, Eritrean, Indian, Jamaican, Lithuanian and Portuguese,
besides Bangladeshi, Pakistani and Somali.[44]

The report was predictably condemned by individuals and
groups eager to see a link between Islam and 'grooming gangs'.
In *The Spectator*, Patrick O'Flynn called it an exercise in obfuscation.[45] Priti Patel came close to joining them in her foreword to
the report, when she called its findings 'disappointing because
community and cultural factors are clearly relevant to understanding and tackling offending'.[46] Here was a British Home Secretary
casting doubt on scientific data and promoting a populist narrative.
Patel's attitude was reflected when the government's child sexual
abuse strategy was published the following month. Ignoring the
report's conclusions that there was no evidence to support the
'grooming gang' narrative, it included a whole section on 'grooming gangs' with dubious calls for profiling of offenders.[47]

Islamic teaching on child rape

Contrary to the claims of Islamophobic writers, the Quran does not excuse or encourage rape still less child rape in any circumstances, and child sexual abusers are destined for torment in this life and the next. Enforced sex of any kind with another person violates a Muslim perpetrator's duties to be chaste: these forbid even looking desirously at another person, let alone sexual congress (Quran 5.5, 23.5, 24.30–31, 70.29).* Moreover, it constitutes oppression and, in Islam, 'oppression is worse than murder' (Quran 2.191 and 2.217).[48]

Any form of violent oppression of children is a special transgression in Islam because all children are a gift of God to their parents. 'To Allah belongs the dominion of the heavens and the earth; He creates what He wills. He gives to whom He wills female [children], and He gives to whom He wills male children. Or he makes them [both] males and females, and He renders whom He wills barren. Indeed, He is Knowing and Competent.'[49] Muslims have a special duty to protect and nurture children – their own or anyone else's.

No Muslim following the Quran – which alone represents the direct word of God to the Prophet and takes priority over anything said or written after – could rape a child and consider himself a good Muslim, although dozens obviously did so, just as many Christian child rapists still considered themselves good

---

* Islamic courts of law have always treated rape as a serious crime, as is made clear in this discussion of evidentiary standards by Professor Jonathan Brown: 'In the Shariah, rape had both a civil and a criminal dimension (here I'm using categories from American law for convenience sake, they are not fiqh categories). The "civil" was the damage done to the woman and for which she could recover compensation. The criminal was the Hadd crime of Zina by the man. In order to prove that the "civil" wrong had been committed, the woman needed only to meet the normal burden of proof (bayyina), which might be no more than her oath along with circumstantial evidence. This is important because it allowed a person to seek justice for rape without having to meet the impossibly high standard of evidence for Zina.' 'The presumption of innocence when too many victims go unheard', April 2018; https://drjonathanbrown.com/2018/the-presumption-of-innocence-when-too-many-victims-go-unheard/

Christians. Religion is simply one of many pretexts which evil people can offer themselves to exculpate their crimes. However, it is a melancholy fact that any online search of 'Quran rape' produces many more anti-Islamic messages than demonstrations of this simple truth. It is buried among stories of Islamist terrorists justifying child rape on religious grounds, and hostile interpretations of Islamic texts, not only from far-right organisations but also from liberal secularists.

It was no surprise that individual campaigners and organisations supporting abused women and children were targeted by the far-Right to press their claim that the destruction of *Islam itself* is a prerequisite for their protection.[50] Such efforts encouraged the idea of an existential struggle between Islam and Western civilisation which, as we have seen, serves to feed extremism within Islam and against it.

All the evidence shows that child sexual abuse – whether committed alone or in groups – is not an Islamic phenomenon, but rather an expression of human depravity which exists in all communities, regardless of faith (or lack of it). Our society has a supreme duty to protect children from all forms of sexual exploitation, abuse and rape. We fail children if we obsess over one form, however horrific, at the expense of others. We fail them even more if we falsely attribute that form to one section of society because of their religious faith.

Moral panic

Child sexual abuse in the UK is under-reported, under-detected, under-recorded, under-prosecuted and under-punished.[51] Our criminal justice system gives us almost no information about child abusers and their origins, motives and methods.

All the inferences derived from convicted 'grooming gang' members are spurious, not only because there is no agreed definition of the tendentious term to allow for an accurate count, but also because we do not know what proportion of child sexual abuse and rapes occur through so-called 'grooming gangs'. The Home Office itself acknowledged the impossibility of distinguishing even 'group-based' child sexual exploitation from existing large scale data. So-called 'grooming gang' offences are very likely to be over-represented in convictions because common sense suggests that they are more likely to become known to the police – networks of people preying on strangers rather than individuals preying on a family member or someone known to them. That said, it is generally agreed that the greatest number of child rapists and abusers are someone known to the victim, a family member or someone in the victim's close circle.[52]

That families are the biggest source of child abuse has always been a painful fact for British government and society. It undermines a cherished ideal. It challenges politicians and opinion formers who extol family values or hard-working families. It challenges commercial interests who use idealised concepts of families to sell goods and services, and media which use these as the foundation of entertainment. All these interests have a huge stake in the ideal of the family and naturally recoil from evidence that some families are imperfect and dysfunctional, and some are toxic places, from which children should be urgently removed. They welcome and prompt any suggestion that cruelty of any kind to children is confined to alien elements outside mainstream society.

The ideal of the family has regularly been buttressed by alarms over threats to children from *outside* the family. Satanic abuse, paedophile networks and reports of individual 'evil' or 'sick' child killers have fulfilled this role. Now, Muslim 'grooming gangs' are held up as public enemy number one, to the detriment of a broader and more informed understanding of child sexual abuse. This is dangerous in itself. Some counsellors have told me that it is actually distracting the vulnerable children they work with: they have seen them pursuing obviously risky relationships with the illusion of safety because these are not with Muslims.

In his celebrated work *Folk Devils and Moral Panics*, the sociologist Stanley Cohen described how:

> societies appear to be subject, every now and then, to periods of moral panic. A condition, episode, person or group of persons emerges to become defined as a threat to societal values and interests; its nature is presented in a stylised and stereotypical fashion by the mass media; the moral barricades are manned by editors, bishops, politicians and other right-thinking people; socially accredited experts pronounce their diagnoses and solutions; ways of coping are evolved or (more often) resorted to; the condition then disappears, submerges or deteriorates and becomes more visible.[53]

This description explains much of the power of the 'grooming gang' narratives; it helps society to look away from the greatest risks to vulnerable children from within their families and close circle, and instead places the danger firmly in the realm of 'them'. The creation of an external enemy deflects blame from 'us'. We've been here before, many times. Other groups that have been and often continue to be targeted have included Jews, Black people, homosexuals and foreigners in general. During the terrifying witch-hunts of the early modern period, women were the main target. These eruptions or irrational hatred, which often turn violent, are based on more than ignorance and bigotry. They often reflect an underlying unease or disequilibrium in society itself and are always subject to political manipulation.

The underage victims of sexual abuse and rape endure real and horrific suffering. For many this is not over, and may never be over. Our society has a solemn moral duty to them. We must not allow their stories to be hijacked to create another moral panic in the interest of political or commercial forces. We need to recognise the scale of child sexual abuse and rape in our country and address all the real factors which put children at risk of them.

'I HAVE BEEN CALLED AN EXTREMIST, AN ISLAMIST, A TERRORIST – ALL THE ISTS'

Over the last few chapters, I have shown how think tanks, working closely with media, have given politicians the script to create a hostile environment for British Muslims. I've demonstrated how the British authorities reverted to the counter-subversion techniques of the Cold War, using some of the same techniques against Muslims as against those earlier thought to have communist sympathies.

I now want to examine the global comparisons between the Cold War against Soviet Communism and today's 'war on terror' against Islamism. Here the parallels are even more striking. The United States and its allies have employed the same techniques against Islamist movements across the Middle East and the wider Muslim world as they did against communists after the Second World War. Post-1945, the US defended its freedom and democracy by entering into a series of paradoxical partnerships with some of the most brutal regimes the world has known. US strategists believed that victory at the polls for communists would lead to suppression of democratic opposition and a one-party state. According to this theory, support for the rule of autocrats and military despots became essential if freedom and democracy were to be preserved.

This policy meant that the US and allies such as the UK

acquiesced in state-sponsored terror: the full gamut of assassination, kidnapping, torture, sabotage, war crimes, denial of human rights and military coups. One beneficiary was apartheid-era South Africa, deemed by the US as an indispensable ally of the free world in its struggle against the USSR. It's no coincidence that the US pulled the plug on apartheid immediately after the end of the Cold War, nor that the tip-off which led to the arrest of Nelson Mandela in 1962 came from the CIA. Indeed Mandela, the first democratically elected president of South Africa, remained on a US terror list until 2008.[1] British prime minister Margaret Thatcher described the African National Congress as a 'typical terrorist organisation'.[2]

Perhaps the most stark example of this Western complicity with state terror concerns the military coup that deposed Salvador Allende, the first Marxist to be voted into power in a South American liberal democracy when he became president of Chile in 1970. His programme – La vía chilena al socialismo (meaning 'the Chilean way to socialism') – included a minimum wage, nationalisation of key industries and sweeping education reform. It was popular among the Chilean working class and trade unions, but less so with the CIA, which declared: 'It is firm and continuing policy that Allende be overthrown by a coup.'[3] After Allende's victory, the Chilean economy was crippled by a series of strikes, most notably by truck drivers, reportedly financed and encouraged by the US.[4] After the military finally struck, on 11 September 1973, dictator General Augusto Pinochet hunted down, rounded up, tortured and executed thousands of Allende supporters.[5] Allende himself died by suicide, reportedly using an AK-47 assault rifle that had been gifted to him by the Cuban leader Fidel Castro.[6]

For Cold War Latin America, read today's Middle East. For Salvador Allende, read Mohamed Morsi, the first democratically elected president of Egypt who was ousted in a military coup in 2013, just over a year after he was sworn in as president. As

New Yorker correspondent Jon Lee Anderson noted: 'Today's Islamists can be yesterday's Marxists, it seems: killable on behalf of notional constructs of law and order.'[7] This doctrine – that Islamism had replaced Soviet Communism as an existential threat to freedom – had been set out very shortly after the end of the Cold War by the US diplomat Edward Djerejian. We have previously visited his speech shortly after the 1992 Algerian coup, but it bears repeating: 'We are suspect of those who would use the democratic process to come to power, only to destroy that very process in order to retain power and political dominance.' Djerejian added that 'while we believe in the principle of "one person, one vote", we do not support "one person, one vote, one time".'[8]

Djerejian's statement explains why the West was complicit in the military coup that called a halt to Algeria's first democratic election. However, as explained in Chapter 14, it had been Western-backed Algerian generals, not the Islamic Salvation Front, the party who looked set to win the election, which had applied the rule of 'one person, one vote, one time'. The Djerejian doctrine was applied again in 2006 when Hamas won Palestinian elections, regarded by observers[9] as free and fair, only to be treated as a pariah by the West. And again when the West backed the coup against Morsi.

When I visited Cairo a few months after the coup, it was like attending a funeral. The atmosphere in the city was subdued, the streets were quiet. Protest was punishable by jail, torture was routine, and the acting president was a puppet while his defence minister General Sisi ran the country. Sisi's picture was everywhere: in shops, in cafés, on street corners, often placed meaningfully alongside those of Nasser and Sadat, the country's two previous strongmen. Sisi was rumoured to have told friends of a series of visions, some dating back decades, in which it was divulged to him that he was destined to emerge as Egypt's saviour.[10] And yet, to this day, not one British Foreign Secretary has uttered the phrase *coup d'état* in relation to the events in Egypt. In a surreal interview on Pakistani TV, US Secretary of State John Kerry hailed General Sisi for 'restoring democracy' and praised him for averting violence.[11]

There are differences between Egypt and Chile. The political opposition to Morsi's socially conservative Muslim Brotherhood presidency came from the country's liberal left, while the hostility towards Allende came from the right. While Allende died by suicide on the day of the Chilean coup, Morsi died in prison six years after he was ousted from power.[12] Also, the CIA was probably not a prime mover in the Egyptian coup, which was supported by Saudi Arabia and the United Arab Emirates with widespread support from neighbouring dictatorships.[13]

The similarities are nevertheless striking. In both Egypt and Chile revolutionary movements sought peaceful political transformation. In Egypt, the United States and the West offered little more than formal protests[14] when the new Egyptian dictator went on to hunt down and kill more than a thousand political activists at Rabaa Square and al-Nahda Square in Cairo. This was around the same number as are thought to have been killed by the Chinese government in Tiananmen Square, although the media coverage was far more restrained, as is so often the case when reporting atrocities committed by a Western ally.[15] The UK never protested about the conditions in which President Morsi was held in jail.* President Sisi was in fact warmly received in Downing Street by David Cameron.[16] The sale of British arms to Egypt continues.

Justifying the slaughter at Rabaa Square in 2013, an Egyptian army spokesman stated that 'when dealing with terrorism, the consideration of civil and human rights is not applicable'.[17] Note the use of the term 'terrorism' here. It was being used on behalf

---

* I contacted the Foreign Office press department and asked for examples of British protests about the treatment of President Morsi. Despite repeated requests, the Foreign Office failed to come up with any examples.

of an illegal military regime, which seized power in a military coup, to describe hundreds of pro-democracy protestors who had been shot down in cold blood. There were, once again, no complaints from the US or the UK. All this is familiar across the Muslim world: US and Western involvement in, or tolerance of, state terror and military coups.

This matters. For many years, one of the biggest selling points for al-Qaeda has been its claim that the Western powers will never allow democracy in the Muslim world – meaning that there was no alternative to armed struggle.[18] They condemn elections as a 'heresy',[19] while mocking the naivety of peaceful Islamist movements, such as Morsi's Freedom and Justice Party, which place their faith in democracy and the rule of law. In fact, these peaceful movements speak for the great majority. Al-Qaeda historian Fawaz Gerges has noted that the great majority of Arabs and Muslims reject al-Qaeda and its cult of violence: 'al-Qaeda's core ideology is incompatible with the universalist aspirations of the Arabs. Arabs and Muslims do not hate America and the West, but rather admire their democratic institutions, including free elections, peaceful transition of leadership, and separation of powers.'[20]

Tragically, Western military strategists, many of whom learned their trade in the Cold War, either cannot or do not want to comprehend this. Just like al-Qaeda, they believe that the world is locked into a mortal struggle between Islam and the West. Again like al-Qaeda, they believe that the stakes are so high that the West has no choice but to become party to assassination, torture and killing. Countless people have suffered or died as a result.

The story of Mohammed Ali Harrath

The West's often misplaced involvement in foreign regimes has shaped global politics over recent decades, but no less important is the impact it has had on the lives of individuals. It has, with disastrous consequences, often led to the reclassification of resistance fighters as terrorists – as already seen, famously, with Nelson Mandela.

Mohammed Ali Harrath appeared in the Prologue – at the end of his Global Peace and Unity Conference in East London when he was bent double with despair. He told me that he had set up the event in order to encourage engagement between British Muslims and wider society, only to be ostracised and snubbed. 'I will never do this again.'

Why the event failed is documented in the Prologue: secret lists circulated round Whitehall; media attacks on those who planned to attend; orders from the party machines not to go. It's hard to blame the politicians. The fact that they had mingled with 'extremists' would be held against them for the rest of their careers, used mercilessly by opponents, written into their profiles, recur in media reports. If you defend a witch in a witch-hunt, you get treated like a witch yourself.

At that time, I knew almost nothing about Harrath, but simply felt there was something profoundly un-British about the way he – and others – were treated. I asked to interview him, and we met a few weeks later in his office. What emerged was a story of remarkable physical courage, high principle and an almost incredibly moral heroism. He has suffered more than most people can conceive for standing up for basic freedoms against dictatorship. This is something we in the West claim to admire. We would have celebrated Mohammed's bravery if he were a Chinese or Iranian dissident. Yet his past has been used pitilessly against him. Instead of a hero, he was treated as a pariah.

This is his story.

Harrath was born in 1963, close to the Tunisian town of Sidi Bouzid, where Mohamed Bouazizi would later set himself on fire on 17 December 2010, the desperate act which literally ignited the Arab Spring. Harrath came from an upper-middle-class family, which dispatched him to what he describes as a 'rigidly conservative boarding school'; it sounded a bit like Gordonstoun, the elite Scottish academy based on tough educational theories, once attended by Prince Philip and later Prince Charles.

Harrath became politically active at the age of thirteen. His first experience involved the preparation of news sheets to be pinned up on the wall of the local mosque. Of course, I asked: why the mosque? One of the central criticisms made in the secular West against so-called Islamists is their failure to distinguish between religion and politics. He gently explained that his local mosque was the only place you could agitate in the Western-backed dictatorship of Tunisia. There were no free newspapers, no political parties, no freedom, no democracy. President Bourguiba – previously encountered in Chapter 13 as a young national independence leader in our discussion of the final years of the French protectorate – ruled a one-party state.

Opponents were locked up or killed. Bourguiba used the same brutal tactics against political opponents that the French state had used against him thirty years earlier. Only now the French were on his side.[21] Tunisia was supposedly independent, but the country remained in many ways a French dependency.

'I was fascinated by the power of the word,' Harrath told me. 'I always believe the word is stronger than the bullet. Sometimes the bullet can silence the word, but then the word prevails.' He was arrested for the first time at the age of eighteen, while a student of textile engineering in Tunis, for 'degrading the status of the president'. He became a founder of the Front Islamique Tunisien (FIT), formed in opposition to the Bourguiba regime.

He spent most of his twenties on the run, in and out of jail. He told me that 'the prison is not the problem. As bad as it is, it cannot be compared to when you go through investigation.' That meant being sodomised with sticks and bottles, with faeces being shoved into your mouth. Victims suffered mock-drowning and electric shocks. Amnesty International has described how some victims were tied to a chair for a week with an apparatus that pierced their neck with a needle whenever their head dropped through exhaustion.[22] 'We were unable to go to the toilet on our own,' Harrath remembered, 'so we were carried by four or five friends.' He knows of thirty people who died under Tunisian government torture. When Bourguiba was removed from power in a coup in 1987, Harrath was on death row, facing execution.

Bourguiba's successor, Zine el-Abidine Ben Ali, promised reforms. Rather than being executed, Harrath was freed. But that moment of hope proved a false dawn. Ben Ali turned out to be even more oppressive than his predecessor.

Harrath told me that at this point, after a decade of struggle, he reassessed his life. He said there came a moment when he realised there was no point fighting the regime in Tunis because Bourguiba and Ben Ali were just puppet rulers. The real enemy, he realised, was France, the former imperial power that provided security assistance and (in part through the European Union) diplomatic and economic backing to keep the dictatorship in power. This was the same insight which famously occurred to Osama bin Laden on his journey from Saudi dissident to terrorist chief. Bin Laden recognised that his real opponent was the 'far enemy' – the United States.[23] Rather than copy Bin Laden's bloodthirsty logic, Harrath abandoned the political struggle and left Tunisia for good.

For five years, Harrath wandered the globe using false documents, 'with a new name and personality every week'. When he arrived in London in 1995, he studied for a degree in politics at the University of Westminster, writing his undergraduate dissertation on Karl Marx ('good on the analysis but bad on the solutions' was Harrath's verdict), and started to dabble in business. 'I was working here and there, buying and selling – I did everything.' This nomadic period was to be used against him by critics who repeated Tunisian government claims – as usual with no evidence – that he worked with al-Qaeda.

For fifteen years, Harrath lived the life of a political exile. Then, in 2004, he set up Islam Channel, a British TV station aimed at Muslims.* It was then, he says, that the harassment began: 'I was vilified.' First to visit, he told me, was the Inland Revenue. 'They came here and stayed for nearly a month going through every single receipt, every single paper. What astonished me is that they were asking politically motivated questions. They are asking about our content, they are asking about programmes. They are the taxman, they have to see whether we are paying our taxes or not. But they went further than that.'

Then the press attacks started. These ranged from a campaign of character assassination led by *The Times* journalist Richard Kerbaj (later to play a prominent role at the *Sunday Times* reporting on the Trojan Horse saga[24]) and ignorant abuse in the *Express* to a rant by Melanie Phillips on her *Spectator* blog.[25] The British media had an easy task. When Harrath fled Tunisia, the Ben Ali regime had accused him of 'counterfeiting, forgery, crimes involving the use of weapons/explosives, and terrorism'. His torturers asked for him to be added to Interpol's Red Notice list, a system of international alerts aimed at detecting suspected criminals or terrorists. The international police agency obliged.

This meant there was no legal risk for journalists in connecting Harrath with terror. Interpol, such a respected international law enforcement organisation, had done the job for them. And no journalist took the trouble to look behind the Interpol designation to the regime that had demanded it. From this moment on, Harrath was fighting battles on two fronts. The Tunisian government and the London media shared a common interest in labelling him an extremist. In 2009, he spoke at a City Hall-sponsored

---

* There were some powerful grounds for criticising Harrath. His channel broke Ofcom's impartiality rules, and one employee won an appeal for unfair dismissal and gender discrimination. More seriously, it broke the broadcasting code by allowing a presenter to condone marital rape and violence against women. Josh Halliday, 'Islam Channel censured by Ofcom', *Guardian*, 8 November 2010. https://www.theguardian.com/media/2010/nov/08/islam-channel-ofcom

event in London. The *Sunday Express* responded with a story head-lined: 'Boris terror link'.

The Times launched an innuendo-filled campaign, opening itself up to the charge of doing Tunisian dictator Ben Ali's job by high-lighting Harrath's alleged links to terrorism, while asserting that he was an adviser to the Metropolitan Police.[26] '[It] was part of the vilification,' he says. 'It was aimed at damaging me within the community.' Harrath insists he was never a police adviser and the claim was based on his having spoken from time to time, like many other Muslims, to the Muslim Contact Unit of the Metropolitan Police. This did not stop the Conservative Party's shadow security minister Baroness Neville-Jones demanding in 2008 that he should be sacked from his non-existent post.[27] In deference to the Ben Ali regime, Neville-Jones declared that 'the Tunisian government, an ally in the fight against terrorism, has asked for extradition of this man'. The Tories, then in opposition, were displaying a shocking readiness to operate within parameters set for them by a North African dictatorship. Ben Ali was then one of the most notorious rulers in Africa. Harrath had fled the country to escape him.

In April 2011, remarkably soon after the fall of Ben Ali, Interpol removed its Red Notice, telling Harrath that, 'after re-examining all the information in the file', the organisation 'considered that the proceedings against you were primarily political in nature'. Interpol has questions to answer. For almost two decades, its system of Red Notices had been used by Tunisia's Ben Ali to harass and torment a leading dissident. Within a few months of the fall of Ben Ali, the Red Notice was removed. The agency's purpose should be to help national police hunt down criminals, not to help round up opponents of dictatorship.[28]

Not one of the newspapers that so eagerly played up Harrath's alleged terrorist past apologised – or even reported that Interpol had lifted him off the Red Notice list. Like the Conservative Party, they were happy to act within the parameters set for them by a dictatorship. I left Harrath's offices feeling upset. Here was a man who arrived in the UK as a refugee from tyranny. Instead of being welcomed, he was treated like a criminal. For years, he has been unable to travel without risk of arrest and extradition. After he set up Islam Channel, a television station popular among the UK's two million Muslims, Harrath's fugitive status was ruthlessly used against him by a new set of persecutors: critics of Islam within the British political and media establishment.

Harrath, who sported a dark, bushy beard, joked: 'I have been called an extremist, an Islamist, a terrorist – all the *ists*.' It wasn't really a joke. Millions of innocent Muslims (and many non-Muslims) are categorised in the same way. Across much of the world, it is actually hard for any supporter of political freedom to avoid being labelled a terrorist. Even if they protest peacefully, they risk arrest and torture, or being shot down by armed police in the streets. If they flee their country, they can find themselves listed as terrorists or hunted down.

I have talked to scores of such 'Islamists' in the near two decades I've spent researching this book. They are brave and principled in a self-sacrificial way that nowadays we rarely encounter in the West, with high standards of personal integrity and public conduct. Otherwise they would not be able to endure torture and enforced exile for their beliefs. But, according to normal discourse in the West, these Islamists are single-minded fanatics hell-bent on the destruction of (to use the phrase much loved of British and American leaders) 'everything that we stand for'. This is false, insulting and, above all, ignorant.

I have found again and again that supporters of political Islam revere the UK and even more so our institutions: Parliament, the rule of law, freedom of the press. Indeed, they admire them all the more keenly for the powerful reason that such institutions can scarcely be said to exist in their own countries and they understand rather better than we do how much they matter. It is true that they criticise the UK (and the West), but this is not because they want to destroy our values, despite what politicians and opinion-formers have repeatedly asserted. They criticise us mainly because we don't cherish our values enough. Our newspapers spread lies and act as propaganda tools. Our governments break the law. Western intelligence services encourage illegal detention and torture. Our armed forces maim and kill with impunity and, in an especially cowardly way, through the use of drones and air power.

Worst of all, as we have seen, the UK is part of the apparatus of repression in Saudi Arabia, Egypt, the United Arab Emirates and elsewhere. We supply arms and provide advice and training for the police and security forces in regimes dedicated to the suppression of democracy and freedom. This means that their opposition becomes our opposition as well.

This explains one reason for hostility towards Islam in the UK. Regimes in Muslim states such as Saudi Arabia and the UAE devote time, influence and, above all, money to discrediting political movements that challenge them.[29] In particular, they have been successful at portraying Islamism as a mortal threat to the West, often defining Islamists as terrorists, thus tying their Western allies closer through a shared enemy.

A note on terrorism

'Terrorism' has become one of the most loaded and feared words of our time. Today, the immediate associations are often Middle Eastern, and yet 'terrorism' first arose in eighteenth-century Europe. The word was invented after the French Revolution. Following the demise of the Bourbon dynasty, the government of the new French Republic fell into more and more radical hands, each with an increasingly shallow political base. The last of these, headed by Maximilien Robespierre, applied a special regime of executions of its opponents, based on denunciation without trial. They described this themselves as the Terror and their policy entered the dictionary as 'Terrorism', with a capital T.

Significantly, the word described a policy adopted by a

government, not an insurrectionary group. The *Oxford English Dictionary* recognised this when it defined terrorism as 'government by intimidation as directed and *carried out by the party in power*' [my italics].[30] If that usage had survived, many governments in the world today would be defined as terrorist. Instead the term fell into disuse, only reappearing in the mid-nineteenth century as a way of getting to grips with anarchist violence, particularly that directed against the Tsarist regime in Russia. It gained further traction as the result of high-profile attacks on ruling dynasties and government ministers in Europe, and on US presidents James Garfield and William McKinley.* The word vanished again after the First World War. The years 1914–45 saw bloodshed and horror on a scale that made the outrages committed by anarchists and nationalists in the West before 1914 – or, for that matter, Islamic terrorists after 2001 – almost inconsequential.

But in the meantime we should note something significant. Terrorism in its original sense – the use of violence by a government for political purposes against its internal enemies – accurately describes many events after 1914. The killing of millions of Russians by Stalin; the British slaughter of Indians at Amritsar; the assaults by Hitler's armies on the civilian populations of Europe (though not the Holocaust, which was genocide): all conform to the original *Oxford English Dictionary* definition. But these governments were very rarely described as terrorist.†

---

* Joseph Conrad's novel *The Secret Agent* concerns one such group, while Fyodor Dostoyevsky's *The Devils* places terrorism in a Russian context. The term covered a wide variety of perpetrators of violence, some isolated and self-directed assassins, others in well-organised movements with clear political objectives, such as the Irish Fenians. It is worth noting that many terrorist movements of that period, particularly in Russia, were thoroughly infiltrated, and even sponsored, by governments.

† George Orwell, an especially attentive student of political language, went to Spain in the late 1930s and wrote about the atrocities carried out by Franco's army and its communist opponents during the Spanish Civil War. Not once, as far as I can discover, did he use the word 'terrorism' – yet a great deal of what he reported would today be regarded as exactly that. (Indeed, Orwell himself might have been classified as a terrorist under contemporary British law as a consequence of fighting with an anarchist militia in the civil war.)

The term did not come back into general use until the 1960s. This time it was largely associated with nationalist groups such as the IRA, PLO and ETA, as well as urban guerrilla movements in South America and Europe, the most notorious of which was Baader-Meinhof. But only after 11 September 2001 did Western leaders identify terrorism as the most serious problem of our time. George W. Bush launched his 'war on terror', while Tony Blair, in 2004, thought that Islamic terror was an 'existential' issue.[31]

By now, it was widely accepted that, however brutally a sovereign government might behave, or however many innocent people it tortured and killed, it could not commit a terrorist act. According to one estimate, the CIA has killed seventy-six children and twenty-nine adults in drone strikes[32] as it hunted down al-Qaeda leader Ayman al-Zawahiri, deaths sometimes described as 'collateral damage', the US military term for unintended or incidental damage during a military operation. As far as is known, Zawahiri survives. According to the human rights organisation Reprieve, by 2014 US drone strikes in northern Pakistan alone had claimed more than 2,500 lives.[33] Saudi Crown prince Mohammed bin Salman paid no price for dispatching an execution squad to murder and then cut up the independent Saudi journalist Jamal Khashoggi.[34]

In a reversal of the original meaning, only individuals or groups can today be labelled terrorist.[35] Today, the US and its allies, such as the UK, retain deep trade and security links with Arab dictatorships. These despotisms – Saudi, Bahrain, Egypt, the UAE and others – belong to Western-sponsored client regimes or families. Political parties are often outlawed, and democratic protest banned. As far as they are concerned, the word 'terrorist' today carries little or no meaning, beyond its use as a term to stigmatise political dissent, rather as it was deployed to delegitimise internal opponents of Western-favoured regimes during the Cold War.

No wonder that, back in 2013, the UK's independent reviewer of terrorism legislation, David Anderson QC, noted the dangers of using the term. 'Many advanced countries managed until recently without special terrorism laws of any kind. The terror label – evocative as it is – risks distorting a thing to which it is attached by its sheer emotional power. Terrorism stands for everything that is extreme, dangerous, frightening and secret – qualities which render it glamorous to all who associate with it.'[36]

He added that 'the very word has such magnetic qualities that ordinary compasses are not to be trusted anywhere near it. It might have been preferable if it had never found its way into the law. For our more sober juridical purposes, something more prosaic – politically motivated violent crime, perhaps – might have been more suitable.'

Eton-educated Anderson now sits in the House of Lords. He's not some wide-eyed ideologue, nor an apologist for hatred and violence. It's difficult to think of a more establishment figure than this Old Etonian son of a famous public schoolmaster, Eric Anderson, who oversaw the education of two British prime ministers, Tony Blair and David Cameron.

Anderson's judgement is sober, scrupulous and well-informed. Few concepts are more widely discussed than terrorism, and few as poorly understood. The idea is constantly reinvented, reshaped and distorted to fit political agendas. As a result, it has become muddled. There is no accepted definition, enabling authoritarian regimes to use the term to disparage and persecute legitimate opponents. In the UK, the concept has been reshaped so that it does not apply only to acts of violence, but also to a range of activities which fall well short of violence.[37] Terrorists are defined not only as using violence, but also as those holding views which can be depicted as threats to the British state or to the values and way of life of the majority of its people. In this way the concept has become part of the apparatus of state control and a channel for popular prejudice and hatred. Like the words 'Islamism' and 'extremism', and the neologism 'non-violent extremism', it has become part of a new political language carefully constructed to denigrate and stigmatise Muslims and other minorities. It's time to think deeply about the way the term is deployed, and perhaps – as Lord Anderson has half-suggested – to abandon it altogether.

PART FIVE

Fate of Abraham

HUNTINGTON'S BLOODY BORDERS

As a lobby correspondent, I often travelled with the press party which accompanies the prime minister on overseas trips. At press conferences with foreign leaders, the local press corps would sit on the left: docile, serious-minded, attentive. The British press corps sat on the right: anarchic, boisterous, contemptuous.

It took me rather too long to understand that British reporters were not the lords of misrule we fancied ourselves to be. We paid no price for our mild, cowardly heresies and studied irreverence. The schoolboyish mayhem was a boorish manifestation of privilege. For us, a courageous piece meant offending a politician who might complain to our editor. In many of the countries I visit, a courageous piece by a local reporter means writing a story that could lead to their disappearance, torture and death. Time and again, truth for them comes at a terrible price, not just for themselves but for their families. I have got to know scores of such journalists and occasionally shared a small part of their tribulations, marvelling all the time at their humour and courage.

And, of course, though we did not have the wit to realise it, we British journalists weren't publishing heretical or difficult material. Our stories fitted an approved official narrative. We ignored the rich complexity of the world – there wasn't time to deal with it. We divided it into good people (us) and bad people (them). This was necessary professionally because it provided a compelling narrative for readers, giving them a reason for taking an interest in events in a faraway part of the world. But it was also important for morale because it enabled us to sustain the myth, greatly cherished by Western reporters, that we were fighting a virtuous battle for truth and freedom.

All of us had interesting and even, many of us may have felt, important lives. We were well paid, with salaries stretching into six figures and some (the ones with opinions and a national following) much more. We knew how to craft stories, and to turn around copy with incredible speed. My colleagues and I could churn out a plausible column of a thousand words or more in an hour, or even less, to deal with a breaking story on a tight deadline. With certain admirable – and generally neglected – exceptions, we enjoyed at best a superficial knowledge of what we were writing about. This was inevitable given the range of subjects we covered, but this meant that our strongly held opinions were backed by remarkably little knowledge. In the absence of genuine understanding, we had no choice but to depend on the prevailing orthodoxy, or agenda-driven briefing, to frame our opinions.

This applied to the foreign countries we wrote about even more than domestic reporting. Even if we had visited the country in question, which was unlikely, it would have been as part of a whistle-stop tour arranged by a lobbyist or government, where we were introduced only to approved official voices, and then not for long.[1] More lengthy visits abroad, especially during the so-called 'war on terror', often took the form of an embed with British or American armed forces. Almost all of us went regularly to the United States. The US embassy had a list of British journalists who were invited to lunches with State Department officials in quiet, tastefully furnished residential houses in the most desirable areas of West London.

We were on first-name terms with Cabinet ministers who, hoping to enhance their reputations by ingratiating themselves with the press, sought us out and shared confidences. If reliable enough, intelligence officers would brief certain British journalists who were flattered by the interest and often jumped to attention. During the Iraq War and thereafter, MI6 and other agencies served up many lies to the British public on the imprimatur of the British state – deniable and, of course, unsourced by reporters who cherished their secret sources too much to expose them.

Think tanks were, and remain, a central part of this world. The most successful organisations provided analysis backed up by facts and arresting examples which brought our copy to life and made it seem authoritative and well researched. Early on, I naively took the term 'think tank' literally. It took me some time to grasp that they were not, as the term implies, places where intellectual endeavour sought out the truth for the public benefit. Even the respectable ones were funded by secretive plutocrats with an agenda.

If you played by the rules, advancement was easy. Editorships and knighthoods lay in wait for the ambitious, while the less successful could move sideways into profitable jobs in commercial lobbying or public relations, or obtain less well-paid but more exciting jobs in government communications. This environment also proved the perfect background for a move into politics. Both Boris Johnson, prime minister at the time of writing, and his Cabinet colleague Michael Gove spent the first half of their careers in British journalism.

Party affiliation didn't matter. Labour (with the telling exception of the years when Jeremy Corbyn was leader from 2015 until 2020) and the Tories are equally part of this game. Floating above it all are the media barons whose primary concern is not the dissemination of impartial and illuminating information; they are businessmen driven by the understandable need to sell newspapers. One of the easiest ways of achieving this is by running inflammatory campaigns against minority groups. There is a financial motive behind the countless fabricated stories about Muslims, both abroad and in the UK. The endlessly repeated idea that Islam poses a mortal threat to the West serves a commercial purpose.

For a long time, too long, I was part of this system. I had a mortgage to pay and a family to support. I believed what I wrote, but perhaps that helps to explain why I was disinclined to upset the bosses. Little by little I started to feel ashamed. I decided to try to understand, rather than judge and condemn from an editorial suite in London. That meant leaving my desk as much as I could. Over the last two decades, I have returned time and again to the 'bloody borders' – which, according to Samuel Huntington, defined the Muslim world – in an attempt to gain a better-informed understanding of these places and their relationship with the West, and to report on the situation as I found it to be, rather than through the lens of a politically or financially motivated news outlet.

Baquba 2005

On the terrible day of the London bombings in July 2005, I was embedded with US forces stationed in Diyala province in eastern Iraq. That evening, I accompanied the commanding officer, Colonel Salazar, to an uneasy dinner at the home of a tribal chief. The food was brought in from outside, not cooked on the premises, an insult in Iraqi culture. The Americans were trying to reach out, but our host was all too evidently fearful of being associated with the occupation.

We spent most of the evening comparing that day's attack in London with the Iraq insurgency. That distant outrage was a convenient (though misleading) method of discussing the problem which was highest on the minds of the occupying American army: how to isolate the militants and gain the support of the mass of the population. It was a conversation that the London bombers themselves might have relished, since they cited the Iraq occupation as a justification for their atrocities.

I admired the American troops I was embedded with. How could you not? They faced hardship and danger, and were regularly struck by suicide bombs and roadside attacks, but they continued doggedly with their mission. I joined them every day on their regular sweeps through the countryside to capture what they called the 'bad guys', although I did wonder how they could distinguish between al-Qaeda and local tribespeople. When soldiers talked to locals, they never looked them in the eye. When I asked an intelligence officer why, he explained he had no choice but to look around because he had to be constantly on the alert for dangers. As far as ordinary Iraqis were concerned, these Americans might as well have come from outer space, with their dark glasses, helmets, sophisticated weapons and communications systems which could call in an F-16 airstrike in less than an hour.

Despite all this, the following year Diyala province had fallen into the hands of al-Qaeda. A few years later, this part of Iraq was captured by Islamic State. More recently still, Iranian-backed militias swept through the province, reportedly ethnically cleansing the area of Sunni Muslims. Western intervention has all but disappeared, though the chaos and bloodshed it brought with it remains.

Darfur 2006

In 2006, I joined a militia unit guarding Chad's eastern border against incursions of the Sudanese Janjaweed Arab raiders. The raiders would come over on horses and camels, armed with automatic weapons and rocket-launchers, murdering and thieving cattle as they went.

News of another atrocity was no surprise. When we reached the scene after a long journey (Darfur is the size of Spain and there are no roads), we found that bodies had been shoved hastily into mass graves. An arm stuck out from under one bush, and the flesh had been eaten by wild animals. A human foot obtruded from another grave. Dried pools of blood stained the ground. The stench of human putrefaction was heavy in the air. Bits and pieces of clothing, spent bullets and the protective amulets used by the Darfuri fighters lay scattered on the ground. One body still lay exposed. The dead man had evidently climbed a tree to escape his attackers, but been shot down from his hiding place.

The Darfuris had used Neolithic weapons: bows and arrows, spears and swords. These were no use against the well-armed Arabs who possessed AK-47s, M14 automatic rifles, grenades and even anti-tank weapons which had been supplied by the Sudanese government. Survivors said the fight lasted on and off for two days and left 118 tribesmen dead. It's not known how many casualties they managed to inflict on the Janjaweed – probably none.

Our guides had brought shovels and pickaxes. They dug a shallow hole in the ground before manoeuvring the body into it. The dead man was a herdsman named Adiet Adam. He was thirty years old and the father of three children. After he was buried, Adam's fellow tribesmen gathered round the grave and recited prayers from the Quran. Then they were anxious to hurry off for fear of attack. According to survivors, the Janjaweed shouted, 'Djaoub al nubia' – 'Kill the Nuba' – during the massacre. The Darfur conflict has its roots in ancient tensions between nomadic Arabs and the pastoral Darfuri people. What made this cocktail utterly poisonous was the emergence in the 1980s and 1990s of a militant Arab ideology. 'You are informed that directives have been issued,' read one instruction from the headquarters of the Janjaweed leader, Musa Hilal, 'to change the demography of Darfur and empty it of African tribes.'

Hilal's father was an avuncular old sheikh who once hunted lions with the British explorer Wilfred Thesiger: the sheikh was one of the very last representatives of a timeless way of life. His son comes from the same nomadic tradition, but it is now horribly mutated. Western writers have made attempts to ratchet the Darfur tragedy into Huntington's 'clash of civilisations' thesis, and it cannot be denied that the genocidal Arab Muslim militias sponsored by Khartoum used a religious justification for their actions, claiming that they were engaged in jihad, a term drawn from the Quran, against the non-Arab population of Darfur.[2]

But the situation is complicated by the fact that most Darfuri people, including the victims of the terrible crime whose aftermath I witnessed, are Muslim too. This means it can be more readily understood as an ethnic conflict rather than one fought out between two religions. The Darfur tragedy is also the result of a battle for land and resources in one of the poorest parts of the planet. We are not talking about religion, or any grand civilisational conflict, but above all the capacity of humanity for evil. Musa Hilal, still a notable public figure in his native Sudan, is a war criminal comparable to Slobodan Milošević or Heinrich Himmler.

Peshawar 2008

Rahad Bibi had been in a coma for twenty days when I visited her hospital bed in Peshawar, the capital of Khyber Pakhtunkhwa province in Pakistan. Her brother-in-law, Sultan Jan, was by her side. 'The shelling started in the evening,' he said. 'It went on all night long. In the morning we decided it was time to leave the village.' In a panic, thirty-six villagers packed themselves into Sultan Jan's pick-up truck. After they had been travelling for an hour, he heard a bang. At first he thought a car tyre had burst.

'Looking up at the skies,' Sultan Jan told me, 'we saw a helicopter hovering above us. It fired at us with volleys of bullets.' His 3-year-old son, Rachim, was killed in front of him. 'He was sitting on my wife's lap in the front seat. His skull was broken on the dashboard. He died pressed against the lips of his mother.'

Doctors said that Rahad Bibi, remarkably, would make a full recovery – but when she woke, she would learn that her two sons, 13-month-old Habibullah and 4-year-old Najibullah, had died in the attack. 'Who do you blame for this?' I asked. He replied: 'We have been targeted by the government of Pakistan – and Britain is an ally of theirs.' Indeed, Pakistan's president Pervez Musharraf had been ordered to co-operate with the Bush–Blair coalition in its assault on Afghanistan or himself face being bombed 'back to the Stone Age'.[3] Musharraf consented, but his enforced decision to become part of the Blair–Bush 'war on terror' condemned Pakistan to a ten-year civil war. The Pashtun tribes that straddle the porous border between Afghanistan and Pakistan comprise the most ancient political societies on earth. They formed their language, loyalties and customs long before the arrival of Islam 1,400 years ago, let alone the creation of Pakistan in 1947. When the Pakistani state, on the orders of the US, attacked them, they retaliated, as tribal custom demanded. Suicide bombings, which have since killed so many thousands of Pakistanis, had been all but unknown before 2001.[4]

By the time I arrived, hundreds of thousands of people had fled from their tribal homes in the mountains to camps to escape attacks by F-16 fighters and long-range cannons. One twelve-year-old boy had lost every one of his eighteen-strong family group. When I got back to Islamabad, friends took me to visit Musharraf in his official commander-in-chief's residence in Rawalpindi. I found him nursing a small dog on his lap in a summer house in a remote corner of a garden the size of a small golf course. I described to him what I had seen. 'That's war', he said, stroking the pooch.

I told everyone about the horror I'd witnessed: diplomats, journalists, aid workers. Nobody was interested. This horrid little war was nothing to do with any clash of civilisations. It was a conflict between the US-supported central government in Islamabad and the northern tribal communities.[5]

Mindanao 2009

The militia leader took me round his defences. Trenches, barricades and bunkers. His *pièce de résistance* was an M30-calibre Second World War machine gun, which had been given to him by the army, and was aimed at some Muslim houses about fifteen yards away. He told us that Muslims had launched attacks 'on many occasions' over the previous twelve months, and burned down 200 Christian homes.

Well dressed, with near-perfect English, he told me that 'we are always under siege. The conflict here is about the land – it's just like Israel and Palestine.' He had 500 militiamen under his command, mainly farmers. They received arms from the government, but he told us they got most of their training from watching Hollywood movies. Some soldiers wore Christian amulets – radiant depictions of the Virgin Mary, the Last Supper or favourite saints – to protect them from bullets. One fighter, Juanin, recalled with relish cutting off the ears of dead Muslims, frying them and eating them, washed down with beer. He said that he made no distinction between ordinary Muslims and Muslim combatants. Recently, so he said, seven of his relations had been killed in a sectarian attack, so he felt that when he killed Muslims, he was simply doing the right thing.

I described in Chapter 2 how the Philippine Moros became the first Muslim subjects of America, which regarded them as barbaric, virtually sub-human, Islamic fanatics fit only for suppression as an obstacle to the advance of Christian civilisation. Nothing had changed. After fighting bravely alongside the Americans against the Japanese in the Second World War, the Muslim Filipino population have been left at the mercy of Christian settlers from the north. In 1945, the majority of the population in the then undivided provinces of Lanao, Cotabato, and the Sulu Archipelago of the Philippines' southern island of Mindanao was Muslim. Today that figure has fallen to around 20 per cent.[6] Many have been driven from their homes by the Philippine army. 'The Christians want to exterminate us, or convert us,' one dispossessed farmer told me. 'But that cannot happen. I was born a Muslim and I will die a Muslim.' When I interviewed a Philippine army general, I asked him why he was wearing an SAS badge. 'They trained me,' he replied. The essential story here, as in Peshawar, has nothing to do with a clash of civilisations. Christian settlers from the north, backed by the Philippine government and supported by the West, are seizing the ancient tribal lands of the indigenous Muslim tribes. It is, as the militia leader so frankly stated, about land.The good news is that there has been peace for the last five years.

Nigeria 2010

Near Jos, a large town in the Nigerian central belt where British prime minister John Major had once been stationed as a banker with Standard Chartered, I walked through the village of Kuru Karama, silent except for birdsong. A villager took me to a little square and pointed out some of the wells into which militants had thrown scores of dead bodies, head downwards. Some bodies were so decomposed that they could not be removed. The stench of death seeped out of the wells.

The villager pointed to a sewage pit, now covered with concrete blocks. He told us that the jihadis had thrown in thirty children, aged between six months and three years old. This pit was now their unmarked grave. All around were burned patches on the ground, in the shape of human bodies, where the jihadis had hacked down their victims, poured fuel on them and set them alight. Every church in the village was burned to ashes, while the two mosques were intact.

Every detail above is true, but I have taken one liberty. Readers of Western media have become accustomed to expect that Muslims carry out terrible acts like these. In fact, the attack had been carried out by Christians against Muslims; the town's two churches were left intact, while the mosques were burned to the ground. Abdullah, my guide, had been away on the day of the attack and returned to discover that he had lost *thirteen* family members, including his wife. He broke down as he told me how, when he helped pull her body out of a well, he saw that her face had been mutilated and he could only recognise her by her clothes.

There were more than 170 dead. There had since been no arrests, and no charges had been pressed. That Sunday, I returned to Kuru Karama. Once more, I walked through the burned-out buildings until I reached a large church untouched by the killers. Above the altar were deep red drapes, in front of which a large banner pronounced: 'Serving God With Purpose'.

Men sat on the right of the church, gorgeously dressed women on the left. A soldier with a gun lounged at the back, stretching and yawning. The singing was beautiful. The pastor intoned: 'We pray for the peace of the nation, we pray for the people of Nigeria.' He devoted much of his sermon to reading from a long, inflammatory and palpably faked document that set out, in great detail, Muslim plans to take over and dominate central Nigeria. It named leading Muslim generals and politicians as part of an organised conspiracy – Christian Nigeria's answer to the *Protocols of the Elders of Zion*.

After the service, I sat down with the pastor, the Reverend Yohanna Musabot. A smallish man, forty-two years old, he told me that he had studied at the Theological College of Northern Nigeria and had been a priest for ten years. I asked him whether he wanted to apologise on behalf of the Christian community for the unspeakably evil acts that had been committed just a few yards away from where we were sitting. He refused to do so, saying that there had been crimes on both sides (this was only too true:

a terrible reprisal attack took place later). I asked him why all the churches in the village were intact, while the mosques were burned. He could not explain. Nor could he name a member of his congregation who had been killed. I asked him what Jesus would have done. 'I believe if Jesus was here, he would not be happy with what happened,' said the pastor.

I don't think he was a bad man, that pastor – simply caught in a situation way beyond his own – or anyone else's – comprehension. He told me that he had tried to stop the killers but failed. When I checked this out, witnesses told me that he had been far more courageous than he claimed: that he had been head-butted and knocked down, and that if he had not run away, he would have been killed. This conduct seems at odds with the inflammatory message he read out in his sermon. Yet every human soul embraces impulses of good and evil. Reverend Musabot was heroic when he confronted the armed killers who invaded his village. I dare say that the bigotry he preached from his pulpit came from elsewhere and did not represent his deepest personal beliefs.

Syria 2014

Broken icons lay on the ground alongside crosses, catechisms, and images of the Virgin Mary. Shell holes let in sun through the ancient limestone walls of the monastery of St Sergius which stands above the sacred town of Maaloula, one of the few places on earth where Aramaic, the language of Jesus Christ, is still spoken. The cliffs that surround the town echoed the sound of machine-gun fire and explosions, and from outside the monastery, smoke was visible, rising from houses below.

Months before, the Christian town had been taken by rebel fighters (according to my Syrian guides, they included Jabhat al-Nusra, the Syrian al-Qaeda affiliate). Syrian army soldiers, fighting alongside local militia and seasoned Hezbollah fighters were on the verge of taking it back. The rebels were supported by the US, the UK, Turkey and Saudi Arabia, all of whom were all too well aware that the anti-Assad coalition contained substantial al-Qaeda elements.[7]

In the monastery library was the visitors' book, recording comments made by the thousands of pilgrims who had visited the monastery of St Sergius over the years. One read:

> This is a very beautiful place to visit and also very inspirational to know that Christians have existed in this area continuously for so many years. May the work here in God's name continue and help to bring peace and understanding to all people in the Middle East and the world, regardless of who or by what means they choose to worship God.

I picked up a small cross, of the kind that is sold to pilgrims, from the floor of the monastery as I left. It's hanging on my wall as I write. It felt like theft, but there was no one to accept payment. One day I will return and pay for it.

A while later and I am on the edges of Islamic State-held Palmyra. Lieutenant Milad's platoon is located as close as the Syrian army gets to the IS fortress. The young artillery officer holds a position about four kilometres west of this ancient city, with a clear view of the citadel. He has a dozen soldiers under his command. They share a single bivouac, outside which I spot a shisha pipe. From this dusty outpost, a soldier peers through powerful field glasses for signs of an IS assault. He tells how they are attacked by IS 'almost every day'. He and his men speak of sudden night-time assaults and daytime ambushes from IS fighters camouflaged to be invisible in the desert sand.

Lieutenant Milad had witnessed IS's grotesque destruction of Palmyra from this hilltop position: the historic temples of Baalshamin and Bel, as well as the three ancient tombs, the oldest of which dates back to just a decade after the death of Jesus. 'We heard and saw the explosion – the noise was very big. They are

killing our history, they are killing our culture, they are killing our families. IS are monsters.' For Milad, there is a unique
pathos in what he has witnessed. He studied archaeology at the
University of Aleppo before the conflict began and on graduation,
narrowly failed to win a place at Cambridge University. In the
irony of ironies, several years earlier, he took part in a dig around
the Bel temple, which he had just witnessed being annihilated.
The dig was supervised by Khaled al-Asaad, the 82-year-old
antiquities scholar who had chosen not to flee the city when IS
captured it. A month later, the terror group beheaded him after
he refused to reveal where valuable artefacts had been moved
for safekeeping. They hung his mutilated body on a column in
Palmyra's main square.

The bearded lieutenant, in his late twenties, told me that he
had been a drummer for a big jazz band during the years of peace
and was hopeful of army leave so that he could get married the
following month. That evening I returned to the nearby city of
Homs, where I drank tea with a Syrian priest and told him about
Lieutenant Milad. To my amazement, the priest knew the young
officer. He recalled that Milad was 'part of the relief of Aleppo.
He came into my church and asked me to bless him, and said "I
want you to pray for me so that I am not killed."'

According to the official ideology of President Bashar al-
Assad's secular regime, all religions are equal. The regime has
been roundly and rightly denounced in the West, and by the
Muslim Brotherhood, for its war crimes and merciless brutality. In this instance, however, Assad's soldiers, with Hezbollah
fighters alongside, were defending Christianity and the essence
of Western civilisation against Islamic State. Nothing is simple.

Turkey 2017

I received a promise of safe passage from the Islamist fighting
group Ahrar al-Sham[8] to visit the north Syrian province of Idlib,

which at the time of writing is still in the hands of the rebels. I travelled with a guide to the border town of Reyhanli, just three miles from the border crossing point of Bab al-Hawa, which has been the busiest highway between Syria and Turkey during the Syrian conflict. But when we reached the border itself, my guide said that he could not advise crossing into Syria, saying that there was a price of 20 million dollars on the head of any kidnapped Western journalist and though he trusted the word of Ahrar al-Sham, feared it might not be able to protect me.

In a safe house we met an Egyptian, Ahmed (not his real name), who had recently come over the border after three years in Syria, where he had fought with a variety of armed groups including the Free Syrian Army, Jabhat al-Nusra and Ahrar al-Sham, as well as other smaller groups. Ahmed, who has a black beard and luminous brown eyes, told us: 'In Egypt, we were just going to get killed. At least here in Syria we are on equal ground.'

Ahmed, who hails from a middle-class Egyptian family, was just twenty-four years old when the Arab Spring was unleashed in 2011. He had a job as a schoolteacher and preached regularly in mosques across Cairo. He immediately became a strong supporter of Morsi's Freedom and Justice Party, even though he was not a member of the Egyptian Muslim Brotherhood. He subsequently became furious with the Brotherhood for its failure to show strength and support to Morsi with power and arms. He recalled in 2012 how when thugs tried to attack the presidential compound, he and his friends wanted to stand up and fight them, but had not been allowed to do so. He told us of his despair that the Brotherhood installed checkpoints for weapons which they seized and handed over to the security services.

The turning point in Ahmed's life was not the victory of Morsi in the Egyptian presidential election of 2012. It was the *coup d'état*, engineered by General Sisi and the Egyptian army in 2013, with subsequent backing from the US and the UK. Like many young Egyptians, he was enraged by the peaceful response of the Muslim

Brotherhood. 'We believed at that moment that our dream needed power to protect it. It was not rational to stand up naked against fire power and aircraft. We didn't have anything to defend ourselves with.' He said that he was convinced that the Muslim Brotherhood's refusal to use force 'was the wrong decision'. He concluded that 'democracy turned out to be a fallacy'.

The military coup against the peaceful and democratic Muslim Brotherhood has sent many young Muslims on the path towards international terror. In the West, we treat democracy as a kind of religion. But we rarely allow it when it produces results we don't like. This selective embrace of democracy across the Muslim world has malign consequences. It has encouraged thousands of political activists like Ahmed to ponder violence, and it has legit-imised al-Qaeda's central message that Western democracy is a sham. When Ahmed backed democratic protest in the shape of the Muslim Brotherhood, the US and the UK supported his bar-barous opponents. When he joined al-Nusra, the Syrian affiliate of al-Qaeda, both countries were on the same side as him.

Myanmar 2017

Belatedly acting on the advice of the leader of the Parliament of the World's Religions (see page 9), I took myself to Sittwe, the capital of Myanmar's Rakhine State. On arrival, at first I could not understand why he had urged me to go. Emerging from my hotel was like walking into a Somerset Maugham short story. Elegant women with parasols to protect against the burning tropical sun walked slowly down well-appointed streets.

Within 200 yards, I found the blackened remains of a mosque, burned down by a Burmese mob five years earlier. Until then, 50,000 of the city's population of around 180,000 had been Rohingya Muslim. Fewer than 3,000 were left, crammed into a ghetto surrounded by barbed wire. Armed guards prevented visitors from entering – and would not let anyone leave.

The Rohingya have been stripped of the right to vote, while new laws suppressed Muslim population growth. Activists smuggled me into one of the camps, about ten miles from the city centre. On the way, we drove through the airy suburbs where Muslims used to live freely. The camp itself was an open-air prison and smelt of sewage.

Mass killings started a few months later. I travelled to Cox's Bazar in Bangladesh, where 600,000 survivors had fled after terrifying jungle journeys. They told how Myanmar soldiers, assisted by Buddhist villagers, raped, burned, mutilated and killed.

The UK was penholder at the United Nations with direct responsibility for Security Council policy towards Myanmar. No sanctions were applied. The British Foreign Secretary, Boris Johnson, didn't even summon the Myanmar ambassador to the Foreign Office. While the slaughter was in progress, Foreign Office minister Mark Field actually defended the Myanmar government, concentrating on provocations by Rohingya with scant reference to the atrocities being carried out against them. In the *Sun*, the columnist Rod Liddle took the same line: 'It's probably true that the Burmese government has been a bit, um, heavy-handed,' he wrote. 'But shouldn't we be told a little more about the causes of the problem? The countless terrorist attacks against Burmese police stations and Buddhists?'[9] Liddle, like Boris Johnson's Foreign Office, was callously echoing Myanmar government talking points. It was certainly true that, according to Myanmar official sources, there had been a series of attacks by Rohingya militants on security positions and civilians who were seen as government collaborators, and the campaign of state-backed violence was prompted by an attack by militants on police and army posts on 25 August 2017.[10] But these were pinpricks in comparison with the carefully organised campaign of ethnic cleansing bordering on genocide that followed. The UN high commissioner for human rights, Zeid Ra'ad Al Hussein, later stressed that 'these operations were organised and planned',

adding that 'you couldn't exclude the possibility of acts of genocide'.[11] The Rohingya, forbidden from travelling outside their
own villages and so poor that most of them can't afford a bicycle,
have been relentlessly portrayed as malign. It was a similar story
to Mindanao. The military machine of a powerful central government, with the West turning a blind eye, turned mercilessly
on the Muslim minority.

Srebrenica 2017

When I arrived in Srebrenica, it immediately became plain that
Europe's only post-war genocide (thus far) had done its job. With
many of the town's former Muslim residents dead or emigrated,
Srebrenica is back in the hands of Bosnian Serbs. Nedzad Avdic, a
genocide survivor who moved back to Srebrenica, told me: 'Our
first child is starting at the local school. They are being taught that
the genocide never happened.' Nedzad Avdic's uncle and father
were killed. He only survived after crawling away, badly wounded,
from a mound of dead men. He told me that he had returned out
of defiance, but now felt he had no choice but to leave again.

Mejra Dzogaz's sons were killed by the Serbs. She told me she
sees the killers in the streets, some holding offices at the local
council or local police force. 'I put so much sugar in my coffee
every morning,' she added, 'but no matter how much I put in, it
still tastes bitter.'

A Bosnian Serb nationalist politician, Mladen Grujicic, was at
the time of writing mayor of Srebrenica. He refuses to use the
word genocide about the atrocities of July 1995 – even though
they are regarded by scholars as the most well-documented and
best-evidenced war crime in history. 'When they prove it to be
the truth,' Grujicic has said, 'I'll be the first to accept it.'[1] The
genocide has been whitewashed from history, and the murderous
propaganda against Bosnian Muslims is ongoing.

Lilian Black, then chair of the Holocaust Survivors' Friendship

Association and director of the Holocaust Heritage and Learning Centre, was on the trip. Black drew comparisons with her own family's terrible experiences. 'It really hurts when people deny the murder of your family. It is just like a dagger to the heart, as if they never even existed.' Germany fully acknowledged and made atonement for the dreadful crimes committed against the Jews. Not so the Serbs. They can strike again.

Islamabad 2021

Eighteen-year-old Jawad comes to see me in an Islamabad guest house. He wants to tell me about his father. He tells me how, when he was a child, his mother explained his father's absence by saying that he was away working in Saudi Arabia, as many Pakistanis do. Jawad first spoke to his father when he was six years old, in a fifteen-minute telephone call arranged by the Red Cross.

His father told him he was in jail.

'I asked him why are you in jail? The jail is supposed to be for bad people. He laughed and didn't reply,' remembers Jawad.

Jawad's father is in Guantanamo Bay. Jawad told me how this knowledge started to affect him when he became a teenager. 'I went to the dark web when I was thirteen or fourteen years old. I was in those groups where they share videos where they tortured people and all those things. So, I do have an idea of how they tortured him, waterboarding or kicking him or playing music that will torture my dad. How they will make miserable his brain. I knew it.

'There was a time that I used to believe my father had committed a crime. That's why he's been tortured, because you don't torture a person for no reason. I used to cry, you know, at night in my room. Just imagine your life without your father for eighteen years. What would you be? If he didn't touch you or care for you or provide you his love, his money, everything? Where would you be?'

Jawad became introverted and tormented. He could never make friends because he felt unable to talk about his family circumstances. The turning point came two years ago when he met Clive Stafford Smith, the British lawyer who has represented more than eighty of the Guantanamo detainees.

'I learned after that meeting that my father is innocent,' Jawad said. 'The second thing is that I shouldn't be ashamed of my father because he's in jail.'

Jawad's father is a Pakistani taxi driver called Ahmed Rabbani, who was kidnapped from his home in Karachi by Pakistan state authorities in September 2002 and taken to the country's capital Islamabad. From there he was transferred to Cobalt, the notorious 'dark prison' near Kabul in Afghanistan, where he was held in CIA custody. The Senate Select Committee report on torture, published ten years ago, has documented what Rabbani and many others experienced.

Cobalt's blacked-out windows left prisoners isolated in total darkness, and often without heat in Afghanistan's freezing winters. They were shackled to bars with their hands forced above their heads, meaning they could never rest. Loud music was played constantly, denying sleep. Some detainees were subjected to cigarette burns. Others were stripped naked, hosed down with water and placed in cold cells. Rabbani has told his lawyers that for days on end he was 'hung by the hand to an iron shackle where my toes hardly touched the ground'. This torture, known as 'strappado', was favoured by the Spanish Inquisition.

After 540 days in Cobalt, Rabbani was rendered to Guantanamo Bay, the offshore military prison where US law does not apply, meaning that the US government is able to hold detainees indefinitely without charge as enemy combatants.

Rabbani is innocent. As the Senate report recorded in 2012, he had been mistaken for an al-Qaeda operative called Hassan Ghul. The United States has known this for a decade, probably much longer. And yet Rabbani is still in Guantanamo as I write, and still to meet his son. Many have suffered in the same way. Rabbani, a Rohingya Pakistani, weighed around 73 kilograms at the time of his arrest. Emaciated from a hunger strike, today he weighs just 30 kilograms. He suffers mentally and finds it hard to remember things.

The United States completely abandoned the rule of law and any pretence of due process with its practice of arbitrary detention and torture – or 'enhanced interrogation'. Britain complied meekly, with the US imprisoning and torturing British citizens without charge. British intelligence was involved in interrogations. Habeas corpus, that famed ancient liberty, which ensures that no one can be imprisoned unlawfully, has been completely disregarded in the 'war on terror'.

Muslims have been deemed by many in the West to be undeserving of basic human rights. It is inconceivable that the British government would have stood by as a white Christian Briton was tortured and imprisoned in Cuba; in the case of British Muslims, however, they appear to consider it unproblematic.

Each one of the 780 prisoners held in Guantanamo over the course of its history has been Muslim. Every single one since the first twenty detainees arrived there twenty years ago, on 11 January 2002. Guantanamo constructs terrorism as an Islamic phenomenon, requiring an alternative legal structure to cope with what was seen as the exceptional horror of Muslim crimes. This helps place in context the well-attested stories of Guantanamo guards deliberately desecrating the Holy Quran.

The prison remains open today. Innocent men are sitting or lying in their cells there as I write these words in January 2022. The prison stands as a reminder of the enduring barbarism and savagery unleashed upon innocent Muslims by the Islamophobia generated in the West after 9/11. The 'war on terror' has often been framed in the West as a mortal struggle against a barbarous, irrational Islam hell-bent on the destruction of freedom and human life. Guantanamo inverts this story.

By coincidence, on the evening I interviewed Jawad, the news came through that, after two decades of incarceration, the US authorities had scheduled Ahmed Rabbani for release. It was wonderful news – but he shouldn't be too hopeful. There are Guantanamo detainees who have been scheduled for release for a decade and have still not been freed.

As for Jawad, he told me his dream that he and his father can open a Rohingya restaurant together in their native Karachi. Let's pray they are not kept waiting for too much longer.

CONCLUSION

THE FATE OF ABRAHAM

Hebron

Jew, Christian, Muslim – all worship the God of Abraham. Abraham was born approximately four millennia ago in Ur, a prosperous city-state in the south of today's Iraq. From there, Abraham, who probably came (like the Prophet Muhammad) from a family of merchant traders, embarked on his momentous journey.

From Ur, he travelled north to Babylon, where he would have seen the great ziggurat Eteme-an-ki, remembered in the Jewish and Christian traditions as the Tower of Babel. Further on, he may have passed what is now Baghdad, then the site of an obscure village, on his way to Nineveh and then Gozan (Tell Halaf) in modern Turkey. Abraham's father Terah died there.

His journey, probably in a convoy of ox carts along well-guarded roads, was easier and safer than it would be today. Abraham passed through Aleppo, the most ancient city in the world, then Damascus. The street called Straight, where St Paul was cured of blindness and along which people still walk today, was already there when Abraham passed through the city. He then crossed the Golan Heights and along the Jordan River before ending his days at Hebron, approximately twenty miles south of Jerusalem.

He fathered two sons. His eldest, Ishmael, was born to Hagar, whom Muslims believe to have been his wife, although in the biblical narrative she is his servant; Ishmael is regarded by Muslims as the ancestor of the Arab nation. Abraham's younger son Isaac, through his wife Sarah, is the ancestor of the Jews. Both Jews and Christians see Isaac as the legitimate heir to Abraham's monotheistic tradition. Christians think that Isaac prefigures Christ. Just as Abraham's readiness to sacrifice his son made atonement for the sins of the children of Israel, so Jesus would do the same for mankind. Abraham is thus the patriarch of the three great monotheistic religions.

The Bible records that Abraham purchased the Cave of Machpelah, as it is called by the Jews, for 400 shekels following the death of Sarah, the first burial (and first commercial transaction) to be recorded in the Bible. Later Isaac and Ishmael buried him there.

I drove to the West Bank city of Hebron. When I typed 'Hebron' into Waze (the Israeli equivalent of Google Maps), a warning flashed up: 'This destination is a high-risk area or is prohibited to Israelis by law.' A settlement was established there in 1979. Perhaps 700 settlers live there now. They occupy an area of houses above the ancient market and are heavily guarded by soldiers from the Israel Defense Forces. These soldiers stand idly by as the settlers harass, persecute and assault the local population. The settlers have created a ghost city in ancient Hebron. The markets are mainly closed because of 'security reasons'. More than a thousand houses have been shut up and around 1,300 shops have been closed. I walked through this desolate area. Zionist slogans such as 'Hevron Yehudit' – 'Hebron is Jewish' – have been scrawled on the walls. The Star of David was sprayed on the doors of many shops, and the names of the streets have been changed from Palestinian to Hebrew ones.

I passed a small settler museum. It was empty and unattended. I called out. A lady came out of a backroom and showed me around. The first room was dedicated to the ancient Jewish presence in Hebron. The second concentrated on the massacre of Jews by Arabs in 1929. It contained horrifying and vivid contemporary photographs of the atrocity, during which sixty-nine Jews were killed. I reached the Tomb of the Patriarchs (the Bible's Cave of Machpelah), where Abraham, Isaac, Sarah, Jacob and Leah are buried. There was an invisible line in the street outside, which Palestinians may not cross. A soldier asked a Palestinian 'Are you Muslim?' as she ventured into the road. Jews could use the public toilets, but not the Palestinians.

As so often in Israel and occupied Palestine, the Tomb of the Patriarchs (as it is often called by Christians; Muslims talk of the Sanctuary of Abraham; Jews talk of the Cave of Machpelah) is divided: one third for Muslims and two thirds set aside for Jews. This partition was built after 1994, when an Israeli settler called Baruch Goldstein entered the building with a machine gun and shot dead twenty-nine Muslim worshippers before being beaten to death. I asked where he was buried: Qiryat Arba, a settlement on the outskirts of Hebron which is home to 7,000 people and where, according to the Bible, Abraham's wife Sarah died.

That evening, I drove up there. A guard nodded me through the entrance gate. Everyone I asked knew where Goldstein was buried, so I found the grave fairly easily. It was behind a row of shops in a public park. The Hebrew inscription read: 'To the holy Baruch Goldstein, who gave his life for the Jewish people, the Torah, and the nation of Israel.' Beside the grave was a glass container in which was two candles and some spent matches. I walked back to the shops and tried to talk to some settlers. Eventually I found a woman who said she had known Goldstein. She said: 'He was my doctor. He was a wonderful man. He was an amazing person who took care of the Arabs and the Jews as well.' She told me that she had come from the United States to Qiryat Arba as a child and that she was 'against violence on both sides'. As for Goldstein, she felt 'there was something that pushed him over. There was a lot of violence on both sides at the time.'

Later, I returned to the Tomb of the Patriarchs. Above it is a powerful rectangular structure, built by King Herod around the time that Christ was born. Since then, it's changed hands between Byzantines, Crusaders, Saladin, the Ottomans, the Jordanians and others. Its ownership is disputed today. Surely it belongs to Abraham alone, patriarch to three great religions and a man of peace. We are all his descendants: the people of the book. We all worship his God. I fell to my knees and I prayed.

A false prophecy

Almost exactly twenty-nine years ago, *Foreign Affairs* magazine published by far the most influential academic treatise of the modern era: Samuel Huntington's 'The Clash of Civilizations?'. This article helped to shape the world and launch wars. It has led to moral and intellectual catastrophe, untold devastation and millions of deaths.

Here's a reminder of Huntington's confidently expressed thesis:

> It is my hypothesis that the fundamental source of conflict in the new world will not be primarily ideological or primarily economic. The great divisions among humankind and the dominating source of conflict will be cultural. Nation states will remain the most powerful actors in world affairs, but the principal conflicts of global politics will occur between nations and groups of different civilizations. The clash of civilizations will dominate global politics. The fault lines between civilizations will be the battle lines of the future.

The most influential part of Huntington's theory concerned Islam. He argued that with the end of the Cold War between the USSR and the West, it would be replaced by a new struggle between two irreconcilable enemies: Islam and the West. As we have seen, the Huntington thesis has inspired a flourishing publishing industry; countless books are calls to arms in the supposed war against Islamism.

But is there indeed a clash of civilisations, as not just Huntington but so many others believe? Certainly, the events of 9/11, when al-Qaeda launched a ferocious attack on the US, gave massive credibility to Huntington's bleak analysis. The wave of Western attacks on Muslim countries in the years that followed appeared to reinforce it, along with the devastating terrorist attacks on London, Paris and other Western cities. Western politicians now speak the language of the clash of civilisations.

But while the events of 9/11 seemed to have fulfilled Huntington's prophecy, in reality they did not. Not a single one of the world's fifty Muslim-majority countries has declared war on the US, nor have we seen an Islamic coalition forming. When one did emerge in 2017 in Yemen, it was Saudi led and sponsored by the US.[2] In Syria, where we have al-Qaeda emerge as a significant Western partner in the war while Assad has defended one of the most ancient Christian communities, the Huntington thesis has collapsed.

Many credible analysts in the Arab world hold the US responsible for creating the conditions that allowed terror groups such as al-Qaeda to flourish – and Islamic State to exist in the first place – when they invaded and occupied Iraq, and destroyed state institutions. Huntington mattered very much. His thesis that the civilised world was fighting 'radical Islam' provided the Western military-industrial complex with the idea of a global, systemic, multinational enemy that replaced communism. It's helped create wars and provoked hatred of Muslims in the United States and among its allies across the globe.

Reclaiming our common humanity

We can start by thinking again about Islam and the West. Recent analysis has been beset by intellectual and moral error. The intellectual error has been to think about Islam in terms of the Cold War. From 1945 until the fall of the Soviet Empire, there really was a clash of ideologies between two military empires, each capable of obliterating the other through force. Even after 9/11, every Muslim state, including the Taliban in Afghanistan, condemned the barbarous attacks on the United States. There were candlelit vigils in Tehran.

This mistaken analysis has led to gross moral error. During the Cold War, Western strategists, wrongly but perhaps understandably, considered the stakes so high that it was legitimate to sacrifice the values that we claim to defend in the mortal combat against Soviet Communism. In the so-called 'war on terror', Western strategists have taken the same view. They conceived that the West (and its supposed Judaeo-Christian values) was engaged in a mortal conflict against Islam (or Islamism), as it had been against the Soviet Union. Just as during the Cold War, they decided that the imperative of an existential struggle against a hostile and violent ideology liberated them to commit terrible crimes. These included illegal wars, torture and a general repudiation of democracy, human rights and decency.

This strategy was wrong in itself. It also awarded a legitimacy to movements such as al-Qaeda and Islamic State. These terror groups had always argued that Western support for liberal democracy was a sham. Western policy since 9/11 validated that al-Qaeda analysis. Both sides have shared a contempt for democracy, human life, the rule of law and due process. In their different ways, both accept the Marxist doctrine that the end justifies the means, up to and including barbaric methods like torture and inflicting civilian casualties.

At the same time, al-Qaeda and the neo-conservatives who have been so influential in forming US foreign policy over the last twenty years share an almost identical analysis of Islam. They both disregard the message of humanity and compassion which lies at the heart of the teaching of the Prophet, insisting instead that Islam is a religion of violence. Osama bin Laden, for example, dismissed the Islamic prohibition against the killing of women and children, meaning that al-Qaeda and other violent Islamic groups in turn awarded a kind of legitimacy to an interpretation of Islam as a militant force hell-bent on the destruction of Western civilisation. In this way, al-Qaeda and the neo-conservatives have been locked into a death embrace. The illegal wars and acts of terror carried out with impunity by the US and her allies have made al-Qaeda's analysis of the West appear all too plausible, while granting a twisted moral sanction to Islamic terror which is not to be found in Islam itself.

A second comparison with Cold War doctrine bears examination. During the post-war era, the US and her allies considered that the mortal threat posed by the USSR enfranchised the West to enter into military alliances with some of the most repulsive regimes the world has known, including Saddam Hussein's Iraq, apartheid South Africa and Pinochet's Chile. This pattern repeated itself after the end of the Cold War. Across the Middle East, the Western countries are aligned with a series of despotisms where human rights are disregarded, the press is controlled and political parties are banned.

This means that democratic Islamist movements, collectively labelled political Islam, found themselves in a desperate predicament. They were not just fighting their own local dictatorships, but the West as well. This is part of the explanation for the rise of a virulent Islamophobia across the West in the last two decades. Some Arab leaders have dedicated significant resources to fuelling suspicion of Islam. They do this to discredit their domestic opposition, who in other circumstances might be regarded in the West as heroic resistance fighters. So we need to think about foreign policy and in particular the alliances we enter into and friendships we make.

We need to reflect on the language we use about Muslims. Words like 'extremist' and 'Islamist' are used by politicians, strategists and the wider media promiscuously to lump terror groups together with non-violent political movements. This strategy, more and more common across Western countries, involves ostracising (or 'cancelling', to use contemporary jargon) Muslim politicians and spokespeople and indeed driving them out of the public sphere. This policing of public discourse means that only two types of voice can be widely heard: officially approved critics of Islam and those Muslims in Western countries who agree with the approved analysis. There is a dark contradiction at work here: Western countries allow free speech, but only for those who accept that non-violent political Islam (Islamism) is at best a threat to the West and at worst part of a wider terror movement.

We urgently need to recognise that the concept of terrorism has been debased. Originally applied to describe state terror, in modern times this usage was abandoned and applied *exclusively* to violence by non-state actors. In recent years, it has mutated once more and is now commonly applied to peaceful opposition movements. By an unnerving paradox, governments which themselves use domestic terror mercilessly against their own populations, deploy the term to criminalise non-violent opposition. Muslim groups are the most numerous – though far from the only – victims. The term is now worse than valueless. It has become actively misleading and needs to be rethought.

It is widely recognised that there is a crisis in public discourse, a problem which stretches way beyond the conversation around Islam. We have lost the ability to listen to each other. To put it another way, we seem increasingly unable to have a civilised conversation with people who disagree with us. We dismiss reasonable criticism as valueless, often attributing bad faith to critics. Social anthropologists define this inability to tolerate disagreement as 'tribal epistemology'.

This brings us to the ugliest manifestation of this closed discourse. The American, British and French media don't report on Muslims. It targets them, fabricating stories and fomenting at best distrust and at worst hatred. In late 2021, Pope Francis made a rare pontifical observation about journalism:

I want in some way to pay homage to your entire working community to tell you that the pope loves you, follows you, esteems you, considers you precious . . . Journalism is not so much a matter of choosing a profession, but rather of embarking on a mission, a bit like a doctor, who studies and works to cure evil in the world. Your mission is to explain the world, to make it less obscure, to make those who live in it less afraid and to look at others with greater awareness.[3]

Newspapers were unknown in the seventh century, but something along the same lines can be found in the Quran: 'O ye who believe! If an evil-lover bring you tidings, verify it, lest ye smite some folk in ignorance and afterward repent of what ye did.'[4] This warning against false and malevolent reporting remains as relevant today as it was in seventh-century Arabia.

Ultimately, the solution is simple. All of the world's great religions have the same golden rule: treat your neighbour as yourself. The sage Hillel the Elder explained Jewish ethics to an enquirer: 'What is hateful to you, do not do to your fellow: this is the whole Torah; the rest is the explanation; go and learn.' Jesus Christ echoed the Torah when he taught 'Thou shalt love thy neighbour as thyself'.

A Bedouin wandered up to the Prophet Muhammad, grabbed the stirrup of his camel and asked: 'O messenger of God! Teach me something to go to heaven with it.' The Prophet answered: 'As you would have people do to you, do to them; and what you dislike to be done to you, don't do to them. Now let the stirrup go!'

NOTES

PROLOGUE

1   Peter Oborne, *The Use and Abuse of Terror: The Construction of a False Narrative on the Domestic Terror Threat* (Centre for Policy Studies, 2006).

2   Peter Oborne, *The Use and Abuse of Terror: The Construction of a False Narrative on the Domestic Terror Threat.* https://cps.org.uk/wp-content/uploads/2021/07/111028102646-20060731PublicServicesTheUseAndAbuseOfTerror.pdf

3   Ginny Dougary, 'The Voice of Experience', *The Times*, 9 September 2006.

4   Christopher Hitchens, 'Martin Amis is no racist', *Guardian*, 21 November 2007. https://www.theguardian.com/uk/2007/nov/21/race.religion

5   Peter Oborne and James Jones, 'Muslims Under Siege: Alienating Vulnerable Communities', in association with Channel 4 *Dispatches* (*Democratic Audit, Human Rights Centre, University of Essex*, 2008) https://www.channel4.com/news/media/pdfs/ Muslims_under_siege_LR.pdf

6   Rob Liddle, 'Warning: This Article May Soon Be Illegal', *The Spectator*. https://www.spectator.co.uk/article/warning-this-column-may-soon-be-illegal

7   This seems to be a reference to a fashion show organised by Muslim women to highlight the latest fashion ideas – illustating 'how modesty can be fabulously stylish': https://issuu.com/islamchannelbrochure/docs/gpu_event_brochure_2013_web2

8   Maajid Nawaz, 'I was radicalised. So I understand how extremists exploit grievances', *Guardian*, 26 February 2015. https://www.theguardian.com/commentisfree/2015/feb/26/tackle-extremism-understand-racism-islamism

9   Roger Scruton, *The Palgrave Macmillan Dictionary of Political Thought* (Palgrave Macmillan, 1982).

10 'CAIR Welcomes AP Stylebook Revision of "Islamist"', CAIR, 5 April 2013. https://www.cair.com/press_releases/cair-welcomes-ap-stylebook-revision-of-islamist/

11 Olivier Roy and Antoine Sfeir, *The Columbia World Dictionary of Islamism* (Columbia University Press, 2007).

12   See Bal Gangadhar Tilak, 'Address to the Indian National Congress, 1907',
     reprinted in William T. de Bary et al., *Sources of Indian Tradition* (New York:
     Columbia University Press, 1958), pp. 719-723.

     'Two new words have recently come into existence with regard to our
     politics, and they are Moderates and Extremists. These words have a specific
     relation to time, and they, therefore, will change with time. The Extremists of
     today will be Moderates tomorrow, Just as the Moderates of today were
     Extremists yesterday. When the National Congress was first started and Mr.
     Dadabhai's views, which now go for Moderates, were given to the public, he
     was styled an Extremist, so that you will see that the term Extremist is an
     expression of progress. We are Extremists today and our sons will call
     themselves Extremists and us Moderates. Every new party begins as
     Extremists and ends as Moderates.'

13   Sasha Ingber, '70 Muslim Clerics Issue Fatwa Against Violence and Terrorism',
     NPR, 11 May 2018. https://www.npr.org/sections/thetwo-way/2018/05/11/
     610420149/70-muslim-clerics-issue-fatwa-against-violence-and-terrorism?t=
     1645118670890;

     For more condemnations of Islamic State by Muslim scholars and leaders,
     see: 'Global Condemnations of ISIS/ISIL', ing.org. https://ing.org/resources/
     for-all-groups/answers-to-frequently-asked-questions/answers-to-frequently-
     asked-questions-about-islam-and-muslims/global-condemnations-of-isis-isil/

14   The idea of a 'conveyor belt' towards terrorism appears to come from the
     United States. The New York Police Department came up with the analogy of
     a conveyor belt to describe radicalisation in 2007. But is the theory true?
     Critics suggest not. In 2013, terrorism expert and former CIA officer Marc
     Sageman told governments to 'stop being brainwashed by this notion of
     "radicalization". There is no such thing. Some people, when they're young,
     acquire extreme views; many of them just grow out of them. Do not
     overreact—you'll just create worse problems.' John Horgan, an expert on the
     psychology of terrorism, has said that 'the idea that radicalization causes
     terrorism is perhaps the greatest myth alive today in terrorism research . . .
     [First], the overwhelming majority of people who hold radical beliefs do not
     engage in violence. And second, there is increasing evidence that people who
     engage in terrorism don't necessarily hold radical beliefs'. French sociologist
     Olivier Roy wrote that 'the process of violent radicalisation has little to do
     with religious practice, while radical theology, as salafisme, does not
     necessarily lead to violence'. And Donatella Della Porta, a leading scholar of
     social movements and political violence, emphasises, as Martha Crenshaw did,
     that radicalisation happens in political contexts and that it cannot be
     understood without examining factors such as Western foreign and domestic
     policy. The West, Della Porta points out, has also become 'radicalised' into
     adopting violence to achieve its ends. See Mehdi Hasan, 'So, prime minister,
     are we to call you an extremist now?'. *Guardian*, 9 June 2011.

https://www.theguardian.com/theguardian/2011/jun/09/cameron-counter-terror-muslims

Katherine Brown, 'This is how Islamist radicalisation actually happens', *Independent*, 24 May 2017. https://www.independent.co.uk/voices/manchester-attack-isis-al-qaeda-radicalisation-risk-factors-a7753451.html

Mitchell D. Silber and Arvin Bhatt, 'Radicalization in the West: The Homegrown Threat', NYPD Intelligence Division, New York City Police Department, https://seths.blog/wp-content/uploads/2007/09/NYPD_Report-Radicalization_in_the_West.pdf.

Sageman quoted in Mehdi Hasan, 'Woolwich attack: overreacting to extremism "could bring back Al Qaeda" ex-CIA officer warns', *Huffington Post*, 28 May 2013. https://www.huffingtonpost.co.uk/2013/05/27/sageman-interview_n_3342206.html

Horgan quoted in John Knefel, 'Everything you've been told about radicalisation is wrong', *Rolling Stone*, 6 May 2013.

https://www.rollingstone.com/politics/news/everything-youve-been-told-about-radicalization-is-wrong-20130506; Jamie Bartlett, Jonathan Birdwell and Michael King, *The Edge of Violence: A Radical Approach to Extremism* (Demos, 2010). https://www.demos.co.uk/files/Edge_of_Violence_-_web.pdf

Olivier Roy, 'Al Qaeda in the West as a Youth Movement: The Power of a Narrative' CEPS, 28 August 2008. https://issuu.com/ufuq.de/docs/microcon2

Donatella Della Porta, 'Radicalization: A Relational Perspective', *Annual Review of Political Science*, May 2018. http://www.start.umd.edu/publication/radicalization-relational-perspective

15 Hansard, Orders of the Day, volume 894: debated on Monday 23 June 1975. https://hansard.parliament.uk/Commons/1975-06-23/debates/c1e4e119-4e30-4c54-b1a9-2789135e870e/OrdersOfTheDay

16 Will Wilkinson, 'On the Saying that "Extremism in Defense of Liberty is No Vice"', *Niskanen Center*, 5 January 2016. https://www.niskanencenter.org/on-the-saying-that-extremism-in-defense-of-liberty-is-no-vice/

17 Malcolm X, 'Oxford Union Debate (December 3, 1964)', *Malcolm X*. http://malcolmxfiles.blogspot.com/2013/07/oxford-union-debate-december-3-1964.html

18 For an example in the context of Northern Ireland, see Hansard: 'Guidance on promoting British values in school published', GOV.UK, 27 November 2014. https://www.gov.uk/government/news/guidance-on-promoting-british-values-in-schools-published

19 Hansard: 'Prevent Strategy'. Volume 529: debated on Tuesday 7 June 2011, Hansard: Parliament UK. https://hansard.parliament.uk/Commons/2011-06-07/debates/11060740000001/PreventStrategy

20 Department for Education and Lord Nash, 'Guidance on promoting British values in schools published', gov.uk, 27 November 2014. https://www.gov.uk/government/news/guidance-on-promoting-british-values-in-schools-published

21 Janet Daley, 'Don't "teach" British values – demand them', *Daily Telegraph*, 14 June 2014. https://www.telegraph.co.uk/news/uknews/immigration/ 10899904/Dont-teach-British-values-demand-them.html

INTRODUCTION

1 For the Judaeo-Christian tradition, I rely heavily on Mark Silk, 'Notes on the Judaeo-Christian Tradition in America', *American Quarterly*, Vol. 36, No. 1, Spring 1984, pp. 65–85.

2 Silk, *op. cit.*

3 Bernard Lewis, 'The Roots of Muslim Rage', *The Atlantic*, September 1990. https://www.theatlantic.com/magazine/archive/1990/09/the-roots-of-muslim-rage/304643/

4 Samuel P. Huntington, 'The Clash of Civilizations?', *Foreign Affairs*, vol. 72, no. 3, 1993, pp. 22–49.

5 Taylor Dafoe, 'Steve Bannon's school for far-right populists can't be evicted from an 800-year-old Italian monastery, a court rules,' Artnet, 27 May 2020. https://news.artnet.com/art-world/ steve-bannons-far-right-school-cant-evicted-800-year-old-italian-monastery-judges-ruled-week-1872006

6 Rowena Mason, 'Nigel Farage: British Muslim "fifth column" fuels fear of immigration,' *Guardian*, 12 March 2015. https://www.theguardian.com/ politics/2015/mar/12/nigel-farage-british-muslim-fifth-column-fuels-immigration-fear-ukip. On Nigel Farage's comments on Judaeo-Christian culture, see: 'Guidance on promoting British values in schools published', GOV.UK, 27 November 2014. https://www.huffingtonpost.co.uk/2013/11/ 02/ukip-nigel-farage_n_4199727.html.

7 Patrick Kingsley, 'A friend to Israel, and to bigots: Viktor Orban's "Double Game" on anti-Semitism,' *New York Times*, 14 May 2019. https://www.nytimes. com/2019/05/14/world/europe/orban-hungary-antisemitism.html

8 Benjamin Ward, 'Europe's Worrying Surge of Antisemitism', Human Rights Watch, 17 May 2021. https://www.hrw.org/news/2021/05/17/ europes-worrying-surge-antisemitism

CHAPTER 1: THE AMERICAN RELATIONSHIP WITH ISLAM

1 Most accounts treat the religions of enslaved Africans as local African religions, with Muslims as slave owners and traders. However, see 'Muslims arrived in America 400 years ago as part of the slave trade and today are vastly diverse', Saeed Ahmed Khan, *The Conversation*, 11 April 2019. https:// theconversation.com/muslims-arrived-in-america-400-years-ago-as-part-of-the-slave-trade-and-today-are-vastly-diverse-113168

2 'The Marine's Hymn: The story behind the song', The Kennedy Center. https://www.kennedy-center.org/education/resources-for-educators/ classroom-resources/media-and-interactives/media/music/story-behind-the-song/the-story-behind-the-song/the-marines-hymn/

3 There are some references to submarines in the book of Ether: Ether: 2:24, Ether 6:7, Ether 6:10, Ether, 2: 19-20. Also see 'Absurdities in the Book of Mormon', Mormon Handbook. http://www.mormonhandbook.com/home/ absurdities-in-the-book-of-mormon.html

4 Ishaan Tharoor, 'Muslims discovered America before Columbus, claims Turkey's Erdogan', *Washington Post*, 15 November 2014. https://www. washingtonpost.com/news/worldviews/wp/2014/11/15/ muslims-discovered-america-before-columbus-claims-turkeys-erdogan/

5 For the story of Istafan and Anthony Jansen van Vaes (or Anthony "the Turk"), who worked for the Dutch, see Kambiz GhaneaBassiri, *A History of Islam in America: From the New World to the New World Order* (Cambridge University Press, 2010), pp. 9–13.

6 See Ibid., pp. 19–34, especially the accounts of Abdul Rahman and Job Ben Solomon. As Job Ben Solomon shows, Africans shaped their own destinies to some extent, even if it is most often true that they became known because 'they were taken up by powerful white men to further political, commercial or religious agendas'. (pp. 30–31).

7 See R. B. Turner, 'African Muslim Slaves and Islam in Antebellum America', in J. Hammer and O. Safi (eds), *The Cambridge Companion to American Islam* (Cambridge University Press, 2013), p. 32.

8 Ibid., pp. 33–35, particularly the accounts of a famous slave, Bilali.

9 Ibid., p. 29–30. Care is needed with the term 'Moorish'. It subsumes African in early accounts and doesn't necessarily mean North African but also sub-Saharan.

10 Turner *op. cit.* pp. 36 and 42.

11 See M. B. Oren , *Power, Faith and Fantasy: America in the Middle East, 1776 to the Present* (Norton, 2007), p. 23.

12 Ibid., pp. 24–26.

13 See J. H. Hutson 'The Founding Fathers and Islam', published by the Library of Congress in May 2002. https://www.loc.gov/loc/lcib/0205/tolerance.html

14 "American Commissioners to John Jay, 28 March 1786," *Founders Online*, National Archives, https://founders.archives.gov/documents/Jefferson/01-09-02-0315. (Original source: The Papers of Thomas Jefferson, vol. 9, 1 November 1785–22 June 1786, ed. Julian P. Boyd. Princeton: Princeton University Press, 1954, pp. 357–359). Cited in Oren, M., *Power, faith, and fantasy : America in the Middle East, 1776 to the present* (New York, 2007), p. 27.

15 Ibid., p. 28.

16 Ibid., pp. 29–31.

17 Naval Act of 1794 quoted in Oren, M., *Power, faith, and fantasy: America in the Middle East, 1776 to the present* (New York, 2007), p. 35.

18 See Angela Sutton, 'White Slaves In Barbary: The Early American Republic, Orientalism and the Barbary Pirates' (MA thesis, Vanderbilt University). https://core.ac.uk/download/pdf/46929407.pdf Sutton notes that 'fictional and forged accounts have much to tell us about how the American public at large conceived of the Barbary pirates'.

19 GhaneaBassiri *op. cit.*, p. 25. See also: Mary Velnet, *The Captivity and Sufferings of Mrs. Mary Velnet, Who Was Seven Years a Slave in Tripoli, Three of Which She Was Confined in a Dungeon, Loaded with Irons, and Four Times Put to the Most Cruel Tortures Ever Invented by Man. To Which Is Added, The Lunatic Governor, and Adelaide, or the Triumph of Constancy, a Tale* (Boston, MA: T. Abbott, 1828), pp. 25-26.

20 Oren *op. cit.*, pp. 178–181.

21 See the citations in 'Christianity And Slavery', published by the World Future Fund. www.worldfuturefund.org

22 Oren, 2007, p. 39.

23 My account of the Barbary Wars is largely condensed from Oren *op. cit.*, pp. 54–77. C. S. Forester, creator of the Horatio Hornblower series, produced a vivid account of American heroism for young readers in *The Barbary Pirates* (first published 1953, republished 2007 by Sterling Point Books).

24 Cathcart, *Tripoli*, p. 111 cited in Oren, *op. cit.* p. 57.

25 Decatur originated the phrase 'my country right or wrong'.

26 For Eaton and his attempt at regime change in Tripoli, see David Smethurst, *Tripoli: The United States' First War On Terror* (Presidio Press, 2006).

27 William Eaton, 'Honourable Secretary of the United States,' April, 1799, p. 117 quoted in Oren, *Power, faith, and fantasy: America in the Middle East, 1776 to the present* (New York, 2007), p. 64.

28 William Eaton 'Honourable Secretary of the United States,' April, 1799, p. 117 quoted in Oren, *Power, faith, and fantasy: America in the Middle East, 1776 to the present* (New York, 2007), p. 65.

29 Oren, 2007, p. 66.

30 Ibid., p. 66.

31 William Shaler, *Sketches of Algiers* (Boston: Cummings, Hillard, 1826), pp. 38, 101, 126-7, 167-68 quoted in Oren, *Power, faith, and fantasy: America in the Middle East, 1776 to the present* (New York, 2007), p. 74.

32 Oren, 2007, p. 75.

33 Ibid., p. 77.

34 J. C. London, 'Victory In Tripoli: Lessons for the war on terrorism' (Heritage Foundation, 2006). https://www.heritage.org/defense/report/victory-tripoli-lessons-the-war-terrorism

35 Joshua London, 'Victory in Tripoli: Lessons for the War on Terrorism', The Heritage Foundation, 4 May 2006. https://www.heritage.org/defense/report/victory-tripoli-lessons-the-war-terrorism; Joshua London, 'America's Earliest Terrorists', National Review, 16 December 2005. https://www.nationalreview.com/2005/12/americas-earliest-terrorists-joshua-e-london/

For reviews that connect the book with modern-day events, see 'Victory in Tripoli: How America's War with the Barbary Pirates Established the U.S. Navy and Shaped a Nation' review, brotherjudd.com, 12 October 2015. http://www.brothersjudd.com/index.cfm/fuseaction/reviews.detail/book_id/1468/

'The degree to which the war(s) connects to our own times necessarily suggests that we apply its lessons today. This seems all the more important when we recall that almost all of our other wars follow the pattern: only reluctantly entered into and then left unfinished. It's too late for us to start the War on Terror on our own initiative--9/11 saw to that. But we can, just this once, refuse to let up in the war until it's truly won. In this instance that will mean getting liberal democratic reform going in every single Middle Eastern state and denying al Qaeda the safe havens it still enjoys in Western Pakistan. Let's not leave another William Eaton to be proved right in retrospect.'

And OU Staff, 'Joshua London, Author of Victory in Tripoli, Joins Orthodox Union's Institute for Public Affairs', Orthadox Union, 8 February 2006. https://www.ou.org/news/joshua_london_author_of_victory_in_tripoli_joins_orthodox_unions_institute_/

'In September 2005, Mr. London's book, *Victory in Tripoli: How America's War with the Barbary Pirates Established the U.S. Navy and Shaped a Nation*, was published by John Wiley & Sons. This history of America's war against North African Muslim pirates under President Thomas Jefferson is a timely and insightful account of America's first interaction with the Arab world, and, more importantly, the story of America's first war against Islamic terror. The National Review calls Victory in Tripoli an "exciting story of the war on terror—circa 1800." Booklist says it is "sound history" and "thoroughly readable."'

36 See Paul Johnson, *A History Of The American People* (Weidenfeld & Nicolson, 1997), p. 308.

37 One curious by-product of the American conquests was the reintroduction of slavery to Texas, where it had been abolished by the Mexicans.

38 William Goodell, *Forty Years in the Turkish Empire* (New York: Robert Carter, 1883). p. 174 quoted in Oren, *Power, faith, and fantasy: America in the Middle East, 1776 to the present* (New York, 2007), p. 131.

39 Lynch, *Narrative of the United States' Expedition*, pp. 360, 415 quoted in Oren, *Power, faith, and fantasy: America in the Middle East, 1776 to the present* (New York, 2007), p. 140.

40 See Raphael Magarik, 'When Native Americans Were The Lost Tribes of Israel', in *Forward* (www.forward.com), 21 April 2020, reviewing Elizabeth Fenton's book *Old Canaan In A New World* (New York University Press, 2020).

41 Victoria Clark, *Allies For Armageddon: The Rise of Christian Zionism* (Yale, 2007), pp. 43–44.

42 Oren *op. cit.*, p. 155. For Haight, see F. Sha'ban, *For Zion's Sake: The Judaeo-Christian Tradition in American Culture* (Pluto Press, 2005), chapter 7.

43 Oren *op. cit.*, pp. 235–237. However, after the American Civil War, Egypt had attracted many Americans through the opportunities created by its modernising spendthrift Khedive Ismail, especially former generals from both sides who retrained his army.

44 Oren *op. cit.*, pp. 238–244 and Sha'ban *op. cit.*, pp. 120–122.

45 GhaneaBassiri *op. cit.*, pp. 199–201.

CHAPTER 2: THE UNITED STATES ACQUIRES MUSLIM SUBJECTS

1   For an outline of the Spanish–American War and the American conquests, see Birdsall S. Viault, *American History Since 1865* (McGraw-Hill, 1993), pp. 134–142.

2   Karine W. Walther, *Sacred Interests: The United States and the Islamic World, 1821–1921* (University of North Carolina Press, 2015), pp. 161–162.

3   Viault *op. cit.*, p. 142.

4   See Mustafa Akyol, *Islam Without Extremes: A Muslim Case for Liberty* (Norton, 2011), p. 159.

5   Walther *op. cit.*, p. 176.

6   See James R. Arnold, *The Moro War* (Bloomsbury, 2011), p. 14.

7   Walther *op. cit.*, p. 171.

8   Ibid., pp. 165–167.

9   Ibid., p. 201.

10 Ibid., p. 183. Sweet was initially an enthusiast for using the Quran to promote law and order among the Moros, see Arnold *op. cit.*, p. 16.

11 Walther *op. cit.*, pp. 184–190.

12 Ibid., pp. 195–197.

13 Ibid., p. 210.

14 For an excellent account see Fred Magdalena, *The Battle of Bayang and other essays on Moroland* (Mindanao State University, 2002).

15 Ibid., p. 216.

16 Arnold *op. cit.*, chapter 17.

17 Ibid., pp. 247–248.

18 For Trump's comments, see Alex Horton, 'Trump said to study General Pershing: Here's what the president got wrong', *Washington Post*, 18 August 2017. https://www.washingtonpost.com/news/retropolis/wp/2017/08/18/after-barcelona-attack-trump-said-to-study-general-pershing-heres-what-the-president-got-wrong/

CHAPTER 3: AFRICAN AMERICANS REDISCOVER ISLAM

1   GhaneaBassiri *op. cit.*, pp. 158–159.

2 Ibid., pp. 136, 163.

3 Oren *op. cit.*, pp. 370–371. It is often forgotten that the United States never declared war on the Ottoman Empire, even though it was fighting with the Central Powers and horrified American public opinion with the Armenian massacres of 1916. Still, few Americans of any race or religion had strong feelings about its fate.

4 S. Howell, 'Laying the groundwork for American Muslim Histories: 1865–1965', in Hammer and Safi *op. cit.*, p. 45.

5 The subject of a compelling novel – *1876* by Gore Vidal.

6 Alexis de Tocqueville, *Democracy in America* (University of Chicago Press, 2nd edn, 2002). Chapter XVIII, 'Future Condition of Three Races in the United States', pp. 312-61.

7 These orders were almost exclusively white. If not formally excluded, African Americans generally found it economically impossible to progress through their secret ranks. Elijah Muhammad, prophet of the Nation of Islam, identified his movement as a means of giving access to Islam without expense. In a radio address, he said: 'Never has any so-called American Negro been taught by white people to believe in Almighty God Allah and his true religion Islam. Only in higher organisations or we say Masonry . . . there is a little teaching at the top . . . that mentions the teachings of Almighty God Allah. But you have to pay a lot of money to become a 33rd degree Mason . . . To buy that kind of teaching does not gain you the hereafter. We must have something that is pure. A Mason cannot be a good Mason unless he knows the Holy Quran and follows its teachings . . .. I say, if you are a true Moslem friend, let's have it out in the open and not in the secret.' GhaneaBassiri, *op.cit.*, p. 202.

8 https://www.tapatalk.com/groups/aalbionic/masonry-and-islam-controversial-information-t285.html

9 GhaneaBassiri *op. cit.*, pp. 220–221, 226.

10 See Aminah McCloud, *African American Islam* (Routledge, 1994) p. 18.

11 GhaneaBassiri *op. cit.*, pp. 219–222.

12 Cited in Richard A. Hill, *The Marcus Garvey and Universal Negro Improvement Papers*, volume 5 (University of California, 1987), p. 21.

13 Thandeka Chapman, 'Foundations of Multicultural Education: Marcus Garvey and the United Negro Improvement Association', *Journal of Negro Education* 73.4 (2004), p. 424.

14 Milton H. Watson, 'Black Star Line'. https://shiphistory.org/wp-content/uploads/2019/02/Black-Star-Line.pdf

15 Colin Grant, *Negro With A Hat: The Rise and Fall of Marcus Garvey* (Jonathan Cape, 2008), pp. 367–71.

16 Karl Evanzz, *The Messenger: The Rise And Fall Of Elijah Muhammad* (Vintage Books, 2001), pp. 204–205 and pp. 402–407.

17 See Kevin Baker, 'Lost-Found Nation' in Byron Hollinshead (ed.), *I Wish I'd*

Been There: Twenty Great Moments in History By Twenty Great Historians (Doubleday, 2006). https://www.historynet.com/lost-found-nation.htm

18   GhaneaBassiri *op. cit.*, pp. 223–224.

19   Ibid., p. 243.

20   Ibid., p. 242.

21   Alexis de Tocqueville, *Democracy in America*, trans H. Reeve and J. C. Spencer (London, 1838). pp. 312–61. In Chapter XVIII of Book 1, he discusses the situation of both the Indians and African-Americans. He argued that while 'The Indians will perish in the same isolated condition in which they have lived, but the destiny of the Negroes is in some measure interwoven with that of the Europeans.' He later added that: 'That it is in the United States that the prejudice which repels the Negroes seems to increase in proportion as they are emancipated, and inequality is sanctioned by the manners while it is effaced from the laws of the country.'

22   C. Eric Lincoln, *The Black Muslims in America* (Beacon Press, 1961), p. 96.

23   GhaneaBassiri *op. cit.*, pp. 231–232.

24   See the obituary of Elijah Muhammad in the *New York Times*, 26 February 1975. https://www.nytimes.com/1975/02/26/archives/elijah-muhammad-dead-black-muslim-leader-77-elijah-muhammad-dead.html

25   See Kevern Verney, *The Debate On Black Civil Rights in America* (Manchester University Press, 2006), p. 118.

26   Richard W. Leeman, *African American Orators* (Greenwood Press, 1996), p. 413.

27   Richard Brent Turner, *Islam in the African American Experience* (Indiana University Press, 2003), p. 197.

28   GhaneaBassiri *op. cit.*, pp. 289–292. In 2010, Farrakhan actually embraced the cult of Scientology and exhorted his followers to study its pseudo-science of dianetics. See Eliza Gray, 'Thetans and bowties: The mothership of all alliances – Scientology and the Nation of Islam', *The New Republic*, 5 October 2012. https://newrepublic.com/article/108205/scientology-joins-forces-with-nation-of-islam

29   For an example of Farrakhan's social conservatism, see Niraj Warikoo, 'Farrakhan urges black unity in Detroit', *USA Today*, 15 May 2013. https://eu.usatoday.com/story/news/nation/2013/05/16/farrakhan-urges-black-unity-in-detroit/2192605/

30   Published by the Pew Research Center, www.pewforum.org, on 30 January 2009.

CHAPTER 4: ISLAM AND THE UNITED STATES AS A GLOBAL SUPERPOWER

1   For an excellent description of American involvement in the 1930s, see Oren *op. cit.*, chapter 23.

2   Oren *op. cit.*, pp. 469–473.

3   Ibid., pp. 412–414. The American contribution to the formation – and presentation – of the Saudi state is assessed by Muriam Haleh Davis in 'The nature of oil: Reconsidering American power in the Middle East', *Jadaliyya*, 12 January 2012. https://www.jadaliyya.com/Details/25122.

4   Bethan McKernan,'Mohammed bin Salman: Saudi Arabia's great young reformer may struggle to control the forces he has unleashed', *Independent*, 7 February 2018.

5   See Deborah Amos, 'Saudi Arabia: The White House loves it. Most Americans? Not so much', www.npr.org, 19 March 2018. https://www.npr.org/sections/parallels/2018/03/19/595018861/trump-may-love-saudi-arabia-but-many-americans-do-not

6   'Read the US intelligence report on the killing of Jamal Khashoggi', *Middle East Eye*, 26 February 2021.

7   See Taylor Nelson, 'North Africa and the Making of American Psychological Warfare and Propaganda 1942–45', thesis. pp. 18–20. https://repository.upenn.edu/curej/254.

8   Oren, *op. cit.*, pp. 446–449.

9   See Robert Satloff, 'Operation Torch and the Birth of American Middle Eastern Policy 75 Years On', Washington Institute for Near East Policy, 9 October 2017. https://www.washingtoninstitute.org/policy-analysis/operation-torch-and-birth-american-middle-east-policy-75-years

10 But not, unfortunately, Algeria, where independence was achieved only after a bitterly destructive war. Nor, for that matter, Vietnam. American anti-colonialism was fatally selective.

11 Oren, *op. cit.*, pp. 450–461.

12 Ibid., pp. 462–466.

13 See Craig Considine, 'Saluting Muslim American Patriots', *Huffington Post*, 10 April 2015. https://www.huffingtonpost.com/craig-considine/saluting-muslim-american-patriots_b_7039866.html

14 See 'Meet the terrifying Moro warriors and heroes of WWII' https://filipiknow.net/moros-during-world-war-2

15 See Barry Rubin, 'America and the Egyptian Revolution 1950-57', *Political Science Quarterly,* vol. 97/1, Spring 1982.

16 GhaneaBassiri *op. cit.*, p. 257.

17 Ibid., pp. 264–267.

18 Sayyid Qutb, *The America I Have Seen*, 1951, p. 5.

19 GhaneaBassiri *op. cit.*, pp. 239–241.

20 Eisenhower's 1957 speech at Islamic Center of Washington is available on the US State Department's website. https://quod.lib.umich.edu/p/ppotpus/4728417.1957.001?rgn=main;view=fulltext

21 Source: US Bureau of the Census: Table 3 World Region and Country or Area of Birth of the Foreign-Born Population 1960-2000, cited in GhaneaBassiri *op. cit.*, pp. 293–294.

22 Zain Abdullah, 'American Muslims in the contemporary world' in Hammer and Safi *op. cit.*, p. 66.

23 GhaneaBassiri *op. cit.*, p. 306.

24 Oren *op. cit.*, pp. 545–546.

CHAPTER 5: APOCALYPSE IMMINENT: GOD'S PLAN FOR ISRAEL

1 See Victoria Clark, *Allies For Armageddon* (Yale University Press, 2007), pp. 40–44; Fuad Sha'ban, *For Zion's Sake* (Pluto Press 2003), p. 42.

2 Herman Melville, *White Jacket* (London, 1850).

3 Abraham Lincoln, Address to the New Jersey State Senate, 21 February 1861. http://www.abrahamlincolnonline.org/lincoln/speeches/trenton1.htm

4 See Sha'ban *op. cit.*, pp. 166 et seq; Clark *op. cit.*, p. 40.

5 For a general account of the Second Great Awakening, sometimes called the Great Revival, see Paul Johnson, *A History Of The American People* (Weidenfeld & Nicolson, 1997), pp. 246–252, and a more sceptical one in Hugh Brogan, *The Penguin History of the USA* (Penguin, 2001), pp. 231–232.

6 Clark *op. cit.*, p. 56.

7 Oren *op. cit.*, pp. 141–142, and Clark *op. cit.*, pp. 82–83.

8 Clark *op. cit.*, p. 80.

9 See Howard Markel, 'The secret ingredient in Kellogg's Corn Flakes is Seventh-Day Adventism', *Smithsonian Magazine*, 28 July 2017.
     https://www.smithsonianmag.com/history/
     secret-ingredient-kelloggs-corn-flakes-seventh-day-adventism-180964247/

10 See the sample in Sha'ban, pp. 210–211. In fairness to Miller, many great minds have wrestled with the chronology of biblical prophecy. Isaac Newton made the uncanny prediction that the Jews would return to Palestine by 1948 – the year the state of Israel was established. Clark *op. cit.*, p. 37.

11 Sutton *op. cit.*, p. 16.

12 Clark *op. cit.*, p. 161.

13 See www.aftertherapturepetcare.com

14 Clark *op. cit.*, pp. 90–93, Sutton *op. cit.*, pp. 8–9.

15 Sutton *op. cit.*, pp. 27, 39.

16 Sutton *op. cit.*, p. 215.

17 Sutton *op. cit.*, p. 220.

18 Clark *op. cit.*, pp. 138-139, and see also Sutton *op. cit.*, p. 127.

19 Sutton *op. cit.*, pp. 281–282.

20 See Clark *op. cit.*, p. 139 and William Vance Trollinger, *God's Empire: William Bell Riley and Midwestern Fundamentalism* (Wisconsin University Press 1990), p. 78.

21 See Sutton *op. cit.*, pp. 279, 291–292.

22 Ibid., pp. 286–288.

23   Sutton *op. cit.*, pp. 300–301.

24   Ibid., pp. 301–302.

25   A point made in a penetrating analysis of Christian Zionism by the theologian Thomas Getman at https://www.wrmea.org/018-may/when-and-how-did-evangelicals-become-zionists.html

26   Sutton *op. cit.*, p. 303.

27   For Truman and Israel, see Clark *op. cit.*, pp. 140–144. I have also relied on the personal knowledge of my contributor, Richard Heller, who chose Truman successfully as a special subject as a contender on BBC Television's *Mastermind* quiz.

28   Sutton *op. cit.*, pp. 310–313.

29   Sutton *op. cit.*, p. 324.

30   For Eisenhower on religion, see the selected quotations by the Eisenhower Foundation at www.dwightdeisenhower.com and William I. Hitchcock, 'How Dwight Eisenhower Found God In The White House', www.history.com, 20 March 2018. https://www.history.com/news/eisenhower-billy-graham-religion-in-god-we-trust. Eisenhower is the only US president to have been baptised while in office.

31   See Patrick Henry, 'And I Don't Care What It Is', *Journal of the American Academy of Religion*, March 1981, which quotes some slight variations in reports of the speech.

32   See David Smith, 'Trump celebrates "shared and timeless values" with Christian evangelicals', *Guardian*, 13 October, 2017. https://www.theguardian.com/us-news/2017/oct/13/trump-religious-conservative-values-voters-summit

33   Under Graham's influence, George W. Bush gave up alcohol and began a major political career.

34   For Graham, see his obituary in the *New York Times*. https://www.nytimes.com/2018/02/21/obituaries/billy-graham-dead.html; Sutton *op. cit.*, pp. 326–27 and p. 343; and the essays on him in the Billy Graham Special Issue of *Christianity Today*, especially by Andrew S. Finstuen.

35   See Zev Chafets, 'How Billy Graham made Israel ok with Evangelicals', Bloomberg, 26 February 2016. https://www.bloomberg.com/view/articles/2018-02-26/billy-graham-made-israel-ok-with-evangelicals. Not surprisingly, Graham was quickly forgiven by Israeli leaders when, in 2002, it was revealed that he had agreed with an anti-Semitic remark by President Nixon.

36   See Christopher Mathias, 'A pastor who said Islam is "evil" is speaking at Trump's inauguration', *Huffington Post*, 17 January 2017. https://www.huffingtonpost.co.uk/entry/franklin-graham-islamophobia-trump-inauguration_us_587e3ea5e4b0aaa369429373; Stephen Prothero, 'Billy Graham built a movement. Now his son is dismantling it', Politico, 24 February 2018. https://www.politico.com/magazine/story/2018/02/24/billy-graham-evangelical-decline-franklin-graham-217077/

37   See Clark *op. cit.*, pp. 151–155, Sutton *op. cit.*, p. 345, and the entry on www.imbd.com for *The Late Great Planet Earth*.

38   Sutton *op. cit.*, p. 371.

39   Clark *op. cit.*, p. 151.

40   See 'Public Sees A Future Full Of Promise And Peril', published by the Pew Research Center, 22 June, 2010.

41   Clark *op. cit.*, pp. 190–191.

42   Sutton *op. cit.*, pp. 335, 354. One major motive behind the formation of Moral Majority was financial, to protest the removal by the Internal Revenue Service of tax-exempt status from private schools and universities which continued to practise racial segregation: see Randall Balmer, *Thy Kingdom Come: How the Religious Right Distorts Faith and Threatens America* (Basic Books, 2006).

43   Jimmy Carter, *White House Diary* (Farrar Straus Giroux, 2010), p. 469.

44   Clark *op. cit.*, p187.

45   Jamin Christopher Carlisle, 'A Dangerous Friendship: Jewish Fundamentalists and Christian Zionists in the Battle for Israel', University of Tennessee, 2007. https://trace.tennessee.edu/cgi/viewcontent.cgi?referer=&httpsredir=1 &article=1300&context=utk_gradthes

46   Clark *op. cit.*, pp. 192–193.

47   See Timothy P. Weber, 'On the road to Armageddon: how Evangelicals became Israel's best friend', BeliefNet. http://www.beliefnet.com/faiths/ christianity/end-times/on-the-road-to-armageddon.aspx

48   See https://www.c4israel.org

49   See https://www.sourcewatch.org/index.php/National_Unity_Coalition_ for_Israel

50   See Weber *op. cit.*, and Clark *op. cit.*, pp. 191, 231–235.

51   Clark *op. cit.*, pp. 193–194.

52   Patrick Allitt, *Religion in America Since 1945: A History* (Columbia University Press, 2003), p. 198.

CHAPTER 6: THE IMPACT OF 9/11

1   See Tara Golshan, 'Donald Trump revives his bogus claim that American Muslims "cheer" terrorism', Vox, 14 June 2016. https://www.vox.com/2016/ 6/14/11931338/donald-trump-muslims-cheering-terrorism

2   Thomas L. Friedman, 'If it's a Muslim problem, it needs a Muslim solution', *New York Times*, 8 July 2005. https://www.nytimes.com/2005/07/08/opinion/ if-its-a-muslim-problem-it-needs-a-muslim-solution.html

3   See John L. Esposito, *The Future Of Islam* (Oxford University Press, 2010), pp. 29–33.

4   http://kurzman.unc.edu/islamic-statements-against-terrorism/

5   Esposito *op. cit.*

6   Edward E. Curtis IV, *Muslims in America: A Short History* (Oxford University Press, 2009), pp. 98–99, 108–110.

7   A. Kundnani, *The Muslims are Coming!: Islamophobia, Extremism, and the Domestic
    War on Terror* (Verso, 2014), pp. 50–51.

8   Nathan Lean, *The Islamophobia Industry* (Pluto Press, 2012), pp. 67–70.

9   See 'Fox host suggests all Muslims are like Isis, says problem should be solved
    "with a bullet to the head"', Media Matters, 20 August 20 2014. https://www.
    mediamatters.org/fox-nation/fox-host-suggests-all-muslims-are-isis-says-problem-
    should-be-solved-bullet-head

10 See Max Fisher, 'It's not just Trump: Islamophobia in America is spiraling out
    of control', Vox, 7 December 2015. http://www.vox.com/2015/12/1/
    9822452/muslim-islamophobia-trump

11 Ibid.

12 See Mona Chalabi, 'Terror attacks by Muslims receive 357 per cent more
    attention, study finds', *Guardian*, 20 July 2018. https://www.theguardian.com/
    us-news/2018/jul/20/muslim-terror-attacks-press-coverage-study

13 'Countering Violent Extremism', April 2017. https://www.gao.gov/assets/
    690/683984.pdf

14 Khaled A. Beydoun, *American Islamophobia: Understanding the Roots and Rise of
    Fear* (University of California Press, 2019), pp. 82–83. A film based on the
    Boston Marathon bombings, *Patriots Day*, was released in 2016 starring Mark
    Wahlberg. Although generally well-reviewed, it was far less successful at the
    box office than *American Sniper*, with a worldwide gross of around $50 million.

15 Lean *op. cit.*, pp. 76–77 and see 'Lowe's pulls ads from TLC's *All-American
    Muslim*', CNN, 9 December 2011. https://edition.cnn.com/2011/12/11/
    showbiz/all-american-muslim-lowes/index.html

16 Daniel Pipes, 'The Muslims are coming! The Muslims are Coming!', *National
    Review*, 19 November 1990. http://www.danielpipes.org/198/
    the-muslims-are-coming-the-muslims-are-coming

17 See Pipes' text and commentary in 'The Muslims are coming, the Muslims are
    coming', *Middle East Forum*, 5 April 2017.

18 Pipes quoted and defended himself in 'A French lesson for Tom Harkin', World
    Net Daily, 5 January 2004, claiming that French Jews were being threatened
    by a Muslim influx. https://www.meforum.org/4198/
    a-french-lesson-for-tom-harkin

19 See Pipes' article 'Bolstering moderate Muslims', the *New York Sun*, 17 April
    2007. http://www.danielpipes.org/4426/bolstering-moderate-muslims

20 See Daniel Pipes, 'Confirmed: Barack Obama practised Islam', *FrontPage
    Magazine*, 7 January 2008. http://www.danielpipes.org/5354/
    confirmed-barack-obama-practiced-islam

21 See Jay Nordlinger's admiring profile 'A witness, part II: the meaning of David
    Horowitz', *National Review*, 15 January 2014. https://www.nationalreview.
    com/2014/01/witness-part-ii-jay-nordlinger/

22 See Lean *op. cit.*, p. 133, and C. J. Werleman, *The New Atheist Threat*
    (Dangerous Little Books, 2015), p. 108.

23   Lean *op. cit.*, p. 134.

24   See Ben Preston, 'David Horowitz provokes extreme response with anti-Arab remarks', *Santa Barbara Independent*, 15 May 2008. https://www.independent. com/news/2008/may/15/david-horowitz-provokes-extreme-response-anti-arab/

25   Cited in Matt Kennard, 'David Horowitz Awareness', *Columbia Spectator*, 27 March 2013. https://www.columbiaspectator.com/2007/10/19/ david-horowitz-awareness/

26   See Michelle Williams, 'Horowitz brings controversial ideas to Student Union', *Massachusetts Daily Collegian*, 25 February 2010. https://dailycollegian. com/2010/02/controversial-author-horowitz-lectures-umass-students/

27   See Paul Farhi, 'Pamela Geller vs Halal Soup from Campbell Soup', The Islamic Workplace, 18 October 2010: 'In an interview, Geller, who was instrumental in whipping up opposition to an Islamic community center and mosque in Lower Manhattan, said she has no objection to the halal certification itself. Rather, she said, she opposes Campbell's decision to have its Canadian products certified by the Islamic Society of North America (ISNA), an organization that government prosecutors alleged had ties to the terrorist group Hamas in a 2007 conspiracy case. "No one is suggesting they refrain from this line," Geller said. "No one is suggesting they not have halal food. I'm not against halal food any more than I'm against kosher food. My issue is who's doing the certifying."'

28   See Brian Montopoli, 'Howard Dean on mosque comments; "I am not going to back off"', CBS News, 20 August 2010. https://www.cbsnews.com/news/ howard-dean-on-mosque-comments-i-am-not-going-to-back-off/

29   See Neda Bolourchi, 'A Muslim victim of 9/11: "build your mosque somewhere else"', *Washington Post*, 5 August 2010. http://www. washingtonpost.com/wp-dyn/content/article/2010/08/06/ AR2010080603006.html

30   See Oshrat Carmiel, 'Condos at NYC's "Ground Zero mosque" site get global financing', Bloomberg, 19 May 2016. https://www.bloomberg.com/news/ articles/2016-05-19/ condos-at-nyc-s-ground-zero-mosque-site-get-global-financing

31   See Lean *op. cit.*, pp. 49–50.

32   See Ali Harb, 'John Bolton hires top staffer from "conspiracy-obsessed" anti-Muslim group', *Middle East Eye*, 30 May 2018. https://www.middleeasteye.net/ news/john-bolton-hires-top-staffer-conspiracy-obsessed-anti-muslim-group

33   See Clark *op. cit.*, pp. 369–370.

34   See Esposito *op. cit.*, p. 164.

35   See Sha'ban *op. cit.*, pp. 151–153.

36   See Esposito *op. cit.*, p. 164. To his credit, Rev. Franklin Graham, responding to criticism of his comments about Islam, said he did not believe Muslims were 'evil people' but lamented evil done in the religion's name. The Associated Press, 'National Briefing I Religion: Graham Modifies Comments', *New York*

Times, 5 December 2001. https://www.nytimes.com/2001/12/05/us/national-briefing-religion-graham-modifies-comments.html

37 Lean *op. cit.*, pp. 78–82.

38 Lean *op. cit.*, pp. 84–90.

39 Esposito *op cit.*, p. 21.

40 Lean *op., cit.*, p. 94.

41 Ibid., pp. 97–99.

42 See James Bennet, 'A day of terror: the Israelis; spilled blood is seen as bond that draws two nations closer', *New York Times*, 12 September 2001.
        https://www.nytimes.com/2001/09/12/us/day-terror-israelis-spilled-blood-seen-bond-that-draws-2-nations-closer.html

43 Sutton *op. cit.*, p. 371.

44 Clark *op. cit.*, p. 162–164, and see 'Pastor John Hagee on Christian Zionism', National Public Radio, 18 September 2006. https://www.npr.org/templates/story/story.php?storyId=6097362&t=1549879457030

45 See Max Blumenthal, 'AIPAC cheers an anti-Semitic holocaust revisionist', *Huffington Post*, 14 March 2007. https://www.huffingtonpost.com/max-blumenthal/aipac-cheers-an-antisemit_b_43377.html

46 Esposito *op. cit.*, pp. 21–23.

47 Ibid., and Clark *op. cit.*, pp. 221–223.

48 Sam Harris, 'Bombing our illusions', *Huffington Post*, 10 October 2005. https://www.huffingtonpost.com/sam-harris/bombing-our-illusions_b_8615.html

49 Sam Harris, 'Mired in a religious war', *Washington Times*, 1 December 2004. https://www.washingtontimes.com/news/2004/dec/1/20041201-090801-2582r/

50 Sam Harris, 'In defense of profiling', www.samharris.org, 28 April 2012. https://samharris.org/in-defense-of-profiling/

51 See the video 'Free Speech', 1 March 2007. http://onegoodmove/org/1gm/1gmarchive/2007/03

52 Christopher Hitchens, 'Bush's secularist triumph', Slate, 9 November 2004. https://slate.com/news-and-politics/2004/11/bush-s-secularist-triumph.html?via=gdpr-consent

53 Christopher Hitchens, 'God-fearing people: why are we so scared of offending Muslims', Slate, 30 July 2007. https://slate.com/news-and-politics/2007/07/why-are-we-so-scared-of-offending-muslims.html

54 Christopher Hitchens, 'Bush's secularist triumph', *op. cit.*

55 Werleman *op. cit.*, p. 38.

56 Werleman *op. cit.*, p. 130, and see Jerome Taylor, 'Atheists Richard Dawkins, Christopher Hitchens and Sam Harris face Islamophobia backlash', *Independent*, 12 April 2013. https://www.independent.co.uk/news/uk/home-news/atheists-richard-dawkins-christopher-hitchens-and-sam-harris-face-islamophobia-backlash-8570580.html

57 See Rogier Van Bakel, 'The trouble is the West', www.reason.com, November 2007. https://reason.com/archives/2007/10/10/the-trouble-is-the-west

58 Interview by David Cohen in the *Evening Standard*, 2 February 2007.

59 See Ayaan Hirsi Ali, 'The ostrich and the owl: a bird's-eye view of Europe', *Los Angeles Times*, 22 October 2006. https://www.latimes.com/archives/la-xpm-2006-oct-22-op-ali22-story.html

60 Werleman *op. cit.*, pp. 95–97.

61 See 'Best of Ayaan Hirsi Ali', in the Agatan Foundation, 14 April 2014.

CHAPTER 7: THE ASSAULT ON ISLAM

1 Esposito *op. cit.*, p. 16, and see Dalia Mogahed, 'Americans' view of the Muslim world', Gallup, 8 February 2006. https://news.gallup.com/poll/21349/americans-views-islamic-world.aspx

2 Kundnani *op. cit.*, pp. 57–66. See also: 'US is "battling Satan" says general', BBC News, 17 October 2003. http://news.bbc.co.uk/1/hi/world/americas/3199212.stm; 'Top General: Could It Be . . . Satan?' CBS News, 18 October 2003. https://www.cbsnews.com/news/top-general-could-it-besatan/

3 Beydoun *op. cit.*, pp

4 In his 2009 memoirs, *The Test Of Our Times*, Ridge claimed to have resisted their pressure to issue a heightened terror alert on the eve of Bush's bid for re-election in 2004.

5 Kundnani *op. cit.*, p. 64.

6 See L. K. Donohue, *The Cost Of Counter-Terrorism* (Cambridge University Press 2008) pp. 254–255.

7 See Neil A. Lewis, 'In Missouri campaign flourishes after the death of the candidate', *New York Times*, 31 October 2000. https://www.nytimes.com/2000/10/31/us/2000-campaign-missouri-senate-race-missouri-campaign-flourishes-after-death.html

8 Kundnani *op. cit.*, pp. 194–195.

9 Beydoun *op. cit.*, pp. 100-101.

10 Esposito *op. cit.*, pp. 162–164.

11 Kundnani *op. cit.*, p. 198.

12 Kundnani *op. cit.*, p. 200. Many more died in the 9/11 attacks, but Muslims present in the United States as visitors carried out these attacks.

13 See 'US Muslims concerned about their place in society but continue to believe in the American dream', Pew Research Center, 9 August 2017. https://www.pewforum.org/2017/07/26/findings-from-pew-research-centers-2017-survey-of-us-muslims/. For McCain and Muslims, see Esposito *op. cit.*, pp. 21–23.

14 Kundnani *op. cit.*, p. 250.

15 Kundnani *op. cit.*, pp. 250–251.

16 Kundani *op. cit.*, p. 252.

17 Cited in Beydoun *op. cit.*, pp. 110–111. Full speech text at www.

obamawhitehouse.archives.gov – 'Remarks by the President at Islamic Society of Baltimore', February 3, 2016

18 Kundnani *op. cit.*, pp. 80–82.

19 Beydoun *op. cit.*, pp. 128–129.

20 Kundnani *op. cit.*, pp. 211–215, 224–225.

21 Beydoun *op. cit.*, pp. 135–139, 146–147.

22 Kundnani *op. cit.*, pp. 188–192.

23 See report in the *Washington Post*, 6 June 2013. https://www.washingtonpost. com/news/post-politics/wp/2013/06/06/ transcript-dianne-feinstein-saxby-chambliss-explain-defend-nsa-phone- records-program.

24 Kundnani *op. cit.*, p. 282.

25 He changed his family name to a Hebrew one meaning 'from Jerusalem'. Lean *op. cit.*, p. 120.

26 Lean *op. cit.*, pp. 123–125.

27 Lean *op. cit.*, pp. 58–59, 64.

28 Lean *op. cit.*, p. 101.

29 Kundnani *op. cit.*, pp. 248–249.

30 Lean *op. cit.*, p. 127–130.

31 See 'State court throws out religion as defense in case involving husband's non- consensual sex with wife', www.nj.com, 2 August 2010. https://www. nj.com/hudson/index.ssf/2010/08/state_court_throws_out_religio.html

32 Kundnani *op. cit.*, pp. 253–254, and see also Andrea Elliott, 'The man behind the anti-Sharia movement', *New York Times*, 30 July 2011. https://www. nytimes.com/2011/07/31/us/31shariah.html

33 See Lean *op. cit.*, pp. 107–109 and Kundnani *op. cit.*, p. 255.

34 Kundnani *op. cit.*, p. 254.

35 Kundnani *op. cit.*, pp. 252–253.

36 In 2011, the liberal Center for American Progress published 'Fear, Inc', a detailed study of the financing of Islamophobic activity in the United States. It found that more than $40 million had flowed to Islamophobic organisations in the previous decade from just seven tax-exempt foundations, and identified five individuals as the main conduits of supposedly expert anti-Muslim analysis: Daniel Pipes, Frank Gaffney, Robert Spencer, Steven Emerson, and David Yerushalmi – all names we have already encountered. A follow-up report, published in 2015, traced between the years of 2001 and 2012 a '$57 million network fuelling Islamophobia in the United States'.

So what are the foundations in question? The Donors Capital Fund is primarily a vehicle for multiple donors to contribute anonymously to conservative causes. It supplied $20.8 million, of which $18.1 million went to the equally anonymous Clarion Fund, which distributed millions of copies of the anti-Islamic 'documentary' *Obsession*. The next largest funder reported was Richard Mellon Scaife Foundations, which is financed by an heir to the Mellon banking fortune and also a major financier of neo-conservative organisations. It gave $7.9 million in total, distributed mainly to three Islamophobic organisations previously mentioned: the Center for Security Policy ($2.9 million), the Counterterrorism and Security Education and Research Foundation ($1.6 million) and the David Horowitz Freedom Center ($3.4 million).

The Lynde and Harry Bradley Foundation was another major supporter of conservative causes: its board included well-known conservatives, such as the columnist George Will and Princeton University professor Robert P. George. It contributed $4.3 million to the David Horowitz Freedom Center, $800,000 to the Center for Security Policy, and $300,000 to the Middle East Forum. It should be noted that it also gave to the mainstream American Islamic Conference, an organisation with the aim of promoting 'tolerance and the exchange of ideas among Muslims and between other peoples'. The Russell Berrie Foundation – which derives its funding from a successful stuffed animal and toy business – supplied $3.1 million to Islamophobic organisations, of which $2.7 million went to the Counterterrorism and Security Education and Research Foundation. The Newton D. & Rochelle F. Becker Foundation was primarily a supporter of Jewish and Zionist causes, but also contributed a total of $1.1 million to Islamophobic organisations. The Anchorage Charitable Fund – together with the William Rosenwald Family Fund and another major contributor to mainstream conservative causes – supplied $2.8 million to the Islamophobic network, principally through $2.3 million given to the Middle East Forum. Finally, the Fairbrook Foundation, controlled by Aubrey and Joyce Chernick, gave $1.5 million to Islamophobic organisations. It was the main source of the funding from the David Horowitz Freedom Center to Robert Spencer's Jihad Watch. Separately, Aubrey Chernick contributed heavily to a blog platform opposed to the Park51 mosque. Many of the purveyors of Islamophobia cross-promoted, and sometimes even employed, each other. Some made a good living from it. In 2013, Pamela Geller paid herself $200,000 a year from her anti-Muslim American Freedom Defense Initiative, while Gaffney collected $300,000 a year from his Center for Security Policy. Horowitz pocketed $525,000 a year from his Freedom Center, which also shelled out $167,000 a year to Robert Spencer.

37 Unless otherwise stated, all figures in this section are from the Stimson Study Group on Counterterrorism Spending, published in May 2018 at www. stimson.org

38 Based not only on spending by the new Department of Homeland Security, but also on related activities by the Departments of State, Defense, Health and Human Services, Justice, and a number of stand-alone agencies. Total homeland security spending more than doubled from $16 billion in 2001 to $33 billion in 2002. It peaked at $74 billion in 2009, then fell back for some years before climbing again to $71 billion in 2017.

39   The DHS was responsible for 51 per cent of total spending in the period ($498
     billion), two thirds of which went to aviation and border security. Defense
     contributed 24 per cent ($232 billion), principally on the protection of crucial
     military infrastructure, bases and facilities. The State Department contributed
     9 per cent ($33 billion) to aviation and border security. Health and Human
     Services contributed 7 per cent ($71 billion) against catastrophic health threats
     (prompted by the anthrax attacks in the wake of 9/11) and on emergency
     preparedness. The Justice Department supplied 4 per cent ($39 billion) on
     domestic counter-terrorism.

     Over this period, around 43 per cent of total homeland security spending
     was allotted to border and transportation security, and 30 per cent to the
     defence of critical infrastructure. Defence against catastrophic threats
     received 9 per cent, emergency preparedness and response 9 per cent, and
     domestic counterterrorism 8 per cent. Remarkably, intelligence and warning
     received just 1 per cent. These proportions changed very little from year to
     year, which might suggest that policymakers made little difference to the
     counterterrorism agenda and that departments and agencies set their own
     priorities.

     Homeland security was remarkably good at creating jobs in both the public
     and private sector. After 9/11, related departments were responsible for nearly
     80 per cent of new government jobs. In 2014, the DHS had 230,000
     employees, second only to the Defense Department, and an equal number
     were employed by the department through private contractors.

40   Alimahomed, Sabrina, 'Homeland Security Inc.: Public order, private profit,
     Race & Class 55 (4), pp. 82–99, p. 86.

CHAPTER 8: DONALD TRUMP AND ISLAM

1   A claim he was still making after he reached the White House. See Tara
     Golshan, 'Donald Trump revives his bogus claim that American Muslims
     "cheer" terrorism', Vox, 14 June 2016. https://www.vox.com/2016/6/14/
     11931338/donald-trump-muslims-cheering-terrorism

2   Jenna Johnson, 'Trump calls for "a total complete shutdown of Muslims
     entering the United States"', *Washington Post*, 7 December 2015. https://www.
     washingtonpost.com/news/post-politics/wp/2015/12/07/donald-trump-
     calls-for-total-and-complete-shutdown-of-muslims-entering-the-united-states/
     ?noredirect=on&utm_term=.3d919c16f29d

3   https://www.thestate.com/news/politics-government/election/Candidate-
     match/article48490700.html

4   'Anti-Muslim violence and the 2016 US presidential election', Bridge, 2 May
     2016. http://bridge.georgetown.edu/islamophobia-and-the-2016-elections/

5   Cited in Daniel Bush, 'Could Trump's anti-Muslim rhetoric influence politics

well beyond 2016?', PBS, 11 December 2015. https://www.pbs.org/newshour/politics/could-trumps-anti-muslim-rhetoric-influence-politics-well-beyond-2016

6   For analysis of Trump's shifting positions, see Ali Vitali, 'In his own words: Donald Trump on the Muslim ban, deportations', NBC News, 27 June 2016. https://www.nbcnews.com/politics/2016-election/his-words-donald-trump-muslim-ban-deportations-n599901

7   Ashley Parker, 'Donald Trump, over 18 Holes in Scotland Plays 20 Questions', *New York Times*, 25 June 2016. https://www.nytimes.com/2016/06/26/us/politics/donald-trump-over-18-holes-in-scotland-plays-20-questions.html

8   Analysis derived from http://www.trumptwitterarchive.com/archive

9   'Transcript of the second debate', *New York Times*, 10 October 2016. https://www.nytimes.com/2016/10/10/us/politics/transcript-second-debate.html

10 David A. Graham, 'Clinton's careful courtship of Muslim voters', *The Atlantic*, 24 October 2016. https://www.theatlantic.com/politics/archive/2016/10/clinton-muslim-outreach/503915/

11 Sarah A. Harvard, '13 percent of Muslim Americans in the CAIE exit poll voted for Donald Trump', Mic, 23 November 2016. https://mic.com/articles/160301/13-of-muslim-americans-in-this-cair-exit-poll-voted-for-donald-trump-here-s-why#.bs6xOQC8K

12 Tucker Higgins, 'Supreme Court rules that Trump's travel ban is constitutional', CNBC, 26 June 2018. https://www.cnbc.com/2018/06/26/supreme-court-rules-in-trump-muslim-travel-ban-case.html

13 Asher Stockler, 'Evangelist Franklin Graham defends Trump against Stormy Daniels reports', NBC News, 20 January 2018. https://www.nbcnews.com/politics/donald-trump/evangelist-franklin-graham-defends-trump-against-stormy-daniels-reports-n839496

14 'Religious Landscape Study', Pew Research Center, http://www.pewforum.org/religious-landscape-study/

15 See the perceptive profile by McKay Coppins, 'God's plan for Mike Pence', *The Atlantic*, Jan/Feb 2018. https://www.theatlantic.com/magazine/archive/2018/01/gods-plan-for-mike-pence/546569/

16 'Transcript of the vice presidential debate', *Time*, 5 October 2016. http://time.com/4517096/vice-presidential-debate-kaine-pence-transcript/

17 Vaughn Hillyard, 'Pence cancels event, says he's "offended" by Trump comments', NBC News, 8 October 2016. https://www.nbcnews.com/politics/2016-election/mike-pence-stands-after-trump-disinvited-n662436

18 Eric Bradner and Cassie Spodak, 'Pence's role: Trump's apologizer-in-chief', CNN, 4 August 2016. https://edition.cnn.com/2016/08/03/politics/mike-pence-donald-trump-apologist-in-chief/index.html

19 See Jessica Martínez and Gregory A. Smith, 'How the faithful voted: a preliminary 2016 analysis', Pew Research Center, 9 November 2016.

https://www.pewresearch.org/fact-tank/2016/11/09/how-the-faithful-voted-a-preliminary-2016-analysis/

20 Kate Shellnutt, 'Trump elected president, thanks to 4 in 5 white Evangelicals', *Christianity Today*, 9 November 2016. https://www.christianitytoday.com/news/2016/november/trump-elected-president-thanks-to-4-in-5-white-evangelicals.html

21 See Maureen Groppe, 'First year of Trump-Pence brings bountiful blessings, religious conservatives say', *USA Today*, 19 January 2018. https://eu.usatoday.com/story/news/politics/2018/01/19/first-year-trump-pence-brings-bountiful-blessings-religious-conservatives-say/1044308001/

22 Morgan Strong, 'Trump, the Evangelicals and the Middle East', *Middle East Eye*, 22 May 2018. https://www.middleeasteye.net/columns/how-evangelicals-learned-manipulate-donald-trump-and-what-it-could-mean-middle-east-85444473

23 Ron Kampeas, 'Mike Pence's faith, Israel and Middle East Policy', *The Jerusalem Post*, 24 January 2018. https://www.jpost.com/Arab-Israeli-Conflict/Mike-Pences-faith-Israel-and-Middle-East-policy-539656

24 F. Brinley Bruton, Lawahez Jabari and Paul Goldman, 'Holy Land Christians feel abandoned by US Evangelicals', NBC, 5 May 2018. https://www.nbcnews.com/news/world/holy-land-christians-feel-abandoned-u-s-evangelicals-n867371

25 'Trump hails "dawn of new Middle East" with UAE-Bahrain-Israel deals', BBC News, 15 September 2020. https://www.bbc.co.uk/news/world-middle-east-54168120

26 See Rakib Ehsan, 'Trump's performance among Muslim-Americans has crucial lessons for the Republicans', capx.co, 21 November 2020. https://capx.co/trumps-performance-among-muslim-americans-has-crucial-lessons-for-the-republicans/ At the time of writing (February 2021), no Muslim government has made any public protest against China's treatment of the Uighurs with the exception of Turkey; President Erdogan criticised China and called what was happening to the Uighurs an embarrassment to humanity. He became more muted for political reasons afterwards. https://ahvalnews.com/uighurs/erdogan-urges-china-treat-uyghurs-equal-citizens-phone-call-xi

27 'Proclamation on Ending Discriminatory Bans on Entry to the United States', 20 January 2021. https://www.whitehouse.gov/briefing-room/presidential-actions/2021/01/20/proclamation-ending-discriminatory-bans-on-entry-to-the-united-states/

28 'Biden names American-Indian Sameera Fazili as deputy director of National Economic Council', *India Times*, 16 January 2021. https://economictimes.indiatimes.com/news/international/world-news/biden-names-indian-american-sameera-fazili-as-deputy-director-of-national-economic-council/articleshow/80298336.cms?utm_source=contentofinterest&utm_medium=text&utm_campaign=cppst

29 Emily Jacobs, 'Biden dismisses Uighur genocide as China's "different norms"',
    New York Post, 17 February 2021. https://nypost.com/2021/02/17/
    biden-says-uighur-genocide-is-part-of-chinas-different-norms/
30 Margaret Brennan, Christina Ruffini and Camilla Schick, 'With China's
    treatment of Muslim Uighurs determined to be genocide, Biden administration
    under pressure to act', CBS News, 27 January 2021. https://www.cbsnews.
    com/news/china-treatment-of-muslim-uighurs-determined-to-
    be-genocide-biden-administration-under-pressure-to-act/
31 'US-China relations: details released of Biden's first call with Xi', BBC News,
    11 February 2021. https://www.bbc.co.uk/news/world-56021205
32 Katrina Manson, 'Joe Biden speaks with Benjamin Netanyahu after being
    accused of snub', *Financial Times*, 17 February 2021. https://www.ft.com/
    content/ac20564f-808f-436d-8ba5-1f1c1bf083d7
33 PBS News Hour interview with Biden: https://www.pbs.org/newshour/show/
    watch-our-interview-with-joe-biden
34 'Over 50 Muslim candidates win US elections', Muslim Mirror, 7 November
    2020. http://muslimmirror.com/eng/
    over-50-muslim-candidates-win-us-elections/

CONCLUSION TO PART ONE

1 The countries were Afghanistan, Iraq, Syria, Yemen, Somalia, Libya, and
   Niger and were acknowledged in a White House report obtained by the *New
   York Times*, 14 March 2018. https://www.nytimes.com/2018/03/14/world/
   africa/niger-green-berets-isis-firefight-december.html
2 'Muslim population in the UK', Office for National Statistics, 2 August 2018.
   https://www.ons.gov.uk/aboutus/transparencyandgovernance/
   freedomofinformationfoi/muslimpopulationintheuk/
3 Besheer Mohamed, 'New estimates show US Muslim population continues to
   grow', Pew Research Center, 3 January 2018. http://www.pewresearch.org/
   fact-tank/2018/01/03/
   new-estimates-show-u-s-muslim-population-continues-to-grow/

CHAPTER 9: FROM BEDE TO ELIZABETH I

1 'Bede felt himself to be perfectly well-qualified to comment in sweeping terms
   upon the Orient, the Saracens and their activities: they are, he says,
   undifferentiatedly shiftless, hateful and aggressive (uagos, incertisque sedibus;
   exosi et contrarii).' Cited in Katharine Scarfe Beckett, *Anglo-Saxon Perceptions of
   the Islamic World* (Cambridge University Press, 2003), p. 20.
2 Jerome lived from AD 342–420 and was instrumental in shaping views of the
   Orient. Bede helped to make Jerome's views more widely known. See

Sophie Gilliat-Ray, *Muslims In Britain* (Cambridge University Press, 2010), pp. 5–8.

3   The Mongols were the most successful conquerors in world history, but most of their vast conquests were of non-Christian territories, and they never had the same impact on Christian imagination as Muslims. The early Mongol emperors were renowned for religious tolerance, Eastern, Roman and Nestorian Christianity all had a foothold in the empire and, in the thirteenth century, the Christian rulers of Byzantium and France made attempts to ally with them. Years later, Edward Gibbon wrote: 'The Catholic inquisitors of Europe who defended nonsense by cruelty might have been confounded by the example of a barbarian [Zingis Khan] who anticipated the lessons of philosophy and established by his laws a system of pure theism and perfect toleration.' He added 'A singular conformity may be found between the religious laws of Zingis Khan and of Mr Locke.' Edward Gibbon, *The History of the Decline And Fall of the Roman Empire* (Strahan & Cadell, 1789), chapter 64.

4   Jerusalem was conquered by Caliph Umar in 637 CE and by Sultan Salah al-Din in 1187 CE. Maher Y. Abu-Munshar, *Islamic Jerusalem And Its Christians: A History of Tolerance and Tensions* (I. B. Tauris & Co, 2007), pp. 175–182.

5   See Andrew Wheatcroft, *Infidels: A History of the Conflict Between Christendom and Islam* (Penguin, 2003), chapter 2, especially pp. 46–56.

6   Wheatcroft *op. cit.*, p. 48.

7   Wheatcroft *op. cit.*, pp. 54–55.

8   Cited in Wheatcroft *op. cit.*, pp. 172, 386 (note 25).

9   Bernard Hamilton, 'Knowing the Enemy: Western Understanding of Islam at the Time of the Crusades', *Journal of the Royal Asiatic Society*, 3rd series, 7.3 (1997), pp. 373–387.

10 Sayeeda Warsi recalls the vivid contrast between English and Muslim narratives of the Crusades, and images of Saladin in *The Enemy Within: A Tale of Muslim Britain* (Penguin, 2017), pp. 12–13. See also Carole Hillenbrand, 'The Evolution of the Saladin Legend in the West'. https://www.academia.edu/1496191/The_Evolution_of_the_Saladin_Legend_in_the_West

11 Stanley Lane-Poole, *Saladin and the Fall of the Kingdom of Jerusalem* (GP Putnam's Sons, 1898), Preface.

12 See the *Oxford English Dictionary* definition of 'crusade'.

13 The Assassins were so abhorred by pious Muslims that, had the Muslim world not been preoccupied with the Crusades, it is probable that they would have undertaken a serious and concerted jihad against the Assassins. See Laurence Lockhart, 'H·asan-i-S·abba‾h· and the Assassins', *Bulletin of the School of Oriental and African Studies*, 1930, 5(4), pp. 675–696.

14 A contingent of Serbian troops took part in the siege and the final attack on Constantinople. During the siege on Vienna in 1683, Louis XIV of France formed an alliance with the Sultan while an army of 100,000 Hungarian Christians assisted the Ottoman attack. During the Crimean War, some

European officers who worked with the Ottomans even converted to Islam, while others adopted Turkish names. See Ian Almond, *Two Faiths, One Banner* (Harvard University Press, 2009), pp. 111, 133–135, 139–140, 219.

15   This claim has not been found in any contemporary source. A. J. Forey, 'Western Converts to Islam (Later Eleventh to Later Fifteenth Centuries)', *Traditio*, vol 68, 2013, pp. 153–231.

16   Adelard translated Euclid's *Elements* from Arabic for the first time and this then became the standard textbook used for teaching geometry to students. He also translated a set of astronomical tables by al-Khwarizmi. Charles Burnett, 'Adelard of Bath', in Thomas Hockey et al (eds), *Biographical Encyclopedia of Astronomers* (Springer, 2014).

17   See Charles Burnett (ed.), *Adelard of Bath: Conversations With His Nephew* (Cambridge University Press, 1998).

18   Gilliat-Ray *op. cit.,* p. 11.

19   Gilliat-Ray *op. cit.,* p. 12.

20   See Warsi *op. cit.,* p. 12, and entry for Geoffrey Chaucer's *Canterbury Tales* at www.muslimmuseum.org.uk

21   See the interesting student paper by Jihoon Ko, 'Economic Impact the Islamic World Had on Christian Europe 11th–14th century', Korean Minjok Leadership Academy. https://www.zum.de>whkmla>jihoon>jihoon. See also 'Europe and the Islamic Mediterranean AD 700-1600', from the catalogue of the Victoria and Albert Museum in London, http://www.vam.ac.uk/content/articles/e/europe-islamic-mediterranean/

22   The Ottomans first established themselves in western Anatolia. From here, they began expanding, capturing Brusa, which became the first Ottoman capital, in 1326. By 1345, the whole coast of the Sea of Marmara and the Asiatic shore of the Dardanelles were now in Ottoman hands. In 1361, they captured Adrianople which was renamed Edirne and became the new Ottoman capital. The newly conquered lands were settled with immigrants from Anatolia. Stephen Turnbull, *The Ottoman Empire, 1326–1699* (Taylor & Francis, 2003), pp. 6–10.

23   The ghazi warriors who had fought for the early Ottoman rulers provided the nucleus for what was to become the Ottoman army. The akinji (raiders) were later used by the Ottomans as an auxiliary militia for intelligence gathering in enemy territory. Renegade Christians could often be found among their ranks. The akinji rode horses and carried a sword, a shield, a scimitar, a lance and a mace. They were commanded by provincial leaders called sanjak bey. In the marches, sipahis (free cavalry) were Muslim Turks who were loyal to their local bey. Madmen (the deli) allowed themselves to be used as human battering rams. Meanwhile, the janissaries were the elite of the Ottoman army and for centuries were considered to be some of the finest infantrymen in Europe. According to the chronicler Chalkondylas, 'I think there is no prince who has his armies and camps in better order, both in abundance of victuals and in the

beautiful order they use in encampment without any confusion or embarrassment'. Ibid., pp. 14–18.

24 In 1366, the Pope proclaimed a crusade to expel the Turks from the Balkans but by 1371, the Ottomans had established themselves in Bulgaria and they killed all of the Serbian leaders on the 26 September 1371 at the Battle of Cernomen. Thessalonica was lost in 1387, Sofia in 1385 and the Serbian city of Nis was occupied in 1386. After the Serbian defeat at the Battle of Kosovo in June 1389, the ruler of Serbia, Stephen Lazarevic, became a loyal Turkish vassal. Bosnia fell in 1391, Bulgaria in 1393 and Bulgarian independence burned out in 1395. The Ottomans then turned their attention to Constantinople. Ibid., p. 21–23.

25 Ibid., p. 23.

26 Ibid., p. 23–4.

27 This was fought at the same site as the 1389 Battle of Kosovo. Initially, both sides fought defensively from behind field fortifications until a series of Ottoman cavalry charges gave the Turks their victory. Stephen Turnbull, *The Ottoman Empire, 1326–1699*, pp. 34–35.

28 Ibid., pp. 36–37.

29 Wheatcroft, *op. cit.*, pp. 207–208.

30 The childless last Emperor Constantine's nephews, heirs to his throne, both survived and assumed high positions under their conquerors. One even became grand vizier (chief minister). See Almond *op. cit.*, pp. 135–136.

31 The Vienna campaign was launched on 10 May 1529 and Suleiman set out with 120,000 men. However, it was unsuccessful and they retreated. However, by 1532, he had returned to Hungary for another attempt to take Vienna, though this was, again, unsuccessful. Turnbull *op. cit.*, pp. 45, 47–51.

32 See Ian Colliard, 'The Consequences of Ottoman Aspirations in Europe for Henry VIII's England', www.tudorstuartperspectives.wordpress.com

33 Established in 1581, the 'Turkey Company' maintained a consul for Syria and, by 1586, Aleppo had replaced Tripoli as the consul's chief residence. Over the course of the seventeenth century, Aleppo emerged as the most important centre for British trade in the Levant. Simon Mills, *A Commerce of Knowledge: Trade, Religion, and Scholarship between England and the Ottoman Empire, 1600–1760*, (Oxford University Press, 2020), pp. 16–17.

34 E. Delmar Morgan & C. H. Coote (eds), *Early Voyages and Travels to Russia and Persia: By Anthony Jenkinson and Other Englishmen* (Cambridge University Press, 2010) pp. XXV, XXXIV, 84.

35 Interest in the Levant trade had developed rather late in England, previously dependent on the Venetians for goods from the East. Until the grant of their national charter of privileges by Murad III in 1580, the English traded in the Levant under the protection of France. After Spain signed a peace treaty, without commercial rights with the Ottomans in 1578, the English sent Harborne to Constantinople to negotiate. They were granted their own treaty

by the Sultan in 1580. S. A. Skilliter, *William Harborne and the Trade with Turkey 1578–1582: A Documentary Study of the First Anglo-Ottoman Relations* (published for the British Academy, London by Oxford University Press, 1977), pp. 1, 4.

36   See Jerry Brotton, 'Elizabethan England's relationship with the Islamic world', www.historyextra.com, 9 March 2018. https://www.historyextra.com/period/elizabethan/
elizabethan-englands-relationship-with-the-islamic-world/

37   A fine book which makes this parallel indirectly is Alice Hogge, *God's Secret Agents: Queen Elizabeth's Forbidden Priests and Their Hatching of the Gunpowder Plot* (Harper Collins, 2005).

38   Richard Wragge, 'A description of a voiage to Constantinople and Syria' in *Early Modern Tales of Orient: A Critical Anthology*, ed. Kenneth Parker (Cambridge University Press, 2013), p. 57.

39   Gerald MacLean & Nabil Matar, *Britain and the Islamic World, 1558–1713* (Oxford University Press, 2011), p. 47.

40   The offer of safe conduct and free trade to the English in the Ottoman Empire (7 March 1579) was confirmed by the first capitulation granted to the English on 16–25 May 1580). Alexander de Groot, 'The Historical Development of the Capitulatory Regime in the Ottoman Middle East from the Fifteenth to the Nineteenth Centuries', *Oriente Moderno*, 22 (83), no. 3, 2003, pp. 575–604.

41   Philip Marshall Brown, 'The Capitulations', *Foreign Affairs*, vol. 1, no. 4, 1923, pp. 71–81.

42   Pugh, *Britain and Islam* (Yale University Press, 2019), p. 44.

43   Gilliat-Ray *op. cit.*, p. 13.

44   Brotton, *op. cit.*

45   According to the historian Miranda Kaufmann, this proclamation never went beyond its draft form. Miranda Kaufmann, 'Caspar van Senden, Sir Thomas Sherley and the "Blackamoor" Project', *Historical Research*, vol. 81, no. 212 (May 2008), pp. 366–371. https://www.bl.uk/collection-items/
draft-proclamation-on-the-expulsion-of-negroes-and-blackamoors-1601#

46   See the section on the Black history of Elizabethan times on the National Archives website. https://www.nationalarchives.gov.uk/pathways/blackhistory/early_times/elizabeth.htm

47   Humayun Ansari, *The Infidel Within: Muslims in Britain Since 1800* (Hurst & Co, 2004), p. 27.

48   Sandys described how the Turks removed their shoes before entering mosques and how the Sofia was frequented by the Sultan himself almost every other Friday. George Sandys, *A Relation of a Journey Begun An: Dom: 1610 foure books: Containing a description of the turkish empire, of ægypt, of the holy land, of the remote parts of italy, and ilands adioyning London* (Thomas Cotes, 1627).

49   One Colonel Anthony Weldon petitioned the Council of State to take action against Ross. No documentary evidence has survived about the proceedings

against Ross, nor about the reasons why there was opposition to the publication of the Quran in English. Nabil Matar, 'Alexander Ross and the First English Translation of the Quarān', *Muslim World*, 88.1 (1998), pp. 81–92.

50 Pugh *op. cit*,. p. 55.

51 See Nabil Matar, 'Britons and Muslims in the early modern period: from prejudice to (a theory of) toleration' in ed M. Malik, *Anti-Muslim Prejudice Past And Present* (Routledge, 2010), p. 13.

52 Ibid., pp. 15–16.

53 Gilliat-Ray *op. cit.*, pp. 22–23. See also Nabil Matar (ed.), *Henry Stubbe And The Beginnings Of Islam* (Columbia University Press, 2013). Stubbe's self-censorship did not help him, as Charles II banished him to Jamaica anyway. When he returned, he was nearly hanged after denouncing Charles's brother, the Duke of York, on account of his Roman Catholic sympathies.

CHAPTER 10: THE FIRST MUSLIM COLONIES

1 Occasionally, the pirates were English, most notably the infamous Peter Eston who commanded a fleet of twenty-five ships based in the west of Ireland as well as Barbary. Eventually, James I dispatched Eston to Newfoundland, where he continued to make a nuisance of himself. See Adrian Tinniswood, *Pirates of Barbary: Corsairs, Conquests and Captivity in the 17th-century Mediterranean*, (Jonathan Cape, 2010), pp. 66–71. See also Ben Johnson, 'Barbary Pirates and English Slaves', Historic UK. https://www.historic-uk.com/HistoryUK/HistoryofEngland/Barbary-Pirates-English-Slaves/

2 Of the £70,000 raised by the levy, only £11,100 ever found its way to Barbary. Tinniswood *op. cit.*, p. 195.

3 Ibid., p. 191.

4 Johnson, *op. cit.*

5 Ibid.

6 See Gilliat-Ray *op. cit.*, p. 16.

7 Johnson, *op. cit.*

8 See Matar in Malik *op. cit.*, p. 20.

9 Ibid., p. 21.

10 Ibid., p. 22.

11 Tony Blair's wife, Cherie, is a lifelong and practising Catholic, along with their children. Blair reportedly took communion at Westminster Cathedral until he was asked to stop as it was causing comment. Stephen Bates, 'After 30 years as a closet Catholic, Blair finally puts faith before politics', *Guardian*, 22 July 2007.

12 Boris Johnson's mother, Charlotte Johnson Wahl, was Catholic and he was baptised as a Catholic. He was confirmed in the Church of England while studying at Eton College. His son, Wilfred Johnson, was also baptised a Catholic on 12 September 2020. Wilfred's mother, Carrie Symonds, is

Catholic. Simon Caldwell, 'Boris Johnson's son baptised Catholic', *The Tablet*, 23 September 2020.

13 Then a presidential candidate, John F. Kennedy delivered a speech to the Greater Houston Ministerial Association on 12 September 1960 on the subject of his faith. Many Protestants questioned whether Kennedy's Roman Catholic faith would allow him to make important decisions free from church influence. From 'Transcript: JFK's Speech on His Religion', NPR, 5 December 2007. https://www.npr.org/templates/story/story.php?storyId=16920600

14 Anthony Zurcher, 'Joe Biden: America's second Catholic president', BBC News, 25 January 2021. https://www.bbc.co.uk/news/world-us-canada-55801307

15 Catherine made one other major contribution to English and Muslim history. She popularised tea drinking. At first a luxury, tea would displace coffee when its price fell, and the English would make great efforts to acquire a source of supply. See Isabel Stilwell, 'Raise Your Cup to Catherine of Braganza', *Historia*, April 2018; and Pugh *op. cit.*, p. 59.

16 See Iain Finlayson, *Tangier: City of a Dream* (Harper Collins, 1992), pp. 26–29.

17 Tangier never attracted a sizeable merchant community and the population consisted almost entirely of the soldiers stationed there and the merchants who supplied them. Tristan Stein, 'Tangier in the Restoration Empire', *The Historical Journal*, vol. 54, no. 4, 2011, pp. 985–1011.

18 While the Portuguese had subsisted on resources from the surrounding countryside, the English preferred to import their provisions from home: salt pork and barrels of other preserved foods which were unsuitable for the conditions of Tangier. Finlayson *op. cit.*, p. 26–28.

19 See John Childs, *The Army Of Charles II* (Routledge, 1976), pp. 136–141.

20 The Jews were expelled in December 1677, but their role in trade was so important that they were readmitted in 1680. T. M. Benady, 'The Role of Jews in the British Colonies of the Western Mediterranean', *Jewish Historical Studies*, vol. 33, 1992, pp. 45–63.

21 His dynasty survived French occupation and still rules Morocco. Mohammed V and his family were exiled to Madagascar by the French on 20 August 1953. They returned to Morocco on 16 November 1955 and were greeted by jubilant crowds. Susan Gilson Miller, *A History of Modern Morocco* (Cambridge University Press, 2013), pp. 150, 153.

22 On 6 February 1684, Lord Dartmouth abandoned the ruins of Tangier after demolishing the Mole. It was then given to Moulay Ismail and the Berber tribesmen of the Rif. Finlayson *op. cit.*, p. 31.

23 Ibid., pp. 29–30, and Mark Patton, 'Dismantling a Colony: Samuel Pepys at Tangiers', English History Authors. https://englishhistoryauthors.blogspot.com/2016/02/dismantling-colony-samuel-pepys-at.html

24 Francis Breton, the East India Company's most senior official in Asia, described how after prayers one Sunday, William Blackwell, the son of the

king's grocer at the court of St James, had 'privately conveighed himselfe to the Governor of ye citty, who, being prepaired, with the Qazi and others attended his comeing; before whome hee most wickedly and desperately renounced his Christian faith and professed himself a Moore, was imediately circumcised, and is irrecoverably lost'. William Dalrymple, 'The White Mughals', *PN Review*, 29.1, 2002, pp. 16–23.

25 See Haig Smith, 'God shall enlarge Japheth and he shall dwell in the tents of Shem', in William A. Pettigrew & Mahesh Gopalan (eds), *The East India Company, 1600–1857* (Routledge, 2017) p. 105.

26 Ibid., p. 93.

27 There are two notable examples in Dalrymple *op. cit.*, pp. 257, 375.

28 Smith *op. cit.*, p. 101.

29 Ibid., p. 102. and see Dalrymple *op. cit.*, pp. 23–24.

30 See Dalrymple *op. cit.*, pp. 25–26.

31 See Philip Lawson, *The East India Company: A History* (Routledge, 1993), chapters 4 and 5 for an account of the company at its financial zenith as a trading company before Clive's victories and later military over-expansion frittered its profits.

32 When the Napoleonic wars drew to a close in 1814, new regulations were introduced for the registration of India-built ships. They decreed that 'no Asiatic sailors, lascars or natives of any territories . . . within the limits of the Charter of the East India Company, although born in territories . . . under the Government of His Majesty or the East India Company, shall at any time be deemed or taken to be British sailors'. Rozina Visram, *Asians in Britain: 400 Years of History* (Pluto Press, 2002), p. 15.

33 See https://www.ourmigrationstory.org.uk/oms/ the-lascars-britains-colonial-era-sailors

34 Frederick Marryat, *Works of Captain Marryatt* (Pennsylvania, 1836), p. 361.

35 Ibid., pp. 27, 32.

36 See Gilliat-Ray *op. cit.*, pp. 24–25, and Ansari *op. cit.*, p. 35.

37 Frey, James W. 'Lascars, the Thames Police Court and the Old Bailey: crime on the high seas and the London courts, 1852–8' (tandfonline.com)

38 See Dalrymple *op. cit.*, pp. 266–269, and Susheila Nasta, *Asian Britain: A Photographic History* (Westbourne Press, 2013), pp. 15–19.

39 In the book, Heathcliff is described as 'a little Lascar, or an American or Spanish castaway.' Brontë, Emily, *Wuthering Heights* (Oxford: Oxford at the Clarendon Press, 1976), p. 40.

40 See Dalrymple *op. cit.*, p. 51 for an example of this. Apart from Lord Liverpool, there is a theory that George III's Queen Charlotte had a distant North African Muslim ancestor. See Stuart Jeffries, 'Was this Britain's first black queen?', *Guardian*, 12 March 2009. https://www.theguardian.com/ world/2009/mar/12/race-monarchy. Naturally, this theory resurfaced at the wedding of Prince Harry to Meghan Markle.

41 Diane Robinson-Dunn, 'Lascar sailors and English converts: the imperial port
    and Islam in late 19th-century England', History Cooperative, 2003. http://
    webdoc.sub.gwdg.de/ebook/p/2005/history_cooperative/www.
    historycooperative.org/proceedings/seascapes/dunn.html

42 Ansari *op. cit.*, pp. 33–34.

43 Quoted in Peter Fryer, *Staying Power: The History of Black People in Britain* (Pluto
    Press, 2010), p. 69.

44 Cited in Lawson *op. cit.*, p. 119.

45 See Lawson *op. cit.*, p. 89, and Rudrangshu Mukherjee, 'Myth of empire – the
    story about the Black Hole of Calcutta refuses to die', *Telegraph India*, 25 June
    2006. https://www.telegraphindia.com/opinion/myth-of-empire-the-story-
    about-the-black-hole-of-calcutta-refuses-to-die/cid/1025320

46 Thomas Babington Macaulay, 'Lord Clive', *Critical and Historical Essays:
    Contributed to the Edinburgh Review* (Longman, Green, Brown & Longman, 1843).

47 See Lawson *op. cit.*, p. 136, and William Dalrymple's brilliant article 'An essay
    in imperial villain-making', *Guardian*, 24 May 2005. https://www.theguardian.
    com/politics/2005/may/24/foreignpolicy.india

CHAPTER 11: ISLAM AND EMPIRE

1   The Asians who moved to Britain in the period before 1914 were a diverse
    group; some were working class, while others mingled with the English upper
    class and some were professionals active in medicine, education, law, business,
    politics and the women's movement. In 1910, the Committee on Distressed
    Colonial and Indian Subjects heard of ayahs in Hornsey, North London and in
    Haywards Heath in Sussex. A 1925 photograph taken in Glasgow also shows
    two nannies from Madras. Visram *op. cit.*, pp. 44–45.

2   Gilliat-Ray *op. cit.*, pp. 24, 29–30.

3   According to the 1881 census, there were eight Egyptians and forty-four Turks
    living on Merseyside. Ansari *op. cit.*, pp. 24–25, 29.

4   Ansari *op. cit.*, pp. 63–65.

5   Gilliat-Ray *op. cit.*, p. 33.

6   Ansari, *op. cit.*, pp. 32–33.

7   Ansari, *op. cit.*, p. 33; Warsi *op. cit.*, p. 10; Visram *op. cit.*, pp. 45–9.

8   Ansari *op. cit.*, pp. 75–79. The relationship between Queen Victoria and the
    Munshi was sensitively observed in Stephen Frears' 2017 film *Victoria and
    Abdul*, starring Judi Dench and Ali Fazal.

9   Gilliat-Ray *op. cit.*, p. 42; F. Halliday, 'The millet of Manchester: Arab
    merchants and the cotton trade', *British Journal of Middle Eastern Studies* 19
    (1992), pp. 159–176.

10 Ansari *op. cit.*, p. 386.

11 In a three-hour speech to the House of Commons on 27 July 1857, Disraeli

declared that 'it was of primary importance to know whether it was a military mutiny or a national revolt'. He blamed the violence on widespread Indian resentment at the whole conduct of British rule. Christopher Herbert, *The Indian Mutiny and Victorian Trauma* (Princeton University Press, 2007), pp. 8–9.

12 See Grace Moore, *Dickens and Empire: Discourses of Class, Race and Colonialism in the Works of Charles Dickens* (Ashgate, 2004), p. 94.

13 See Nicola Frith, *The French Colonial Imagination: Writing the Indian Uprisings, 1857–1858, from the Second Empire to Third Republic* (Lexington Books, 2014) p. 64 et seq.

14 Cited in Biswamoy Pati (ed.), *The 1857 Rebellion* (Oxford University Press, 2007), pp. 30–31.

15 See Ansari *op. cit.*, p. 61.

16 The East India Company made a virtue of religious tolerance, which outraged the British religious establishment. See Herbert *op. cit.*, pp. 41–44.

17 Frith, *op cit.*, pp. 67–8.

18 See ibid., p. 66. France still had a colony in India at the time of the uprising, but Napoleon III, anxious to preserve his understanding with Britain, ignored all pleas for support from the rebels. Nana Sahib is a central character in Jules Verne's fantasy novel *The Steam House*. His religion is ambiguous, but he certainly co-operates with the Muslim Mughal family members who murder the English colonel Sir Charles Munro.

19 See below and in particular Warren Dockter, *Churchill And The Islamic World* (I B Tauris, 2015), pp. 201–210.

20 See Daniel J. Mount, 'G. A. Henty and the Christian Worldview (Condensed)', Daniel J. Mount Archives. https://danielmount.com/archives/g-a-henty-and-the-christian-worldview-condensed/

21 See Brooke Allen, 'G. A. Henty and the vision of empire', *The New Criterion*, 20.8, April 2002. https://newcriterion.com/issues/2002/4/g-a-henty-the-vision-of-empire

22 See Bill Heid, 'Was Winston Churchill G.A. Henty's Biggest Fan?', Live The Adventure Letter!, 31 May 2018. https://www.livetheadventureletter.com/worldview-training/was-winston-churchill-g-a-hentys-biggest-fan/

23 G. A. Henty, *With Clive In India: Or, the beginnings of an empire* (Blackie and Son, 1884), p. 362.

24 G. A. Henty, *With Kitchener in the Soudan: A Story of Atbara and Omdurman* (Blackie and Son, 1903), chapter 18.

25 Henty *op. cit.*, p. 248.

26 Ibid., p. 378.

27 See Andrew Hough, 'Revealed: David Cameron's favourite childhood book is *Our Island Story*', *Daily Telegraph*, 29 October 2010. https://www.telegraph.co.uk/culture/books/booknews/8094333/Revealed-David-Camerons-favourite-childhood-book-is-Our-Island-Story.html

28 H. E. Marshall, *Our Island Story* (T. C. & E. Jack, 1905), pp. 435–436.

29 Henty, *With Clive In India*, *op. cit.*, p. 299. In a recent account by William Dalrymple, he states that more recent assessments of the evidence suggest that 64 entered the Black Hole and 21 survived. William Dalrymple, *The Anarchy: The Relentless Rise of the East India Company* (London: Bloomsbury, 2019) p. 106.

30 Sayyid Ahmad Khan urged his fellow Muslims to learn the language of their rulers, believing that by failing to learn English, the Indian Muslims 'self-excluded' themselves from the mainstream society in India. Belkacem Belmekki, 'Sir Sayyid Ahmad Khan's Framework for the Educational Uplift of the Indian Muslims during British Raj', *Anthropos*, vol. 104, no. 1, 2009, pp. 165–172.

31 Mark Curtiss, *Secret Affairs: Britain's Collusion With Radical Islam* (Serpent's Tail, 2012), pp. 2–4.

CHAPTER 12: BRITAIN AND ISLAM, 1914–45

1 The repression of religious minorities by the Ottoman Empire had long-since been used as a pretext for European countries to interfere in Ottoman affairs. Christine Philliou, *Biography of Empire: Governing Ottomans in the Age of Revolution* (University of California Press, 2010), and Albert Hourani, *Arabic Thought in the Liberal Age, 1789–1923* (Oxford University Press, 1962), pp. 54-55. The Crimean War is also another example, see: Richard Cavendish, 'The Crimean War', *History Today*, vol. 54, no. 3. Retrieved 18 February 2022.

2 The Germans helped to finance the railway line from Scutari to Ankara, the first stage of a line which would later become the Baghdad Railway. In 1902–03, the Ottoman Railway Company secured a concession to extend the railway to Baghdad and the Persian Gulf, with a branch line to Khanikin, a small town on the Persian boarder. By 1914, this line had reached Ras el Ain, some 200 miles beyond Aleppo, though tunnels through the Taurus and Amanus mountains remained incomplete. Alexander Lyon Macfie, *The End of the Ottoman Empire, 1908–1923* (Longman, 1998), pp. 99–100.

3 The reinstatement of the Ottoman constitution (first introduced in 1876 but suspended within two years by Sultan Abdul Hamid II) on 23 July 1908 marked the beginning of the second constitutional period of the empire. During the Young Turk Revolution, parliamentary rule and liberties were introduced. Hasan Kayali, *Arabs and Young Turks: Ottomanism, Arabism, and Islamism in the Ottoman Empire, 1908–1918* (University of California Press, 1997), introduction.

4 Sultan Abdul Hamid II rejected constitutional reform and opted for the preservation of the traditional system of government which was based on the absolute sovereignty of the sultan and the supremacy of the Muslim millet. He

enjoyed considerable support among the Muslim peoples of the Ottoman
Empire due to his promotion of traditional Islamic values. Macfie *op. cit.*, pp.
15, 17, 21.

5   In 1910–11, the Albanians rose up in revolt. In 1912–13, a league of Balkan
states (Serbia, Bulgaria, Greece and Montenegro) launched an assault on the
empire with the object of expelling the Ottomans from Europe and, in 1911,
Italy occupied Tripolitania (Libya). The Italian occupation of Tripolitania and
the ensuing war exposed the weaknesses of the Ottoman Empire. It also
exposed the unwillingness of the European powers to intervene to save the
Empire, a factor which was to prove crucial in the next few years. Macfie *op.
cit.*, pp. 2, 70.

6   German influence in the Ottoman Empire had been steadily increasing and, in
the 1890s, the German Levant Line established a shipping route between
Hamburg and Istanbul while trading posts were set up in the Persian Gulf.
Meanwhile, Krupp received contracts for the supply and equipment of the
Ottoman army. In the 1880s, Lieutenant-Colonel Baron Colmar von der Goltz
was dispatched to reform the Ottoman army and in 1913, following the
Ottoman defeat in the Balkans, the Germans dispatched a military mission,
led by General Otto Liman von Sanders. The Russians viewed this as placing
the Straits under German control. Macfie *op. cit.*, pp. 99–100.

7   Churchill cultivated the Young Turk leaders personally on a supposedly private
visit to Constantinople in 1910. Dockter, op. cit., pp. 49–50, 64. See also
chapter 2 for an overview of the relationship between Britain and the Ottoman
Empire.

8   See Eugene Rogan, *The Fall Of the Ottomans: The Great War in the Middle East,
1914–1920* (Penguin, 2016), pp. 47–8.

9   There is a vivid account of this episode in Barbara W. Tuchman's *The Guns Of
August* (Macmillan, 1962), chapter 10.

10 Rogan, 2016, *op. cit.*, p. 69.

11 The great Cairo trilogy of novels by Egypt's Nobel Prize winner Naguib
Mahfouz brilliantly traces the political and emotional impact of these events on
an Egyptian family.

12 The Germans had encouraged the sultan to call a jihad against Britain and
France as the millions of Muslims in the British and French empires would
likely cause them a problem. However, this call for jihad had little impact on
Muslims internationally. Eugene Rogan, *The Arabs: A History* (Allen Lane,
2009), p. 202.

13 Rogan, 2016, *op. cit.,* pp. 70–1.

14 See 'The Role of Muslims During The First World War', www.britishlegion.
org.uk

15 Rogan, 2016, p. 71.

16 Rogan, 2016, pp. 72–4.

17 Rogan, 2016, p. 189.

18 Ross Anderson, 'The Battle of Tanga, 2–5 November 1914' in *War in History*, Vol. 8, No. 3 (July 2001), pp 294-322.

19 HC Debs 29 March 1928 col 1389.

20 See Mihir Bose, *From Midnight To Glorious Morning?: India Since Independence* (Haus Publishing, 2017), chapters 1 and 2 to demonstrate how the Empire, and India, was often viewed with a mixture of indifference and contempt.

21 During the period September to October 1920, the British completed their conquest of Iraq with force, using heavy artillery and aerial bombardment. A journalist in Najaf described the British onslaught thus: 'They attacked the houses of tribal shaykhs and burned them down, contents and all. They killed many men, horses and livestock.' Rogan, *The Arabs*, p. 232. Air power was also used in 1919 during the third Anglo-Afghan War; Irfan Ahmad, 'Role of Airpower for Counterinsurgency in Afghanistan and FATA (Federally Administered Tribal Areas)', Naval Postgraduate School thesis, 2009; A. J. Young, 'Royal air force north-west frontier, India 1915-39'. *The RUSI Journal*, 127, 1, 1982), p. 59.

22 N. C. Fleming, 'Cabinet Government, British Imperial Security, and the World Disarmament Conference, 1932–1934', *War in History*, vol. 18, no. 1, 2011, pp. 62–84.

23 David Killingray, '"A Swift Agent of Government": Air Power in British Colonial Africa, 1916-1939', *The Journal of African History*, vol. 25, no. 4, 1984, pp. 429–444.

24 For a thorough study of Churchill and air power, see Dockter *op. cit.,* chapter 3.

25 By the early 1940s, the population of 2,500–3,000 Arabs, Somalis, Indians, Malays and Egyptians in Cardiff was overwhelmingly Muslim. Humayun Ansari, *The Infidel Within: Muslims in Britain since 1980* (Hurst, 2004) p.44.

26 The Alien Restriction (Amendment) Bill had been introduced in early 1919 by the Lloyd-George government. The controls were further strengthened with the Aliens Order of 1920. Joynson-Hicks, who had been prominently 'anti-alien' in the 1905–06 agitation, brought in the 1925 Special Restrictions Order to stop England being 'flooded with the whole of the alien refuse from every country in the world'. It was revoked in 1943 due to manpower shortages caused by the war. Ansari *op. cit.,* pp. 42–43.

27 Lawrence James, *Churchill and Empire: A Portrait of an Imperialist* (Weidenfeld & Nicolson, 2013), p. 227. Also see Azeem Ibrahim, 'How Muslims won the Second World War', *Huffington Post*, 24 June 2014. https://www.huffpost.com/entry/how-muslims-won-the-secon_b_5202541

28 James *op. cit.,* p. 301.

29 Ansari *op. cit.,* pp. 119, 50.

30 James *op. cit.,* p. 236.

31 James *op. cit.,* chapters 25 and 26, and pp. 304–6.

32 See Parveen Usmani, 'Out Break of the Second World War and Attitude of the All India Muslim League', *IOSR Journal of Humanities and Social Science*, vol 22 issue 7, 2017.

33 See, for example, 'Impact of the Second World War', Story of Pakistan. https://storyofpakistan.com/impact-of-the-second-world-war/

34 See Nastassja Shtrauchler, 'How Nazis courted the Islamic world during WWII', DW, 13 November 2017. https://www.dw.com/en/how-nazis-courted-the-islamic-world-during-wwii/a-41358387; David Mikics, 'The Nazi romance with Islam has some lessons for the United States', Tablet, 24 November 2014. https://www.tabletmag.com/sections/arts-letters/articles/nazi-romance-with-islam

35 See Antony Beevor, *The Second World War* (Weidenfeld & Nicolson, 2013), p. 178.

36 See Orit Bashkin, 'Egypt Didn't Shill for the Nazis in World War II', Haaretz, 15 July 2018. https://www.haaretz.com/middle-east-news/egypt/.premium-shattering-the-myth-about-egyptian-elites-supporting-the-nazis-in-wwii-1.6264715

37 There is an excellent account of British struggles against the fakir in Mihir Bose's *Silver: The Spy Who Fooled The Nazis* (Fonthill, 2016), a biography of the astonishing Indian spy, Bhagat Ram Talwar. Characteristically, the British warmed to the fakir after the war and he received a warm tribute in his *Times* obituary in April 1960.

38 Vappala Balachandran, 'Netaji's ideal national army', *Tribune India*, 24 October 2018. https://www.tribuneindia.com/news/archive/comment/netajiper centE2per cent80per cent99s-ideal-national-army-672629

39 Welldon had a lot of influence in forming Churchill's world view. Churchill had gone out to India for 'self-education'. Dockter *op. cit.*, pp. 9–10.

40 Churchill wrote home to his mother about how he would send pictures in which she would be able to see him 'fiercely struggling with a turbaned warrior'. Dockter *op. cit.*, pp. 24–25.

41 It has also been argued that, at this point, Churchill was going through an anti-religious phase and that he tended to be very critical of major religions. Dockter *op. cit.*, pp. 7–8.

42 Dockter *op. cit.*, pp. 9, 34–35.

43 Dockter *op. cit.*, p. 36. In time, as often happens, the British warmed to their former enemies. Whirling dervishes became a stock 'turn' in British music hall, as in American vaudeville. See https://arabkitsch.com/orientalism-in-american-vaudeville-songs-and-stories/ and Mark Sedgwick, *Western Sufism: From the Abbasids to the New Age* (Oxford University Press, 2016), chapter 4. By the 1920s, the Mahdist movement was regarded as a moderate force in the Sudan and a guarantee of the loyalty of local Muslims. See Curtis *op. cit.*, p. 3.

44 Dockter *op. cit.*, p. 12.

45 Dockter *op. cit.*, pp. 37–49.

46 British public opinion in general admired the Young Turks. The term passed into the English language as a metaphor for any impatient innovator.

47 James *op. cit.*, pp. 106–108.

48 Dockter *op. cit.*, p. 49. Churchill was not totally wrong in his hopes for Enver's alliance: the latter was killed after the Great War leading the Muslim Basmachi revolt against Churchill's hated enemy, the Bolsheviks. See Rogan *op. cit.*, p. 390.

49 James *op. cit.*, pp. 108–111; Dockter *op. cit.*, p. 82.

50 Dockter *op. cit.*, pp. 86–89, James *op. cit.*, p. 127.

51 Dockter *op. cit.*, pp. 92–93, 99–101.

52 Dockter *op. cit.*, pp. 190–91.

53 After the war, Churchill wrote to Inonu saying that the Allies had 'staunch friends and allies and not least among them is Turkey'. Dockter *op. cit.*, pp. 229–230.

54 Michael J. Cohen, *Churchill and the Jews* (Routledge, 2003), p. 90.

55 Dockter *op. cit.*, pp. 172–176.

56 Dockter *op. cit.*, pp. 236–237.

57 Dockter *op. cit.*, pp. 132–135.

58 Mayo concluded that Islam was inherently more democratic than Hinduism due to the untouchability of the lower castes in Hindu society. She also argued that the divisions between the two communities in India would lead to civil war and that the British presence in India had prevented such a catastrophe. Churchill echoed this point in a speech at the Royal Albert Hall on 18 March 1931: 'Were we to wash our hands of all responsibility and divest ourselves of all our power, as our sentimentalists desire, ferocious civil wars would speedily break out between Moslems and Hindus.' Dockter *op. cit.*, pp. 204–205, James *op. cit.*, pp. 190–191.

59 James, op. cit., pp. 185, 190-1.

60 Dockter *op. cit.*, p. 208.

61 James *op. cit.*, pp. 297–298.

62 Dockter *op. cit.*, p. 243.

63 Dockter *op. cit.*, pp. 248–249, James *op. cit.*, pp. 344–345.

64 The writer and archaeologist Gertrude Bell documented how Faisal I was groomed by Britain and became king of Iraq because that was what the British wanted. Paul Collins & Charles Tripp, *Gertrude Bell and Iraq: A Life and Legacy* (Oxford University Press, 2017) pp. 197–199.

65 Richard M. Langworth, 'Churchill Red Herrings: On a Federal Europe and "Keep Britain White"', 21 September 2019. https://richardlangworth.com/europe-federal-england-white

    Ian Gilmour, *Inside Right: A Study of Conservatism* (Hutchinson, 1977), p. 134.

66 Priyamvada Gopal, 'Why can't Britain handle the truth about Churchill?', *Guardian*, 17 March 2021. https://www.theguardian.com/commentisfree/2021/mar/17/why-cant-britain-handle-the-truth-about-winston-churchill

67 Winston Churchill, *A History of the English-Speaking Peoples, Volume 1: The Birth of Britain* (Weidenfeld & Nicolson, 1956), chapter 2. I am grateful to Dr Abdul Wahid, executive chairman of the British branch of Hizb ut-Tahrir, for bringing this quotation to my attention.

CHAPTER 13: FRANCE AS A COLONIAL POWER

1 Quoted by Fitzroy Morrissey, *A Short History of Islamic Thought* (Head of Zeus, 2021), p. 174.

2 Conrad Hackett, 'Five facts about the Muslim population in Europe', Pew Research Center, 29 November 2017.

3 Michèle Tribalat, 'Marriages "mixtes" et immigration en France', Espace populations sociétés, 2 (2009), pp. 203–214.

4 Alessandro Barbero, *Charlemagne: Father of a Continent* (University of California Press, 2004), p. 10, and James T. Palmer, 'The fake history that fuelled the accused Christchurch shooter', *Washington Post*, 4 June 2019. https://www.washingtonpost.com/outlook/2019/03/18/fake-history-that-fueled-accused-christchurch-shooter

5 On 9 January 2015, two days after the *Charlie Hebdo* attack in Paris, Jean-Marie Le Pen said 'I am not Charlie, I am Charles Martel', recalling the man who defended France from a Muslim invasion at Poitiers in AD 732. Michel Pauron, 'France: quand l'extrême-droite ressuscite Charles Martel', *Jeune Afrique*, 12 August 2015.

6 Under the Ancien Régime, the Church had been closely associated with the State; indeed, Tocqueville – in his *L'Ancien Régime et la Révolution* – cited this as being one of the primary causes of what he considered to be 'irreligion' in France. During the revolution, the Constituent Assembly nationalised Church property in November 1789 and then, on 12 July 1790, the Assembly unilaterally replaced the Concordat of Bologna with the Civil Constitution of the Clergy. On 27 November 1790, all priests holding office were required to swear an oath to uphold the Constitution or be dismissed. The clergy was split into those who accepted the Civil Constitution (juring priests) and those who did not (refractory priests). Prohibitions of public displays of religion and against the wearing of a religious habit in public were then included on the revolutionary decrees on the separation of Church and State in the 1790s. Napoleon later tried to heal this rift. Though the later Constitutional Charter of 1833 'brought back religious freedom and denominational pluralism', anti-clerical and secular attitudes continued into the 19th century and, when Napoleon III lost the Franco-Prussian War in September 1870, the Second Empire gave way to the Third Republic and the war between the 'two Frances' of secularists and believers resumed. In this period, the traditionalists on the right and the socialists on the left sought to unbalance the bourgeois heirs of the revolution, and religion became a key battleground. In the election of 1879, the supporters of the Third Republic stressed the need to secularise France and they began with education, banning religious teaching congregations in 1880 and in 1882, religious instruction in state primary schools was prohibited. C. M. A. McCauliff, 'Dreyfus, Laïcité and the Burqa', *Connecticut Journal of International Law* 117, 28 (2012).

7   Olivier Roy, *Secularism Confronts Islam* (Columbia University Press, 2007), p. 22.

8   The quotation is taken from article 10 of the Declaration of Rights of Man and the Citizen asserted by the National Constituent Assembly in 1789, reasserted in the French Constitution of the Fifth Republic.

9   I am relying on Rim-Sarah Alouane, 'Publicly French, Privately Muslim: The Aim of Modern Laïcité', Berkley Forum, 13 May 2021. https://berkleycenter. georgetown.edu/responses/publicly-french-privately-muslim-the-aim-of-modern-laicite

10 See Eric Ciotti: 'Mass immigration of predominantly Arab Muslim origins is menacing France's Enlightenment heritage and our Judeo-Christian civilisation', tweet from 14th November 2021 when he was still a candidate for Les Républicains party's presidential candidate: Romain Brunet, 'Présidentielle : face à Marine Le Pen et Éric Zemmour, la surenchère droitière des candidats LR', France 24, 15 November 2021. https://www.france24.com/fr/france/ 20211115-pr%C3%A9sidentielle-face-%C3%A0-marine-le-pen-et-%C3%A9ric-zemmour-la-surench%C3%A8re-droiti%C3%A8re-des-candidats-lr;

       Eric Ciotti also talked about enshrining the 'Judeo-Christian' roots of France in the Consistitution: Marie-Pierre Bourgeois, 'INSCRIRE LES RACINES "JUDÉO-CHRÉTIENNES" DANS LA CONSTITUTION, EST-CE POSSIBLE?', 1 September 2021. https://www.bfmtv.com/politique/elections/ presidentielle/inscrire-les-racines-judeo-chretiennes-dans-la-constitution-est-ce-possible_AN-202109010353.html

11 Alouane *op. cit.*

12 Jonathan Wyrtzen, *Making Morocco: Colonial Intervention and the Politics of Identity* (Cornell University Press, 2015), pp. 73, 75, 221–223.

13 James McDougall, *A History of Algeria* (Cambridge University Press, 2017).

14 For example, Jean-Auguste-Dominique Ingres' 'La Grande Odalisque' is an expression of the sexual fascination many Westerners had with the Orient, particularly with life in the harem. Meanwhile Pierre-Auguste Renoir's 'Parisian Women Dressed as Algerians' demonstrates how this sexualised attitude to the Orient was taken up in the metropole.

15 J. H. Hutton, 'Census of India, 1931. Vol 1: India. Part 1: Report', 1933. According to the 1931 Census, the total returned as European-British subjects in India, including Burma, was 155,555, though the total number of those who were returned as born in Great Britain and Ireland was 100,150. The total population of India at the time was 256,859,787.

16 By 1911, the settler population of Algeria stood at 752,043, of which just less than half a million were French, with the balance largely made up of Spaniards and Italians. Between 1871 and 1885, half a million hectares of land passed into European hands. By 1944, 23 per cent of Algerian agricultural property was in the hands of 1.7 per cent of the population. McDougall, *op. cit., A History of Algeria* (Cambridge, 2017) pp. 98–99.

17 Andrea L. Smith, *Colonial Memory and Postcolonial Europe: Maltese Settlers in Algeria and France* (Indiana University Press, 2006), p. 68. Over the half-century following the conquest, nearly half of the immigrants to Algeria were French nationals, usually from the regions bordering the Mediterranean and Corsica. However, French nationals were outnumbered by migrants from across southern Europe, along the Mediterranean and from Sardinia, the Balearic Islands, Sicily, Malta, Pantelleria and the Lipari Islands, and in lesser numbers from Portugal, Germany, Russia and Greece. Many of these immigrants were peasant farmers and agricultural labourers who had been negatively impacted by war and agricultural reforms. McDougall *op. cit.*, p 107. In addition to almost half a million French Algerians, the 1911 Census found 137,746 Spaniards and 36,795 Italians.

18 Smith *op. cit.*, p. 64.

19 McDougall *op. cit.*, p. 110.

20 Ibid., p. 116.

21 Albert Memmi, from *Portrait du Colonisé* (Buchet-Chastel, 1957), quoted in Nicholas Harrison, *Our Civilizing Mission: The Lessons of Colonial Education* (Liverpool University Press, 2019), p. 232.

22 Harrison *op. cit.*, p. 223.

23 During the First World War, some 500,000 out of the eight million troops mobilised for French forces were from the colonies. While not all of these were Muslims, they undoubtedly made up a large proportion of this number. Joseph Downing, *French Muslims in Perspective: Nationalism, Post-Colonialism and Marginalisation Under the Republic* (Palgrave Macmillan, 2019), p. 83.

24 An estimated 2.5 million Muslims contributed to the allied cause, either as soldiers or labourers. An estimated 200,000 Algerians, 100,000 Tunisians, 40,000 Moroccans, 100,000 West Africans and 5,000 Somalis and Libyans fought in the French army. Vivek Chaudhary, 'The forgotten Muslim heroes who fought for Britain in the trenches', *Observer*, 12 November 2017. https://www.theguardian.com/world/2017/nov/12/forgotten-muslim-heroes-fought-for-britain-first-world-war

25 High import costs provoked an upward trend in consumer goods, while an array of taxes increased the burden on the Tunisian population. The most hated of these taxes was the 'colonial third', a salary supplement first given to French officials in 1919. Kenneth J. Perkins, *A History of Modern Tunisia* (Cambridge University Press, 2004), p. 81.

26 Murtaza Hussain, 'Liberté for whom: French Muslims grapple with a Republic that codified their marginalisation', The Intercept, 23 February 2019. https://theintercept.com/2019/02/23/france-islamophobia-islam-french-muslims-terrorism/. See also David Yamaguchi, 'The Muslim Soldiers of World War II', *The North American Post*, 19 May 2016. https://napost.com/2016/the-muslim-soldiers-of-world-war-ii/

27 Philippe Masson, *Histoire de l'armée française de 1914 à nos jours* (Tempus, 2002),

quoted in 'Débarquement de Provence: l'Armée d'Afrique y a été déterminante', Le Point Afrique, 14 August 2019. https://www.lepoint.fr/afrique/debarquement-de-provence-les-soldats-venus-d-afrique-en-premiere-ligne-14-08-2019-2329922_3826.php

28 The French divide the war in Indochina into three phases: the 1945–46 attempt to reassert control; the local colonial war period which lasted until the end of 1950; and the final stage which culminated in the defeat at Dien Bien Phu in 1954. This defeat marked the end of French involvement in the war and the beginning of her withdrawal from the area. In total 11,000 Frenchmen were killed with a further 4,500 missing, 20,899 wounded and 5,000 prisoners; 7,500 members of the Légion were killed with 3,000 missing and 5,439 prisoners; 4,500 North and Black Africans were killed, 2,500 missing and 6,000 prisoners together with 24,347 Légion, North and Black Africans wounded. Anthony Clayton, The Wars of French Decolonisation (Longman, 1994). Pp. 39, 68, 70–71, 74.

29 Jennifer Yee and Kathryn Robson (eds), France and 'Indochina': Cultural Representations (Lexington Books, 2005), pp. 2, 5.

30 Though many in the French army felt that they had been betrayed by the Americans, they also laid some of the blame at the door of the politicians in Paris for the reluctance to send conscripts to Indochina and for the failure to take the perceived realities of the conflict home to the general public. Clayton op. cit., p. 75.

31 Martin Evans, Algeria: France's Undeclared War (Oxford University Press, 2012).

32 Quoted in Evans op. cit., p. 130.

33 The total number of people killed in the war is subject to debate, but French army losses are thought to have numbered around 25,000 men, with European settler losses around 4,000–5,000 people. Meanwhile, Harki community activists have claimed that there were as many as 150,000 Harki deaths while historians' estimates range anywhere between 15,000 and 75,000 people. While 'one and a half million martyrs' is the official number of Algerian combatants and civilians killed during the war from 1954 until 1962, historians have put the actual number of deaths at between 350,000–400,000; of these, up to 150,000 may have been combatants. Natalya Vince, The Algerian War, The Algerian Revolution (Palgrave, 2020), pp. 1–2.

34 Although the Algerian War might have been undeclared, by spring 1956 the French people could be under no illusions about the scale of the violence as 400,000 troops were deployed. Evans op. cit., p. 348.

35 For a discussion of Le Pen's Algerian experience and its influence over him and the French Right, see Catherine Fieschi, 'Muslims and the secular city: how far-right populists shape the French debate over Islam,' Brookings, 28 February 28, 2020. https://www.brookings.edu/research/muslims-and-the-secular-city-how-right-wing-populists-shape-the-french-debate-over-islam/

36 Juan Cole, *Napoleon's Egypt: Invading the Middle East* (Palgrave Macmillan, 2007), pp. 17–19. The 2,000 passengers aboard the *Orient* included many members of the Commission on Sciences and Arts.

37 Ibid., pp. 55–57, 73.

38 Saliha Belmessous, *Assimilation and Empire: Uniformity in French and British Colonies, 1541–1954* (Oxford University Press, 2013). pp 135–136. In 1863, Napoleon III had proclaimed that Algeria was not a colony but a *royaume arabe*, which indicated that he wanted to break with the assimilationist theory and modernise Muslim institutions with the help of Muslims themselves. This policy was violently opposed by the European settlers who eventually joined the republicans when the Second Empire collapsed in the midst of the 1870 Franco-Prussian war.

39 Cole *op. cit.*, pp. 123–124, 128–132.

40 Ibid., p. 75.

41 Ibid., pp. 123–124, 122.

42 Jérôme Louis, *La Question de l'Orient sous Louis-Philippe* (Sciences de l'Homme et Société, 2011), pp. 31–36.

43 McDougall, *op cit.*, pp. 51–52.

44 See John Ruedy, *Modern Algeria: The Origins and Development of a Nation* (Indiana University Press, 2005): 'the name itself – Algerie, coined by the French *philosophe*, Bernard le Bouyer de Fontenelle in the early eighteenth century – did not become official until made so by French Royal Ordinance of October 14, 1839.'

45 James McDougall, 'The emergence of nationalism', in Amal Ghazal and Jens Hanssen (eds), *The Oxford Handbook of Contemporary Middle Eastern and North African History* (Oxford University Press, 2020). By the end of the 1860s, a combination of famine and epidemic had combined to kill perhaps a third of the pre-conquest-level population. It has been estimated that the pre-conquest population of Algeria was three million. While England's population in America almost doubled from 1550 to 1650, by 1608 as many as eighteen epidemics had reduced the Powhatans of the Virginia coast from perhaps 50,000 to no more than 14,000. According to Russell Thornton, there had been seven million people living north of the Rio Grande in 1492, but by 1800 there were only 600,000. Ben Kiernan, *Blood and Soil: A World History of Genocide and Extermination from Sparta to Darfur* (Yale University Press, 2007), pp. 219, 364. In comparison, Libya was taken over by the Italians and, between 1912 and 1943, 250,000–300,000 Libyans died (the pre-conquest population was between 800,000 and one million). Dirk Vandewalle, *A History of Modern Libya* (Cambridge University Press, 2012) pp. 31–32, 34.

46 McDougall *op. cit.*, pp. 65–66, 69.

47 Between 1871 and 1885, more than half a million hectares of land passed into European ownership. By the time the First World War had broken out, Algerian peasants had lost the ownership or use of almost 11.6 million hectares of farm, pasture and other land. Algerian landholdings were also reduced in

size due to market pressures. McDougall *op. cit.*, p. 98–99. The expanse of land which was to become the modern Popular and Democratic Republic of comprised some 219 million hectares. John Ruedy, *Land Policy in Colonial Algeria: The Origins of the Rural Public Domain* (University of California Press, 1967), p. 1.

48 Andrew Hussey, *The French Intifada: The Long War Between France and its Arabs* (Granta, 2014), pp. 94–95.

49 David Prochaska, *Making Algeria French: Colonialism in Bône, 1870–1920* (Cambridge University Press, 2004), pp. 22.

50 Vince *op. cit.*, p. 7. The Sénatus-consulte of 14 July 1865 set out the boundaries of whom in Algeria was entitled to full citizenship. To avoid the settler population being outnumbered by the indigenous population, the 'indigenous Muslim' was declared French.

51 Paul Smith, *Feminism and the Third Republic: Women's Political and Civil Rights in France, 1918–1945* (Oxford University Press, 2011), pp. 9–10.

52 Ernest Renan, *De la part des peoples sémitiques dans l'histoire de la civilisation* (Michel Lévy Frères, 1862). quoted in Hussey *op. cit.*, p. 112.

53 Vince *op. cit.*, p. 9.

54 Ibid., pp. 21, 23. In total, 172,019 Algerian soldiers were brought into the French army, with around 120,000–125,000 of these seeing frontline action. Nearly 26,000 Algerians were killed or disappeared and 72,000 were injured. It is also estimated that, during the First World War, between 120,000 and 130,000 Algerians went to France to work in war factories or on the farms of conscripted French soldiers.

55 The Etoile Nord Africaine (ENA) was born from the French communist and trade union movement, and sought to recruit from among the North African workers in France. Ibid., p. 29.

56 The Blum-Violette project would have permitted approximately 20,000–25,000 Algerians who could show evidence of French culture or service to France to receive the 'political rights of French citizenship'. However, it failed due to settler pressure. Senator Pierre Roux-Freissineng, representing the Departement of Oran, declared in a speech that 'the French of Algeria will never accept such a project because . . . in reality it would place them sooner or later under native domination'. William B. Cohen, 'The Colonial Policy of the Popular Front', *French Historical Studies*, vol. 7, no. 3, 1972, pp. 368–393.

57 Evans *op. cit.*, p. 76. Vichy's National Revolution appealed to many of the European settlers and they embraced many of the new state's measures, including the Jewish Statute of October 1940 which revoked the Crémieux Decrees and stripped Jews of their status as French citizens.

58 Darlan served as minister of the marine and then, in 1941, he took over as vice president of the council, minister of foreign affairs, minister of the interior and minister of national defence. According to the 'Darlan Deal', he would be recognised as High Commissioner of France in Africa in return for ordering all

French forces to join the allies. George E. Melton, *Darlan, Admiral and Statesman of France, 1881–1942* (Praeger, 1998), chapter 21.

59 In the summer of 1944, 60 per cent of 633,000 men in the French army were 'indigenous' soldiers, many of which were Algerian. They played a key role in the liberation of France and Italy. Vince *op. cit.*, pp. 41–42.

60 Giraud and de Gaulle had been co-presidents of the French Committee of National Liberation and Free French Forces. Giraud lost the co-presidency in November 1943. G. Ward Price, *Giraud and the African Scene* (Macmillan, 1944), chapter 11.

61 Maxime Benatouil, 'On VE Day, French Colonists launched a massacre in Algeria', *Jacobin*, 5 May 2020. https://www.jacobinmag.com/2020/05/ ve-day-victory-europe-algeria-france-setif-guelma-kherrata

62 McDougall *op. cit.*, chapter 5.

63 Ibid., p. 199.

64 This speech has been made by both Pierre Mendes-France and François Mitterrand (who made it in front of the National Assembly in Paris on 12 November, 1954). Vince *op. cit.*, p. 67; Alistair Horne, *A Savage War of Peace: Algeria 1954–1962* (New York Review, 2006), p. 98.

65 Hussey *op. cit.*, p. 164.

66 Vince *op. cit.*, pp. 65–67. On 1 November 1954, a series of assassinations, bomb explosions and acts of sabotage took place across Algeria, accompanied by a proclamation issued by the FLN declaring that its new goal was 'national independence'. The FLN began to try to establish itself as the sole representative of Algerian nationalism and to oust the MNA, which was led by Messali Hadj.

67 David Carroll, *Albert Camus the Algerian: Colonialism, Terrorism, Justice* (Columbia University Press, 2007). Albert Camus was born in French Algeria and his dual French and Algerian identities created a complex issue throughout his life. During the Algerian War of Independence, he was critical of the violence and torture employed by all sides, including the FLN.

68 Vince *op. cit.*, p. 92. In January 1957, just as the 'Algerian Question' was scheduled to come up on the UN agenda, the FLN gave the order to organise another strike, building upon the student strike of May 1956. Beginning on 28 January, it was scheduled to last for eight days. Around 8,000 French soldiers took up positions in the capital, surrounding the Casbah with checkpoints and barbed wire. The strike was then brutally broken up, with the army forcing workers back to their factories and offices, and smashed shops to re-open. A prominent revolutionary leader, Larbi Ben M'Hidi, was arrested and killed in custody.

69 James McDougall, 'The Impossible Republic: The Reconquest of Algeria and the Decolonisation of France, 1945–62', *Journal of Modern History*, vol. 89, pp. 772–881. Furthermore, the attempt by the generals Lagaillarde, Ortiz and Susini to carry out a military putsch in response to the referendum of 8

January 1961 convinced the metropole that Algeria risked destabilising the
French Fifth Republic and that she should, therefore, be cut off from it.

70   This was announced on 5 October 1961. Pascal Blanchard et al (eds), *Colonial
     Culture in France Since the Revolution* (Indiana University Press, 2014).

71   Blanchard et al *op. cit.*, pp. 385–386. Some were even thrown from the
     Saint-Michel bridge in the very heart of Paris. Thousands of Algerians were
     rounded up and interned in the Palais des Sports, the Coubertin Stadium
     and the Vincennes Camp. Once there, they were brutally beaten by
     'welcome committees'. One estimate is that around 200 people were killed
     on 17 October and the days following. For the media silence, see Maria
     Flood, 'Politics and the Police: Documenting the 17th October 1961
     Massacre', *Contemporary French and Francophone Studies*, 20:4-5, 2016, pp.
     599–606.

72   Robert Boyce 'The Trial of Maurice Papon for Crimes Against Humanity and
     the Concept of Bureaucratic Crime', in R. A. Melikan (ed.), *Domestic and
     International Trials, 1700–2000: The Trial in History, Volume 2* (Manchester
     University Press, 2003).

73   Taken from testimony by Djalli Soummoud on the torture he experienced in a
     Lyon police station. Blanchard et al *op. cit.*, p. 382.

74   Colonial legacy in France book, pp. 383–384.

75   Blanchard et al *op. cit.*, pp. 385.

76   Boyce *op. cit.* Papon's trial for ordering the arrest and detention of nearly 1,600
     Jews in Bordeaux to the transit camp of Drancy, from where they were
     deported to Auschwitz, took place over the winter of 1997–98. He was found
     guilty on 430 of the 788 counts and was sentenced to ten years' imprisonment,
     suspended pending appeal.

77   'Hollande reconnaît la répression du 17 octobre 1961, critiques à droite,' *Le
     Monde*, 17 October 2012. https://www.lemonde.fr/societe/article/2012/10/
     17/francois-hollande-reconnait-la-sanglante-repression-du-17-octobre-1961_
     1776918_3224.html

78   Assiya Hamza, 'Macron appelé à reconnaître la respónsabilité de l'État dans le
     massacre du 17 octobre 1961', France 24, 17 October 2017. https://www.
     france24.com/fr/
     20171017-france-algerie-macron-guerre-responsabilite-etat-massacre-
     manifestation-17-octobre-1961

79   Evans *op. cit.*, chapter 11. In this period, OAS violence struck out in several
     directions: at the riot police, the Europeans looking to leave, and Algerian
     professionals – all with the explicit aim of eliminating the Algerian elite.
     Operation Rock and Roll of 5 March 1962 produced 120 explosions across
     Algiers in two hours. On 21 March, OAS groups in Bab-El-Oued launched
     mortar bomb attacks at passing Algerians on the Place du Gouvernement,
     killing twenty-four and wounding fifty-nine. On 23 March, a lieutenant and
     five young conscripts died in an OAS firefight in Bab-El-Oued. However, three

days later, it was clear that the insurrection had failed and that the OAS groups had been dismantled.

80 Pierre Daum, *Ni valise ni cercueil, les Pieds-Noirs restés en Algérie après l'indépendance* (Solin-Actes Sud, 2012), p. 44.

81 Evans *op. cit.*, chapter 11. When it became clear that the insurrection had failed, the OAS adopted a 'scorched earth policy', burning down town halls, schools and public buildings.

82 Hussey *op. cit.*, pp. 204–205.

83 Ibid., pp. 208–214.

84 *'France remembers the Algerian War, 50 years on'*, France 24, 16 March 2012. There is a parallel dispute between France and Algeria over the nuclear bombs which the former detonated on Algerian soil, some even after independence, which Algeria now claims to have brought premature death to 42,000 Algerians. See also Lamine Chikhi, 'French nuclear tests in Algeria leave toxic legacy', Reuters, 4 March 2010, and Adam Bensaid, 'France detonated 200 nuclear bombs in colonies but never answered for it', TRT World, 12 October 2018.

85 Martin Thomas, *Fight or Flight: Britain, France and Their Roads from Empire* (Oxford University Press, 2014), p. 289.

86 Horne *op. cit.*, p. 25.

87 Sally N. Cummings and Raymond A. Hinnebusch (eds), *Sovereignty After Empire: Comparing the Middle East and Central Asia* (Edinburgh University Press, 2011).

88 Perkins *op. cit.*, pp. 49, 52–53. Against the backdrop of the establishment of the French Protectorate in Tunisia, the Italian premier, Francesco Crispi, described Tunisia as 'an Italian colony occupied by France'. At the same time, the Italian population of Tunisia increased by 88 per cent during the first decade of the protectorate. By 1896, Italians living in the country outnumbered French citizens by a ratio of five to one.

Around 400,000 hectares had come into French hands by 1892 and the Enfida and Sidi Thabit holdings of the Société Marseillaise de Crédit, along with 30,000 hectares controlled by five other investment companies, accounted for 88 per cent of all French property in the country. The remaining 12 per cent was divided among thirty-four owners. Speculation on land drove the price too high for most Tunisians to afford and so they continued to work the land, mostly as renters but also as sharecroppers.

Susan Gilson Miller, *A History of Modern Morocco* (Cambridge University Press, 2013), p. 113. In the years 1917 to 1931, 1,600 people settled on 620,000 acres, but after 1931, the number of new settlers to Morocco completely dried up.

89 Hussey *op. cit.*, pp. 274–277.

90 Miller *op. cit.*, p. 90. Lyautey believed that Morocco, unlike Algeria, should not be annexed but rather that 'modernity' should be brought to it while still conserving its original 'soul'. Quoted from Hubert Lyautey, *Lettres de Tonkin et de Madagascar (1894–1899),* 2 volumes (A. Colin, 1920).

91   C. R. Pennell, *Morocco Since 1830: A History* (New York University Press, 2000), p. 175.

92   Miller *op. cit.*, pp. 107–109. Pétain was France's most distinguished war hero while Franco first gained national attention after his performance at the Battle of Anwal.

93   Hussey *op. cit.*, p. 289.

94   Miller *op. cit.*, pp. 142–143.

95   Perkins *op. cit.*, pp. 42–43.

96   Ibid., p. 49. The Italian government did not intend to relinquish the dispensations secured in the 1868 Italo-Tunisian treaty, though by 1896 France acquiesced to the Italian insistence that they honour most of the privileges accorded in this treaty.

97   Ibid., p. 79. Young Tunisian exiles in Istanbul contributed to the German and Ottoman war effort, often by writing anti-French propaganda.

98   Hussey *op. cit.*, pp. 358–361. The first general strike was actually called on 20 November 1937. During this strike, six Tunisians were killed and dozens injured on 8 January 1938. Another strike was called on 8 April 1938.

99   Perkins *op. cit.*, chapter 4, pp. 110–112. Following the capitulation of France in June 1940, the Vichy regime sent Admiral Jean Esteva to Tunisia. In November 1942, British and French troops landed in Morocco and Algeria. The aim of the North African campaign was to capture Tunisia and use it to launch an invasion of Sicily. However, after the Vichy commanders negotiated a cease-fire, Germany seized the Vichy-administered area of France and Tunisia. The country then became a key battleground in the North African campaign.

100   Hussey *op. cit.*, p. 363.

101   Miller *op. cit.*, p. 151. Mohammed V and his family remained in exile in Madagascar until they were allowed to return on the eve of independence in 1955.

CHAPTER 14: FRANCE'S COLONIAL LEGACY

1   For example, from 1947 to 1953, North African arrivals officially numbered 740,000, with returns estimated at 560,000. While the official number of North Africans in France is difficult to estimate due to the ease of immigration, official statistics indicate that, by 1953, there were 220,000 in France. Blanchard et al *op. cit.*, pp. 372–379.

2   Hussey *op. cit.*, p. 369.

3   See ibid., p. 303, and Jim House, 'The Colonial and Post-Colonial Dimensions of Algerian Migration to France', *History in Focus*, No.11, autumn 2006.

4   House *op. cit.*

5   Ibid., and see Hussey *op. cit.*, p. 20.

6   House *op. cit.*

7 'Macron seeks "forgiveness", vows recognition for Harkis who fought for France in Algeria', France24, 20 September 2021. https://www.france24.com/en/europe/20210920-macron-seeks-new-step-towards-the-algerian-harkis-who-fought-for-france

8 See Olivier Esteves, 'A Historical Perspective: Secularism, "White Backlash" and Islamophobia in France', in Irene Zempi and Imran Awan (eds), *The Routledge International Handbook of Islamophobia* (Routledge, 2019).

9 House *op. cit.*

10 Hussey *op. cit.*, p. 303.

11 Blanchard et al *op. cit.*, pp. 376.

12 House *op. cit.*

13 Adam Bensaid, *'France's "Muslim" problem and the unspoken racism at its heart'*, TRT World, 19 February 2020. https://www.trtworld.com/magazine/france-s-muslim-problem-and-the-unspoken-racism-at-its-heart-33939

14 Hussey *op. cit.*, pp. 43–44.

15 Ibid., pp. 40–41, and Hussain *op. cit.*

16 Esteves *op. cit.*

17 See 'La Visibilite De L'Islam: Un "Problème" Pour Le FN', Derrière Le Front, 29 February 2016. https://blog.francetvinfo.fr/derriere-le-front/2016/02/29/la-visibilite-de-lislam-un-probleme-pour-le-fn.html

18 Marc-Olivier Bherer, 'Le "Marxisme culturel", fantasme préféré de l'extrême droite', Le Monde, 28 August 2019. https://www.lemonde.fr/idees/article/2019/08/28/le-marxisme-culturel-fantasme-prefere-de-l-extreme-droite_5503567_3232.html

19 On 19 October 1989, Fatimah (14), Leila (15) and Samira (14) were not allowed to enter their classes at Creil's high school. Their teachers asked them to remove their veils and they refused. 'Rebondissement dans l'affaire du port du voile Les trois musulmanes de Creil de nouveau exclues des cours', *Le Monde*, 21 October 1989. https://www.lemonde.fr/archives/article/1989/10/21/rebondissement-dans-l-affaire-du-port-du-voile-les-trois-musulmanes-de-creil-de-nouveau-exclues-des-cours_4136188_1819218.html

20 Esteves *op. cit.*, pp. 102–103.

21 'Avis n° 346.893 du Conseil d'Etat, Assemblée générale, 27 novembre 1989'. This decision can be seen at http://affairesjuridiques.aphp.fr/textes/avis-n-346-893-du-conseil-detat-27111989-port-du-foulard-islamique/

22 'LOI n° 2004-228 du 15 mars 2004 encadrant, en application du principe de laïcité, le port de signes ou de tenues manifestant une appartenance religieuse dans les écoles, collèges et lycées publics'. https://www.legifrance.gouv.fr/jorf/id/JORFTEXT000000417977/

23 In November 2017, Manuel Valls suggested that French society had a 'problem' with Islam and the Collectif Contre l'Islamophobie (CCIF) has frequently denounced him for what they perceive to be Islamophobia. However, Valls has

criticised the use of the word 'Islamophobie', preferring instead to refer to 'anti-Muslim' acts as he believes that the word drives French Muslims further away from the republic. 'Valls pointe un "problème des musulmans" dans la société française', *Le Parisien*, 21 November 2017, https://www.leparisien.fr/politique/valls-pointe-un-probleme-des-musulmans-dans-la-societe-francaise-21-11-2017-7407054.php; Eugénie Bastié, 'Manuel Valls, bête noire du Collectif contre l'islamophobie (CCIF)', *Le Figaro*, 8 December 2016, https://www.lefigaro.fr/actualite-france/2016/12/08/01016-20161208ARTFIG00161-manuel-valls-bete-noire-du-comite-de-lutte-contre-l-islamophobie.php; 'Manuel Valls: "L'islamophobie est le cheval de Troie des salafistes"', *L'Obs*, 31 July 2013, https://www.nouvelobs.com/politique/20130731.OBS1612/manuel-valls-l-islamophobie-est-le-cheval-de-troie-des-salafistes.html

24   Fieschi *op. cit.*, and for the French left, see Timothy Peace, 'Islamophobia and the Left in France', in Zempi and Awan *op. cit.*, chapter 9.

25   McDougall *op. cit.*, pp. 256–257. Between 1963 and 1967, workers', women's, youth and peasants' organisations were folded into a single-party system. Between 1972 and 1976, sovereign debt grew from 18 per cent of gross national income to 40 per cent. By 1978, it had reached 50 per cent.

26   Ibid., p. 286.

27   Ibid., p 287. The FIS was founded by Ali Belhadj, a popular preacher in the Bab el-Oued mosque, and Abbassi Madani, a veteran Islamic activist.

28   Interview with Slimane Zeghidour, *Politique Internationale* (Autumn 1990): pp. 156, 180.

29   Gilles Kepel, *Jihad: The Trail of Political Islam*, (I.B. Tauris & Co, 2002), p. 170.

30   Martin Meredith, *The Fate of Africa: From the Hopes of Freedom to the Heart of Despair – A History of Fifty Years of Independence* (Public Affairs, 2005), p. 453.

31   McDougall *op. cit.*, p. 289.

32   Ibid., pp. 303–304. After thirty years in opposition and exile, Boudiaf was brought back to serve as president of the council. Thousands of FIS sympathisers were detained. On 29 June 1992, he was shot dead by one of his bodyguards while addressing a televised meeting in Anaba.

33   The religious identity adopted by young Muslims is not necessarily a 'radicalised' form of the religion. Some young Muslims have chosen a more fundamentalist view. However, numerous studies have shown that the majority of young Muslims consider their religious identity to be largely symbolic and the majority of them do not observe religious traditions. Imène Ajala, 'The Muslim Vote and Muslim Lobby in France: Myths and Realities', *Journal of Islamic Law and Culture*, 12, 2010.

34   Martin *op. cit.*, p. 307.

35   Luis Martinez, *The Algerian Civil War, 1990–98* (Hurst & Company, 1998), pp. 93, 228–229. The financial backing of the Algerian government by France since 1992 has been a source of discontent among Islamists. The financial package was worth six billion francs.

36 Some suggest the assassination was the work of an isolated soldier with Islamist sympathies, while others insist that the entire army was implicated. See McDougall *op. cit.*, p. 315. Also Lounis Aggoun and Jean-Baptiste Rivoire, *Françalgérie: Crimes et Mensonges d'États* (Editions La Découverte, 2005), pp. 281–293.

37 Martin *op. cit.*, p. 308.

38 Hussey *op. cit.*, p. 239.

39 See 'Vigipirate: 3 niveaux d'alerte face à la menace terroriste', www.service-public.fr, December 2018.

40 Islam Abdel-Rahman, *'The Refutation of the Djerejian Doctrine,'* OpenDemocracy, 12 November 2014. https://www.opendemocracy.net/en/north-africa-west-asia/refutation-of-djerejian-doctrine/

41 Blanchard et al *op. cit.*, p. 522. Zyed and Bouna were fleeing from arrest on 27 October 2005 when they entered an EDF power transformer in Clichy-sous-Bois.

42 Gil Kaufman, 'Violence continues across France; President vows to crack down on rioters', MTV, 7 November 2005.

43 Blanchard et al *op. cit.*, pp. 524–525.

44 Hussey *op. cit.*, chapter 2, and Hussain *op. cit.*, Also, 'Brixton en France', *Le Monde*, 17 April 1981.

45 Valérie Amiraux, 'Islam: le voil qui cache le débat', *Libération*, 25 April 2003. https://www.liberation.fr/tribune/2003/04/25/islam-le-voile-qui-cache-le-debat_462589/; Cécile Chambraud and Matthieu Goar, 'L'islam, variable électorale de Sarkozy', *Le Monde*, 3 June 2015.
    https://www.lemonde.fr/politique/article/2015/06/04/l-islam-variable-electorale-de-sarkozy_4646083_823448.html

46 Bensaid *op. cit.,* and 'French Muslim Council in troubled waters,' France 24, 6 June 2008. https://www.france24.com/en/20080606-french-muslim-council-troubled-waters-islam-france

47 Karina Piser, 'A new plan to create an 'Islam of France', *The Atlantic*, 29 March 2018. https://www.theatlantic.com/international/archive/2018/03/islam-france-macron/556604/

48 Hussey *op. cit.*, chapter 3, and Andrew Hussey, 'France: a country at war with itself', *New Statesman*, 30 March 2012.

49 See Hussain *op. cit.*

50 See Richard Wike, Bruce Stokes and Katie Simmons, 'Europeans fear wave of refugees will mean more terrorism, fewer jobs', *Pew Research*, 11 July 2016. https://www.pewresearch.org/global/2016/07/11/europeans-fear-wave-of-refugees-will-mean-more-terrorism-fewer-jobs/

51 Fieschi *op. cit.*

52 Ibid.

53 Macron was opposed to 'multiculturalisme', which has different contexts to the English translation of 'multiculturalism', saying on France 2 in 2017: 'I am against multiculturalism, but for integration which is not the same as assimilation.' In this period, he highlighted the diversity of French culture.

54   'Emmanuel Macron: "La colonisation est un crime contre l'humanité"', *Le Point*,
     15 February 2017. https://www.lepoint.fr/presidentielle/emmanuel-macron-la-
     colonisation-est-un-crime-contre-l-humanite-15-02-2017-2105177_3121.php

55   'Le programme d'Emmanuel Macron concernant les questions religieuse et la
     laïcité', En Marche. https://en-marche.fr/emmanuel-macron/le-programme/
     questions-religieuses-et-laicite

56   Violaine Morin and Mattea Battaglia, 'Après la mort de Samuel Paty,
     "l'enchaînement des faits" détaillé par l'inspection Générale,' *Le Monde*, 4
     December 2020. https://www.lemonde.fr/societe/article/2020/12/04/apres-
     la-mort-de-samuel-paty-l-enchainement-des-faits-detaille-par-l-inspection-
     generale_6062175_3224.html.

57   According to the French anti-terrorist prosecutor, Jean-François Ricard, the
     attacker, who was seriously wounded by the police, was a twenty-one-year-old
     Tunisian national who had arrived in France earlier that month. He was named
     as Brahim Aioussaoi. 'France attack: three killed in "Islamist terrorist"
     stabbings', BBC News, 29 October 2020. https://www.bbc.co.uk/news/
     world-europe-54729957

58   See Adam Sage, 'Parents face jail for home-schooling in French curbs on
     Islamic extremism', *The Times*, 19 November 2020. Also Chloé Benoist, 'Is
     France's response to Samuel Paty murder deepening divisions?', *Middle East
     Eye*, 23 October 2020. https://www.middleeasteye.net/news/
     france-samuel-paty-murder-macron-muslim-repression

59   https://www.francetvinfo.fr/societe/religion/religion-laicite/ecole-a-
     domicile-strictement-limitee-fin-de-la-formation-des-imams-a-l-etranger-les-
     annonces-d-emmanuel-macron-sur-le-separatisme-islamiste_4126193.html

60   Rym Momtaz, '5 things to know about France's bill to combat Islamist
     radicalism', Politico, 9 December 2020. https://www.politico.eu/article/
     france-law-emmanuel-macron-islamist-separatism-security/ See also Marwan
     Muhammad, 'France is weaponising its "republican values" as a means of
     exclusion', *Middle East Eye*, 26 November 2020. https://www.middleeasteye.
     net/opinion/how-france-weaponising-its-ideals-and-values-means-exclusion.
     Also Mustafa Akyol, 'Yes, Islam is facing a crisis. No, France isn't helping solve
     it,' *Foreign Policy*, 20 November 2020.

61   Macron has frequently asserted his opposition to 'Muslim separatism'. This
     was asserted in his *Financial Times* piece: Emmanuel Macron, 'Letter: France is
     against "Islamist separatism" – never Islam', *Financial Times*, 4 November 2020.
     https://www.ft.com/content/8e459097-4b9a-4e04-a344-4262488e7754

62   'Gérald Darmanin: déclaration polémique sur les rayons halal et casher des
     supermarchés', Franceinfo, 21 October 2020. https://www.francetvinfo.fr/
     societe/religion/religion-laicite/gerald-darmanin-declaration-polemique-sur-
     les-rayons-halal-et-casher-des-supermarches_4150921.html and 'Christophe
     Castaner liste les signes de radicalisation? "Vous avez une barbe vous-même",
     lui répond un député', Europe1, 9 October 2019. https://www.europe1.fr/

politique/christophe-castaner-liste-les-signes-de-radicalisation-religieuse-vous-avez-une-barbe-vous-meme-lui-repond-un-depute-3924324. See also Anasse Kazib, 'Barbe, prière, ramadan . . . la chasse aux musulmans est ouverte!', Révolution Permanente, 10 October 2019. https://www.revolutionpermanente.fr/
Barbe-priere-ramadan-la-chasse-aux-musulmans-est-ouverte

63 The site was launched on 28 January 2015. https://www.gouvernement.fr/
sites/default/files/risques/pdf/fiche-prevention-et-signalement-des-cas-de-radicalisation-djihadiste.pdf

64 The number of calls to the hotline increased by 45 per cent in the year between April 2015 and April 2016. Around 2,700 men and women were the subjects of 'relevant' reports in this period. Clémence Apetogbor, 'Radicalisation: Le nombre d'appels au numéro vert "anti-djihad" a explosé en un an', 20minutes, 27 April 2016. https://www.20minutes.fr/societe/
1834931-20160427-radicalisation-nombre-appels-numero-vert-anti-djihad-explose-anv

65 Bénédicte Lutaud, 'Dissolutions du CCIF et de Baraka City: que sait-on de ces associations visées par Darmanin?', *Le Figaro*, 19 October 19, 2020. https://
www.lefigaro.fr/actualite-france/
dissolutions-du-ccif-et-de-baraka-city-que-sait-on-de-ces-associations-visees-par-darmanin-20201019

66 Marwan Muhammad, *op. cit.* This article is an especially cogent analysis of how enlightenment values are being used for authoritarian purposes.

67 Ibid.

68 Geoffrey Bonnefoy, '"Pas de leçon de morale, Judas!": Le Pen tance Darmanin dans l'hémicycle', *L'Express*, 13 July 2017. Marine Le Pen cried 'Not a moral lesson, Judas', which was an allusion to the political career of Darmanin, who went from Les Républicains to Macron's government. Darmanin replied: 'Unlike you, Ms Le Pen, Judas will go down in history.' https://www.
lexpress.fr/actualite/politique/pas-de-lecon-de-morale-judas-le-pen-tance-darmanin-dans-l-hemicycle_1927147.html

69 Abel Mestre, 'Débat entre Marine Le Pen et Gérald Darmanin: la dédiabolisation par procuration', *Le Monde*, 12 February 2021. https://www.
lemonde.fr/politique/article/2021/02/12/debat-marine-le-pen-gerald-darmanin-la-dediabolisation-par-procuration_6069774_823448.html

70 See 'France is not the free-speech champion it says it is', Amnesty International, 12 November 2020. https://www.amnesty.org/en/latest/news/
2020/11/france-is-not-the-free-speech-champion-it-says-it-is/

71 Courtney Freer, 'Understanding the Saudi, Emirati religious authorities' "excommunication" of the Muslim Brotherhood', The New Arab, 24 November 2020. https://english.alaraby.co.uk/opinion/
understanding-saudi-emirati-excommunication-muslim-brotherhood

72 Omar Soliman, 'My brother is one of Egypt's 60,000 political prisoners – and

Trump is happy to let him rot in jail', *Independent*, 17 January 2020. https://www.independent.co.uk/voices/moustafa-kassem-abdel-fattah-el-sisi-trump-egypt-us-prisoner-a9288401.html. Political prisoners are currently imprisoned by Abdel Fattah el-Sisi. People are often kept in pre-trial detention for up to 150 days before being given access to any judicial process. Judges can then renew their detention for up to two years, after which some are released but others disappear or are re-charged. See also Patrick Kingsley, 'Egypt massacre was premeditated, says Human Rights Watch,' *Guardian*, 12 August 2014. https://www.theguardian.com/world/2014/aug/12/egypt-massacre-rabaa-intentional-human-rights-watch. The killing of 817 people at Rabaa Square in Cairo in August 2013 was reportedly planned. See also 'Macron gave Sisi France's highest award on Paris visit: official', France24, 10 December 2020. https://www.france24.com/en/live-news/20201210-macron-gave-sisi-france-s-highest-award-on-paris-visit-official

73 https://www.middleeasteye.net/opinion/how-british-media-are-enabling-macrons-anti-islam-campaign

74 Emmanuel Macron, 'Letter: France is against "Islamist separatism" – never Islam', *Financial Times*, 4 November 2020. https://www.ft.com/content/8e459097-4b9a-4e04-a344-4262488e7754

75 Peter Oborne, 'Freedom of speech in France extends to Macron's critics as well', *Middle East Eye*, 10 November 2020. https://www.middleeasteye.net/opinion/freedom-speech-france-extends-macron-critics

CHAPTER 15: THE COLD WAR ON ISLAM

1 Tilak, quoted in William T. de Bary, *op. cit.*, 719–723. Also referenced in Fitzroy Morrissey, *A Short History of Islamic Thought* (Apollo, 2021), p. 174.

2 Winston Churchill, 'The Sinews of Peace' speech (aka the 'Iron Curtain Speech') made at Westminster College, Fulton, Missouri, on 5 March 1946.

3 Francis Fukuyama, in his famous article 'What Is History?', set out his belief that Western liberalism had triumphed over the alternatives: 'not just . . . the passing of a particular period of post-war history, but the end of history as such. That is, the end-point of mankind's ideological evolution and the universalisation of Western liberal democracy as the final form of human government.' Francis Fukuyama 'What is History?' in Stephen Eric Bronner (ed.), *Twentieth Century Political Theory: A Reader* (Psychology Press, 2005) p.421.

4 Fukuyama proclaimed that the twentieth century, which had begun with self-confidence in the 'ultimate triumph of Western liberal democracy', was now 'returning full circle to where it started': not an 'end of ideology' or a convergence between capitalism and socialism, as earlier predicted, but to an unabashed victory of economic and political liberalism.' Francis Fukuyama, 'The End of History?', *The National Interest*, no. 16, 1989, p. 1.

5 Policy planning staff memorandum, Washington DC, 4 May 1948. https://
   history.state.gov/historicaldocuments/frus1945-50Intel/d269

6 Herman Kahn, *On Thermonuclear War* (Princeton University Press, 1960).

7 Fred Kaplan, 'Truth stranger than "Strangelove"', *New York Times*, 10 October
   2004. https://www.nytimes.com/2004/10/10/movies/truth-stranger-than-
   strangelove.html

8 Angel Rabasa, Cheryl Benard, Lowell H. Schwartz and Peter Sickle, *Building
   Moderate Muslim Networks* (RAND Corporation, 2007), xv.

9 Ibid., p. 37.

10 Ibid., xi. Note the pointed ambivalence of the term 'to varying degrees'.

11 Ibid., xii.

12 Ibid., p. 32.

13 Ibid., xv and 32.

14 Ibid., p. 3.

15 Ibid., p. 143.

16 See Andrew Defty, *Britain, America and Anti-Communist Propaganda 1945–53*
    (Routledge, 2013), p. 65. There are no guarantees that the 'moderate' version
    will remain acceptable subsequently. Jeremy Corbyn's social democracy was
    no more left wing than Attlee, yet he was portrayed as an extremist in the
    2019 general election.

17 Frances Stonor Saunders, *The Cultural Cold War: The CIA and the World of Arts and
    Letters* (The New Press, 2013), p. 1.

18 David Leigh, 'Death of the department that never was', *Observer*, 27 January
    1978. http://www.cambridgeclarion.org/e/fo_deceit_unit_graun_
    27jan1978.html

19 Hugh Wilford, 'The Information Research Department: Britain's Secret Cold
    War Weapon Revealed', *Review of International Studies*, Vol 24, issue 3, July
    1998, pp. 356–357.

20 Scott Lucas, 'Rear Window: The British Ministry of Propaganda', *Independent*,
    26 February 1995. https://www.independent.co.uk/voices/letters/rear-
    window-cold-war-the-british-ministry-of-propaganda-1574950.html

21 Frances Stonor Saunders, *The Cultural Cold War: The CIA and the World of Arts and
    Letters* (The New Press, 2013), p. 14.2

22 Paul Lashmar and James Oliver, *Britain's Secret Propaganda War, 1948–77*,
    (Sutton Publishing, 1998), p. 137–8.

23 Michael Holzman, *Guy Burgess: Revolutionary in an Old School Tie*, (Chelmsford
    Press, 2013), pp. 278–279.

24 Leigh, *op. cit.*

25 See Paul Lashmar, Nicholas Gilby and James Oliver, 'Slaughter in Indonesia:
    Britain's secret propaganda war', *Observer*, 17 October 2021. https://www.
    theguardian.com/world/2021/oct/17/slaughter-in-indonesia-britains-secret-
    propaganda-war; See also Jess Melvin, *The Army and the Indonesian Genocide:
    Mechanics of Mass Murder* (Routledge, 2018), p. 1.

26 *The Muslims Are Coming!: Islamophobia, Extremism and the Domestic War on Terror*,
    Arun Kundnani (Verso, 2015), p. 157.In the 2011-12 budget, Prevent was given
    an annual budget of £46 million. This increased year on year, to £47.3 million
    in the 2018/19 budget. 'Counter-terrorism: Expenditure', Question for Home
    Office, UK Parliament, 13 May 2019. https://questions-statements.parliament.
    uk/written-questions/detail/2019-05-13/253602

27 Ibid., p. 159.

28 Ibid., p.166.

29 Ian Cobain, 'How a book on Cold War propaganda inspired British counter-
    terror campaign,' *Middle East Eye*, 21 November 2018. https://www.
    middleeasteye.net/news/
    how-book-cold-war-propaganda-inspired-british-counter-terror-campaign

30 Ian Cobain, Alice Ross, Rob Evans and Mona Mahmood, 'Revealed: UK's
    covert propaganda bid to stop Muslims joining Isis', *Guardian*, 2 May 2016.
    https://www.theguardian.com/uk-news/2016/may/02/
    uk-government-covert-propaganda-stop-muslims-joining-isis

31 Ian Cobain, 'This is Woke: the media outfit that's actually a UK counter-terror
    programme', *Middle East Eye*, 15 August 2019. https://www.middleeasteye.
    net/news/
    revealed-woke-media-outfit-thats-actually-uk-counterterror-programme

32 Ian Cobain, 'UK government fighting to keep details of counter-extremism
    radio shows secret', *Middle East Eye*, 17 January 2019. https://www.
    middleeasteye.net/news/
    uk-government-fighting-keep-details-counter-extremism-radio-shows-secret

33 Ian Cobain, Alice Ross, Rob Evans and Mona Mahmood, 'Government hid fact
    it paid for 2012 Olympics film aimed at Muslims', *Guardian*, 3 May 2016.
    https://www.theguardian.com/uk-news/2016/may/03/
    government-hid-fact-it-paid-for-2012-olympics-film-aimed-at-muslims

34 Ian Cobain, Alice Ross, Rob Evans and Mona Mahmood, 'Help for Syria: the
    "aid campaign" secretly run by the UK government', *Guardian*, 3 May 2016.
    https://www.theguardian.com/world/2016/may/03/
    help-for-syria-aid-campaign-secretly-run-by-uk-government

35 Intelligence and Security Committee Annual Report 2011–2012 (chairman:
    The Rt Hon. Sir Malcom Rifkind MP), p. 31. To view the complete report,
    see: https://www.gov.uk/government/publications/
    intelligence-and-security-committee-annual-report-2011-2012

36 Narzanin Massoumi, 'Exceptional measures', *Red Pepper*, 11 November 2020.
    https://www.redpepper.org.uk/exceptional-measures/

37 Ian Cobain and Alice Ross, 'UK counter-extremism propaganda unit
    extending reach around the globe', *Middle East Eye*, 10 June 2020. https://
    www.middleeasteye.net/news/
    uk-prevent-export-tunisia-iraq-reach-around-globe

38 Ian Cobain, 'How a book on Cold War propaganda inspired British

counter-terror campaign', *Middle East Eye*, 21 November 2018.
https://www.middleeasteye.net/news/how-book-cold-war-
propaganda-inspired-british-counter-terror-campaign

39 'Schedule 7 declared "unjust" by European Court of Human Rights', *Mend*, 12
March 2019. https://www.mend.org.uk/
schedule-7-declared-unjust-european-court-human-rights/

40 'Operation of police powers under the Terrorism Act 2000, quarterly update
to December 2015: data tables', Home Office, GOV.UK, 17 March 2016.
https://www.gov.uk/government/statistics/operation-of-police-powers-
under-the-terrorism-act-2000-quarterly-update-to-december-2015-data-
tables; 'What you should know about the terror arrests stats', *CAGE*, 7 April
2016. https://www.cage.ngo/what-you-should-know-about-terror-
arrests-stats

41 Alan Travis, 'Schedule 7 detainees have right to see solicitor, court rules',
Guardian, 6 November 2013. https://www.theguardian.com/law/2013/nov/
06/schedule-7-detainees-solicitor-court

42 Ibid.

43 'Schedule 7 declared "unjust" by European Court of Human Rights', *Mend*, 12
March 2019. https://www.mend.org.uk/
schedule-7-declared-unjust-european-court-human-rights/

44 See 'Can the Muslim world really unite?', published at www.hizb.org.uk, 4
March 2010. https://www.hizb.org.uk/islamic-culture/can-the-muslim-world-
really-unite/

45 See HT Britain's media information pack, 2010, p. 14. For the contrary view,
see James Brandon, 'Hizb-ut-Tahrir's Growing Appeal in the Arab World',
Terrorism Monitor, December 2006, and Zeyno Baran, 'Hib ut-Tahrir: Islam's
Political Insurgency', published by the Nixon Center, 2004, p. 53.

46 Ed Husain, *The Islamist: Why I Joined Radical Islam In Britain, What I Saw Inside
and Why I Left* (Penguin, 2007), p. 100–1.

47 Ibid, pp. 151–153.

48 Ibid, p 240–41.

49 Ibid, pp 282–284.

50 Riazat Butt, 'How Mohammed became Ed', *Guardian*, 9 May 2007. https://
www.theguardian.com/commentisfree/2007/may/09/
thereismuchexcitementabout

51 Maajid Nawaz, *Radical: My Journey Out Of Islamist Extremism* (W.H. Allen, 2013),
chapters 5 and 11.

52 Ibid, chapters 24–26, pp. 212–3, 228 and 230.

53 Peter Oborne, '"Extremist is the secular word for heretic": the Hizb ut-Tahrir
leader who insists on his right to speak', *Guardian*, 24 July 2015. https://www.
theguardian.com/uk-news/2015/jul/24/
david-cameron-extremism-struggle-generation-abdul-wahid

54 Nawaz received death threats in 2014 after tweeting a cartoon of the Prophet

Muhammad and Jesus. He also claimed that he was ordered to install a home panic alarm by anti-terror police after ISIS called for his death in 2015 when photos of him having a private lap dance at a strip club on his stag night emerged. Anna Dubuis, 'Maajid Nawaz sent death threats by ISIS and installs panic alarm at home because of lap dance CCTV', *Evening Standard*, 15 April 2015. https://www.standard.co.uk/news/london/maajid-nawaz-sent-isis-death-threats-and-installs-panic-alarm-at-home-because-of-lap-dance-cctv-10177562.html; Jonathan Brown and Ian Johnston, 'Nick Clegg attacks death threats against Maajid Nawaz' *Independent*, 26 January 2014. https://www.independent.co.uk/news/uk/politics/nick-clegg-attacks-death-threats-against-maajid-nawaz-lib-dem-candidate-who-tweeted-a-cartoon-of-the-prophet-mohammed-and-jesus-greeting-each-other-9086469.html

55   Nawaz *op. cit.*, p. 219.

56   Maajid Nawaz on *Newsnight*, 11 September 2007. https://www.youtube.com/watch?v=57y-dQMnqMk

57   Nawaz, *op .cit.*, p. 330.

58   Ian Cobain, Alice Ross, Rob Evans and Mona Mahmood, 'Inside Ricu, the shadowy propaganda unit inspired by the cold war', *Guardian*, 2 May 2016. https://www.theguardian.com/politics/2016/may/02/inside-ricu-the-shadowy-propaganda-unit-inspired-by-the-cold-war

59   Ibid., chapter 29, p. 249.

60   Ibid., pp. 349–353; Nafeez Mosaddeq Ahmed, 'UK's flawed counter-terrorism strategy', *Le Monde diplomatique*, 9 December 2013. https://mondediplo.com/outsidein/uk-s-flawed-counter-terrorism-strategy; Charles Moore, 'An insider's exposé of Islamist extremism', *Telegraph*, 30 July 2012. https://www.telegraph.co.uk/comment/columnists/charlesmoore/9437550/An-insiders-expose-of-Islamist-extremism.html

61   Nawaz *op. cit.*, chapter 30. Also see 'State multiculturalism has failed, says David Cameron', BBC News, 5 February 2011. https://www.bbc.co.uk/news/uk-politics-12371994

62   Quilliam Foundation, Form 990, 2011. https://projects.propublica.org/nonprofits/organizations/264293228

63   Spencer had been due to speak at an English Defence League march. For the Home Office letter to Spencer, see http://archive.is/c1E6m

64   Quilliam Foundation, Form 990, 2011. https://projects.propublica.org/nonprofits/organizations/264293228

65   According to IRS corporate filings, the US branch received an annual grant of approximately $265,000 under the patronage of Gen Next Inc. This was transferred to 'grant recipients' in Europe. Up to the end of 2013, Gen Next had provided the think tank with $813,000. Nafeez Ahmed, 'How violent extremists hijacked London-based "Counter-Extremism" think tank', AlterNet, 28 April 2015. https://www.alternet.org/2015/04/how-violent-extremists-hijacked-london-based-counter-extremism-think-tank/

66 Stuart Family Foundation, Form 990, years 2011–2015.
    https://projects.propublica.org/nonprofits/organizations/363422731
    Donations are also cited in 'Why Counter-extremism Organisations like
    Quilliam do more harm than good', Mend, 12 December 2018. https://www.
    mend.org.uk/counter-extremism-organisations-like-quilliam-harm-good/
    For the anti-Muslim stance of Frank Gaffney Jr., see: 'Frank Gaffney Jr.',
    Southern Poverty Law Center (SPLC). https://www.splcenter.org/fighting-
    hate/extremist-files/individual/frank-gaffney-jr

67 Templeton Foundation, Form 990, 2011–2015.

68 Quilliam Foundation, Form 990, 2012.

69 Gatestone Institute Statement.

70 Chuka Umunna, Home Affairs Committee meeting, 1 December 2015. See
    also: https://5pillarsuk.com/2015/12/04/how-quilliam-foundation-crumbled-
    in-front-of-home-affairs-select-committee/

71 Tom Griffin, 'The problem with the Quilliam Foundation', openDemocracy, 7
    November 2016. https://www.opendemocracy.net/en/opendemocracyuk/
    problem-with-quilliam-foundation/
    Nafeez Ahmed, 'The Charmed Life & Strange, Sad Death of the Quilliam
    Foundation', *Byline Times*, 11 May 2021. https://bylinetimes.com/2021/05/11/
    the-charmed-life-and-strange-sad-death-of-the-quilliam-foundation/
    For a live recording of the Home Affairs Committee session on 1 December
    2015, see: https://www.parliamentlive.tv/Event/Index/
    f2a86e88-262c-44b7-8a94-40f1dd936cad

72 'The Quillam Foundation crumbled in front of Home Affairs Select Committee',
    5 Pillars UK, 4 December 2015. https://5pillarsuk.com/2015/12/04/
    how-quilliam-foundation-crumbled-in-front-of-home-affairs-select-committee/

73 The relationship between Quilliam and right-wing donors in the US has been
    well documented. See, for example, https://www.opendemocracy.net/en/
    opendemocracyuk/problem-with-quilliam-foundation/

74 For Quilliam's American finance, see Ahmed *op. cit.*, and J. Spooner and Jono
    Stubbings, 'Maajid Nawaz and Quilliam: The Money Trail Behind the
    Propaganda', loonwatch.com, 6 March 2017. http://www.loonwatch.com/
    2017/03/06/
    maajid-nawaz-and-quilliam-the-money-trail-behind-the-propaganda/

75 Matthew Bell, 'Who is an anti-Muslim extremist?' The World, 1 November
    2016. https://theworld.org/stories/2016-11-01/who-anti-muslim-extremist

76 See Raya Jalabi, 'A history of Bill Maher's "not bigoted" remarks on Islam',
    Guardian, 7 October 2014. https://www.theguardian.com/tv-and-radio/
    tvandradioblog/2014/oct/06/bill-maher-islam-ben-affleck; Hamid Dabashi,
    'When it comes to Islamophobia, we need to name names', Al Jazeera, 31
    March 2019. https://www.aljazeera.com/opinions/2019/3/31/
    when-it-comes-to-islamophobia-we-need-to-name-names

77 'SPLC Statement regarding Maajid Nawaz and Quilliam Foundation,

www.SPLCenter.org, 18 June 2018. https://www.splcenter.org/news/2018/
06/18/splc-statement-regarding-maajid-nawaz-and-quilliam-foundation

78   'Quilliam facilitates Tommy Robinson leaving the English Defence League',
     Dorset Eye, 8 October 2013. https://dorseteye.com/quilliam-facilitates-
     tommy-robinson-leaving-the-english-defence-league1/

79   Adrian Goldberg, 'Tommy Robinson: The man behind the British version of
     Pegida', BBC News, 29 January 2016. https://www.bbc.co.uk/news/
     magazine-35432074

80   See Tom Belger, 'How Tommy Robinson won the support of the global alt-
     right,' *Financial Times*, 31 May 2018. https://www.ft.com/content/
     f8f2b174-6409-11e8-90c2-9563a0613e56

81   On the subject of the lawyer and politician Sayeeda Warsi, Robinson said that
     she had 'been made a baroness based simply on being Muslim and female'.
     Robinson described how the British state was 'sponsoring this effective fifth
     column infiltration wherever you look'. Tommy Robinson, *Enemy of the State*,
     (The Press News, 2015), pp. 254–265, 271.

82   Nafeez Ahmed, 'David Cameron's "counter-extremism" experts work with
     far-right Donald Trump sympathisers', Insurge Intelligence, 17 December
     2015. https://medium.com/insurge-intelligence/
     donald-trump-s-trojan-horse-in-britain-bdb40f7d1867

83   See Steven Hopkins, 'Tommy Robinson, former EDL leader, claims Quilliam
     paid him to quit far-right group', *Huffington Post*, 4 December 2015. https://
     www.huffingtonpost.co.uk/2015/12/03/tommy-robinson-claims-quilliam-
     paid-him-to-leave-edl_n_8710834.html

84   See 'Why Counter-Extremism Organisations like Quilliam do far more harm
     than good', MEND, 12 December 2018. https://www.mend.org.uk/
     counter-extremism-organisations-like-quilliam-harm-good/

85   See Miqdaad Versi, 'The government has caved to the ideologues opposed to
     the APPG definition of Islamophobia', *New Statesman*, 16 May 2019. https://
     www.newstatesman.com/politics/2019/05/
     government-has-caved-ideologues-opposed-appg-definition-islamophobia

86   Rafiq, H. (2018) [Twitter] 26 November. Available at: https://twitter.com/
     harasrafiq/status/1067055457007820800

87   See the statement 'To My Fellow Muslims', https://www.
     quilliaminternational.com/quilliam-files/euuk1126/

88   See, for example, Douglas Murray, 'The false equivalence between
     "Islamophobia" and anti-Semitism,' *The Spectator*, 9 March 2019. https://www.
     spectator.co.uk/article/
     the-false-equivalence-between-islamophobia-and-anti-semitism-8-march-2019

89   See Vanessa Thorpe, 'LBC's Maajid Nawaz's fascination with conspiracies
     raises alarm', *Guardian*, 31 January 2021. https://www.theguardian.com/tv-
     and-radio/2021/jan/31/
     lbcs-maajid-nawazs-fascination-with-conspiracies-raises-alarm

90 Brian Cathcart, 'The closure of Quilliam: some questions for Maajid Nawaz', Byline Times, 29 April 2021. https://bylinetimes.com/2021/04/29/the-closure-of-quilliam-some-questions-for-maajid-nawaz/

91 See Nafeez Ahmed and Max Blumenthal, 'The self-invention of Maajid Nawaz: fact and fiction in the life of the counter-terror celebrity', AlterNet, 4 February 2016. https://www.alternet.org/2016/02/self-invention-maajid-nawaz-fact-and-fiction-life-counter-terror-celebrity/

92 Erasmus, 'A liberal Muslim and a non-believer in search of common ground', *The Economist*, 3 October 2015. https://www.economist.com/erasmus/2015/10/03/a-liberal-muslim-and-a-non-believer-in-search-of-common-ground

93 *Islam and the Future of Tolerance* (Amazon Prime Video, 2018). Directed by Jan Shapiro and Desh Amila, performance by Sam Harris, Maajid Nawaz, Douglas Murray and Ayaan Hirsi Ali, produced by Aaron Louis and Suzi Jamil. https://www.amazon.co.uk/Islam-Future-Tolerance-Sam-Harris/dp/B07L6N9HXN.

94 See Peter Baehr, 'The Informers: Hannah Arendt's appraisal of Whittaker Chambers and the ex-Communists', *European Journal of Cultural and Political Sociology*, vol. 1 no. 1, 2014.

95 According to the Home Office, Quilliam last received funding of £26,993.34 in 2011–2012. 'Home Office funding to the Quilliam Foundation, 2008 to 2012', gov.uk, 29 January 2014. https://www.gov.uk/government/publications/home-office-funding-to-the-quilliam-foundation-from-2008-to-2012

96 Alex MacDonald, 'Quilliam: British "counter-extremist" group closes citing lack of funds', *Middle East Eye*, 9 April 2021. https://www.middleeasteye.net/news/uk-quilliam-foundation-controversial-counter-extremist-closes

CHAPTER 16: POLICY EXCHANGE: HOW A NEO-CONSERVATIVE THINK TANK DEFINED BRITISH MUSLIMS

1 Peter Coaldrake, 'Deregulation and marketisation in English higher education – lessons from Australia', Policy Exchange, 9 September 2016. https://policyexchange.org.uk/event/deregulation-and-marketisation-in-english-higher-education-lessons-from-australia/; Lucian J. Hudson and Iain Mansfield, 'Universities at the Crossroads: how higher education leadership must act to regain the trust of their staff, their communities and the whole nation', Policy Exchange, 23 February 2020. https://policyexchange.org.uk/publication/universities-at-the-crossroads/; Sally Weale. 'Universities brace for government scrutiny after Policy Exchange report', *Guardian*, 1 March 2020. https://www.theguardian.com/education/2020/mar/01/universities-government-scrutiny-policy-exchange

2 Dominic Casciani, 'Hearts and minds: London's street battle with al-Qaeda', BBC News, 9 September 2011. http://www.bbc.co.uk/news/mobile/uk-14844988

3   The views of Conservative Party activists are strikingly similar to those of
     everyday worshippers at Finsbury Park mosque. These activists are also
     disproportionately older than the average voter (the average age is fifty-seven)
     and also overwhelmingly white, male and middle class, which may also be a
     reason for the prevalence of some of these views. See Tim Bale et al,
     'Grassroots: Britain's party members – who they are, what they think, and
     what they do' (Mile End Institute/Queen Mary University of London, 2018).
     https://esrcpartymembersprojectorg.files.wordpress.com/2018/01/
     grassroots-pmp_final.pdf

4   Phillips detailed how London hosted 'radicals' such as Abu Hamza, Abu
     Qatada, Omar Bakri Mohammed and Mohammed al-Massari. Abu Hamza was
     jailed in February 2006 for soliciting murder and inciting racial hatred. Even
     after Hamza was banned from preaching inside the mosque, he held prayers
     outside the building until he was eventually put on trial; sometimes he even sat
     on the pavement in an armchair as he embraced his followers. According to
     Phillips, individuals such as Hamza were often viewed as mere 'pantomime
     villains'. Phillips described how former Home Secretary David Blunkett had
     claimed that the authorities, the security service MI5 and prosecuting
     authorities had accused him of exaggerating the threat posed by Hamza. His
     role in the Finsbury Park mosque is well documented in the book. According
     to Phillips, the answer to the question of why authorities allowed 'the growth
     of a hostile separatism among British Muslims' requires 'understanding a
     society that even now is in denial about the threat that it faces, and whose
     institutions have all been captured by a mindset that poses a lethal danger to
     the British state by weakening its defences from within against the threat from
     without'. Melanie Phillips, *Londonistan: How Britain Has Created a Terror State
     Within* (Gibson Square, 2012, new edition), pp. 12–13, 49, 52–56, 82–83.

5   Joe Murphy, 'Exciting times at the Tories' feeder school', *Evening Standard*, 22
     July 2008. https://www.standard.co.uk/news/mayor/comment-exciting-
     times-at-the-tories-feeder-school-6805259.html

6   Tom Mills, Tom Griffin and David Miller, *The Cold War on British Muslims: An
     Examination of Policy Exchange and the Centre for Social Cohesion* (Public Interest
     Investigations, 2011), p. 39.

7   Hugh Wilford, 'American Labour Diplomacy and Cold War Britain', *Journal of
     Contemporary History*, vol. 37, no. 1, 2002, pp. 45–65.

8   Shiraz Maher and Martyn Frampton, *Choosing Our Friends Wisely: Criteria for
     Engagement with Muslim Groups* (Policy Exchange, 2009), p. 18.

9   On 29 February 1988, Reagan said: 'On my desk in the Oval Office, I have a
     little sign that says: "There is no limit to what a man can do or where he can go
     if he doesn't mind who gets the credit."' https://www.reaganfoundation.org/
     ronald-reagan/reagan-quotes-speeches/remarks-at-a-meeting-of-the-white-
     house-conference-for-a-drug-free-america/

10   We are entering deep waters. Those curious about the Institute for European

Defence and Strategic Studies might (with a health warning) try reading:
https://pinkindustry.wordpress.com/the-institute-for-european-defence-and-strategic-studies/. According to the abstract of a report by William Clark, a researcher at the University of Strathclyde: 'The general hypotheses is that the Institute for European Defence and Strategic Studies (IEDSS) was not an impartial independent think tank, but that it was part of large-scale US public diplomacy and propaganda strategies to influence UK domestic politics, funded by the Central Intelligence Agency and a small group of foundations.' https://ethos.bl.uk/OrderDetails.do?uin=uk.bl.ethos.605968.

11 Information about Dean Godson is scanty and hard to obtain. I have therefore resorted to Wikipedia (https://en.wikipedia.org/wiki/Dean_Godson#cite_note-15), though I have done my best to corroborate information found there.

12 Maggie Brown, 'Newland unleashed', *Guardian*, 15 November 2004. https://www.theguardian.com/media/2004/nov/15/thedailytelegraph.mondaymediasection

13 In April 2020, they were Munira Mirza, Rupert Reid, Blair Gibbs, Jack Airey, David Shiels and Iain Mansfield.

14 Martin Bright, *When Progressives Treat with Reactionaries: The British State's Flirtation with Radical Islamism* (Policy Exchange, 2006).

15 Jason Burke, a foreign correspondent for the *Observer*, wrote the preface.

16 Bright, *op. cit.* p. 12.

17 Ibid., pp. 12, 28.

18 Ibid., p. 11.

19 Munira Mirza, *Living Apart Together: British Muslims and the Paradox of Multiculturalism* (Policy Exchange, 2007), p. 92.

20 Ibid., p. 66.

21 Ibid., p. 72.

22 Ibid., p. 6.

23 James Slack and Benedict Brogan, 'Agenda of hate in UK mosques', *Daily Mail*, 30 October 2007, p. 1; Toby Helm, 'Many mosques "continuing to spread messages of hate"', *Daily Telegraph*, 30 October 2007, p. 1; Sean O'Neill, 'Lessons in hate found at leading mosques', *The Times*, 30 October 2007, p. 1.

24 Charles Moore, 'Newsnight told a small story over a big one', *Daily Telegraph*, 15 December 2007. https://www.telegraph.co.uk/comment/columnists/charlesmoore/3644727/Newsnight-told-a-small-story-over-a-big-one.html

25 Mills, Griffin & Miller, *op. cit.*, p. 42.

26 Marko Attila Hoare, 'Alan Mendoza's putsch in the Henry Jackson Society', Greater Surbiton blog, 13 August 2012. https://greatersurbiton.wordpress.com/2012/08/13/alan-mendozas-putsch-in-the-henry-jackson-society/

27 Maher & Frampton, *op. cit.*, p. 2.

28 Shiraz Maher, 'How I Escaped Islamism', *Sunday Times*, 12 August 2007. https://www.thetimes.co.uk/article/how-i-escaped-islamism-zptlgrsjrvz

29 Maher and Frampton, *op. cit.*, p. 68.

30 'Prevent duty guidance', GOV.UK, 12 March 2015. https://www.gov.uk/
    government/publications/prevent-duty-guidance

31 'Revised Prent dury guidance: for England and Wales', GOV.UK, 1 April
    2021. https://www.gov.uk/government/publications/prevent-duty-guidance/
    revised-prevent-duty-guidance-for-england-and-wales

32 'Individuals referred to and supported through the Prevent Programme, April
    2020 to March 2021', Home Office, GOV.UK, 18 November 2021. https://
    www.gov.uk/government/statistics/individuals-referred-to-and-supported-
    through-the-prevent-programme-april-2020-to-march-2021

33 Ibid.

34 'People's Review of Prevent', 15 February 2015, p. 63. https://
    peoplesreviewofprevent.org/

35 'False Positives: the Prevent counterextremism policy in healthcare' report by
    MEDACT, which can be found here: https://www.vice.com/en/article/
    xg8ae4/asians-and-muslims-more-likely-to-be-referred-to-the-uks-anti-
    terror-programme; see also 'Counter-Radicalization: A Critical Look into a
    Racist New Industry' by Dr Tarek Younis for Yaqeen Institute, which can be
    read here: https://yaqeeninstitute.org/read/paper/
    counter-radicalization-a-critical-look-into-a-racist-new-industry

36 Caroline Mortimer, 'Eight-year-old questioned after teachers mistake t-shirt
    slogan for Isis propaganda', Independent, 1 August 2016. https://www.
    independent.co.uk/news/uk/home-news/isis-propaganda-t-shirt-boy-east-
    london-teachers-mistake-terrorism-terror-a7164941.html

37 Vikram Dodd, 'School questioned Muslim pupil about Isis after discussion on
    eco-activism', Guardian, 22 September 2015. https://www.theguardian.com/
    education/2015/sep/22/school-questioned-muslim-pupil-about-isis-after-
    discussion-on-eco-activism

38 Eleanor Busby, 'Students' university essays reported to police under
    "overzealous" government counter-terrorism measures', Independent, 15
    February 2020. https://www.independent.co.uk/news/education/education-
    news/students-university-police-essays-terrorism-free-speech-a9289301.html

39 Gordon Brown, speech at a seminar on Britishness at the Commonwealth Club
    London, February 2007.

40 See this illuminating essay – Dr Saffron Karlsen, 'Hard Evidence: How British
    Do British Muslims Feel?', Policy Bristol blog, 25 January 2016.
    https://policybristol.blogs.bris.ac.uk/2016/01/25/hard-evidence-
    how-british-do-british-muslims-feel/

CHAPTER 17: THE CONSERVATIVE PARTY AND BRITISH ISLAM

1 'The Weightless Decade' is the title of a chapter in Michael Gove's book
   Celsius 7/7: How The West's Policy Of Appeasement Has Provoked Yet More

Fundamentalist Terror — And What Has To Be Done Now (Weidenfeld & Nicolson, 2006).

2   For the charge that John Major and, later, Tony Blair went soft on the IRA, see Gove *op. cit.,* pp 45–46. See also: Ed Vulliamy, 'Major, the chicken turned hawk', *Guardian*, 11 April 1999. https://www.theguardian.com/world/1999/apr/11/balkans11

3   In 2010, membership was estimated at 177,000. By 2013, it had fallen to 134,000. In July 2019, it had risen to 180,000. https://www.theguardian.com/politics/blog/2010/oct/05/tories-fears-falling-membership;
    http://researchbriefings.files.parliament.uk/documents/SN05125/SN05125.pdf;
    http://www.dailymail.co.uk/debate/article-5240801/Peter-Oborne-Tories-wither-away-not-act.html

4   Janan Ganesh, *George Osborne: The Austerity Chancellor* (Biteback Publishing, 2012), p. 158.

5   HC Deb (14th September 2001), vol 372, col. 653. Available at: https://hansard.parliament.uk/commons/2001-09-14/debates/82da0642-328b-4155-a224-5f35d68758bf/CommonsChamber

6   By contrast, another fashionable term, neo-liberalism, is conceptually hard to distinguish from classical liberalism as defined by John Stuart Mill or Adam Smith – that is, personal liberty and free markets.

7   'Neoconservatism's Marxist roots are showing', *The Atlantic*, 15 June 2010. https://www.theatlantic.com/daily-dish/archive/2010/06/neoconservatisms-marxist-roots-are-showing/185857/

8   Nicholas Watt and Harriet Sherwood, 'David Cameron: Israeli blockade has turned Gaza Strip into a "prison camp"', *Guardian*, 27 July 2010. https://www.theguardian.com/politics/2010/jul/27/david-cameron-gaza-prison-camp

9   William Hague, speaking in the House of Commons on 20 July 2006. HC Deb (20th July 2006) vol 449, col. 523. Available at: https://hansard.parliament.uk/commons/2006-07-20/debates/3b53cbc9-87fd-46c3-b98b-1d5e465c683f/CommonsChamber

10 He visited a Manchester mosque in 2013, and the Makkah mosque in Leeds in 2016. 'David Cameron chops onions at Manchester Mosque', BBC News, 7 August 2013. https://www.bbc.co.uk/news/av/uk-23609451; 'Muslim women who don't improve their English now face deportation, warns Cameron in Leeds', *Yorkshire Evening Post*, 18 January 2016. https://www.yorkshireeveningpost.co.uk/news/politics/muslim-women-who-dont-improve-their-english-now-face-deportation-warns-cameron-leeds-629144

11 David Cameron, 'What I learnt from my stay with a Muslim family', *Guardian*, 13 May 2007. https://www.theguardian.com/commentisfree/2007/may/13/comment.communities

12 Gove *op. cit.,* p. 9.

13   Ibid., p. 11. See also Alan Travis, 'Michael Gove book offers clue to Trojan horse row and his views on Islamism', *Guardian*, 6 June 2014. https://www.theguardian.com/politics/2014/jun/06/michael-gove-trojan-horse-islam

14   Peter Oborne, 'The cowardice at the heart of our relationship with Israel', *Daily Telegraph*, 12 December 2012. I wrote this ten years ago but, as far as I am aware, no Tory MP or Conservative Friends of Israel representative has challenged my estimate. This statistic dates back to 2014, and there is currently no up-to-dates statistics on membership. https://web.archive.org/web/20140802055821/https://cfoi.co.uk/AboutCFI/Whatwedo/

15   See William Dalrymple's review of Michael Gove's book for the *Sunday Times*, 'A global crisis of understanding', *Sunday Times*, 24 September 2006. https://www.thetimes.co.uk/article/a-global-crisis-of-understanding-jjvgb9j079k

16   'How demographic decline and its financial consequences will sink "the European Dream"', New Frontiers Foundation, 2005, pp. 19–20.

17   Niall Ferguson, 'The way we live now: Eurabia?', *New York Times*, 4 April 2004. https://www.nytimes.com/2004/04/04/magazine/the-way-we-live-now-4-4-04-eurabia.html

18   Dominic Cummings, 'Gesture without motion from the hollow men in the bubble, and a free simple idea to improve things a lot which could be implemented in one day (Part I)', dominiccummings.com, 16 June 2014.

19   For an early study of fabrications from the Murdoch press and other newspaper organisations, see James Jones' and my study for Channel 4: https://www.channel4.com/news/media/pdfs/Muslims_under_siege_LR.pd. For other examples of the Murdoch press problem with Muslims, see David Folkenflik, 'Former Murdoch Executive Says He Quit Over Fox's Anti-Muslim Rhetoric', NPR, 21 March 2019. https://www.npr.org/2019/03/21/705441083/former-murdoch-executive-says-he-quit-over-foxs-anti-muslim-rhetoric?t=1645449190027f

20   The document can be accessed here: https://www.scribd.com/document/34834977/Secret-Quilliam-Memo-to-government

21   This period saw US senator Joseph McCarthy of Wisconsin produce a series of investigations and hearings in an attempt to expose communist infiltration of the US government. Paul. J. Achter, 'McCarthyism', *Encyclopedia Britannica*, 13 January 2021.

22   McCarthy was a first-time senator in Wisconsin, having won there in 1946. He was propelled into the national spotlight after his speech at the Ohio County Women's Republican Club in Wheeling, West Virginia in February 1950. He declared that he had a list of 205 known members of the Communist Party involved in US government. 'Joseph McCarthy', History.com, 29 October 2009.

23   In 1946, Nixon scored a victory against Jerry Voorhis by emphasising his anti-communism. He used the same strategy to win his 1950 Senate campaign. 'Joseph McCarthy, and other facets of the 1950s Red Scare', American History USA. https://www.americanhistoryusa.com/

joseph-mccarthy-and-other-facets-of-1950s-red-scare/. For Nixon and anti-communism, see Michael P. Riccards, 'Richard Nixon and the American Political Tradition', *Presidential Studies Quarterly*, Vol. 23, No. 4, *The Managerial, Political and Spiritual Presidencies* (Fall, 1993), p. 740.

24 Buckley was a prolific author and influential newspaper columnist. George W. Bush said that he 'brought conservative thought into the political mainstream, and helped lay the intellectual foundation for America's victory in the Cold War'. Douglas Martin, 'William F. Buckley Jr. is dead at 82', *New York Times*, 27 February 2008. https://www.nytimes.com/2008/02/27/business/media/27cnd-buckley.html

25 Francis Coker, review of William F. Buckley Jr. and L. Brent Bozell, *McCarthy and his Enemies: The Record and Its Meaning*, *The Journal of Politics*, vol. 17, no. 1, 1955, pp. 113–122.

26 Homosexuals at the time faced ruin from exposure and were therefore by necessity more secretive. At the time, the 'red scare' was accompanied by a 'lavender scare' in which suspected homosexuals were investigated, interrogated and dismissed by both government officials and private employers. Andrea Friedman, 'The Smearing of Joe McCarthy: The Lavender Scare, Gossip, and Cold War Politics', *American Quarterly*, vol. 57, no. 4, 2005, pp. 1105–1129.

27 The notorious House Un-American Activities Committee (HUAC) carried out highly public inquisitions into Hollywood personalities. In fact, McCarthy's direct victims were relatively few. He was not involved in the cases of Alger Hiss (which made the reputation of Richard Nixon), nor the Rosenberg spy ring. He did not promote any legislation, unlike his contemporary Senator Pat McCarran who gave his name to the anti-Communist National Security Act. In spite of his status as the US's leading anti-communist, he did not form any domestic political movement and had no role in the many private freelance anti-communist organisations which sprang up in his time. (These included *Red Channels*, the publication which denounced Bob Heller, father of my friend and collaborator Richard Heller, who has helped me greatly with this book.)

CHAPTER 18: THE TROJAN HORSE AFFAIR

1 Interview between the author and Tahir Alam.

2 John Holmwood, *Countering Extremism in British Schools? The truth about the Birmingham Trojan Horse affair* (Policy Press, 2017), p. 131.

3 Dorothy Lepkowska, 'The first "outstanding" school of 2012 reveals all', *Guardian*, 13 February 2012. https://www.theguardian.com/education/2012/feb/13/outstanding-osted-for-birmingham-school

4 Holmwood *op. cit.*, p. 150.

5 Keith Brown, 'Letter to Park View Students', published in Ofsted's *Inspection*

Report for Park View Business and Enterprise School, 2012. https://files.api.ofsted.gov.uk/v1/file/1889019

6　Quoted in Andrew Gilligan, 'Extremists and the "Trojan Horse" approach in state schools', *Daily Telegraph*, 9 March 2014. https://www.telegraph.co.uk/news/uknews/terrorism-in-the-uk/10685418/Extremists-and-the-Trojan-Horse-approach-in-state-schools.html

7　Quoted in Richard Adams, 'Ofsted inspectors make U-turn on "Trojan Horse" school, leak shows', *Guardian*, 30 May 2014. https://www.theguardian.com/education/2014/may/30/ofsted-u-turn-trojan-horse-park-view-school-leak

8　Quoted in Peter Clarke, 'Report into allegations concerning Birmingham schools arising from the "Trojan Horse" letter', 2014. http://dera.ioe.ac.uk/20549/1/Report_into_allegations_concerning_Birmingham_schools_arising_from_the_Trojan_Horse_letter-web.pdf

9　Richard Kerbaj and Sian Griffiths, 'Top academy investigated for "sidelining" non-Muslim staff', *Sunday Times*, 23 February 2014. https://www.thetimes.co.uk/article/top-academy-investigated-for-sidelining-non-muslim-staff-xdgxw66qk62

10　Richard Kerbaj and Sian Griffiths, 'Islamist plot to take over schools', *Sunday Times*, 2 March 2014. https://www.thetimes.co.uk/article/islamist-plot-to-take-over-schools-655mhbw0vtc

11　'Trojan Horse probe headed by ex-Met chief Peter Clarke', BBC News, 15 April 2014. https://www.bbc.co.uk/news/uk-england-birmingham-27031941

12　Patrick Wintour, 'Schools face new curbs on extremism after Birmingham Trojan horse affair', *Guardian*, 22 July 2014. https://www.theguardian.com/politics/2014/jul/22/schools-face-curbs-extremism-birmingham-trojan-horse-affair

13　Clarke, *op. cit.*

14　'Extremism in schools: the Trojan Horse Affair', parliament.uk, 17 March 2015. https://publications.parliament.uk/pa/cm201415/cmselect/cmeduc/473/47304.htm

15　'Direction: Tahir Alam barred from managing independent schools', decision from the Department of Education and The Rt Hon Baroness Nicky Morgan, GOV.UK, 9 September 2015. https://www.gov.uk/government/publications/direction-tahir-alam-barred-from-managing-independent-schools

16　'Regulation of school managers and governors: prohibition direction', Department for Education, September 2015. https://assets.publishing.service.gov.uk/government/uploads/system/uploads/attachment_data/file/459386/Regulation_of_school_managers_and_governors_Tahir_Alam.pdf

17　The Muslim Council of Britain, in a statement released shortly after the publication of the report, said that 'Mr Clarke's approach . . . chooses to ascribe guilt by association . . . by conflating conservative Muslim practices to a supposed ideology and agenda to "Islamise" secular schools'. https://mcb.org.uk/press-releases/the-muslim-council-of-britain-responds-to-peter-clarkes-trojan-horse-letter-report/

18 'Extremism in schools: the Trojan Horse affair', March 2015, https://
    publications.parliament.uk/pa/cm201415/cmselect/cmeduc/473/47302.htm

19 Alexander Robertson and Eleanor Harding, 'Senior teachers at the centre of
    Trojan Horse plot cleared', *Daily Mail*, 30 May 2017. https://www.dailymail.
    co.uk/news/article-4555910/Senior-teachers-centre-Trojan-Horse-plot-
    cleared.html; Olivia Rudgard, '"Trojan Horse" case against five Birmingham
    teachers thrown out by tribunal', *Daily Telegraph*, 30 May 2017. https://www.
    telegraph.co.uk/news/2017/05/30/trojan-horse-case-against-five-birmingham-
    teachers-thrown-tribunal/; '"Trojan Horse": Cases against teachers dropped',
    BBC News, 30 May 2017. https://www.bbc.co.uk/news/uk-england-
    birmingham-40094333. The NCTL (or Teaching Regulation Agency) is an
    independent agency of the Department for Education, as is Ofsted.

20 Andrew Gilligan and Sian Griffiths, 'Teachers' college slated over Trojan
    Horse plot', *Sunday Times*, 4 June 2017.

21 Andrew Gilligan, '*Trojan Horse* reviewed by Andrew Gilligan – the man who
    helped report the scandal', *The Times*, 2 September 2018. https://www.
    thetimes.co.uk/article/trojan-horse-reviewed-by-andrew-gilligan-the-man-
    who-helped-report-the-scandal-sh966t2sw

22 John Holmwood, *Countering Extremism in British Schools?: The Truth about the
    Birmingham Trojan Horse Affair* (Policy Press, 2017), p. 207.

23 Nick Timothy, 'It's a fiction to suggest that there was no plot by Islamist
    hardliners to take over state schools', *Daily Telegraph*, 9 August 2018. https://
    www.telegraph.co.uk/news/2018/08/09/
    fiction-suggest-no-plot-islamist-hardliners-take-state-schools/

24 See: https://www.compare-school-performance.service.gov.uk/school/
    138059/rockwood-academy/secondary

25 I have not spoken to the teachers. I am relying on information provided by
    Professor John Holmwood, who knows them well.

26 'Counter-Extremism Strategy', presented to Parliament by the Secretary of
    State for the Home Department by Command of Her Majesty, October 2015.
    https://assets.publishing.service.gov.uk/government/uploads/system/
    uploads/attachment_data/file/470088/51859_Cm9148_Accessible.pdf

27 Department for Education and Lord Nash, 'Guidance on promoting British
    values in schools published', gov.uk, 27 November 2014. https://www.gov.uk/
    government/news/guidance-on-promoting-british-values-in-schools-published

CHAPTER 19: A FALSE NARRATIVE
ABOUT MUSLIM 'GROOMING GANGS'

1   See for example this summary by the *Daily Express* https://www.express.
    co.uk/news/uk/839509/Britain-towns-cities-asian-grooming-gangs-Newcastle-
    Rochdale-Rotherham

2   The *Daily Telegraph* suggested that the girls suffered 'at the hands of a nine-strong paedophile gang of Asian men who preyed on vulnerable white girls they saw as "easy meat"'. Girl C, who became pregnant at thirteen by Adil Khan, said 'Pakistani men pass you around like a ball, they're all in a massive circle and put a white girl in the middle'. One of the men on trial later implied that the fate of the girls was the fault of British society as a whole: 'You white people train them in sex and drinking, so when they come to us they are fully trained.' Nigel Bunyan, 'Rochdale grooming trial: how the case unfolded', *Daily Telegraph*, 8 May 2012. https://www.telegraph.co.uk/news/uknews/crime/9347305/Rochdale-grooming-trial-how-the-case-unfolded.html

3   'Mushin Ahmed death: two men jailed over racist Rotherham killing', BBC News, 29 February 2016. http://www.bbc.co.uk/news/uk-england-south-yorkshire-35688543

4   Fiona Hamilton, 'Driver Darren Osborne "ran Muslims down after TV grooming drama"', *The Times*, 23 January 2018. https://www.thetimes.co.uk/article/driver-darren-osborne-ran-muslims-down-after-tv-rochdale-grooming-drama-three-girls-5x2bt3h9m

5   Tom Davidson, 'Evil New Zealand gunman had "For Rotherham" written on ammo used in shooting', *Daily Mirror*, 15 March 2019. https://www.mirror.co.uk/news/world-news/evil-new-zealand-gunman-for-14138715

6   Peter Walker, 'Tommy Robinson appointed as UKIP's "grooming gangs adviser"', *Guardian*, 22 November 2018. https://www.theguardian.com/politics/2018/nov/22/tommy-robinson-ukip-grooming-gangs-adviser

7   In Rochdale, Shatter Boys (a group for child sexual abuse survivors) said that it had been approached on several occasions by senior UKIP figures who offered to introduce them to doors in exchange for them raising the alarm on 'grooming gangs'. Josh Halliday, 'Far right "infiltrating children's charities with anti-Islam agenda"', *Guardian*, 5 March 2019. https://www.theguardian.com/world/2019/mar/05/far-right-infiltrating-childrens-charities-with-anti-islam-agenda

8   Andrew Norfolk has has been criticised for misreporting Muslims. According to an investigation by Brian Cathcart and Paddy French, 'our analysis of Norfolk's methods indicates that important facts were omitted or marginalised, untrustworthy or inadequate witnesses were relied on, quotations were taken out of context, expert testimony was ignored – and there were clearly shortcomings in verification'. https://inforrm.org/2019/06/28/unmasked-the-andrew-norfolk-report-in-10-points-brian-cathcart/. In addition, see the response by *The Times*: https://pressgazette.co.uk/times-condemns-extraordinary-personal-attack-on-journalist-andrew-norfolk-anti-muslim-reporting-claim/

9   Norfolk's awards include Journalist of the Year at the British Press Awards 2014, the Paul Foot Award in 2012 and the Orwell Prize in 2013.

10 See Jayne Senior, *Broken And Betrayed* (Pan, 2016), chapter 17, and Sammy Woodhouse, *Just A Child* (Blink, 2018), chapters 36 and 37.

11 For detailed criticism of Norfolk by one of the UK's leading experts on child
    sexual exploitation, see Ella Cockbain, 'Grooming and the "Asian sex gang
    predator": the construction of a racial crime threat', *Race & Class*, vol. 54(4),
    2013, pp. 22–32. https://journals.sagepub.com/doi/pdf/10.1177/
    0306396813475983; also J. Spooner and J. Stubbs, 'Making a monster: How
    The Times created the Asian "grooming gang"', Regressive Left Media, 24
    February 2018. https://medium.com/@Reg_Left_Media/
    making-a-monster-how-the-times-created-the-asian-grooming-gang-
    f944ad598822

12 'Group-Based Child Sexual Exploitation: Dissecting Grooming Gangs', Home
    Office, GOV.UK, December 2020. https://assets.publishing.service.gov.uk/
    government/uploads/system/uploads/attachment_data/file/944206/Group-
    based_CSE_Paper.pdf

13 Ibid., introduction.

14 Steve Bird, 'Grooming gangs of Muslim men failed to integrate into British
    society', *Daily Telegraph*, 9 December 2017. https://www.telegraph.co.uk/news/
    2017/12/09/grooming-gangs-muslim-men-failed-integrate-british-society/

15 Elizabeth Burden, 'Grooming gang study reveals 84 per cent are Asian', *The
    Times*, 11 December 2017. https://www.thetimes.co.uk/article/
    child-groomer-study-by-quilliam-think-tank-finds-84-are-asian-0r3csrbmb

16 Tom Barnes, 'British-Pakistani researchers say 84 per cent of grooming gang
    members are Asian: "It's very important we talk about it"', *Independent*, 10
    December 2017. https://www.independent.co.uk/news/uk/home-news/
    quilliam-grooming-gangs-report-asian-abuse-rotherham-rochdale-newcastle-
    a8101941.html

17 The questions were put by my collaborator Richard Heller.

18 http://journal.quilliaminternational.com/2018/11/10/taking-grooming-gangs-
    seriously/ For Ella Cockbain, see her account 'When bad evidence is worse
    than no evidence: Quilliam's "grooming gangs" report and its legacy', Policing
    Insight, 20 March 2019. https://policinginsight.com/features/analysis/when-
    bad-evidence-is-worse-than-no-evidence-quilliams-grooming-gangs-report-
    and-its-legacy/; and (with Waqas Tufail) 'Failing victims, fuelling hate:
    Challenging the harms of the "Muslim grooming gangs" narrative', *Race & Class*,
    6 January 2020. https://journals.sagepub.com/doi/full/10.1177/
    0306396819895727. For personal attacks, see also Kenan Malik, 'We're told 84
    per cent of grooming gangs are Asian. But where's the evidence?', *Guardian*, 11
    November 2018. https://www.theguardian.com/commentisfree/2018/nov/11/
    84-per-cent-of-grooming-gangs-are-asians-we-dont-know-if-that-figure-is-right

19 Quilliam report, *op. cit.*, p. 24.

20 Allison Pearson, 'It's not racist to tell the truth about grooming gangs', *Daily
    Telegraph*, 12 December 2017. https://www.telegraph.co.uk/women/politics/
    not-racist-tell-truth-grooming-gangs/

21 'Ukip spokesman accused of being "alarmist" after calling grooming gangs

"holocaust of our children"', ITV News, 21 September 2018. https://www.itv.com/news/2018-09-21/muslim-sex-gangs-responsible-for-holocaust-of-our-children-claims-ukip

22 House of Lords debate, Hansard: HL Deb. (13th March 2018) Vol. 789 cols 1504-5. Available at: https://hansard.parliament.uk/Lords/2018-03-13/debates/87943d7d-0572-4c63-a1c7-d635502b94ee/LordsChamber

23 'Muhammad Fraser-Rahim counters extremism from within', The AHA Foundation. https://www.theahafoundation.org/muhammad-fraser-rahim-counters-extremism-within/

24 https://www.meforum.org/search.php?cx=partner-pub-2951801646144412 per cent3Ap24ltemdv6f&cof=FORID per cent3A9&ie=UTF-8&q=Quilliam+grooming+gangs&sa=Search

25 Douglas Murray, 'Tommy Robinson drew attention to "grooming gangs": Britain has persecuted him', National Review, 31 May 2018. https://www.nationalreview.com/2018/05/tommy-robinson-grooming-gangs-britain-persecutes-journalist/

26 See N. Lowles and S. Cressy. 'The BNP Past of the EDL Leader', Searchlight, vol. 421, July 2010, pp. 284-5.

27 Haroon Siddique and Ben Quinn, 'EDL: Tommy Robinson and deputy Kevin Carroll quit far right group', Guardian, 9 October 2013. https://www.theguardian.com/uk-news/2013/oct/08/tommy-robinson-english-defence-league; 'EDL Leader Tommy Robinson quits group', BBC News, 8 October 2013. https://www.bbc.co.uk/news/uk-politics-24442953. See Chris Allen, 'Opposing Islamification or Promoting Islamophobia? Understanding the English Defence League', Patterns of Prejudice, vol. 45 (4), 2011, pp. 279–294. doi:10.1080/0031322X.2011.585014.

28 See above, pp. oo.

29 Cahal Milmo, 'EDL founder Tommy Robinson addresses Pegida anti-Islam rally in Holland', Independent, 12 October 2015. https://www.independent.co.uk/news/uk/politics/edl-founder-tommy-robinson-addresses-pegida-antiislam-rally-in-holland-a6691406.html

30 See Josh Halliday, Lois Beckett and Caelainn Barr, 'Revealed: the hidden global network behind Tommy Robinson', Guardian, 7 December 2018. https://www.theguardian.com/uk-news/2018/dec/07/tommy-robinson-global-support-brexit-march

31 Maya Oppenheim, 'Tommy Robinson arrested after "trying to film Muslims" outside court', Independent, 12 May 2017. https://www.independent.co.uk/news/uk/home-news/tommy-robinson-arrest-muslims-filming-court-a7733156.html

32 'Amazon bans book co-written by Tommy Robinson from their website', Independent, 7 March 2019. https://www.independent.co.uk/news/uk/home-news/amazon-ban-tommy-robinson-website-koran-a8812111.html

33 Peter McLoughlin and Tommy Robinson, Mohammed's Koran: Why Muslims Kill

for Islam (Peter McLoughlin, 2017). http://www.pmclauth.com/muhammads-quran/summary-muhammads-quran

34 David Batty and agencies, 'White girls seen as "easy meat" by Pakistani rapists, says Jack Straw', *Guardian*, 8 January 2011. https://www.theguardian.com/world/2011/jan/08/jack-straw-white-girls-easy-meat. The book was first published in 2016 by the New English Review Press (which also published the right-wing *New English Review*), itself a subsidiary of the US anti-Muslim World Encounter Institute.

35 Reviewing the book (glowingly) for the right-wing *American Thinker*, Janet Levy said: 'McLoughlin explains how sex as rape has historically been used as a weapon of war to assert Islamic supremacy. Islamic doctrine encourages the rape and enslavement of non-Muslims, even with married infidel women as a legal and moral enterprise . . . Further, the required first and foremost allegiance to the Umma, or Muslim community, and the inbred obligation of enmity toward non-Muslims facilitates the pimping of non-Muslim girls and hinders any attempts at exposing its criminality and eventual prosecution. Sexual slavery has historically been used as a religious weapon to advance the domination of Islam.' Janet Levy, 'A Look Inside Britain's Muslim Sex Grooming Gang Scandal', American Thinker, 6 April 2016. https://www.americanthinker.com/articles/2016/04/a_look_inside_britains_muslim_sex_grooming_gang_scandal.html

36 Its terms were misquoted then and after by *The Times* and other media, so I shall quote his letter (to the two chairs of the All-Party Parliamentary Group on Child Sexual Exploitation) in some detail. The relevant section opened: 'Improving our understanding of the scale and nature of *all forms of child sexual exploitation and abuse* [my emphasis] is a priority for this government.' He referred to the work of the special Centre of Expertise (operated by the children's charity Barnardo's) which 'will help us to identify the similarities and differences between child sexual exploitation by organised networks and other types of offending which will support a more targeted response by the police and other agencies'. He continued: 'Offending involving grooming by organised networks is of particular concern. I am fully committed to taking the steps necessary to improving our understanding of how this particular form of offending can best be prevented. To this end, my officials have been working with investigating officers in relevant cases and with the National Crime Agency, to establish the particular characteristics and contexts associated with this type of offending. We are looking at what this data set can tell us about the characteristics of offenders, victims and the wider context of abuse, all of which have critical bearing on the effective targeting of prevention activity.'

37 Andrew Norfolk, 'Sajid Javid orders research into ethnic origin of sex grooming gangs', *The Times*, 26 July 2018. https://www.thetimes.co.uk/article/sajid-javid-orders-research-into-ethnic-origin-of-sex-grooming-gangs-v97lc5mdk

38 Isabella Fish, 'Javid orders probe into the ethnicity of sexual grooming gangs', *Daily Mail*, 26 July 2018. https://www.dailymail.co.uk/news/article-5993379/Javid-orders-probe-ethnicity-sexual-grooming-gangs.html

39 https://twitter.com/sajidjavid/status/1053336915850739714?lang=en

40 '"Wrong to ignore" ethnicity of grooming gangs – Javid', BBC News, 26 December 2018. https://www.bbc.co.uk/news/uk-46684638

41 Lizzie Dearden, 'Grooming gang review kept secret as Home Office claims releasing findings "not in public interest"', *Independent*, 21 February 2020. https://www.independent.co.uk/news/uk/home-news/grooming-gang-rotherham-review-home-office-findings-a9344896.html

42 Lizzie Dearden, 'Grooming gangs review: almost 50,000 people sign petition demanding release of government research into characteristics', *Independent*, 6 March 2020. https://www.independent.co.uk/news/uk/home-news/grooming-gangs-review-release-petition-home-office-rotherham-rochdale-a9380981.html

43 Arj Singh, 'Exclusive: Priti Patel orders officials to explain status of grooming gang review', *Huffington Post*, 6 February 2020. https://www.huffingtonpost.co.uk/entry/grooming-gang-review-priti-patel-home-office_uk_5e3b21b1c5b6bb0ffc0a55ee

44 Lizzie Dearden, 'Grooming gangs come from "diverse backgrounds", says Home Office as review finally published', *Independent*, 15 December 2020. https://www.independent.co.uk/news/uk/crime/grooming-gangs-review-race-religion-home-office-b1774161.html

45 Patrick O'Flynn, 'The Home Office's grooming report is an exercise in obfuscation', *The Spectator*, 15 December 2020. https://www.spectator.co.uk/article/the-home-office-s-grooming-report-is-an-exercise-in-obfuscation

46 Arj Singh, 'Child grooming gang members mainly white men, Home Office finds', *Huffington Post*, 15 December 2020. https://www.huffingtonpost.co.uk/entry/child-sexual-abuse-gangs-white-men_uk_5fd8fb35c5b6218b42ecd70f

47 See Ella Cockbain, 'Continuing to Racialise Child Sexual Abuse by Focusing on "Grooming Gangs" Won't Lead to Systemic Change', *Byline Times*, 2 February 2021. https://bylinetimes.com/2021/02/02/continuing-to-racialise-child-sexual-abuse/

48 'Rape – Quran's perspective and misconceptions', submission.org, https://submission.org/Rape.html.

49 Cited in *Peace, Love, Tolerance: Key Messages From Islam And Christianity On Protecting Children From Violence And Harmful Practices* (UNICEF, 2017). https://www.unicef.org/egypt/reports/peace-love-tolerance

50 See https://www.independent.co.uk/news/uk/home-news/muslims-extremism-women-far-right-tommy-robinson-rape-a9143671.html and https://www.theguardian.com/world/2019/mar/05/far-right-infiltrating-childrens-charities-with-anti-islam-agenda

51 Karika Karsna and Professor Liz Kelly, 'Measuring the scale and nature of child sexual abuse', Centre of expertise on child and sexual abuse. https://

www.csacentre.org.uk/our-research/the-scale-and-nature-of-csa/
measuring-the-scale-and-nature-of-csa/

52 See *Office for National Statistics, Abuse During Childhood: findings from the Crime Survey for England and Wales, year ending March 2016* (Newport: office for National Statistics, 2016); L. Radford, S. Corral, C. Bradley, H. Fisher, C. Bassett, N. Howat and S. Collishaw, *Child Abuse and Neglect in the UK Today* (London: NSPCC, 2011).

53 Stanley Cohen, *Folk Devils and Moral Panics*, 3rd edition, (Routledge, 2002), p. 1.

CHAPTER 20: 'I HAVE BEEN CALLED AN EXTREMIST, AN ISLAMIST, A TERRORIST – ALL THE ISTS'

1 'Nelson Mandela: CIA tip-off led to 1962 Durban arrest,' BBC News, 15 May 2016. https://www.bbc.co.uk/news/world-africa-36296551

2 Josh K. Elliott, 'Why anti-apartheid hero Nelson Mandela was once labelled a terrorist', Global News, 27 April 2019. https://globalnews.ca/news/5201623/nelson-mandela-apartheid-terrorist-south-africa/; Martin Plaut, 'Did Margaret Thatcher really call Nelson Mandela a terrorist?', *New Statesman*, 29 August 2018. https://www.newstatesman.com/politics/2018/08/did-margaret-thatcher-really-call-nelson-mandela-terrorist

3 'The CIA and Chile: Anatomy of an Assassination', National Security Archive. https://nsarchive.gwu.edu/briefing-book/chile/2020-10-22/cia-chile-anatomy-assassination

4 Seymour M. Hersh, 'CIA is linked to strikes in Chile that beset Allende', *New York Times*, 20 September 1974. https://www.nytimes.com/1974/09/20/archives/cia-is-linked-to-strikes-in-chile-that-beset-allende-intelligence.html

5 'Chilean president Salvador Allende dies in coup', history.com. https://www.history.com/this-day-in-history/allende-dies-in-coup

6 'Chilean president Salvador Allende committed suicide, autopsy confirms,' *Guardian*, 20 July 2011. https://www.theguardian.com/world/2011/jul/20/salvador-allende-committed-suicide-autopsy

7 I am indebted to Jon Lee Anderson's arresting *New Yorker* article, 'Egypt's Dirty War?', for a comparison between the Chilean military coup and the fall of President Morsi. https://www.newyorker.com/news/daily-comment/egypts-dirty-war

8 Islam Abdel-Rahman, 'The refutation of the Djerejian doctrine', Open Democracy, 12 November 2014. https://www.opendemocracy.net/en/north-africa-west-asia/refutation-of-djerejian-doctrine/; for a direct citation of the speech, see Edward P. Djerijian, 'The US and the Middle East in a changing world', US Department of State Dispatch, vol 3, no. 23, 8 June 1992.

9 The EU delegation judged 'there was nothing which would indicate that the final result was not the outcome chosen by the voters'. 'MEPs oversee historic

Palestinian election', European Parliament, 30 January 2006. https://www.europarl.europa.eu/sides/getDoc.do?type=IM-PRESS&reference=20060130STO04803&language=EN

10 James M. Lindsay, 'Hello (Ahlan), Abdul Fattah al-Sisi: President of Egypt', Council on Foreign Relations, 9 June 2014. https://www.cfr.org/blog/hello-ahlan-abdul-fattah-al-sisi-president-egypt

11 'Egypt Army "restoring democracy", says John Kerry', BBC News, 1 August 2013. https://www.bbc.co.uk/news/world-middle-east-23543744

12 'Egypt's ousted president Mohammed Morsi dies during trial', BBC News, 17 June 2019. https://www.bbc.com/news/world-middle-east-4866894; https://www.middleeasteye.net/news/audio-forensics-experts-authenticate-sisis-voice-leaked-tapes

13 David Butter, 'Egypt and the Gulf: Allies and Rivals', Chatham House, 20 April 2020, pp. 5-7. https://www.chathamhouse.org/2020/04/egypt-and-gulf/sisis-debt-his-gulf-arab-backers

14 A useful summary of international reaction can be found here: 'U.S. condemns killings of Egypt protesters, Turkey wants U.N. action', Reuters, 14 August 2013. https://www.reuters.com/article/us-egypt-protests-reaction-idUSBRE97D11920130814

    Britain, as well as other European nations, restricted exports of equipment and arms, although in the case of the UK, this was short-term. https://www.aljazeera.com/news/2013/8/21/eu-restricts-arms-sales-to-egypt

15 'Egypt: Rab'a killings likely crimes against humanity', Human Rights Watch, 12 August 2014. https://www.hrw.org/news/2014/08/12/egypt-rab-killings-likely-crimes-against-humanity; Patrick Kingsley, 'Egypt massacre was premeditated, says Human Rights Watch', Guardian, August 12, 2014. https://www.theguardian.com/world/2014/aug/12/egypt-massacre-rabaa-intentional-human-rights-watch

16 Joint press conference with Prime Minister Cameron and President Sisi, 5 November 2015. https://www.gov.uk/government/speeches/joint-press-conference-david-cameron-and-president-sisi

17 Army spokesman Ahmed Ali is quoted in Anderson op. cit.

18 See Peter Bergen's verdict on the aftermath of the Egyptian coup: 'Now Zawahiri gets to say "I told you so." Earlier this month Zawahiri posted a 15-minute recording on militant websites. In the recording Zawahiri explained that the military coup that deposed Egypt's elected president, Muslim Brotherhood leader Mohamed Morsy, proved that democracy had failed.'" Peter Bergen, 'Al Qaeda leader's "I told you so" on Egypt', CNN, 15 August 2013. https://edition.cnn.com/2013/08/15/opinion/bergen-zawahiri-egypt/index.html

    The reflections of torture victim Mohamad Soltan on the coup are harrowing on the consequences for democracy: 'In Egypt the regime has polarised the country and suffocated all avenues of peaceful expression and dissent through politics, civil society or media, leaving many dead, disappeared, imprisoned, hiding or exiled. The anti-protest and anti-terrorism laws have left no space for any meaningful dialogue in Egypt, let alone dissent.'

'This is not only true for the demonised Islamist camp: the crackdown has reached every voice of opposition across the ideological and political spectrum. However, the current environment is fertile ground for radicalisation, as many disenfranchised young Egyptians find themselves questioning the ideals of freedom and democracy that they once cherished when they see the free world silent in the face of Sisi's repression.' Mohammed Soltan, 'I got 643 days of torture. My tormentor get's Cameron's red carpet', Guardian, 31 October 2015. https://www.theguardian.com/commentisfree/2015/oct/31/643-days-torture-cameron-general-sisi-egyptian-radicalisation?CMP=twt_gu

Moreover, Gehad El Haddad provides an important eyewitness accounts of prison life in Egypt and the debates that are taking place between Daesh and the democratic current. 'In the cases where people did leave the Muslim Brotherhood to embrace violence, they did so specifically because they found no path in our philosophy, vision of society or movement for such extremism. A great many of these extremists – if not all – consider us apostates and politically naïve. This is not an issue as simple as distaste for our political naïveté, but is in fact recognition that our philosophy renders their extremist ideology irrelevant.' Gehad El-Haddad, 'Opinion: I Am a Member of the Muslim Brotherhood, Not a Terrorist', *New York Times*, 22 February 2017. https://www.nytimes.com/2017/02/22/opinion/i-am-a-member-of-the-muslim-brotherhood-not-a-terrorist.html

19 Abu Musab al-Zarqawi, 'Zarqawi and other Islamists to the Iraqi People: Elections and Democracy are Heresy', Middle East Media Research Institute, Institutional Scholarship. 23 January 2005. https://scholarship.tricolib.brynmawr.edu/handle/10066/4808

20 Fawaz A. Gerges, *The Rise and Fall of al-Qaeda* (Oxford University Press, 2011), p. 5.

21 https://www.theguardian.com/news/2000/apr/07/guardianobituaries1 suggests 'Bourguiba always saw the French as his ultimate protectors' https://uca.edu/politicalscience/dadm-project/middle-eastnorth-africapersian-gulf-region/tunisia-1956-present/ has a summary of events. It states (after an attack by Tunisian Resistance in 1980) that 'The French government provided military assistance . . . beginning on January 28 1980, and deployed eight warships.. on January 30, 1980'.

22 'Amnesty International Report', Amnesty, 1 January 1978, pp. 142-3: https://www.amnesty.org/en/documents/pol10/001/1978/en/ See also: Eqbal Ahmad and Stuart Schaar, 'Human Rights in Morocco and Tunisia: A Critique of State Department Findings', Middle East Research and Information Project (MERIP), No. 67 (May, 1978), pp. 15-17; 'The Final Comprehensive Report: Executive Summary', Truth and Dignity Commission, May 2019, pp. 159-164.

23   Dominic Tierney, 'The Twenty Years' War', *The Atlantic*, 23 August 2016.
     https://www.theatlantic.com/international/archive/2016/08/twenty-years-
     war/496736/

24   Richard Kerbaj and Dominic Kennedy, 'Terrorism advisor to Met is on wanted
     list', *The Times*, 15 December 2008. https://www.thetimes.co.uk/article/
     terrorism-adviser-to-met-is-on-wanted-list-gvxt658mg8x

25   John Plunkett, 'PCC investigates Melanie Phillips' Spectator blog', *Guardian*, 18
     March 2011. https://www.theguardian.com/media/2011/mar/18/pcc-melanie-
     phillips-spectator-blog; Ted Jeory, 'Boris's terror link', *Sunday Express*, 25 October
     2009. https://www.express.co.uk/news/uk/136063/Boris-s-terror-link

26   Kerbaj and Kennedy, *op. cit.*

27   Chris Irvine, 'Police Adviser Should Be Sacked Over Terror Links, Says
     Baroness Neville-Jones', the *Telegraph*, 16 December 2008. https://www.
     telegraph.co.uk/news/uknews/law-and-order/3779430/Police-adviser-
     should-be-sacked-over-terror-links-says-Baroness-Neville-Jones.html

28   There is now overwhelming evidence that Interpol's channels have assisted
     secret police from some of the world's most vicious regimes as they target and
     then persecute internal dissidents. See Peter Oborne, 'Is Interpol fighting for
     truth and justice, or helping the villians?', *Daily Telegraph*, 22 May 2013. https:/
     /www.telegraph.co.uk/news/uknews/law-and-order/10073483/Is-Interpol-
     fighting-for-truth-and-justice-or-helping-the-villains.html?fb

29   One well-documented example is the UAE's lobbying campaign which sought
     to shape UK government policy, both towards British Muslims and towards UK
     and US foreign policy in the Middle East. According to journalists Alex
     Delmar-Morgan and David Miller, the then Tory prime minister David
     Cameron appears to have been vulnerable to this lobbying. Delmar-Morgan and
     Miller obtained emails suggesting the UAE devoted substantial effort to
     influencing MPs and journalists. They claimed that Quiller Consultants, a
     lobbying company, was asked to draw up names of Emirati dissidents in London
     who had claimed asylum, as well as identify BBC journalists who were deemed
     unsympathetic to the UAE for their alleged links to the Muslim Brotherhood.
     An intensive lobbying campaign was directed at journalists. Alex Delmar-
     Morgan and David Miller, 'The UAE Lobby: Subverting British democracy?',
     School for Policy Studies, University of Bristol. https://research-information.
     bris.ac.uk/en/publications/the-uae-lobby-subverting-british-democracy

30   Bruce Hoffman, *Inside Terrorism* (Columbia University Press, 1998). https://
     archive.nytimes.com/www.nytimes.com/books/first/h/hoffman-terrorism.
     html?_r=2

31   George W. Bush's post-9/11 address to a joint session of Congress and the
     American people, 20 September 2001. https://www.theguardian.com/world/
     2001/sep/21/september11.usa13; Tony Blair speech addressing the terror
     threat to the UK, 5 March 2004. http://news.bbc.co.uk/1/hi/uk_politics/
     3536131.stm

32 'You Never Die Twice: Multiple Kills in the US Drone Program', Reprieve, 2014. https://reprieve.org/wp-content/uploads/sites/2/2020/07/Report_YouNeverDieTwice_2014.pdf

33 'Get the Data: Drone Wars', Bureau of Investigative Journalism. http://www.thebureauinvestigates.com/category/projects/drones/drones-graphs/

34 Michael Safi and Julian Borger, 'Khashoggi fiancée: Saudi crown prince must be "punished without delay"', *Guardian*, 1 March 2021. https://www.theguardian.com/world/2021/mar/01/khashoggi-fiancee-saudi-crown-prince-must-be-punished-without-delay

35 The FBI defines international terrorism as 'violent, criminal acts committed by individuals and/or groups who are inspired by, or associated with, designated foreign terrorist organisations or nations (state-sponsored)'. https://www.fbi.gov/investigate/terrorism. Four countries at the time of writing (December 2021) were designated by the US as 'state sponsors of terrorism': Cuba, Iran, North Korea and Syria: https://www.state.gov/state-sponsors-of-terrorism/

36 David Anderson Q.C. 'Shielding the Compass: How to Fight Terrorism Without Defeating the Law', 15 June 2003, Available at SSRN: https://ssrn.com/abstract=2292950

37 Anthony Richards, 'Characterising the UK Terrorist Threat', *Journal of Terrorism Research*, vol. 3 (1), 2012, pp. 17–26. 'https://repository.uel.ac.uk/download/40eac52bfdafb8c936df22bdd7874b696b95f6911a1dc21dfc2ca1c702da2302/1412330/Characterising per cent2520the per cent2520UK per cent2520Terrorist per cent2520Threat.pdf

CHAPTER 21: HUNTINGTON'S BLOODY BORDERS

1 Foreign correspondents sometimes knew better. Hugh Pope, in his book *Dining With Al-Qaeda: Three Decades of Exploring the Many Worlds of the Middle East* (Thomas Dunne Books, 2010), describes how the opinion section at the *Wall Street Journal* ignored his far better-informed opinions in the run-up to the Iraq invasion.

2 See this contemporary *New York Times* report: 'Mr. Hilal's claim that he has no control over any militia does not bear scrutiny, said Alex de Waal, an Africa scholar who studies Sudan. "He is at the center of all of this," Mr. de Waal said. In letters to government officials and other tribal leaders, Mr. Hilal has repeatedly said his fighters are engaged in a jihad, or holy war, and will not disarm even if the government demands it. "We will not retreat," he wrote in one such letter in 2004 to the leaders in Khartoum. "We continue on the road of jihad." Trying to disarm his men, he wrote, would be "cowardly", and impossible to enforce.' Lydia Polgreen, 'Over tea, sheikh denies stirring Darfur's torment', *New York Times*, 12 June 2006. https://www.nytimes.com/2006/06/12/world/africa/12darfur.html

3   Suzanne Goldenberg, 'Bush threatened to bomb Pakistan, says Musharraf', *Guardian*, 22 September 2006. https://www.theguardian.com/world/2006/sep/22/pakistan.usa

4   Christopher Finnigan, 'Pakistan: suicide bombing's deadliest victim?' LSE blog, 27 March 2019. https://blogs.lse.ac.uk/southasia/2019/03/27/pakistan-suicide-bombings-deadliest-victim/

5   See Akbar Ahmed, *The Thistle and the Drone: How America's War on Terror Became a Global War on Tribal Islam* (Brookings Institution Press, 2013). Ahmed was a political agent in the tribal agency of South Waziristan, which lay at the epicentre of George Bush and Tony Blair's 'war on terror'. Now a social anthropologist, he says that 'if there is a clash it is not between civilisations based on religion: rather, it is between central governments and the tribal communities on the periphery'. He argues that these tribes have always flourished outside state systems, with their own language, territory and traditions. To illustrate the point, he quotes the Pashtun leader Wali Khan: 'I have been a Pashtun for 6,000 years, a Muslim for 1,300 years, and a Pakistani for twenty-five.' These tribes, Akbar Ahmed points out, are the most ancient political structures in the world. 'No ancient society – the Greek city states, the Roman Empire, the Indian kingdoms – survives today, with one exception: tribes that were organised along the segmentary lineage system.'

6   International Religious Freedom Reports, US Department of State. https://www.state.gov/international-religious-freedom-reports/

7   This was set out clearly by Joe Biden when serving as vice president in 2014. He told Harvard University's Kennedy School of Government in a question-and-answer session that 'our allies in the region were our largest problem in Syria. The Turks were great friends, and I have a great relationship with Erdogan, [who] I just spent a lot of time with, [and] the Saudis, the Emirates, etcetera.

'What were they doing? They were so determined to take down Assad, and essentially have a proxy Sunni-Shia war. What did they do? They poured hundreds of millions of dollars and tens of tons of weapons into anyone who would fight against Assad – except that the people who were being supplied, [they] were al-Nusra, and al-Qaeda, and the extremist elements of jihadis who were coming from other parts of the world.

'Now, you think I'm exaggerating? Take a look. Where did all of this go? So now that's happening, all of a sudden, everybody is awakened because this outfit called ISIL, which was al-Qaeda in Iraq, when they were essentially thrown out of Iraq, found open space and territory in [eastern] Syria, [and they] work with al-Nusra, who we declared a terrorist group early on. And we could not convince our colleagues to stop supplying them.' Adam Taylor, 'Behind Biden's gaffe lie real concerns about allies' role in rise of Islamic State', *Washington Post*, 6 October 2014. https://www.washingtonpost.com/news/worldviews/wp/2014/10/06/

behind-bidens-gaffe-some-legitimate-concerns-about-americas-middle-east-allies/. See also my video report from Maaloula for the *Daily Telegraph*: https://www.youtube.com/watch?v=YAwLUB_BPuI; for my BBC Radio 4 report on the unspoken alliance between the UK and al-Qaeda, listen here: https://www.bbc.co.uk/programmes/b06s0qy9

8   The group's full name is Harakat Ahrar al-Sham al-Islamiyya, which translates as Islamic Movement of the Free Men of the Levant.

9   Rod Liddle, 'When Theresa May needs to save herself and scrap cap on public sector pay – there really is a magic money tree', *Sun*, 13 September 2017.

10 For a helpful discussion of the role of violent resistance and the Arakan Rohingya Salvation Army, see Jonathan Head, 'Rohingya crisis: Finding out the truth about Arsa militants', BBC News, 11 October 2017. https://www.bbc.co.uk/news/world-asia-41521268. See also Simon Lewis, 'Myanmar sees insurgents behind Rohingya killings in northwest', Reuters, 20 July 2017. https://www.reuters.com/article/us-myanmar-rohingya-attackers-idUSKBN1A515L

11 'Myanmar army investigating mass grave in Rakhine', mizzima.com, 20 December 2017. https://www.mizzima.com/news-domestic/myanmar-army-investigating-mass-grave-rakhine

CONCLUSION: THE FATE OF ABRAHAM

1   Reuters, 'Srebrenica elects as mayor Serb who denies massacre was genocide', *Guardian*, 17 October 2016. https://www.theguardian.com/world/2016/oct/17/srebrenica-elects-mladen-grujicic-mayor-serb-denies-massacre-genocide

2   'Saudi-led Islamic military alliance: counterterrorism or counter Iran?', *Deutsche Welle*, 26 November 2017. https://www.dw.com/en/saudi-led-islamic-military-alliance-counterterrorism-or-counter-iran/a-41538781

3   Cindy Wooden, 'Pope Francis' Three Tips For Journalists Today', *America*, 15 November 2001. https://www.americamagazine.org/politics-society/2021/11/15/pope-francis-journalists-241836

4   Quran, 49:6. Translation by Professor Abdel Haleem.

FURTHER READING

In *The Fate of Abraham* we have ranged widely across history, across the globe, and across many topics. There are conversations of immense importance to be had on these themes, and there is a wealth of literature exploring them. While not exclusive, the books and articles discussed below will give you a starting point should you wish to read further in this subject.

We begin with a politician. Michael Gove has exercised more influence on British government policy towards Muslims than any other politician. This makes his *Celsius 7/7* (Weidenfeld & Nicolson, 2006) an essential read. William Dalrymple exposed many of Gove's errors of fact and interpretation in a *Sunday Times* review that has since been taken down, but can still be found on Evernote online.

Melanie Phillips' *Londonistan: How Britain is Creating a Terror State Within* (Encounter Books, 2007) is better researched than Gove's book, and her polemic anticipates today's controversy over 'Londongrad'. Though the two authors have different perspectives, her book can be read alongside Mark Curtis' *Secret Affairs: Britain's Collusion with Radical Islam* (Serpent's Tail, 2010), an arresting study of British government collaboration with Muslim terror groups overseas, most strikingly al-Qaeda, overseas.

Douglas Murray's *The Strange Death of Europe: Immigration, Identity, Islam* (Bloomsbury, 2017) domesticates Renaud Camus' 'Great Replacement' theory, as set out in his influential *Le*

Grand Remplacement (Chez l'auteur, 2011). See also Murray's *Neoconservativism: Why We Need It* (Encounter Books, 2006) and *Islamophilia: A Very Metropolitan Malady* (emBooks, 2013). Roger Scruton's *Where We Are: The State of Britain Now* (Bloomsbury, 2017), an assessment of British identity post-Brexit, argues that use of the term 'Islamophobia' is an attempt to 'silence those who champion our inheritance of freedom and law against its extremist opponents'.

Several pamphlets produced by Policy Exchange in the noughties are crucial to an understanding of official policy towards Muslims. Munira Mirza's *Living Apart Together: British Muslims and the Paradox of Multiculturalism* (Policy Exchange, 2007) foreshadowed government policy during her term as head of policy in Downing Street as part of the Johnson government. Shiraz Maher and Martyn Frampton's *Choosing Our Friends Wisely* (Policy Exchange, 2009) helped to create today's security environment for British Muslims. It can be seen as one of the most influential public policy pamphlets this century.

Nick Cohen's compellingly written *What's Left?* (Fourth Estate, 2007) illuminates one of the most paradoxical aspects of public discourse around Muslims, namely the shared analysis between the far right and the mainstream left. Majid Nawaz' *Radical* (W. H. Allen, 2012) and Ed Hussein's *The Islamist* (Penguin, 2007) are lively examples of conversion literature which articulate Whitehall thinking.

For an alternative perspective Arun Kundnan's *The Muslims are Coming!: Islamophobia, Extremism, and the Domestic War on Terror* (Verso, 2014) is a powerful analysis of the development of domestic counter-terrorism measures after 9/11 in both Britain and America. Maha Hilal's *Innocent Until Proven Muslim* (Broadleaf Books, 2022) was published as this book went to press.

For a rebuttal of Bernard Lewis and Samuel Huntington's 'Clash of Civilisations' thesis, see Mahmood Mamdani's *Good Muslim, Bad Muslim: America, The Cold War and the Roots of Terror*

(Three Leaves Press, 2005). See also 'The People's Review of Prevent' (2022) by Layla Aitlhadj and John Holmwood for a recent incisive demonstration of Prevent's ineffectiveness, disproportionality and discriminatory targeting of Muslims. Rob Faure Walker's *The Emergence of Extremism* (Bloomsbury, 2021) dissects the language of counter-extremism. *Leaderless Jihad* (University of Pennsylvania Press, 2008) by former CIA analyst Mark Sagemen challenges official wisdom about terrorists.

Sayeeda Warsi, Britain's first female Muslim cabinet minister, provides an insider's insight into recent government attitudes towards Islam in *The Enemy Within: A Tale of Muslim Britain* (Penguin, 2017), along with her compelling personal story. Her book should be read alongside Uday Singh Mehta's portrait of Edmund Burke in his *Liberalism and Empire* (University of Chicago Press, 1999), which suggests the founding philosopher of British Conservatism would have been horrified by the coercive liberalism of today's Conservative Party.

John Holmwood and Therese O'Toole's *Countering Extremism in British Schools? The Truth about the Birmingham Trojan Horse Affair* (Policy Press, 2018) is the definitive study into the Trojan Horse affair, rigorously examining what occurred in the schools involved, and showing how a fake event was used to justify the expansion of a broad and intrusive counter-extremism agenda. Though no critic has been able to point to any errors, Holmwood and O'Toole's book was not reviewed in mainstream media, and they and their work have been cut out of media discourse, leaving space for less well-informed voices to make arguments without challenge. In early 2022, the *New York Times* and Serial Productions produced an eight-part investigative podcast on the Trojan Horse affair (https://www. nytimes.com/interactive/2022/podcasts/trojan-horse-affair. html). It is a far deeper investigation than anything previously undertaken, and drew a number of hostile as well as favourable reactions. The response by British humanists, alleging unfair reporting, can be found here: https://humanists.uk/2022/02/23/humanists-uk-comment-on-trojan-horse-affair-pod.

K. A. Beydoun's *American Islamophobia: Understanding the Roots and Rise of Fear* (University of California, 2018) charts United States' hostility to Islam from the antebellum South to the Trump administration. J. L. Esposito, Professor of Religion, International Affairs, and Islamic Studies at Georgetown University, has challenged the mainstream narrative with a series of learned works, among them *The Future Of Islam* (Oxford University Press, 2010). In *The Islamophobia Industry* (Pluto Press 2012) Nathan Lean follows the money trail. C. J. Werleman's *The New Atheist Threat* (Dangerous Little Books, 2015) intriguingly portrays the muscular atheism championed by Sam Harris and the late Christopher Hitchens as a secular religious cult. In this way he follows Emile Durkheim, who argued that secularism is a form of civic religion and can itself become a version of fundamentalism.

For more on the Moro Muslim minority in the Philippines see Federico V. Magdalena, 'Moro-American Relations in the Philippines', *Philippine Studies*, Vol. 44, No. 3 (1996): 427–438; 'Dabao-kuo and the Winning of Mindanao', *The Mindanao Forum*, Vol. XXII, No. 1 (2009): 1–20; see also J. R. Arnold, *The Moro War* (Bloomsbury 2011). See also Fred Magdalena, *The Battle of Bayang and other essays on Moroland*, Mindanao State University; Marawi City, Mindanao, 2002, 68 p; 22 cm.

On US foreign policy M. B. Oren, *Power, Faith And Fantasy: America in the Middle East, 1776 to the present* (Norton, 2007), is a mighty work as is K. GhaneaBassiri, *A History of Islam in America: from the New World to the New World Order* (Cambridge University Press, 2010).

For the Barbary Wars see D. P. Smethurst, *Tripoli: The United States' First War On Terror* (Mass Market Paperback, 2006) and Adrian Tinniswood, *Pirates of Barbary* (Vintage, 2010). For an interpretation of the Barbary Wars as America's first war against Islamic terror see Joshua London's *Victory in Tripoli: How America's*

War with the Barbary Pirates Established the U.S. Navy and Shaped a Nation (John Wiley & Sons, 2005).

K. Evanzz, *The Messenger: The Rise And Fall Of Elijah Muhammad* (Vintage, 2001), is valuable for an understanding of the Nation of Islam, as is Muhammad Fard, *The Supreme Wisdom, The Final Call* (1993). The autobiography of Malcolm X, supremely well ghosted by Alex Haley, is a great work of literature. For the physical and moral horror of Guantanamo Bay see former inmate Moazzem Begg's *Enemy Combatant* (Free Press, 2006). Few have done more for Guantanamo inmates than human rights lawyer Clive Stafford-Smith, whose *The Eight O'Clock Ferry to the Windward Side: Fighting the Lawless World of Guantanamo Bay* (Nation, 2007), is a classic.

The novels of G. H. Henty, which I devoured at prep school, remain readable and give a vivid insight into the British imperial mentality. A good start might be *With Clive in India* (Blackie and Son, 1884). More than any other writer, Thomas Babington Macaulay created the British liberal imperial myth. His *Critical and Historical Essays* are works of genius which nourished the imagination of more than a century of English schoolchildren. They are now out of print, and would perhaps be unpublishable today. The Everyman edition (1961) is best. For a life of Macaulay, including his time with the East India Company, read John Clive, *Macaulay: The Shaping of the Historian* (Vintage, 1973). *Sikunder Burnes: Master of the Great Game* (Birlinn Ltd, 2017) by the renegade British diplomat Craig Murray is a fine description of the Great Game, and a reminder of British treachery. Anyone who has not read Kipling's *Kim* on the same subject should go and do so at once. The same applies to Peter Hopkirk's *The Great Game: On Secret Service in High Asia* (John Murray, 1990).

Pankaj Mishra's unputdownable *From the Ruins of Empire* (Allen Lane, 2012) places pan-Islamic resistance movements against the British empire alongside other Asian resistance movements. His portrait of the Muslim public intellectual, journalist and man of mystery Jamal al-Din al-Afghani is unforgettable. On a similar subject see Nikki R. Keddie's *An Islamic Response to Imperialism* (Berkley, 1966) and his *Sayyid Jamal al-Din 'al-Afghani': A Political Biography* (Berkley, 1972).

Like Winston Churchill and many other Britons, Imran Khan's *Pakistan* (Transworld, 2011) romanticises the Pashtun tribespeople of the North West Frontier. He also has much to say about Islamophobia. Khan's book should be read alongside Akbar Ahmed's *The Thistle and the Drone: How America's War on Terror Became a Global War on Tribal Islam* (Harper Collins India 2013). The author, a former political agent in South Waziristan Agency in Pakistan, argues from deep personal experience and academic study that George W. Bush's 'War on Terror' quickly mutated into a war on tribal peoples, waged by the United States with the cooperation of local governments.

James Barr's *A Line in the Sand* (Simon & Schuster, 2011) is a superbly researched history of the Anglo/French carve up of the Middle East after the First World War. I have relied on Warren Dockter's masterly *Churchill and the Islamic World* (IB Tauris, 2015).

Zachary Karabell's *People of the Book* (John Murray, 2007) is a haunting study of the boundless connections between the three Abrahamic religions. John V. Tolan's *Faces of Muhammed: Western Perceptions of the Prophet of Islam from the Middle Ages to Today* (Princeton, 2019) traces the continuity between mediaeval anti-Muslim diatribes and contemporary polemic. Tarif Khalidi's *The Muslim Jesus: Sayings and Stories in Islamic Literature* (Harvard University Press 2001) is a collection of representations of Jesus in Islamic literature. This rich and deep work demonstrates the close links which bind Christianity and Islam. Karen Armstrong has written a series of masterpieces which explore the same theme including *The Bible* (Atlantic Books, 2007). Her *Islam: A Short History* (Weidenfeld & Nicolson, 2000) and *Muhammad: A Biography of the Prophet* (HarperCollins, 1992) are ideal introductions to the subject and can be read alongside her *St Paul: The Misunderstood Apostle* (Atlantic Books, 2015) and her *Jerusalem: One*

City, Three Faiths (Knopf, 1996). Maxime Rodinson's *Muhammad* (Club Francois de Livre, 1961 and Penguin,1971) is another fine biography of the Prophet (for Tariq Ali's fine recent essay on Robinson see: https://www.lrb.co.uk/the-paper/v43/n12/tariq-ali/winged-words). Fitzroy Morrissey's *A Short History of Islamic Thought* (Head of Zeus, 2021) provides an elegant field guide to Islam's intellectual and spiritual traditions. Martin Lings, *Muhammad: His Life Based on the Earliest Sources* (Allen & Unwin, 1983), is based on very early Arab sources and as a result gains freshness and immediacy. J. H. Hexter's *The Judaeo-Christian Tradition* (Yale University Press, 1966) is a model short history.

For Islam and violence read Muhammad Haniff Hassan's *Civil Disobedience and Islam: A Contemporary Debate (*Palgrave Macmillan, 2017). Karen Armstrong's *Fields of Blood: Religion and the History of Violence* (Bodley Head, 2014) is a model of compassion and erudition. Fawaz Gerges' *The Rise and Fall of Al-Qaeda* (Oxford University Press, 2011) is a text of deep learning and good sense. His *Making the Arab World: Nasser, Qutb, and the Clash That Shaped the Middle East* is a dazzling investigation into the two political traditions which shaped the modern Middle East. I found *Jihad, Radicalism and the New Atheism* by Mohammad Hassan Khalil (Cambridge University Press, 2017) enlightening and helpful.

For a readable and fair-minded corrective on contemporary British myths about Islam I suggest Tauseef Khan's *The Muslim Problem: Why We're Wrong About Islam and Why it Matters* (Atlantic Books, 2021). Those in search of serious, well-informed analysis of Islamic thought should read, and then re-read, Jonathan A. C. Brown's *Misquoting Muhammad: The Challenge and Choices of Interpreting the Prophet's Legacy (*One World, 2014*)*. Brown's *Slavery and Islam* (One World, 2020) handles a complex subject with skill and understanding. *Useful Enemies* (Oxford University Press, 2019) by Noel Malcolm, former political correspondent of the *Spectator*, explores how prejudice shaped Western discourse about the Ottoman Empire in early modern Europe.

On Britain's historical engagement with Islam, Jerry Brotton's *This Orient Isle: Elizabethan England and the Islamic World* (2016) documents the often-amicable relations between Elizabethan England and the Muslim world. I learnt a great deal from between Christopher de Bellaigue's *The Islamic Enlightenment: the Modern Struggle Between Faith and Reason* (Bodley Head, 2017). My narrative often follows Andrew Wheatcroft's glorious *Infidels: A History of the Conflcit Between Christianity and Islam* (Penguin, 2003). William Dalrymple's *The Company Quartet* (Bloomsbury, 2021) tells the story of the British East India Company's takeover of India, with a particular focus on British interactions with Indo-Islamic culture. See also a recent translation of Yusuf Samih Asmay's *Islam in Victorian Liverpool: An Ottoman Account of Britain's First Mosque Community* (Claritas Books, 2021) for an insight into the early Muslim presence in Britain. I have drawn on Hamayun Ansari's *The Infidel Within* (Hurst & Co., 2004), an authoritative and at times very affecting study of the arrival, settlement and establishment of British Muslims. *They* by Sarfraz Manzoor (Wildfire, 2021) is an honest and hopeful account of being brought up in a Pakistani Muslim family in Luton.

I have also relied on Martin Pugh's ambitious, wise, easy-to-read *Britain and Islam: A History from 622 to the Present Day* (Yale University Press, 2019). Ian Almond exposes many contemporary misunderstandings about the relation between Islamic and Western powers in his *Two Faiths, One Banner: When Muslims marched with Christians across Europe's battlegrounds* (Harvard University Press, 2009). Innes Bowen's *Medina in Birmingham Najav in Brent* (Hurst and Co., 2014) is based on solid research into British Muslim communities.

There is an urgent need for a book detailing the role of media in spreading lies and fabrications about Islam and Muslims. This is even more of a problem today than when Edward Said drew attention to it forty years ago in *Covering Islam: How the Media and the Experts Determine How we see the Rest of the World* (Vintage, 1981).

Two recent works point the way to a better public discourse. Nesrine Malik touches on this ugly subject in her groundbreaking *We Need New Stories: Challenging the Toxic Myths Behind our Age of Discontent* (Weidenfeld & Nicolson, 2020), but does not go into detail when it comes to Islam, though her regular *Guardian* column repays close reading. Jon Yates' *Fractured: Why our societies are coming apart and how we put them back together* (HarperNorth, 2021) attempts to describe a route to a more generous public conversation, not just with Muslims.

Detailed studies of actual reporting are rare. *Unmasked: Andrew Norfolk, The Times Newspaper and Anti-Muslim Reporting – A Case To Answer* (Unmasked Books, 2019), by Brian Cathcart and Paddy French, forensically unpicks three series of articles relating to Muslims by the chief investigative reporter of *The Times*, Andrew Norfolk. The writers concluded that Norfolk's central allegations were unfounded, that he failed to observe ethical standards of reporting and that the articles consistently and unjustifiably presented Muslims as a threat. In an editorial on 27 June 2019 *The Times* called this an ideologically motivated smear. The authors published a follow-up pamphlet (*The Revealing Response To The Unmasked Report*) calling *The Times*' response 'little more than dishonest bluster'. *The Times* leader can be read here: https://www.thetimes.co.uk/article/the-times-view-on-media-campaigners-and-andrew-norfolk-press-gang-7fd352sds. See also Cathcart and French on the grooming gang narrative: https://bylinetimes.com/2020/12/17/home-office-study-trashes-the-times-muslim-grooming-gangs-narrative/

Ella Cockbain and Waqas Tufail have done remarkable work exposing the fallacies in reporting of Muslim grooming gangs in their article 'Failing victims, fuelling hate: challenging the harms of the "Muslim grooming gangs" narrative', which can be found online: https://journals.sagepub.com/doi/abs/10.1177/0306396819895727

For several years Miqdaad Versi of the Muslim Council of Britain has earned the enmity of Fleet Street editors by repeatedly expos-ing media falsehoods on Islam. In November 2021 former *Times* reporter Faisal Hanif produced his compendious *British Media's Coverage of Muslims and Islam (2018–2020)*. Stretching over 318 pages, Hanif's book is an indispensable companion for any analy-sis of British press coverage of Islam or Muslims. Fourteen years ago the television producer James Jones and I wrote a pamphlet, 'Muslims Under Siege' (Open Democracy, 2008), exposing the poisonous press reporting of Muslims, to accompany a Channel 4 documentary *It Shouldn't Happen to a Muslim* (2008). Sadly, it is still relevant today. Simon Walters' *The Borisaurus* (Biteback, 2020) contains many example of derisive language used by the British prime minister against Muslims (and other minorities).

On France's troubled relationship with its Muslim citizens, see *Republic of Islamophobia* (Hurst & Co., 2018) by James Wolfreys. Juan Cole's *Napoleon's Egypt: Invading the Middle East* (Palgrave Macmillan, 2007) is an excellent account of the first major attempt to incorporate a large Middle Eastern state into a Western empire, in the name of liberty and tolerance. Everything by Olivier Roy is worth reading. The English language reader might start with *Secularism Confronts Islam* (Columbia University Press, 2007), Roy's meditation on the hard to translate French concept of *laïceté*. For an alternative point of view read Roy's antagonist Gilles Keppel, whose latest work is *Away from Chaos: The Middle East and the Challenge to the West* (Columbia University Press, 2020). Despite its problematic title there is value to be had in Andrew Hussey's *The French Intifada: The Long War Between France and its Arabs* (Granta, 2014).

For a vivid overview of the conquest of Algeria see Jennifer Sessions, *By Sword and Plow: France and the Conquest of Algeria* (Cornell University Press, 2011). David Prochaska, *Making Algeria French: Colonialism in Bône, 1870–1920* (Cambridge University Press, 1990) explores settler society in one Algerian city. Though outdated, Alistair Horne, *A Savage War of Peace: Algeria, 1954–62*

(London, 1977) remains an outstanding account of the Algerian War of Independence.

On India and Islam, Christophe Jaffrelot's *Modi's India: Hindu Nationalism and the Rise of Ethnic Democracy* (Princeton University Press, 2021) provides a valuable analysis of the rise of Hindu nationalism and its consequences, while Rana Ayyub's extraordinary investigation, *Gujarat Files: Anatomy of a Cover Up* (CreateSpace, 2016), exposes governmental complicity in the anti-Muslim riots of 2002. The novelist Arundhati Roy gives a horrifying explanation of the Hindutva agenda, written before the mass protests over the Citizenship Amendment Act in *The Nation*, 'India: Intimations of an Ending': https://www.thenation. com/article/world/arundhati-roy-assam-modi/. For an engaging short introduction to Indian Prime Minister Narendra Modi, read Mihir Bose, *The Yogi of Populism* (Bite Sized Books, 2021).

For renewed tensions in the Balkans barely a quarter century after the Srebrenica genocide read Janine di Giovanni's article in *Vanity Fair*, 'Bosnia Redux': https://www.vanityfair. com/news/2021/12/bosnia-redux-are-the-balkans-headed-for-another-civil-war. For genocide denial after Srebrenica see Lamija Grebo's article in Balkan Insight, 'Bosnian Serb Decree Rejecting Genocide Denial Law Sparks Uncertainty': https:// balkaninsight.com/2021/10/13/bosnian-serb-decree-rejecting-genocide-denial-law-sparks-uncertainty/

Anne Norton's *On the Muslim Question* (Princeton University Press, 2013) argues that contemporary Islamophobia often reflects the West's own anxieties about itself. See also Ismail Adam Patel's *The Muslim Problem: From the British Empire to Islamophobia* (Palgrave Macmillan, 2021) for a rigorous study into the presentation of Muslims in the British imagination over time. Joseph Massad's *Islam in Liberalism* (University of Chicago Press, 2015) examines how liberal discourse presents Islam as misogynistic, homophobic and anti-democratic in contrast to the West, suggesting that Muslims must be cured by liberalism.

Last year Human Rights Watch declared that the Chinese government has committed crimes against humanity in China's north-west region of Xinjiang, which most of the indigenous population, the Uyghur Muslims, call East Turkestan. Its report, 'Break their lineage, break their roots', can be read on their website: https://www.hrw.org/report/2021/04/19/break-their-lineage-break-their-roots/chinas-crimes-against-humanity-targeting. *The War on the Uyghurs* by Sean Roberts (Manchester University Press, 2020) documents how China has used the discourse of the 'war on terror' to target the Uyghur Muslims in what he terms a cultural genocide.

TIMELINE

AH signifies dates in the Am Al-Fil Islamic Calendar*

General Abrahamic Timeline

American Timeline

c.2150 BCE Birth of Abraham

c.1300 BCE Birth of Moses, the most important prophet in Judaism and deeply significant in Christianity, Islam and other Abrahamic faiths

587 BCE Destruction of the first Temple in Jerusalem; Babylonian exile begins

1200–165 BCE Old Testament written down

First century CE New Testament books written

30 CE Crucifixion of Jesus Christ

70 CE The Romans destroy the second Temple after the siege of Jerusalem

570 CE Prophet Muhammad is born in Mecca

610 CE Prophet Muhammad receives the first revelations of the Quran in a cave on Mount Hira

622 CE (1 AH) Prophet Muhammad and his followers flee from Mecca to Medina journey known as the *Hijra*) founding the first Muslim city

629 CE (8 AH) First pilgrimage (*umrah*) made by Prophet Muhammad and his followers to Mecca since they migrated to Medina

630 CE (9 AH) Prophet Muhammad returns to Mecca and gains control of the city

632 CE (11 AH) Prophet Muhammad participates in his only Hajj pilgrimage

632 CE (11 AH) Prophet Muhammad dies in Medina

680 CE (60 AH) Imam Husayn killed at Battle of Karbala

711 CE (92 AH) Jewish 'Golden Age' begins in Muslim-controlled Spain

827 CE (211 AH) Muslim conquest of Sicily

833 CE (217 AH) The 'Mihna': Abbasid caliph al-Ma'mun fails to impose the Mu'tazila doctrine on Muslims

1058 CE (449 AH) Theologian and philosopher al-Ghazali is born

1095 CE (488 AH) First Crusade
1099 CE (492 AH) Crusaders take Jerusalem

---

* All Hijri dates have been lifted from this source: https://habibur.com/hijri/

Britain and Islam Timeline

638 Muslims seize Jerusalem, and rule with a general tolerance of Christianity and other faiths

731 Bede publishes his *Ecclesiastical History of the English People*

1009 Caliph Al-Hakim initiates the destruction of the Holy Sepulchre and other churches in Jerusalem

1095 Pope Urban II launches the First Crusade

France Timeline

732 Battle of Poitiers – Charles Martel expels Muslim invaders from France, a turning point for the Islamic incursion into Europe

1095 CE (488 AH) First Crusade
1099 CE (492 AH) Crusaders take Jerusalem

General Abrahamic Timeline   **American Timeline**

1187 CE (531 AH) Saladin captures Jerusalem for the Muslims

1273 CE (672 AH) Birth of scholar and poet Jalaluddin Rumi

1299 CE (698 AH) Beginning of Ottoman Empire

1389 CE (791 AH) Ottomans defeat Serbs at Kosovo

1453 CE (857 AH) Ottomans conquer Byzantine Constantinople

1478 CE (883 AH) The Spanish Inquisition begins

1492 CE (897 AH) The Nasrid kingdom of Granada falls to the Christian Reconquista

1492 CE (897 AH) The Ottomans accept thousands of Sephardic Jews fleeing from Spain

1526 CE (932 AH) Foundation of the Mughal Empire as Babur enters India

1529 CE (935 AH) The Ottomans fail to capture Vienna

1537–1540 CE (944–947 AH) Ottoman–Venetian War

1300s Portuguese Muslims create navigation charts that Christopher Columbus later uses to discover the New World

1492 Christopher Columbus discovers the New World of the Americas

1636 Harvard University is founded and teaches Hebrew to the sons of ministers

1765 CE (1178 AH) Shah Alam is forced to sign the Treaty of Allahabad, marking the end of any real Mughal power

1798 CE (1213 AH) Napoleonic conquest of Egypt

1783 The United States of America is granted independence; North African pirates begin preying on American merchant ships

1801 CE (1216 AH) Commencement of the First Barbary War
1805 CE (1220 AH) End of the First Barbary War
1815 CE (1230 AH) Second Barbary War, won by the Americans

Britain and Islam Timeline

France Timeline

*c.*1107–1135 Adelard of Bath writes *Quaestiones Naturales*, ascribing any especially daring advanced idea to Arabs

1187 CE (531 AH) Saladin captures Jerusalem for the Muslims

1213 King John sends England's first diplomatic mission to a Muslim power – the Sultanate of Morocco

1600 Queen Elizabeth I receives envoy from the Ottoman Sultan to negotiate a military alliance against Spain

1600 The East India Company is founded

1645 Barbary pirates seize 240 men, women and children on Cornish coast

1648 Alexander Ross, Charles I's chaplain, publishes the first English translation of the Quran

1664 In the Battle of Tangier Ahmad Al Khadir ibn Ali Ghaylan inflicts the first defeat of an English force by a Muslim army since the Crusades

1756 Siraj ud-Daulah, last independent ruler of Bengal, reputedly holds 146 British prisoners overnight in a cell intended for three people at most; 123 of the prisoners die – an event remembered as The Black Hole of Calcutta

1536 Franco-Ottoman Alliance between Francis I and Suleyman the Magnificent

1765 CE (1178 AH) Shah Alam is forced to sign the Treaty of Allahabad, marking the end of any real Mughal power

1799 Tipu Sultan, the ruler of Mysore, is killed in the Second Mysore War

1796 France aids Tipu Sultan in fighting the British East India Company

1798 Napoleon invades Egypt

1801 CE (1216 AH) Commencement of the First Barbary War
1805 CE (1220 AH) End of the First Barbary War
1815 CE (1230 AH) Second Barbary War, won by the Americans

General Abrahamic Timeline

1821 CE (1236 AH) Odessa Pogroms mark the beginning of the nineteenth century pogroms against Jews in Tsarist Russia

1839 CE (1255 AH) The Tanzimat reforms begin in the Ottoman Empire, liberalising and modernising governance

1864 CE (1281 AH) Genocide is committed by the Russian Empire against the Circassian Muslims

1905 CE (1323 AH) Muhammad Iqbal, the Indian Muslim philosopher and poet credited with the idea of Pakistan, begins his studies at Trinity College, Cambridge

1909 CE (1327 AH) Sultan Abdul Hamid II is overthrown by the modernising Young Turks

1914 CE (1332 AH) The Ottomans enter the First World War on Germany's side

1915 CE (1333 AH) The Ottomans begin a campaign of genocide, involving mass deportation and massacres against the Armenians

1917 CE (1335 AH) Basmachi Revolt – Muslims in Central Asia rebel against Russian rule

1922 CE (1340 AH) Egypt gains independence

1923 CE (1341 AH) Collapse of the Ottoman Empire

1924 CE (1342 AH) Abolition of the Caliphate

1938 CE (1357 AH) Oil is found in the Dammam oil field in Saudi Arabia

1938 CE (1357 AH) Thousands of Jewish shops attacked and more than 1,000 synagogues targeted in 9–10 November Pogrom known as Kristallnacht (night of broken glass)

1941 CE (1360 AH) The Holocaust, also known as the Shoah, begins. Nazi Germany and its collaborators systematically murder some six million Jews

American Timeline

1863 The Seventh-Day Adventist Church founded

1898 America is victorious in the Spanish–American war and acquires Spain's Pacific possessions, including the Philippines and its population of 300,000 Muslims

1898 Sultan Abdul Hamid II writes a letter appealing to the Sulu Muslims to submit to the Americans (after being approached by the American ambassador to the Ottoman Empire)

1901–13 The Moro Wars are fought by the Filipino Moros and the Americans

1904 The St Louis World Fair displays captive Moros as an exhibit of barbaric and bloodthirsty Muslims

Early 1900s Muslim Revival among African American communities in the United States

1913 Timothy Drew (aka Noble Drew Ali) founds the Moorish Science Temple of America, the first specifically Muslim organisation in the United States

Summer 1919 The United States sees its worst spate of interracial violence in history

1921 The first permanent mosque is founded in the United States in Michigan

1930 Wallace Fard Mohammad founds the Nation of Islam in Detroit

1933 Bilateral relations between Saudi Arabia and the United States begin with the establishment of diplomatic relations. This alliance was formalised in 1951 with the signing of the Mutual Defence Assistance Agreement

1934 Leadership of the Nation of Islam passes to Elijah Muhammad. He holds this position until his death in 1975

1937 Immense quantities of oil are discovered in Saudi Arabia, making it a focal point of American oil interests

1942 District Judge Tuttle denies Ahmed Hassan, a Yemeni Muslim, citizenship on the basis of his religion

1942 The United States launches Operation Torch, invasion of Algeria and Morocco, in an attempt to create a 'second front' against the Axis

1947 CE (1366 AH) **Commencement of the Cold War**
1948 CE (1367 AH) **State of Israel founded**

Britain and Islam Timeline

1838 Britain invades Afghanistan

1847 The Ottomans send aid to Ireland during the Great Famine, bypassing a British blockade

1857 Indian War of Independence (known in Britain as the Indian Mutiny)

1858 Beginning of the British Raj

1878 The second British invasion of Afghanistan

1911 Winston Churchill becomes the First Lord of the Admiralty, and orders the Royal Navy not to fire on vessels taking pilgrims on the hajj

1914–18 The Indian army sends 1.5 million men to fight for the British Empire overseas, including at least 400,000 Muslims

1917 The Balfour Declaration establishes British support for the creation of a Jewish state

1919 The third British invasion of Afghanistan

1921 Winston Churchill, amongst other attendees of the Cairo Conference, agrees to the creation of the Arab states of Iraq and Transjordan

1924–29 The Home Office, under the leadership of Sir William Joynson-Hicks, introduces a series of orders reducing Muslims in Britain to Aliens, virtually without rights

1928 MP Colonel Applin opposes lowering the age of voting for women from thirty to twenty-one because of its impact on Muslims in the empire

1932 The Kingdom of Saudi Arabia begins, supported by Britain

1940 The Lahore Declaration serves as the first official expression of ambition for an independent nation to be known as Pakistan

1947 Pakistan is established as Britain leaves India

France Timeline

1830 French invasion of Algeria

1865 Napoleon III offers Algerian Arabs a pathway into French citizenship, on the condition that they renounce their 'Muslim personal status' in matters of family law

1871 The Franco-Prussian war sparks the start of French presence in Tunisia

1881 France occupies Tunisia

1881 The Indigénat law subjects Algerians to many demeaning and racist measures and punishments, clearly setting them apart from other French citizens

1883 A treaty signed between the Tunisians and the French makes the sultan little more than a French puppet

1905 The passing of the Separation of Churches and State law forbids the French state from recognising any religion, imposing neutrality on civil servants in order to protect freedom of conscience

1914 Some 34,000 Moroccan Muslims enlist for France in the First World War

1930 Protests break out in Tunisia against a Catholic Congress in Carthage

1931 Protests break out in Tunisia against French celebrations of fifty years of colonial rule, to which the French response is the expulsion of Habib Bourguiba, the leading nationalist leader

1937 The fall of the Popular Front government in Tunisia sees the renewed repression of Tunisians by the French authorities

1938 A general strike and student demonstration in Tunis are met with the declaration of a state of emergency, renewed expulsion of Bourguiba and outbreaks of shooting

1939 Hundreds of thousands of North African Muslims join the French army at the outbreak of the Second World War

1943 The Anglo-American invasion brings hope to Moroccans of a new, independent future, but the restoration of French control by the Allied Forces quickly dashes this hope

1947 CE (1366 AH) Commencement of the Cold War
1948 CE (1367 AH) State of Israel founded

General Abrahamic Timeline	American Timeline

General Abrahamic Timeline

1948 CE (1367 AH) The First Arab–Israeli War and the Nakba (about half of Palestine's population) flee or are expelled from their homes

1967 CE (1387 AH) Six-Day Arab–Israeli War

1971 CE (1391 AH) Bangladesh, formerly East Pakistan, is created after a bloody civil war

American Timeline

1949 Evangelical Billy Graham rises to national prominence with the Hearst Press' coverage of his Los Angeles crusade

1952 Second-generation American Muslims form the Federation of Islamic Associations of the United States and Canada

1953 President Eisenhower first uses the term 'Judaeo-Christian' to describe the American government

1953 CIA and MI6 help depose the democratically elected Iranian leader, Mohammad Mossadegh

1957 President Eisenhower opens the Islamic Centre in Washington DC

1960 Billy Graham takes his Evangelical Crusade to Israel, cementing the relationship between Israel and American Evangelicals

1961 The Nation of Islam publishes its own newspaper, *Muhammad Speaks*, with Malcolm X as founder-editor

1961 Heavyweight boxing champion Muhammad Ali attends his first Nation of Islam meeting

1965 Members from the Nation of Islam assassinate Malcolm X

1965 The United States removes discriminatory policies against Muslim countries

1967 CE (1386 AH) Israel is victorious in the Six-Day War

1973 The Arab oil embargo on the United States sees the price of oil quintuple

1978 President Carter brokers the Camp David Peace Accord

1979 Ayatollah Khomeini uses the term the 'Great Satan' to describe the United States

1979 CE (1399 AH) The Iranian revolution

1979 CE (1399 AH) USSR Invades Afghanistan. The Mujahideen, funded by the US, fight the Soviets.

1995 CE (1416 AH) Genocide against Muslims in Bosnia

1983 Yechiel Eckstein, an Orthodox Jewish rabbi, founds the International Fellowship of Christians and Jews, cementing Israeli–Evangelical relations

Britain and Islam Timeline	**France Timeline**

1954 War for Algerian Independence starts

1954 The Front de Libération Nationale (FLN) is founded in Cairo

1956 Algerian War of Independence enters second stage with FLN terrorist attacks against Algiers which trigger the French government's deployment of the army under one of its toughest generals, Jacque Massu

1956 Tunisia is granted independence from France

1961 Tunisians, angry with the continued presence of the French naval base at Bizerte, decide to reclaim it by force – 630 Tunisians and 24 French are killed in three days to no avail; the port was only handed back to Tunisia in 1963 after the end of the Algerian war

1961 A crackdown on the Algerian population of Paris sees the deaths of up to 300 people, with countless bodies being thrown into the Seine

1962 France grants Algeria its independence, formally ending the French African colonial empire, embodied by some 350,000 *colons* fleeing to France

1967 CE (1386 AH) Israel is victorious in the Six-Day War

1979 CE (1399 AH) The Iranian revolution

1983 Over 100,000 North Africans march from Marseilles to Paris in protest against labour discrimination, police brutality, and hate crimes against Arabs and Africans

1987 Jean-Marie Le Pen's National Front releases its first specifically anti-Muslim poster

1989 Three Muslim girls are suspended from their high school for refusing to remove their headscarves, though later that year the French administrative High Court rules that the wearing of the headscarf is compatible with the principle of *laïcité* unless it threatens public order

General Abrahamic Timeline　　　　**American Timeline**

1989 CE (1409 AH) End of the Cold War

1990–1991 The First Gulf War

1996 Samuel Huntington publishes *Clash of Civilisations*, claiming that that 'Islam has bloody borders'

11 September 2001 CE (1422 AH) Al-Qaeda hijacks four airplanes in a terrorist attack against the United States, crashing two of them into the Twin Towers of the World Trade Centre in New York, claiming 2,996 lives

27 September 2001 American and overseas Muslim clerics issue Fatwa condemning the 9/11 attacks and authorising Muslims' participation in the US-led actions against al-Qaeda

2001 America invades Afghanistan

2002 Detention site Guantanamo Bay is opened in Cuba; the only detainees are Muslim

2003 Invasion of Iraq

2003 Robert Spencer launches Jihad Watch

2008 Barack Obama is elected US President, with 92 per cent of the American Muslim vote

2010 CE (1431 AH) The self-immolation of street vendor Mohamed Bouazizi in Tunisia triggers the start of the Arab Spring

Britain and Islam Timeline	France Timeline

1989 CE (1409 AH) End of the Cold War

1990–91 The First Gulf War sees the largest use of British troops in one deployment since WW2

1990 Algeria has its first free elections, and the people elect the Islamic Salvation Front (FIS) as their local leaders, and its co-founder Ali Belhadj proclaims his intention to 'ban France from Algeria'

1991 Before the FIS can secure an absolute majority in Algerian parliament, the army cancel elections, dissolve FIS, and install the exiled independence fighter Mohamed Boudiaf as the president of the Council, triggering a decade of conflict

1992 FIS begins to develop links with French mosques and Boudiaf is assassinated when he tries to head off the FIS by helping the Mitterrand government restructure Algeria's debt and oil and gas infrastructure

1992 The murder of President Boudiaf is met by a wave of terrorist attacks by a new Islamist coalition, the Groupe Islamique Armé (GIA), which is considerably more violent than FIS

1994 GIA violence spreads to metropolitan France with the air hijacking and murder of a prominent imam who acted as a go-between for the French government and the FIS

11 September 2001 CE (1422 AH) Al-Qaeda hijacks four airplanes in a terrorist attack against the United States, crashing two of them into the Twin Towers of the World Trade Centre in New York, claiming 2,996 lives

2001 The fourth British invasion of Afghanistan, this time supporting the American War on Terror

2002 The first of nine British citizens is held by the US in Guantanamo Bay

2003 Britain joins America in invading Iraq

2003 The Prevent policy is introduced by the Labour government as part of its counter-terrorism approach

2005 Four Muslim suicide bombers with rucksacks full of explosives attack central London, killing fifty-two people and injuring hundreds more in the worst single terrorist atrocity on British soil

2003 Sarkozy sets up an official council charged with creating an 'Islam of France'

2005 A wave of domestic riots in fifteen French towns and cities breaks out, following the deaths of two Muslim boys in a police chase

2010 CE (1431 AH) The self-immolation of street vendor Mohamed Bouazizi in Tunisia triggers the start of the Arab Spring

General Abrahamic Timeline

2010 CE (1431 AH) The Arab Spring begins

2014 CE (1435 AH) The Gaza War

2018 CE (1439 AH) Human Rights Watch reports on China's imprisonment of Uyghur Muslims in 're-education' camps and the criminalisation of Islam in Xinjiang

2019 CE (1440 AH) Passing of the Citizenship Amendment Act in India, which explicitly discriminates against Muslims seeking citizenship

2020 CE (1441 AH) Massacre of Muslims in Delhi

2020 CE (1441 AH) It is revealed that China has built nearly 380 detention camps for Uyghur Muslims

2021 CE (1442 AH) Israeli troops storm and desecrate Masjid al Aqsa, the Holy Mosque in Jerusalem, during Ramadan

American Timeline

2011 The Obama administration's Countering Violent Extremism strategy, relying heavily on informants, is rolled out nationwide

2015 Muslim terrorists kill fifteen and injure many more in San Bernardino

2015 The November Paris attacks trigger Donald Trump's first specific pledge against Muslims – a database tracking all Muslims in the US and surveillance of all mosques

2016 A Muslim terrorist murders forty-nine and injures fifty-three others in a shooting at a gay nightclub in Orlando

2017 Donald Trump bans travel to the United States from Syria, Libya, Iran, Somalia and Yemen

2017 President Trump recognises Jerusalem as the capital of Israel

2018 Saudi Journalist Jamal Khashoggi is murdered

2021 America leaves Afghanistan as the Taliban takes control of the country

Britain and Islam Timeline

2014 The Trojan Horse affair; a forged letter leads to fears that schools in Birmingham are being 'radicalised' in an Islamic plot

2015 Saudi Arabia begins its war on Yemen, supported by Britain

2015 Prevent is made into a legal duty for public sector workers, who have to report signs of extremism to the programme

2015 British 'counter-extremism' experts promote Prevent to officials in Xinjiang, China as Uyghur Muslims are held in re-education camps

2017 Devastating Manchester terrorist attack kills twenty-three. One Muslim man is killed in June near Finsbury Park mosque in north London. The case against the teachers accused of misconduct in the Trojan Horse affair collapses

2017 The government-backed mass killing of Rohingya Muslims begins in Myanmar, and British foreign office minister Mark Field openly defends the Myanmar government in response

France Timeline

2015 Al-Qaeda-linked terrorists kill twelve people and injure eleven others in the office of French magazine *Charlie Hebdo*. Islamic state linked terrorists kills four French Jews in the Hypercacher supermarket siege. In November the attacks on the Stade de France and mass shootings at the Bataclan theatre leave 130 people dead

2015 French government responses to the terrorist attacks include a state of emergency that allows security forces to carry out raids, shut down private institutions and limit individuals' movement

2019 President Macron revives Sarkozy's plan to create a 'French' version of Islam, hoping to create a moderate domestic Islam to conquer adherents from 'foreign' versions

2020 Two terrorist attacks are carried out by Muslims in France – the first a beheading of a teacher and the second the stabbing of three civilians – leading to a fierce government crackdown on the expression of Islamic identity in the public realm and Islamic institutions generally

2021 President Macron asks the *hakris* from the Algerian War of Independence for forgiveness and vows to recognise their contributions

ACKNOWLEDGEMENTS

I have acquired more debts than I can ever repay while researching and writing this book. I am especially grateful to *Middle East Eye*, its Editor-in-Chief David Hearst and the staff on the website. Thanks to MEE I have been able to travel widely across the Muslim world, and especially the Middle East, exploring the themes and stories that have shaped this book. In the later stages Mr Hearst allowed me ample time off to write.

Endless conversations (including frequent disagreements) with my friend and frequent collaborator Richard Heller, a secular liberal, tested my arguments and enabled me to reach more balanced and informed conclusions. Richard's family history in Lebanon and later the United States has enabled me to understand the immigrant experience of the United States, while his father Bob Heller's personal experience of McCarthyism gave me insight into present pressures on Muslims in Western countries to hold acceptable beliefs, and the sanctions they may face when they do not.

Carl Arrindel, former head of news at the Islam Channel, has been a constant source of advice, information and good analysis. I acknowledge the support of Professor Conor Gearty, then Director of the Institute of Public Affairs at LSE, for the many fruitful conversations I had while a visitor in that institute. Dr Maria W. Norris, Assistant Professor of International Relations, gave me tutorials on Prevent and the UK Counterterrorism Strategy. At a relatively late stage, Imran Mulla was a vital pillar of support.

Professor John Holmwood generously shared his limitless knowledge of the Trojan Horse affair and gave me a crash course in sociology. I thank Tahir Alam, Jehangir Akbar, Nick Timothy, Adrian Packer CBE and others involved in or knowledgeable about the Trojan Horse controversy for allowing me to interview them.

Ella Cockbain and Waqas Tufail have been generous with their time explaining the false narrative on grooming gangs. Lord Anderson of Ipswich, former terrorism reviewer, has instructed me about terrorism law and the use of the term 'extremism'. So have Ali Bajwa QC, Farooq Bajwa, Catherine Oborne and Tayab Ali.

Federico V. Magdalena, Associate Specialist & Deputy Director at the University of Hawaii, has shared his learning about the Moros. Dr Warren Dockter gave me an enjoyable tutorial about Winston Churchill and Islam. I learnt a great deal touring Britain with the Commission for Islam in Public Life under the chairmanship of Dominic Grieve MP QC. Oliver McTernan, Julian Weinberg, Harry Higginson and Jordan Morgan of Forward Thinking have provided new perspectives and opened their contact book to me. Mohammad Ali Harrath kindly allowed me to interview him. I thank Fadi Esber for his rich insight into the haunting symmetry between Neo-Conservativism and al-Qaeda. Aisling Byrne and Alastair Crooke of Conflicts Forum generously allowed me to attend their seminars in Beirut where I heard many wise and well-informed voices, Italian diplomat Marco Carnelos and Seyed Mohammad Marandi, professor of English Literature and Orientalism at the University of Tehran, among them. The Centre for Policy Studies allowed me to explore at an early stage some of the ideas and stories embraced here in a pamphlet. Peter Jukes and Hardeep Matharu at *Byline Times* have been immensely supportive. Asim Qureishi, Azad Ali and Moazzem Begg from CAGE have been generous with their time and knowledge.

Mujib Gallagher gave me insights into the mysterious closure of bank accounts of British Muslims. BBC producer Anna Meisel made important discoveries about how and why they happened. Two victims were Anas Altakriti and Mohammad Kozbar of the Finsbury Park Mosque. They allowed me to interview them about that, and more besides. Robert Lambert, formerly of the Metropolitan Police Muslim Contact Unit, spoke to me about the police operation which dislodged Abu Hamza. Historian Humayun Ansari has advised me about the historical experience of British Muslims. Miqdaad Versi of the Muslim Council of Britain has repeatedly picked up the telephone to answer my queries about British media coverage of Islam. His colleague Faisal Hanif has published powerful research. Dr Abdul Wahid of Hizb ut-Tahrir has been generous with his time and insight, as was Lord Pickles when Secretary of State for Communities and Local Government.

Michael Gove is criticised in this book, but during the early stages he was generous with his time and open to discussion. I am intensely grateful to the formidable Baroness Cox, who has allowed me to accompany her and her team on memorable trips to South Sudan, Armenia and Nagorno-Karabakh. Several conversations with Baroness Sayeeda Warsi were valuable. Crispin Blunt MP has been helpful during his time as chair of the Foreign Affairs Committee. William Hague, when British Foreign Secretary, took me to Algeria, Libya, Morocco and Mauritania, while David Miliband when Foreign Secretary, generously allowed me to hitch a lift with him across Iraq. Despite occasional differences of opinion, Lord Polak of Conservative Friends of Israel has always been kind, courteous and helpful. Mohamed Okda took me to southern Turkey and the Syria border, sharing his knowledge, contacts and profound understanding of the region.

I have travelled frequently to Pakistan where I have been greatly helped and elevated by Abdul Rauf, Irfan Ashraf, Shandana Khan, Shoaib Sultan Khan, Sabin Agha and Ramma Cheema. Many thanks too to the Pakistan High Commission, above all the press secretary Muneer Ahmed. Karachi novelist Masood Lohar guided me up the Sind valley, where he showed me how different religions can coexist with good humour and mutual understanding. Sarkis Karkassian took me round much of Syria at the height of the war, including to the relief of Maloula. Azzam Tamimi hosted me in Jordan, and has provided insight and wisdom. Lubna Masarwa has guided me around Jerusalem and the West Bank. Bishop Riah, former Anglican Bishop of Jerusalem, took me round Nazareth and Galilee. I also thank Father Mario, who allowed me to visit him at the Church of the Holy Family in Gaza. Ola Lubbad at the University of Gaza tolerantly endeavours to teach me Arabic over Skype.

Dorothy Byrne, Head of News and Current Affairs at Channel 4, allowed me to explore the predicament of Muslims in Britain and overseas. As a result, I have been fortunate to work with a number of outstanding TV director/producers including James Brabazon, James Jones, Robin Barnwell, Richard Cookson, Andy Wells, George Waldrun, Alex Nott, Ed Braman, Richard Sanders, Chris Boulding, Paul Yule and Marc Perkins. Much of this work was courtesy of Channel 4's *Unreported World* and I owe a heavy debt to its Executive Producer Eamonn Matthews, Head of Production Natalie Triebwasser and the team at Quicksilver. I am grateful to Paul Dacre, when editor of the *Daily Mail*, for allowing me to write about British complicity in torture and certain domestic Muslim issues, though not as much as I wanted. Tony Gallagher was inspirational and supportive when I worked under his editorship at the *Daily Telegraph*. I also thank Anthony Barnett and Mary Fitzgerald at Open Democracy for their help in publishing awkward material. Leaf Kalfayan and Chris Deerin are always cheerful and wise.

For the history of France and Islam I am especially grateful to Hatem Nafti (Tunisia), Adlène Meddi (Algeria) and Elodie Farge of *Middle East Eye*. I also benefitted greatly from a long conversation with Marwan Mohammad. In Paris, Peter Allen has been generous with his knowledge, time and advice. Thanks also to

Professor Jeremy Jennings, historian of French thought. Natasha Voase has helped immensely with fact-checking and footnotes for the French section.

I am grateful to human rights lawyer Clive Stafford-Smith for instructing me about torture, extraordinary rendition and, most recently, for introducing me to Jawad Rabbani, whose innocent father, Ahmed Rabbani, has been held in Guantanamo Bay for nearly two decades.

All or parts of this book have been read by Simon Walters, Nadia Roeske, Robert Gallimore and Imran Mulla. I am very grateful for the fact-checking services of Nadia Roeske, Natasha Voase, Asa Breuss-Burgess, George Poyser, Lewis Clabby and not least Tom Griffin. Mahdi Mustafa and Nadia Roeske have done superb research over many years. As have Jan Westad, Richard Assheton, Alastair Sloane (who suggested the title, and urged that I should think more about France), Fabia Martin, Livvy Moore and Alex Delmar Morgan. Lindsay Codsi has provided her usual capable, level-headed administrative back-up and kept me in good order.

Thanks again to my agent Andrew Gordon. I am grateful to Simon and Schuster for the faith and commitment they have shown in this book and in particular to Ian Marshall, Kat Ailes (whose wise and sensible suggestions have greatly improved the text) and Sophia Akhtar, upon who I placed many unfair burdens. The book's copyeditor and proofeader, Nige Tassell and Clare Hubbard, were also very helpful in editing the text into shape. Above all I thank my wife Martine, who puts up with a lot.

INDEX